INTERPRETING JESUS

Essays on the Gospels

N.T. Wright

ZONDERVAN
ACADEMIC

ZONDERVAN ACADEMIC

Interpreting Jesus
Copyright © 2020 by N. T. Wright

Requests for information should be addressed to:
Zondervan, *3900 Sparks Dr. SE, Grand Rapids, Michigan 49546*

Also published in Great Britain in 2020
Society for Promoting Christian Knowledge
36 Causton Street
London SW1P 4ST
www.spck.org.uk

ISBN 978-0-310-09864-5 (hardcover)

ISBN 978-0-310-09865-2 (ebook)

Cover Design: Brand Navigation

Printed in the United States of America

20 21 22 23 24 25 26 27 28 29 30 /LSC/ 20 19 18 17 16 15 14 13 12 11 10 9 8 7 6 5 4 3 2 1

For the principal, staff and students
at Wycliffe Hall, Oxford

Contents

Contents

Preface

Jesus and the four gospels have been near the heart of my work, both scholarly and popular, throughout my adult life. Though I have published more overall on Paul and his letters, I have constantly come back to the questions raised by the four gospels. The present volume collects together the essays that led up to *Jesus and the Victory of God* (1996) and that have tried to take forward various related discussions from that point.

I am grateful to the many publishers and editors who have given permission for these pieces to be made available in this way, and to my friends and publishers at SPCK and Zondervan for their work behind the scenes. I am greatly indebted to my research assistants Simon Dürr and Ethan Johnson for their painstaking work in scanning the original documents, inserting pagination with relevant page numbers in square brackets, lightly editing where typographical mistakes had crept in, and inserting occasional references to relevant material published subsequently (including to other essays in the present volume). No attempt has been made, of course, to smooth out any internal contradictions or indeed repetitions. My views on various subjects displayed here have undergone a mostly gentle development, though not without some sudden leaps, and anyone interested in observing such changes will find plenty of material here.

Throughout the present volume, unless otherwise stated, quotations in English from the New Testament are either my own translation or taken from my published translation *The New Testament for Everyone* (SPCK, 2019), known in the USA as *The Kingdom New Testament* (Zondervan HarperCollins, 2012). As in that work, I always use lower-case 's' for 'spirit', not because I hold a 'low' view of the third person of the Trinity but because, in the first century, the early Christian use of the common and polysemous word *pneuma* had to make its own way without such help. Quotations from the Old Testament are either my own translation or taken or adapted from the New Revised Standard Version with Apocrypha, Anglicized (1995 edition). When quoting from the NRSV, I have replaced the term 'the LORD' with the name YHWH.

N. T. Wright
St Mary's College, St Andrews
Trinity 2019

Abbreviations

1 Stylistic Shorthands

ad loc.	at the [relevant] place
cf.	confer
ch(s).	chapter(s)
contra	against
cp.	compare
ed(s).	edited by, editors
edn.	edition(s)
e.g.	for example
esp.	especially
et al.	and others
etc.	et cetera
f.	and the following
frag.	fragment
i.e.	that is
n.	(foot/end)note(s)
pace	with all due respect to different opinion
par.	parallel (in the synoptic tradition)
passim	throughout
refs.	reference(s)
repr.	reprinted
rev.	revision/revised by
sic	thus (acknowledging an error in the original)
s.v.	under the word(s)
tr.	translation/translated by
v(v).	verse(s)
vol(s).	volume(s)

2 Primary Sources

1 En.	*1 Enoch*
1 Macc.	1 Maccabees
1QS	Rule of the Community

1QSa	Rule of the Congregation
2 Macc.	2 Maccabees
4 Ez.	*4 Ezra*
4 Macc.	4 Maccabees
4Q174	Midrash on Eschatology
4Q246	Apocryphon of Daniel
4Q521	Messianic Apocalypse
4QDibHam	Words of the Luminaries
4QMMT	Halakhic Letter
Barn.	*Barnabas*
bYom.	Babylonian Talmud, Yoma
Eus. *Hist. Eccl.*	Eusebius, *Ecclesiastical History*
Gos. Thom.	*Gospel of Thomas*
Jos.	Josephus (*Ant.*=*Jewish Antiquities*; *War*=*The Jewish War*)
jTa'an.	Jerusalem Talmud, Ta'anit
Jub.	*Jubilees*
LAB	*Liber Antiquitatum Biblicarum* (=Pseudo-Philo)
LAE	*Life of Adam and Eve* (=*Apocalypse of Moses*)
LXX	Septuagint version of the Old Testament
MT	Masoretic Text (of the Hebrew Bible)
Mt. Pol.	*Martyrdom of Polycarp*
NT	New Testament
OT	Old Testament
Philo *Opif. Mun.*	Philo, *De Opificio Mundi* (On the Creation of the World)
Plut. *Princ. Iner.*	Plutarch, *Ad Principem Ineruditum* (To an Uneducated Ruler)
Sib. Or.	*Sibylline Oracles*
Sir.	Sirach
T. Jud.	*Testament of Judah*
Tg. Neb.	*Targum of the Prophets*
Wis.	Wisdom of Solomon

3 Secondary Sources, etc.

AB	Anchor Bible
ABD	*Anchor Bible Dictionary*, ed. D. N. Freedman. 6 vols. New York, NY: Doubleday, 1992.
ABRL	Anchor Bible Reference Library
AGJU	Arbeiten zur Geschichte des antiken Judentums und des Urchristentums

Abbreviations

BDAG	*A Greek-English Lexicon of the New Testament and Other Early Christian Literature.* 3rd edn, rev. and ed. F. W. Danker, W. Bauer, W. F. Arndt and F. W. Gingrich. Chicago, IL and London: University of Chicago Press, 2000 [1957].
CBQMS	Catholic Biblical Quarterly Monograph Series
COQG	Christian Origins and the Question of God
FAT	Forschungen zum Alten Testament
HTS	Harvard Theological Studies
ICC	International Critical Commentary
IRT	Issues in Religion and Theology
JSNTSup	Journal for the Study of the New Testament Supplements
LCL	Loeb Classical Library
NA (25)	Nestle-Aland *Novum Testamentum Graece* (25th edn.)
NIGTC	New International Greek Testament Commentary
NRSV	New Revised Standard Bible
PTMS	Princeton Theological Monograph Series
SBEC	Studies in the Bible and Early Christianity
SBL	Society of Biblical Literature
SBT	Studies in Biblical Theology
SNTSU	Studien zum Neuen Testament und seiner Umwelt
SNTW	Studies of the New Testament and Its World
STDJ	Studies on the Texts of the Desert of Judah
SV	Scholars Version
TLS	*Times Literary Supplement*
UBS (5)	United Bible Societies *Greek New Testament* (5th edn.)
WUNT	Wissenschaftliche Untersuchungen zum Neuen Testament

I

Towards a Third 'Quest'?
Jesus Then and Now

When I arrived at McGill University, Montreal, in September 1981 as Assistant Professor of New Testament, my main academic work, including my DPhil dissertation, had been on Paul. But I had already been working on various issues to do with the 'historical Jesus' – as this and subsequent essays will indicate. In part this was in order to teach undergraduates in Cambridge (1978–81), and in part it was my own fascination. I had come from the study of Ancient History to the study of Theology in 1971, and had been startled at the cheerfully unhistorical approach to the gospels taken by so many scholars at the time. We had read Bultmann, but nobody had explained to us where he was coming from intellectually or culturally; it was assumed that he was an extremely learned German whose 'findings' were part of the 'assured results' of critical study which it would be intellectual suicide to doubt. The 'New Quest', on which more below, appeared to be what it was: an attempt to rearrange the Bultmannian deckchairs on a sinking ship. But in the late 1970s there were signs of a change, and this article notes them. In particular, the work of the late Ben F. Meyer of McMaster University, whom I would get to know as a colleague in the Canadian Society of Biblical Studies, was clearly pointing to a different *kind* of 'quest' from either the pre-Schweitzer or the post-Bultmann movements. The present essay, delivered as a paper at the McGill 'Doktorklub' and then published in the Faculty's in-house journal *ARC*, was thus the first outing for the idea, which has caught on widely though not always with full understanding, that what we were witnessing was a 'Third Quest', not just a 'new wave' of study but a new *type* of history, relying far more on the Jewish sources (marginalized both by Bultmann and by his successors). I recall my friendly colleague Professor Fred Wisse saying, after the Doktorklub meeting, that my paper would send him running back to Bultmann. For me, this was the first small milestone in my journey in the opposite direction.

[20] Karl Barth's *Romans*, so the saying goes, fell like a bombshell on the playground of the theologians.[1] The same thing could have been said of Albert Schweitzer's famous review *The Quest of the Historical Jesus*.[2] In neither case has the dust yet settled. I do not intend in this article to rebuild the playground, or to hunt for survivors from the explosions. I want, if anything, to lay a few more detonators.

It is common knowledge that the 'Quest', though its epitaph was written by Schweitzer, has refused to lie down and stay dead. Schweitzer himself constructed his famous portrait of Jesus the failed apocalyptic visionary. Bultmann, while working towards his equally famous view that the preaching of Jesus constitutes a presupposition for, rather than a part of, New Testament theology, wrote his *Jesus and the Word* to portray Jesus as the great preacher of existentialist self-understanding.[3] Post-Bultmannian scholars, even while paying lip-service to the dogma that the gospels do not really contain 'biographical' data, have continued to write about Jesus, although their work, held together with caveats and alternative possibilities, often looks decidedly shaky. The so-called 'New Quest of the Historical Jesus', rising like a phoenix from the ashes of the old one, attempts to combine the Bultmannian premise (that the early church was not interested in the earthly Jesus) with the apparently contradictory result of redaction-criticism, namely, that the writing of Mark is evidence of a desire to 'earth' the exalted Christ of the kerygma by identifying him with the Jesus of history.[4] Meanwhile, scholars in other traditions have continued to write about Jesus, not (to be sure) uncritically, but at least in the belief that we can know several things about him with reasonable certainty. Anthony Harvey's recent Bampton Lectures, *Jesus and the Constraints of History*, are an excellent example, as is Ben Meyer's *The Aims of Jesus*. The larger works by Schillebeeckx and Dunn[5] are further evidence of the continuing possibility of serious work not merely on the primitive Christian community in which the gospel materials were transmitted but on Jesus himself.

A proper preliminary task for such work would be an examination of the imposing facade of the dominant paradigm in gospel criticism, and a demonstration that it not only contains cracks and fissures but is actually built on

---

1 Barth 1933.
2 Schweitzer 1954.
3 Bultmann 1934.
4 Käsemann 1964; Perrin 1970, 76.
5 Schillebeeckx 1979; Dunn 1980.

shaky foundations. This alarming news is already being understood in various (and widely differing) quarters.[6] In the present paper I must be content with a few abbreviated remarks.

First, asking questions about Jesus must be reckoned a valid historical project. Any historian of the first century must face the problem of the rise of Christianity, and any serious historian will not be content to attribute the phenomenon merely to the enthusiasm of a Jewish sect and the brilliance of a wandering missionary and letter-writer. The 'primitive [21] community' and Paul are not enough, by themselves, to explain the Christianity of Clement, Ignatius and Polycarp. Something must be said about Jesus.

But how? It is a commonplace of modern scholarship that the gospels are evidence not for Jesus but for the evangelists and/or their sources and/or communities; and this would appear to leave us with only a very few bits of information – the brief, biased accounts in Jewish and pagan sources, and the few sayings and biographical details that even the most radical critics would allow through the net. But (this is my second point) this 'commonplace' of scholarship needs to be challenged, as follows.

One of the odd quirks in the history of ideas is that philosophical theories, themselves long out of fashion, continue to beget recognizable offspring in other areas of study. What we are witnessing in the field of gospel criticism is the application to the biblical literature of phenomenalism, the theory that insists on understanding statements about the external world in terms of the speaker's 'sense-data'. Ultimately, of course, this movement of thought leads to solipsism. That is one of various good reasons why its force as a serious philosophical option is now largely spent. But it survives in its literary-critical grandchildren: 'We must take as our starting point the assumption that the Gospels offer us directly information about the theology of the early church and not about the teaching of the historical Jesus'.[7] 'Every text is first and foremost evidence for the circumstances in and for which it was composed, and in this respect texts serve as documentary evidence for the time of writing'.[8]

But the only sense in which this 'assumption' or 'analytical principle' is valid is also a fairly trivial one: that all human writings, including the New Testament, are just that – human writings, not self-created or produced by unmediated divine activity. Wise readers will always take a writer seriously

---

6   E.g. Meyer 1979; Petersen 1978, 9–48.

7   Perrin 1970, 69.

8   Petersen 1978, 15, describing this as an 'analytical principle'.

as a person, and even when this is impossible (for example, in reading an anonymous poem) they will at least be aware of a probable context. But in fact (this is the equivalent of the realist's reply to the phenomenalist) few writers write their lines in order to have readers read between them to discover the writer's personality or background, and readers who try to do that will almost certainly fail to hear what the writer wanted to say. Worse, the apparent 'objectivity' of phenomenalist literary criticism, which gains its strength from the obvious need to understand the viewpoint and bias of a writer, masks a deeper subjectivity: released from the constraints of the prima facie subject-matter, the critic's imagination is free to create psychological or sociological entities, not infrequently in a dangerously anachronistic form.

A third weakness in the twentieth-century 'quests' for Jesus has been the failure to appreciate the original aims of form-criticism itself. For Bultmann, the thing that *mattered* in the New Testament, the thing worth hunting for, was not the 'historical Jesus' but the faith of the early church. Though some of his [22] followers have used form-criticism as a tool to probe back within the tradition towards Jesus himself, it was designed to do, and is of course much better at doing, something different – creating a picture of the primitive community preaching, praying, counselling one another, and so on. That was the 'normative' thing. This task is not really part of the quest for the historical Jesus. It is the quest for the kerygmatic church.

It is true that the 'New Quest'[9] marks an important step on the road. Käsemann spotted a flaw in Bultmann's scheme. It was vital, he pointed out, that the Christ of faith should be identified with the human Jesus who died on the cross, since otherwise he would remain a docetic figure, removed from our world. But this means, ultimately, that the writing of gospels is not, after all, evidence for a failure of nerve on the part of the early church, a lapse back into history-faith. The gospel-writers had a good reason, it appears, to be interested in the Jesus of history – as of course scholars outside the narrow Bultmannian tradition had always maintained.[10] Nevertheless, the 'New Quest' has not proved itself markedly more successful than the old one, not least perhaps because of this tension or even contradiction within its presuppositions. Recent work[11] indicates that scholars from several backgrounds are eager to discover new ways forward, building on the strengths of old models

---

9   See Käsemann 1964; Robinson 1959.

10   E.g. Dodd 1971; Manson 1931; Moule 1967; and now Harvey 1982; Stanton 1974.

11   Meyer 1979; Harvey 1982; Riches 1980.

while attempting to eliminate weaknesses. It is in that hope that I offer a few suggestions in the second half of this article.

Many criticisms have been advanced against the 'criteria of authenticity' set up by Perrin and Fuller as tests of synoptic material.[12] But even on the most stringent criteria, certain points emerge more or less beyond dispute: that Jesus began his ministry at the time of John's baptism, that he proclaimed the kingdom of God, that he had a well-earned reputation as a healer and exorcist, that he gathered around him a group of close associates, sometimes kept dubious company, engaged in controversy with the Jewish religious teachers, and that, as a result of this, he was finally crucified 'under Pontius Pilate'.[13] In Perrin's famous sentence, 'that . . . is all that we can know: it is enough'.[14]

But – enough for what? For Perrin's own (Bultmannian) theological scheme, perhaps, in which anything more than a bare outline of Jesus' story is too much. But enough, also, for us to know one fact about Jesus which, though almost laughably obvious, is scarcely ever given any prominence at all,[15] while being, I believe, of great significance. It is this: the total ministry of Jesus takes place in the context of *the hope of Israel*. And that hope was not, in essence, universalizable. It could not be transplanted into other nations or cultures or times. It was, specifically, not a generalized human hope. It was the hope that now, at last, God would act in history to vindicate both his own [23] name and his covenant people Israel. This hope that God would take his power and reign was therefore a hope for national restoration. God would exalt Israel to occupy the role for which the Torah had fitted it, that of being his right-hand nation, ruling over those outside. This hope, variously expressed, was in essence the result of the tension between Israel's vocation in the Torah and Prophets and the actuality of first-century politics. It is important to note that only in comparatively rare cases did it include specific messianic expectation. Conversely, when such an expectation existed, it was as part of the larger whole, God's purposes for his chosen race.[16]

It was within this context that Jesus appeared, like John, as a prophet, declaring that the time promised of old had now been fulfilled. It is at this point (I believe) that a good deal of Christian reading of the gospels has gone

---

12   See Perrin and Duling 1982, 405f.; for some criticisms see Hooker 1972; 1975.

13   This is an abbreviated version of Perrin's minimal account. Perrin and Duling 1982, 411f.

14   Perrin and Duling 1982, 412.

15   Meyer 1979; Caird 1965; and Flew 1938 are good exceptions.

16   See now Harvey 1982, 77f.

wrong, jumping too quickly, in the interests of contemporary relevance, away from the specifically Jewish context of the ministry and teaching of Jesus. In fact, neither John nor Jesus was preaching a set of 'timeless truths'. Their message was one of sharp local relevance. Jesus was not sent 'except to the lost sheep of the house of Israel' (Matthew 15.24; cf. 10.6). The message – of apocalyptic urgency – was not a universalized prediction of the imminent end of the world, but a specific prediction (couched, of course, in appropriate apocalyptic imagery) of what, from a Jewish point of view, would be conceived as *the end of the present world order*, namely that state of affairs in which Israel according to the flesh was the chosen people through whom God would act in the world. That is why the predictions of the destruction of Jerusalem are irrevocably intertwined with those usually interpreted as referring to a final cataclysm. As John warned that the axe was laid to the roots of the tree (the tree being, in context, Israel as the people of God), so Jesus, in proclaiming the fulfilment of God's promises to Israel, necessarily announced the final warning to a people whom he saw as failing in their divine vocation.

This framework provides, I believe, a historically credible and theologically appropriate context for a good deal more synoptic material than normally survives critical scrutiny. The preaching of the kingdom, in particular, is to be understood in a threefold fashion. First, it is the declaration that God is at last fulfilling his promises, reigning as king and, in doing so, vindicating his people. Second, however, it is the *explanation* (particularly in the 'parables of the kingdom') that this fulfilment is not taking the shape commonly expected. Third, therefore, it is the urgent summons ('Repent, and believe the good news') to prove oneself truly a member of the eschatological people of God, to respond not merely to the message but to the messenger himself, the prophet whose aim seems to have been to gather the nucleus of the true Israel around himself.[17]

If this picture is accurate, the criterion of coherence will show that a good deal of synoptic material, whatever its subsequent use in the church, can be seen as belonging in a peculiar sense in the ministry of Jesus. The [24] healing miracles, for example, are not mere philanthropy, nor even merely a fulfilment of (for example) Isaiah 35. The healing of lepers, deaf and dumb, paralysed people and so on was first and foremost the restoration to covenant membership of those who had been ritually excluded (compare 1QSa). This activity corresponds to the open table-fellowship with outcasts: 'today

---

17   See Meyer 1979 etc.

salvation has come to this house, inasmuch as he too is a child of Abraham'
(Luke 19.9).

Within this context, too, there is scope for a renewed assessment of Jesus'
so-called 'self-understanding'. We can at least say that he was conscious of
a vocation to proclaim that God was at last doing what he had promised,
and this consciousness (perhaps we should say 'belief') seems to have
included the belief that God's kingdom was in some way bound up with
his own proclamation and activity. Jesus appears, in fact, to draw on to
himself the role marked out in God's purposes for *Israel itself*: God is ruling,
and redeeming, the world through his obedient Man. And this inevitably
effects the *reconstitution* of Israel around the Man. The prophetic word of
judgment and mercy is acted out by the prophet himself in his death and
resurrection, as he accomplishes, for Israel and for the world, what Israel
was called to do but failed to do. It is when we raise the further question,
of the *appropriateness* of this fulfilment of God's redemptive purposes, that
new christological perspectives are opened up which it is here impossible to
pursue further.

This all too brief reconstruction suggests a new kind of criterion for further
synoptic research. Paradoxically, we meet up at this point with the results
of some recent redaction-critical work, in which Matthew and Luke see
the time of the ministry of Jesus as a special time, a sort of 'sacred time'.[18]
Our suggestion is that, while these analyses of Matthew and Luke may need
further adjustment, the insight is fundamentally correct, in two senses. First,
Matthew and Luke (and for that matter Mark) *do* see the time of the ministry
as *sui generis*; second, they were right so to see and describe it. Certain sorts of
event were appropriate then, so to speak, which were appropriate at no other
time. Only then was Jesus walking round Palestine preaching and acting in
just that way.

Two results follow at once. First, if the evangelists made a clear distinction –
as the redaction-critics and the 'New Quest' are now saying – between the
ministry of Jesus and the time of the church, the old form-critical presupposition that 'early church' material could without difficulty be transposed
back into the life of Jesus looks decidedly shaky. Second, it is possible to use
this basic picture of the ministry of Jesus as a *theological* 'criterion of dissimilarity', as opposed to the regular history-of-religions one. According to such
a criterion, certain sorts of *event* (not merely teaching) would be appropriate
for the time of the ministry, and certain others would not.

---

18   Perrin and Duling 1982, 289, 303ff.

Like all good historical proposals, such a point of view would function as an hypothesis in need of verification or falsification. The tests, as in scientific work, would be whether the hypothesis succeeded, at least more than its rivals, in (1) making clear and coherent sense of as much of the basic data [25] as possible, and (2) helping to solve other problems in addition to those for which it was designed. I believe that the suggestions I have made here, albeit dangerously brief, could in principle be expanded into an hypothesis that would fulfil the first condition. Further research on other New Testament areas, not least Pauline theology, might help towards satisfying the second. Such is my present proposal for some new detonators to be placed in the theologians' playground. Whether they explode or not, and if so which toys would remain undamaged, it is beyond the scope of this article to predict.

2

Jesus, Israel and the Cross

In the autumn of 1982, a few months after writing the previous article, I was for the first time teaching an introductory course on the whole New Testament, and I was gearing up for the section on Jesus himself. As part of my background work, I reread the booklet *Jesus and the Jewish Nation* by my teacher George Caird, while on a homeward train from work, passing through the West Island of Montreal. The historical work I had been doing since the first time I had read it prepared me now more fully to grasp one of Caird's central emphases, and the way in which he drew together the historical meaning of standard Jewish 'apocalyptic' language into a dramatic, though very abbreviated, statement of Jesus' own historical intentions as he went to the cross. I spent some time brainstorming what I saw as the possible implications and ramifications, and wrote to Caird rather cautiously to see if he would approve of the direction I was taking. Back came a letter by return, expressing delight that someone was at last taking seriously things he had been 'banging on about' for years, and pushing the line of thought further.

This was one of several sudden stimulants for the fourteen years of further research, teaching, conference discussions and writing which finally issued in *Jesus and the Victory of God* in 1996. A second was my reading of Marcus Borg's book *Conflict, Holiness, and Politics in the Teachings of Jesus*; Marcus had studied with Caird before my time, but he and I became close friends, despite a considerable theological gap, as his book made its impact in the mid-1980s. It was a public discussion of that book, at the 1984 Annual Meeting of the Society of Biblical Literature (SBL), which generated the present paper for a follow-up session the next year. It is fascinating, rereading this essay after thirty-five years, to see how themes that I now regard as absolutely necessary for the understanding of early Christianity were already making their appearance – even though I would now put them in a larger framework and with a different nuance.

[75] Like naughty children whispering after a command to silence, and then, greatly daring, talking openly and with increasing volume, New Testament

scholars, so long forbidden to talk about Jesus of Nazareth, have begun in the last decade to do so with renewed vigour. Twenty or so years ago the late Bishop Stephen Neill could write, 'It is just the fact that the *historical* reconstruction of the life and history of Jesus has as yet hardly begun';[1] those words, true at the time, are now quite out of date. Neill went on to say that 'The materials for further work are all there. What we need now is historians'. They have duly appeared: Caird (1965), Bowker (1973a), Vermes (1973), Meyer (1979), Riches (1980), Hengel (1981b; German original, 1968), Harvey (1982) and now Borg (1984)[2] and Sanders (1985), sharing (despite their wide differences of approach and results) the conviction that it is possible to know quite a lot about Jesus of Nazareth and that to discuss him as a figure of history is worthwhile.[3] There is space here neither to review this 'Third Quest' nor to justify it theologically.[4] My intention, in response to the suggestion of the Historical Jesus Consultation in the 1984 SBL meeting, is simply to attempt an answer to the question: if it is true that Jesus' life and ministry are to be understood within the framework of Judaism, and in particular if it is true that his aims and intentions were bound up with the fate of the Jewish nation (this loose way of putting it is designed to cover the positions of most of the above writers: in what follows, however, there will be space only for limited interaction with others, with the exception of Borg and Sanders), what sense can be made of his suffering and death?

A few words about the background and nature of this question will be in order before we can begin to look at it for itself.

I

There is, for a start, the problem of the 'if' in the question as formulated. It was axiomatic for some previous generations of scholars that Jesus' life and ministry had to be divorced from their Jewish setting: at best it provided the dark backcloth against which the sparkling jewel could better be seen.[5]

---

1 Neill 1964, 283.

2 And see now Borg 1987b.

3 I use the phrase 'Jesus of Nazareth' in preference to 'the historical Jesus' because of the overtones of earlier debates, and of unfortunate positions within them, carried by the latter. For other positions of importance within the present stage of debate, see Stanton 1974; Goppelt 1981; Lohfink 1984.

4 For some reflections on this issue, see Wright 1982 (ch. 1 in the present volume).

5 See Sanders 1977, 1–59, for what must now be regarded as a standard refutation of [76] this retrojection of the Protestant view of sixteenth-century church history – the dark Middle Ages, the bright jewel of Martin Luther – into the first century of the era. See Sanders's criticism of Käsemann (1985, 331 and elsewhere), and the chapter 'The agonised attempts to save Jesus from apocalyptic: continental New Testament scholarship' in Koch 1972, ch. 6.

Jesus, it was thought, taught a lofty **[76]** message of universal significance: interest in his own Jewish people, their problems and their politics, would stand awkwardly apart from virtually all other situations. Worse (for the line of thought we are describing), it would have tied him not just to a particular historical situation but to a *Jewish* frame of thought, which was just the sort of thing that much post-Enlightenment religion regarded with distaste or worse. Thus, in order to make Jesus not only theologically relevant but theologically correct, he must be universalized, and with him his background. Judaism becomes a typical example of the wrong sort of religion: Jesus, the announcer of the right sort.

It is without a doubt the problems that this view poses for anyone wishing to make sense of the history of first-century Palestine that have caused people acting (no doubt) with the highest of motives to argue that the 'Jesus of history' is more or less irrelevant for Christian faith, and to retroject that argument, too, into the first century by claiming that the evangelists were no more interested in him than a good neo-Kantian or Heideggerian ought to be. But the historical problems will not go away. As F. C. Burkitt pointed out in his preface to the first edition of Schweitzer's *Quest*:

the true view of the Gospel [by which he meant, of course, the accounts of Jesus' life in the gospels] will be that which explains the course of events in the first century and the second century, rather than that which seems to have spiritual and imaginative value for the twentieth century.[6]

And what is to be explained is just what the view I have criticized cannot explain: why Jesus of Nazareth, who began his ministry in close association with a preacher of repentance to Israel, and whose followers, after his death, still shared in some ways the apocalyptic hope of their Jewish contemporaries, should have met his death on a Roman cross outside the gates of Jerusalem. Just as it makes sense to ask why the Peloponnesian War occurred, and why Athens eventually lost it (not to mention whether Thucydides, the first to raise the questions, got the answers right), it makes sense to ask why Jesus did what he did during his evidently brief ministry, and why he met the death he did – and whether the evangelists, who may have been the first to raise these questions, got the answers (historically) right.

---

6 Burkitt 1954 [1910], xix. See Sanders 1985, 333: history and exegesis are to be set free 'from being obligated to come to certain conclusions which are pre-determined by theological commitment'.

It is, of course, possible to suggest an answer to this question without leaving the usual framework of thought: Jesus offended the religious beliefs and vested interests of his contemporaries, and died (in effect) as a martyr for the right sort of religion. But this view, too, has large problems to surmount. First, the evidence of the gospels themselves does not suggest that the opposition which eventually led to Jesus' death was what (in this view) would usually count as specifically religious, or theologically motivated. The trial narratives do not obviously go back to Jesus' reported attacks on Torah, his sabbath violations, his rude remarks about the food laws. However the charge of blasphemy is to be interpreted, it is only connected by the occasional slender thread (for example Mark 2.7 and parallels) to the controversies that surrounded Jesus during his ministry. Second, this view has great difficulty in explaining how Jesus' death as a martyr to the cause of universal spiritual religion could be seen, within a decade or two at least, as possessing atoning significance; this point could be sharpened by asking how it was that Paul could write, about twenty years later, that 'the son of God loved me and gave himself for me' (Galatians 2.20). This second problem, however, is shared by some at least of the works repre-[77]-sented in the newest Quest, and it is the task of this paper to show how, within the parameters set by the current discussion, a satisfactory answer may be found.

The alternative approach offered by writers in the Reimarus–Brandon line[7] has of course had its own solution to the problem: Jesus was a Jewish freedom-fighter who suffered, predictably, the punishment that the Romans characteristically meted out to revolutionary leaders. This view, though not (as we will see) without strengths that must be taken into account in any eventual hypothesis, runs into problems of its own. The actual evidence we have makes it extremely unlikely that Jesus was an advocate of revolutionary violence,[8] and this view, too, fails to explain either why Jesus' death was regarded so soon as atoning or, as Sanders has pointed out (1985, 226, 228, 231, 295, 318, 329), why his disciples were not at once rounded up and rooted out.[9] Nevertheless, the reaction to Brandon has too often been of the form: Jesus was not a violent revolutionary, therefore (or is it 'because'?) his message is apolitical,

---

7   See Bammel 1984.

8   Harvey 1982, ch. 1; Bammel and Moule 1984, *passim*. Sanders 1985, 326, claims that it is 'certain or virtually certain' that neither Jesus nor his disciples 'thought that the kingdom could be established by force of arms'.

9   The Domitianic persecution of the family of Jesus as though its members belonged to a royal house with political aspirations (Eus. *Hist. Eccl.* 3.19f., following Hegesippus) does not of course disprove this point, but rather highlights the fact that the earliest disciples did not suffer such persecution.

spiritual, timeless, universal. I regard it as one of the many great strengths of Borg's book that he attacks this standard view and suggests that there are more than two possible positions here.[10] To split 'religion' and 'politics' as neatly and apparently self-evidently as post-Enlightenment western thought does is one thing; to project that view into the first century (or even, for that matter, the sixteenth) is to commit gross anachronism, especially when what is at stake is the historical understanding of a people who were committed, for reasons we would today call 'religious', to a particular territory and social lifestyle. There is, then, more than meets the eye to the *titulus* on the cross: Jesus' death may after all have had something to do with the hope of Israel, though not perhaps in the way Brandon thought.[11] But this is to run ahead of the argument.

It is, happily, less incumbent on a writer today than it was ten years ago to write a massive section of his treatment of Jesus explaining and justifying his method.[12] One or two remarks, however, are in order at this stage. Like Sanders (1985, 47), I agree wholeheartedly with Meyer in his argument that, as historians, we must proceed on the assumption that historical knowledge is real knowledge, and that the route by which it is to be reached is that of hypothesis and verification. Insofar as some of the famous 'criteria' for adjudging synoptic authenticity lend themselves to use within this scheme, they are to be valued; but they are not of very much value even there, as will be readily apparent from the constant disagreements even among those who agree in theory on the tools they are using. The much-vaunted 'criterion of dissimilarity', in particular, was never really a *critical* tool in the first place, however 'objective' it may have appeared to the outsider. It was designed as a blunt instrument for implementing a double theological programme: Jesus is to be divorced from his Jewish context, and the early church **[78]** is to have no interest in the historical Jesus. This is actually an odd combination, since if Jesus really was separate from Judaism, the teacher who challenged people to existentialist decision, it should have been quite safe for the early church, or indeed the modern one, to be interested in him: hence Bultmann's *Jesus*. The idea that ancient and modern Christians are better off with the Christ of

---

10   1984, 1–20; and such summaries as 235: 'Jesus' attitude towards Rome was not based on an apolitical stance, but on the conviction that in the political affairs of the world the judging activity of God was at work.'

11   See Meyer 1979, 19f.: Reimarus was right to insist on the Jewish political context (which the nineteenth century promptly forgot), wrong in how he interpreted it. See below for an analogous analysis of Schweitzer.

12   See Schillebeeckx 1979, 41–102; Meyer 1979, 23–110. [I did, however, write a substantial essay to this effect in Part II of *The New Testament and the People of God* (Wright 1992a).]

faith than with the Jesus of history offers tacit recognition that Jesus cannot, after all, be divorced from his Jewish matrix. Hence the need for the other blunt instrument: demythologization.

In practice, writers of all stripes this century have in fact used the hypothesis-model: sayings and incidents that would be suspect on strict application of the criteria are retained because they are close to the heart of what the writer assumes to be bedrock in our knowledge of Jesus, and the criteria are often wheeled in only as convenient ways of eliminating those bits of evidence that do not fit the hypothesis.[13] This has resulted in the strange situation that one of the age-old criteria for a good *hypothesis* – in any field of enquiry from a police investigation to a metaphysical conundrum – has been quietly set aside: one must 'save the appearances', must include as far as possible all the evidence. The 'criteria' have provided a convenient waste-basket where 'appearances' that the hypothesis cannot 'save' may be deposited without anyone feeling guilty about it. The strength of Harvey's argument, and, *mutatis mutandis*, those also of Meyer, Borg and Sanders, is that they provide hypotheses in which significantly more of the 'appearances' are 'saved' than in many previous treatments; and by 'appearances' I mean the texts of the synoptic gospels.[14] We need, then, hypotheses, and these recent works suggest some; I shall offer my own, or rather a summary outline of that part of my own which bears on the specific topic in hand. The strength of a hypothesis is its essential simplicity, its 'saving' of the 'appearances', and its ability to make sense of data not part of the present puzzle. I regard all the works already cited as possessing these strengths in varying degrees over against the main line of writing about Jesus that preceded them in the twentieth (or, for that matter, the nineteenth) century; and this paper is an attempt to modify and re-present part, at least, of the overall hypothesis that seems to be emerging.

II

The case I wish to advance has three stages, almost syllogistic in overall form. The first may be stated, in advance, as follows: *Jesus warned his contemporaries*

---

13 See the comments of Caird (1965, 5) on Bultmann's actual practice; and of Borg (1984, 22) on Perrin's.

14 Borg 1984 frequently (e.g. 132f., 142, 173) resorts to the argument that, even if a certain passage is not from Jesus, it is from the early Palestinian church, which shared his aims and outlook. This seems to me fine as far as it goes, though it is, of course, open to the rejoinder that if the continuity is strong enough for the argument to stand it is hard to see why the passage cannot, at least hypothetically, be ascribed to Jesus himself.

of imminent divine judgment. This is in some ways the required starting-point for this paper, since it was requested as a sequel to a discussion of Borg's book, where the point is made central, and established at some length.[15] But just here there is a conflict with most of the other recent writers about Jesus. Meyer and Sanders, for instance, regard a message of judgment as almost peripheral in Jesus' ministry. The point must therefore be set out in some detail.

We may begin on solid ground.[16] (1) Jesus' ministry took its historical origin from that of John the Baptist, who, as is widely agreed, warned Israel of 'the wrath to come' and urged it to turn while there was time. He can be safely located on the map of [79] Jewish apocalyptic expectation, as can the early church, whose half-misunderstandings (for example Acts 1.6) are still recorded at a time when such issues had lost their immediate relevance. Paul, too, shows constant signs of being grounded in the Jewish apocalyptic expect-ation, whether we judge such signs to be indications of his major theological emphases or whether, with Käsemann, we place them at the periphery. If Jesus had not shared these expectations, he would have been more than an historical oddity: he would have been incomprehensible and irrelevant in the eyes of his contemporaries. This, which is similar to Harvey's overall thesis (though he does not develop it in relation to the hope of *Israel*), amounts to the simple argument: Jesus must have taught and lived in this context, otherwise he would not have made sense. More: he would not have been crucified. A nineteenth-century moralist or teacher of pure, spiritual religion, or a man who proclaimed that God was 'near' as opposed to remote (a fact of which many Jews were already well aware), would not, it is safe to say, have ended up on a cross.[17] Jesus lived, taught and died in a context of what Sanders calls 'Jewish restoration eschatology'.

(2) But in what did this 'apocalyptic hope' consist? Space forbids the detailed discussion this question warrants. Perhaps the best that can be done is to register my agreement with the line taken by Caird (1965; 1976; 1980) and Borg (as above), following the interpretation of apocalyptic given by S. B. Frost in particular: the 'apocalyptic' hope of Israel was not an expec-tation that God would soon end the entire space-time order, but was the hope that he would soon, within the continuing course of history, act to vindicate his own name by delivering his covenant people from their current political

15 Borg 1984, 201–27, 265–76.
16 See Sanders 1985, *passim*.
17 So, rightly, Borg 1984, 319 n. 115.

15

and social predicaments. The language used by many writers (though by no means all) as the vehicle of this hope has systematically misled generations of scholars into imagining that the referent is 'the end of the world', whereas its purpose is rather to invest the future space-time events that are the actual referents with their true theological significance. The classic example of a scholar thus misled is of course Albert Schweitzer, who was so right in his insistence that Jesus is to be seen in the context of Jewish eschatology and so wrong in his interpretation of it, just as Reimarus and Brandon were right to make politics the setting and wrong to make Jesus an armed revolutionary.[18] When God acts in this way, he will be ushering in *ha'olam haba'*, the new age. This is akin to Jeremiah's prophecy that 'the day of the Lord' was soon to break on the people of Israel: the Babylonian invasion was to be identified as the coming of that day. The historical and political events were invested with theological significance. This point is particularly striking in the interpretation of Daniel 7. No-one imagines that the beasts are to be taken as actual animals, but many assume that the figure like a son of man is to be taken as just that, a human figure. It is hard to maintain the symbolic interpretation, and the consequent this-worldly reference, of the New Testament apocalyptic language when faced with an overwhelming tradition that insists on taking it literally, but I believe this is the only way forward if justice is to be done to the literature itself, let alone its relevance to the New Testament. Even Borg (for example p. 212) stops short of Caird's position (1965, 18–22) when it comes to the 'son of man' sayings.

(3) Jesus warned, then, of the approach, not of 'the end of the world' in the sense of the cessation of the present space-time continuum, but of *the end of the present socio-political state of affairs*.[19] (I used to use the phrase 'the end of the present world order', but in his new book Sanders has used it with a different sense, and I therefore avoid it for the sake of clarity. Sanders, it seems to me, never quite grasps the nettle. He sees that [80] in some cases the hope must be seen as this-worldly, but persists in maintaining the traditional view that many expressions of it have an otherworldly referent.) Jesus' statements about an imminent 'end' are to be read against their characteristic Jewish-apocalyptic background: there will be events in the immediately future history which will constitute God's action in history to fulfil the covenant and bring in at last the new age when God's people will be vindicated after

---

18 See esp. Borg 1984, 216ff., and the references there, especially that (367 n. 45) to the work of Amos Wilder; also Caird 1976; 1980 chs. 12–14.

19 See Borg 1984, 202: 'what faced the hearers of Jesus was not the imminent . . . end of the world, but the imminent . . . destruction of Israel.'

their long desolation. It is this which gives to his preaching its character-istic urgency, so rightly noted and so wrongly interpreted by both Schweitzer and Bultmann. It is this, too, that gave him relevance to his contemporary situation: the smouldering conflicts between Jew and gentile, and between Jew and Jew, that characterized the outwardly peaceful society of Palestine in the first thirty years of the era[20] were directly addressed by one who claimed, and put his claim into action, that God was about to act to set things right. Only in this context can we understand how his message – especially his language about the kingdom – could have been more than the timeless philosophy to which scholarship still so often reduces it.

(4) If Jesus' language about the kingdom thus resonated with the expect-ation of his contemporaries that God would act in history to vindicate his name and his people, it is also clear that what he said about the kingdom challenged and disturbed those current expectations. His message is, to that extent, like that of Amos 5.18: why do you desire the day of YHWH? It is a day of darkness, and not of light. A good many of the parables are devoted to saying: *this*, and not that, is what the kingdom (for which you have longed) is like. It is like a net full of fish, good and bad together; like wheat mingled with tares; like a man sowing seed in his field. It is a time of judgment for Israel, not deliverance merely. Many will come from east and west, and sit down with Abraham, Isaac and Jacob in the kingdom, while the children of the kingdom are cast out. If these statements and others like them are read simply as retrojections of the later church into the ministry of Jesus, it will be impossible (I believe) to understand that ministry in its true colours.

(5) In particular, it will be impossible to understand why Jesus was referred to as a *prophet*. This attribution should be distinguished from the frequently discussed question of whether Jesus was thought of, or thought of himself as, 'the eschatological prophet'; there is, in fact, comparatively little evidence for that reference to Deuteronomy 18.15–22 in the gospels, John 6.14 and one or two other passages being exceptions. There is plenty of evidence that the primary category seized on by Jesus' contemporaries to explain who he was was 'prophet' in the sense not of national leader but of national disturber: John the Baptist, Elijah, Jeremiah were the models chosen, according to Matthew 16.14 and parallels. Good evidence, too: the great majority of refer-ences come very definitely into the 'dissimilarity' test, since Judaism was not noticeably expecting a prophet who, like Elijah and Jeremiah, would warn that the covenant God had a quarrel with his people, and the early church very

---

20 For this view of the period see Borg 1984, 27–72.

quickly abandoned the category in favour of others more clearly honorific. Matthew 16.14 itself might be held to be an exception, since the passage is clearly leading up to a statement of Jesus' Messiahship, and the references to the prophets might be held to be introduced simply for the sake of contrast. But this will not do in the light of the other evidence. Herod apparently put Jesus into the category of 'prophet'; so did the disciples; and so did Jesus himself – 'it is impossible that a prophet should perish outside Jerusalem'; 'a prophet is not without honour except in his own country'. Even when the context cries out for at least a messianic statement, Matthew has the crowds at the Entry announce, 'This is the prophet, Jesus, from Nazareth in Galilee.' And the characteristic message of the prophet is to warn the people of God that they are off course, and that God will shortly act to punish them, and to deliver those who (in this sense) mend their ways. [81]

(6) Into this developing picture the numerous explicit *warnings* of the synoptic gospels fit comfortably. The fig tree has one more year to bear fruit, and 'if not, then you can cut it down': those who perished in one of Pilate's characteristically provocative suppressions of Jewish feeling will set the pattern for all – unless they repent. There will be a separation of righteous and unrighteous, of wheat and chaff. Israel will be like a steward about to be put out of service for mismanagement, and unless it makes alternative provisions quickly its plight will be sorry. If Sanders is right – and I think he is – then the action in the Temple can be seen within exactly the same context: not basically as a cleansing, as though Jesus thought either to make it fit for continuing use or to register a protest against the 'materialistic' concerns of Judaism (again, anachronism has made nonsense of the setting), but as a symbolic act of destruction.[21] Here the theme that we are observing in the sayings material finds a grounding in indisputable fact.[22] But, against Sanders's repeated assertions, I believe (a) that there is no good reason to deny that Jesus preached, repeatedly and centrally, the warning of impending judgment which the action in the Temple symbolized; and (b) that there is nothing in the synoptic tradition (and only John 2.18–22 outside it) to warrant the assertion that the main thing in Jesus' mind in the Temple-incident was not judgment but restoration. (It is ironic how one of the few 'sayings' attributed

21 At the same time, Sanders's view needs to be put together with the brilliant suggestions made by Borg (1984, 170–7). If this is done the incident can be interpreted as an acted parable of judgment, and the saying that accompanies it fits perfectly. The Temple, and its concern for 'holiness' of the 'separation' variety, is the actual centre of that Jewish resistance to Rome which Jesus sees as courting theological/political disaster. See too Meyer 1979, 198, explaining the incident by reference to the prophecy of Zech. 14.21 (that there would, in the eschaton, be no traders in the Temple).
22 See Sanders 1985, 61–76.

to Jesus which Sanders allows to become part of his 'bedrock' is that put into his mouth by the false witnesses in the trial – and even they could not agree on it. It could of course be said that the setting reflects the embarrassment of the evangelists, but that is odd, since (i) they happily 'report' several other predictions of the Temple's destruction and (ii) the Johannine explanation of the 'rebuilding' idea was ready to hand.) The fig-tree incident, which clearly goes with the Temple-incident and interprets it, suggests that Luke 13.35 is closer to the mark: the Temple is abandoned by God, as in Ezekiel 10, and is therefore defenceless against the enemy.[23] One of the great advantages – if it is an advantage – of this view is that Mark 13 and parallels no longer stand out like a sore thumb from the rest of the tradition, but fit comfortably within it and indeed draw it to a climax: Jesus' whole ministry is one of apocalyptic warning of the immediately future judgment that will come on Israel unless it repents.

(7) The warnings appear to have a definite and concrete referent. Just as Babylon, and Assyria before it, were seen by the prophets as God's instruments for purging his sinful people, so Rome will be God's means of bringing judgment on those who refuse to heed the warnings of Jesus (or, for that matter, of John the Baptist). The axe is laid to the roots of the tree: Rome, with its blasphemous standards and coinage, already pollutes the holy land, and the pollution will be complete – 'unless you repent'. It is at this point that the extraordinariness of Jesus' message becomes fully apparent. The Jewish hope, in a nutshell, was that God would act to save his people *from* Rome (as the concrete historical manifestation of his faithfulness to the covenant). Where messianic expectations existed, as we shall see, they functioned within that wider, and more widespread, national hope. Jesus, however, while declaring that the kingdom of God is imminent, stands the concrete form of the hope on its head. Hope lies, not in large-scale **[82]** national deliverance from an enemy without, but in a national turning to a new form of aspiration – which is already appearing *entos hymōn*, 'in your midst', as a grain of mustard seed, small but growing. The paradox of Jesus' ministry is this: that, in claiming to herald the fulfilment of Israel's hope, he radically redefines that hope. Caird and Borg both make the point that, for Jesus, the referent of the warnings is specific and concrete: if you persist in nationalist ambition, sooner or later Rome will crush you. Left in that form, it may be said (and Sanders does say it) that it did not take much political astuteness to make such a prediction. True; but what the synoptic writers assert is that Jesus did not leave it in that

---

23   See Borg 1984, 181ff.

form. He warned that the 'national hope', followed in the way it was being followed, would lead to the wrath of Rome, *and that in that wrath was to be seen the wrath of God.* That is the point at which the political and historical referent of the warning is invested with theological significance, the insight that went beyond mere political or historical shrewdness.

(8) The (so-called) ethical teaching of Jesus is to be seen, in this light, not in terms of a mere interiorization of 'external' Torah, nor indeed as a new Torah, but as the summons to Israel to *be* Israel – under Jesus' guidance. The Torah means what it says, that the very ideas of murder and adultery are hateful to God. God means what he says that he is a father to Israel, but to treat him as such will involve rethinking many practices of current piety. Here Borg makes one of his most important contributions to the discussion: Jesus offers Israel an alternative paradigm, the 'mercy code' (Luke 6.36 summarizing 6.27–36 and its Matthaean parallel) instead of the 'holiness code'. Instead of conceiving its national task as a holiness that involved separation, Jesus invites Israel to find its vocation in a different sort of *imitatio Dei*,[24] which will mean forgiving enemies instead of exacting vengeance against them, going the second mile on behalf of the hated Roman soldier, taking the pain and anger of the present situation and offering love in return. The table-fellowship with sinners is not merely the acting out of grace to sinners: it is an acted parable of what Israel should be like, a welcoming, mercy-offering community, rather than an exclusivist company concerned with separation from defilement and hence always likely to run into conflict with Rome (so Borg, ch. 4 and frequently). This is a revolutionary Jesus of a rather different sort from Brandon's, but, as Borg so clearly shows, one who was making a definite political statement none the less. He who is not with the national hope is against it; he who announces that it is fulfilled, and yet systematically undermines it, is a traitor. The parallel with Elijah, and particularly with Jeremiah, could hardly be clearer.[25]

Each of these eight points is of course controversial in its own right in terms of present scholarship, and I do not suppose for a moment that I have

---

24 Borg 1984, *passim*, and esp. ch. 5.

25 From this point it would be possible to suggest a new solution to the problem tackled so interestingly by Sanders (1985) on pp. 222ff., that the sayings material seems not to fit the overall 'Jewish restoration eschatology' which he finds to be the correct matrix for understanding Jesus. This, of course, is why he spends so much time in the book arguing that the sayings are the wrong place to begin – a point with which, for my own reasons, I am in agreement. I think, in fact, that the sayings, understood as I have suggested, fit very well with the theme of Israel's reconstitution. The further question, whether Jesus thought the judgment inevitable (Schweitzer) or merely contingent (Borg, Caird and most others), is harder, and must be pursued at a later point.

here presented a complete, let alone a convincing, case for them. My intention is merely to suggest the outline of what I believe to be a comprehensible and coherent picture, as far as it goes, of Jesus: as 'a prophet mighty in word and deed', announcing like John the Baptist a message of imminent judgment on the people of God. The judgment will be an historical event, a fall of Jerusalem in history like that predicted by Jeremiah, but, also like [83] that event, it must be understood as God's judgment on his people and, particularly, on the holy city and the Temple.

III

The second point of the syllogism has the effect of restoring the balance that some may feel is lost in the presentation of the first. Jesus did not merely proclaim judgment against the people of God: *he identified himself with Israel.* His summons, his welcome, his offer form the positive side of the ministry, which, as we shall see, dovetails exactly into the negative side outlined above. This is, if anything, a more controversial claim than the first, and must likewise be presented step by step.[26]

(1) In a prima facie reading of the synoptics, it appears that, when Jesus warned of judgment to come he also invited his hearers to follow him and so become part of the incipient new people of God that he was summoning into being. There is now growing agreement that the category of 'the twelve' goes back to Jesus himself, and that it signifies his intention to remake the people of God;[27] this is just one of many symptoms of his underlying aim. Those who followed him were those who had heeded the warning, and who were, in principle at least, prepared to forswear the outlook and aspirations of their contemporaries, though the muddles they retained, preserved against the natural tendency in the synoptic tradition, are evidence that they were still fairly unclear as to precise implications. But the fact of their being *twelve* carries an implicit meaning about the place of Jesus himself in the whole scheme. He is not himself one of the twelve, not even *primus inter pares.* He stands over against them, calling them into being: they are the beginnings of the reconstituted Israel insofar as they are his followers. It is important not to read too much into this, but equally important not to

---

26 Among scholars who have pursued this line one thinks particularly of Caird (e.g. 1982), Manson 1931 and Moule 1967.

27 See now Sanders 1985, 95–106.

read too little. I suggest that the natural implication is that they are 'Israel' *because he is Israel.*[28]

(2) This interpretation is reinforced by a consideration of other actions that are now almost universally acknowledged as historical: Jesus welcomed 'sinners' and ate with them, and he healed those afflicted with a variety of physical and mental ailments. Jesus restores to membership in Israel those who had been on the margins of the holy society, whether through physical defects (compare 1QSa 2.4–9) or moral or social blemishes. The healing miracles and the table-fellowship with sinners are, in fact, all of a piece, and very instructive for the hypothesis I am developing. Jesus' physical contact with lepers, with the woman suffering from the haemorrhage, with corpses, and so on, render him unclean just as did his eating with Matthew, or with Zacchaeus. Those two stories, in fact, could be seen as paradigmatic for this aspect of the ministry. Jesus *identifies himself with sinful Israel,* and thus contracts its uncleanness: nevertheless, when he emerges from Zacchaeus's house to face the accusing crowd, it is not he who is unclean but Zacchaeus who is 'a son of Abraham'. The miracles and the welcome to outcasts thus invite the same interpretation as I have given to the call of the 'twelve': they only make sense if Jesus, who eats with the sinners, is himself the centre-point of the reconstituted Israel that is being called into existence. Unless this nexus between Jesus and the people of God is clearly seen, the welcome becomes vacuous: who is he, to 'welcome' anyone?[29] **[84]**

(3) Putting this point together with the first part of the syllogism, I therefore prefer to speak not of Israel's 'restoration', as does Sanders, but of its 'reconstitution'. Sanders (it seems to me) is absolutely right to draw attention to the Israel-dimension of the ministry of Jesus, and this marks him out from many other writers even in what I have called the 'Third Quest'.[30] But his suggestion, both explicitly and by implication, is that Jesus' primary aim is to restore Israel, with judgment only an ancillary warning. My suggestion is that Jesus sees Israel passing into a crisis – its last crisis: this generation will see the end of the present situation of the people of God. Like Jonah at Nineveh, his message could be summarized as 'yet forty years, and Jerusalem shall be

---

28 See the careful, but ultimately inconclusive, discussions in Sanders 1985, 321ff., 333, etc.

29 We are here at the point argued forcefully by George Caird in some of his last articles (1982; 1983), picking up and developing hints from Moule and others. This para-**[84]**-graph deliberately leaves on one side the question, raised now sharply by Sanders 1985, ch. 6, as to who precisely the 'outcasts' were.

30 See particularly Harvey, whose argument would be strengthened and clarified at several points by the recognition of the significance of Israel in the ministry of Jesus.

overthrown'. Yet, like Isaiah gathering a remnant around him, his message is also one of salvation through the judgment; and this salvation is already inaugurated in the course of his ministry: 'today salvation has come to this house'. The announcement of the kingdom has therefore a present as well as a future sense, which seems to me a better way of putting it than to sit on the fence by calling it 'imminent'.[31] It is as though the kingdom – God's sovereign rule put into effect over Israel and, through Israel, over the world[32] – is present where Jesus is, because he is identified with, and indeed identified as, God's people. Where he is, God is ruling the world as he always intended. The hope of Israel is fulfilled in the present, in him, and when the future events occur to which his warnings and promises refer they will be seen as the outworking of what has already begun in the course of the ministry.

(4) It is thus that we should, I believe, make sense of the 'son of man' problem which still causes so much vexation. There is no difficulty in granting that the phrase, whatever its original Aramaic form, could have meant 'one' or 'someone like me'.[33] But there should also be no difficulty in granting that Jesus, in whose ministry the themes that characterize Daniel 1—7 were prominent (the kingdom of God and its vindication, together with the vindication of the faithful people of God, over all idolatry), should have used the symbol that occurs at the climax of the book (in the canonical form in which it will have been as familiar to him as to us) to express both the hope of Israel and his own identification with that hope. In the chapter as a whole, whatever the original intent of its component parts, the figure of the son of man clearly represents those who are vindicated by God after their suffering at the hands of the 'beasts': the picture, as has often been pointed out, is drawn from the mythological scheme in which, as in Genesis 1—2, Adam is given dominion over the animals. In the context of the Jewish expectations of the last two centuries BC and the early years of the common era, the entire first seven chapters of Daniel would have the obvious message: remain true to God, and he will vindicate you over those idolaters who are at present oppressing you. This clarifies still further what is to be understood by 'the kingdom of God' at this point in Jewish history: God's rule, and the vindication of his true people, over the pagan nations. Jesus, in using the term 'son of man' with

---

31 See Sanders 1985, 150ff., quoting Caird.

32 I take this (which is close to the first meaning of 'kingdom of God' listed by Sanders 1985 on pp. 141ff., though ironically it is closer to the meaning he identifies as the rabbinic one than to that which he regards as the New Testament equivalent) to be the primary meaning of the phrase, though of course there is no room to argue the point here.

33 See Vermes, Lindars etc.

at least characteristic ambiguity, leaves open the possibility of interpreting his sayings to mean that he identified himself, and his ministry, as the [85] fulfilment of that national hope. It is through him that God is setting up the kingdom that cannot be shaken: he is the one in whom Israel is to find its redemption.[34]

(5) It is in this light, too, that some of the other christological titles may be more clearly understood. Harvey[35] pointed out that messianic expectations, which were not as widespread as is sometimes thought, were not free-standing, but were a function of the national hope:

> As sociologists would be quick to tell us, it would be rare for beliefs about a coming deliverer to be anything but secondary to a general belief in the coming deliverance. It may of course happen that a particular individual, by the performance of notable exploits, comes to be recognised as a messianic figure. But this will be the case only if there is already a powerful expectation of a new age to come.

He goes on to suggest that Jesus regarded himself as Messiah, and was so regarded by his followers during his lifetime, a conclusion which (due to the anachronistic impression that still persists among scholars that 'Christ' is a 'divine' title) is resisted by many others. Contrary to much repeated assertion, it is quite comprehensible, historically and psychologically, that a human being growing up in a situation charged with national expectation should come to believe that he or she is the one through whom that expectation is to be realized. The particular features of the situation in first-century Palestine which sharpen this general statement into a specific one result in the suggestion that it is quite comprehensible that Jesus, growing up with the expectation that God would bring in his kingdom and vindicate Israel over its enemies, should come to believe that God would accomplish this through him; and an individual who believed something like that believed also that he was the Messiah, the representative of Israel as David was the representative of the people of God.[36] The phrase 'son of God' is likewise to be understood, without the anachronism of later christological terminology, as messianic and, like 'Messiah' and 'son of man', as capable of carrying the overtones of 'Israel's

---

34 See Caird 1965, 19–22.

35 1982, 77f.

36 See Caird 1983, 43–6; Wright 1980, 12f. See too Sanders 1985, 234ff., for the reasons why the disciples understood Jesus to be the Messiah.

representative' – Israel itself being seen as God's son in several biblical and post-biblical passages.[37]

It is historically probable, then, that Jesus not only proclaimed the judgment of God against Israel, but also, in summoning men and women to follow him and in his healing miracles and table-fellowship with outcasts, enacted the inauguration of the reconstituted Israel of the new age, an idea and an entity which only attains coherence if he in some sense represents or embodies Israel in himself. This latter point, incidentally, is where I begin to go beyond the argument of Borg's book, which however is (I believe) thereby strengthened.[38] These two basic features of Jesus' ministry, each of which could be set out, established and illustrated at much greater length than is possible here, invite us to complete the syllogism as follows. [86]

IV

The question with which we began, which we saw to be among the most pressing questions facing historians of the ministry of Jesus, was: what was the connection between Jesus' ministry and his death? This is one form of the deceptively ambiguous question: why did Jesus die? To illustrate the ambiguities, and the nature of the problem that confronts us, I cite the two quite different answers given to the question by members of a grade 6 Sunday school class: some, reaching for the security of the tradition, said 'Jesus died because of our sins', whereas others, attempting to think historically, produced various hypotheses about Jesus' running foul of the Jewish and/or Roman authorities. The division between the two answers is instructive. Both are clearly present in a variety of forms in the New Testament. It would, I think, be claimed by many scholars that they have nothing to do with each other (Lessing's ugly ditch separates them, after all, into the eternal truth of atonement and the contingent historical fact of Jesus' execution). But this is not, I think, the view of the New Testament writers themselves.

My suggestion is that *Jesus, as Israel's representative, took on himself the judgment which he pronounced against the nation.* This is, obviously, the result of putting together my two earlier suggestions; and I believe that, while each part of the syllogism can be supported individually, the combination of all three produces a coherence which gives it the force of a cumulative case.

---

37 E.g. Ex. 4.22f.; Jer. 31.9; Wis. 9.7; 18.13; *Sib. Or.* 3.702; *4 Ez.* 5.28; *Jub.* 1.25–28; 4QDibHam 3.4ff.

38 See e.g. Borg 1984, 338 nn. 43, 47, where Borg seems to overlook the point that, precisely because of the David–Israel nexus, the ministry of Jesus as he (Borg) has described it carries implications which make Davidic overtones not 'over-subtle' but almost predictable.

It must be emphasized that this is, at the moment, an historical hypothesis, not a theological construct. I am suggesting that Jesus saw Israel as courting political and historical disaster by that national ambition which would lead Rome to crush it, as so many other peoples had been crushed; and that he identified himself, as a matter of vocation, with Israel. In that context it would be a matter of logic, not of 'supernatural' prophecy (and hence not, either, of a *vaticinium* after the event), that would lead him to say that the son of man had to be crucified by the Romans. He was to suffer the characteristic fate of those who rebelled against Rome. He was, in fact, to die Israel's death.

The central evidence for this suggestion is found in the most controversial section of the synoptic gospels, namely the trial narratives. (It is perhaps necessary to say at this stage that, though one cannot ignore questions of modern relevance, not least questions of Jewish–Christian relations, it is quite out of the question to let the historical enquiry be predetermined by such considerations. At the same time it is interesting to note that Sanders, the last person one would accuse of a lack of sympathy towards the Jewish position, is compelled by the evidence to take a different line from that of, say, Winter or Rivkin, and to conclude that the Jewish leaders, representing the interests of mainline Judaism as a whole, acted to have Jesus put to death by the Romans.)

We may begin with the clearest point. Luke leaves us in no doubt that, for him at least, Jesus died because of charges that amounted to *sedition*: he was forbidding people to pay taxes to Caesar, and giving himself out to be King of the Jews. The *titulus* renders the latter part of the charge extremely likely; and whether or not the former admits of an historian's verdict 'probable' it is clear that the force of the charge is that Jesus dies as an apparent martyr for the Jewish hope of liberation from the Romans.

This is the point at which the Reimarus–Brandon thesis is both right and wrong. (1) Jesus dies because of the (national, political) hope of Israel. It is nationalist Messiahs who end up getting crucified. Had he given in to pressure (from proto-'zealot' factions – or quite possibly from inside himself, as he identified with his helpless people, overrun by harsh, provocative and pagan Roman rule) and become the sort of Messiah that would fit with the hope for a national political liberation, it is extremely likely that he would have been crucified on the same charge. (2) Luke's readers, however, know that the charge is (in the sense in which Pilate must have heard it and implemented it) exactly false. Jesus is innocent of the charges laid against him (it is in this precise sense that we should take, for instance, Luke 23.41b). Hence the irony, unperceived in the literalness of the Brandon [87] thesis: Jesus dies on charges of which, while he is innocent, (many at least of) those with whom he identified himself were guilty. On the cross Jesus 'becomes' a zealot, just as he 'became' unclean when touching a leper, or 'became' a sinner by sitting down to eat with Zacchaeus. At last, when there is no risk of misunderstanding, he can identify himself fully with the national aspirations of his people. He cannot preach Israel's national hope, but he can die for it.

Before taking this line of thought further, we must examine more closely the trial narrative in Mark and Matthew. It is commonly said that it contains inconsistencies both with itself and with historical probability. While it is impossible here to go into the details of the discussion, several important points may be made.

First, it is historically likely that Jesus said, perhaps more than once, things which are more or less reflected in the charge laid by the 'false witnesses': 'This fellow said, "I am able to destroy the Temple of God, and to build it in three days"' (Matthew 26.61), or 'We heard him say, "I will destroy this Temple that is made with hands, and in three days I will build another, not made with hands"' (Mark 14.58). Jesus' prediction of God's judgment against Israel found, as we saw (in agreement with Sanders), a natural centre in the Temple. I regard the so-called apocalyptic discourse (Mark 13 and parallels), which is given such prominence in all three synoptics, as of great importance not only as part of the apocalyptic preaching of Jesus but also within the historical explanation offered by the evangelists for Jesus' death. Jesus predicts the destruction of the Temple; he warns the disciples about false national leaders ('Messiahs') who will arise; and he predicts, absolutely in line with standard Jewish hope as expressed in, for instance, Daniel 1—7, that God will vindicate 'the son of man'. That, at least, is how I would interpret Mark 13.26 – though I am of course aware that most scholars still attempt to take it literally, and either use it as part of the 'end-of-the-world Jesus', the Jesus who expected a 'heavenly' event, the 'coming' from heaven to earth either of himself or of another as 'son of man', or reject its authenticity because that Jesus is incredible or undesirable. As it stands, read in the way I have suggested, the apocalyptic discourse joins very closely the three themes that often appear so disparate in the trial narrative of the next chapter: the destruction of the Temple, the identity of the Messiah, and the vindication of the son of man.[39]

---

39   [38] It is at least clear that this is how Luke read Mark: Lk. 21.7 makes the disciples' question refer unambiguously to the destruction of the Temple, and breaks off the discourse (21.33) at the point where, according to this interpretation, the break occurs (between Mk. 13.31 and 32) between apocalyptic sayings about the Temple and the vindication of the son of man and the warnings about being prepared in view of the disciples' ignorance of the 'day'. Was Luke reacting, as in 19.11f., to an overliteral reading of Mark in the early church?

They are joined, in any case, by their actual significance. As is clear from the cryptic answer given to the question about authority (Mark 11.27–33 and parallels), that which gives Jesus his authority over the Temple is the status he possesses in virtue of his baptism by John – which, as the reader of any one of the synoptics already knows, is the status of 'son of God', that is, Messiah; the heavenly voice, and the echoes of Davidic theology (compare 1 Samuel 16.13), indicate that the baptism is to be understood as the anointing of Jesus as Messiah, the time when he is identified with the people of God and equipped for the task thereby entailed. As has been recently argued,[40] it is the coming king who has authority over the Temple. This reinforces the 'messianic' overtones of the whole triumphal-entry sequence: to put it negatively, if Jesus did *not* want to be thought of in any way as Messiah, the Entry and the action in the Temple were extremely unwise things to undertake. When, therefore, the question about the destruction of the Temple (Mark **[88]** 4.57–60 and parallel) is at once followed by the question 'Are you the Christ, the Son of the Blessed?' (14.61 and parallel), it should not be supposed that the two form a non sequitur. To claim that one has the right to overthrow the Temple *is* to make a messianic claim, and if Jesus will not respond to the charge in which this is implicit he must be made to face the question direct.

This is not, as it stands, an argument that the 'trial' must have actually happened like this, only that the sequence is natural and comprehensible. But the larger claim, that something like this took place between Jesus' arrest and his death, becomes considerably less difficult to entertain once this point is grasped. And the further question, concerning the relevance of Jesus' reported answer to the high priest, is also comprehensible. He has acted and spoken in such a way as to claim an identification with the people of God: their destiny in the purposes of God is bound up with his. Now, in response to the question, he replies not with a qualified affirmative (if you must call me 'Messiah', I will accept the term, but insist that you understand it in terms of 'son of man') as much conservative scholarship has thought, but with the double affirmation: yes – and you will see that God will vindicate me as the true representative of his people. The discussion is hereby tied in to the Jewish idea of martyrdom, of God's vindication of the righteous Israelite(s) who maintain(s) fidelity to the covenant in the face of threats, persecution and death.[41] Daniel 7 belongs in the centre of this theme; so, if my argument is correct, does the trial. Jesus is claiming to be the true Israelite, the nation's representative, and is asserting

---

40   [39] Runnals 1983.

41   [40] See Sanders 1985, 412 n. 31.

that God will vindicate him as such.[42] If the referent of Mark 14.62, as of 13.26, is understood not as the *parousia* but as the vindication of Israel's representative, then several of the arguments against its authenticity, for example those of Vermes, are undermined. It may be that this gives the real reason for the charge of 'blasphemy'. It is not that Jesus was claiming identity with 'the son of man' as a well-known 'heavenly figure' who was to come to earth at the end of time. Two other possibilities are open. Either his identification of his own cause with that of the true people of God was felt to be a direct affront to God's honour, or his combination of Daniel 7 and Psalm 110 came close to the 'two powers' heresy.[43]

What is the result of this line of thought for the question: why did Jesus die? The answer is very close to that which was reached more simply through Luke 23.2: he died because he, the one who was reputed to be announcing Israel's imminent overthrow, claimed to be the royal representative of the people of God. There is another irony in the account at this point. It is customarily said that the Jewish 'trial' was a religious one, that before Pilate a political one, and that the charges in the former were simply framed in such a way as to be easily translatable into terms of the latter. But such a distinction, as we saw earlier, is totally anachronistic in terms of first-century Palestine. For Jesus to claim the status of Messiah, or to be the representative of the true people of God, or to have authority over the Temple, was to make at the same time a statement of the greatest possible political and religious significance. It was to claim that God's plans, and Israel's national destiny, revolved around him and his fate. There were only two courses open to his hearers: either believe him and accept the consequences, or get rid of him – both courses involving, again, theological belief and 'political' action. It is therefore possible, taking the accounts of the trial as they stand, to say that, according to the evangelists, *both* the Jewish 'court'[44] *and* the Roman one condemned Jesus for claiming [89] to be the king of the Jews, in each case for reasons that can be described as 'political' without denying the constant theological overtones. The matter is summed up in the parable of the wicked tenants: when the son comes to claim the inheritance, the tenants say 'Come, let us kill him, *and the inheritance will be ours.*' Whether this represents Jesus' interpretation of his death or that of Mark and the others, it fits very closely with the rest of the narrative. The role

---

42 [41] See too Caird 1965, 20–2.

43 [42] See Segal 1977; and on the trial in general Meyer 1979, 179f.

44 [43] Begging, for the purpose of this paper, the question of the composition of the body that interrogated Jesus prior to his handing over to Pilate. That some interrogation by Jewish leaders took place I regard, in terms of historical arguments, as virtually certain.

assigned to Jesus is that of Israel; those who themselves claim to represent Israel are naturally offended.

It is Luke, once more, who highlights this interpretation in his account of the Barabbas incident. In 23.25 he writes: 'He [Pilate] released the man who had been thrown into prison for insurrection and murder, whom they asked for; but Jesus he delivered up to their will.' Jesus dies, quite literally, the death meant for Barabbas (the point is repeated in the narrative of the two thieves, to which we referred earlier); and Barabbas is the one 'whom they asked for', the one whose acts of violent rebellion are taken by Luke as expressing the secret desires of the people. Jesus receives the punishment the Romans characteristically meted out to rebels. As if to emphasize the point, Luke follows this with the warning to the daughters of Jerusalem (23.27–31), in which Jesus identifies himself explicitly with the national aspiration: if they do this when the wood is green, what will happen when it is dry? This is what the Romans do even to one not guilty of rebellion; how much more when the sons of the women at present bewailing him take up actual arms and fight for God and country.

Finally, the scene of the cross itself is replete with the same irony. The mocking, both of the crowds and of the rulers, echoes the themes of the trial: if he is the Christ, if he is the one who was going to destroy the Temple and rebuild it, he must demonstrate his claim by coming down from the cross. But, in the intention of the evangelists (signalled by the extra incidents, such as the two thieves or the remark of the centurion), this charge rebounds: it is precisely because he is Messiah that he must stay on the cross, must die Israel's death. The *titulus*, intended no doubt insultingly by Pilate and protested, for the same reason, by the Jewish leaders, is used by the evangelists to express their belief that Jesus, having announced the imminent downfall of Israel at the hands of the Romans, was taking Israel's fate on himself as its representative king.

The train of thought we have been following leads to a conclusion which, though by now it may be obvious, needs none the less to be stated. Just as Jesus identified himself with Zacchaeus, becoming a 'sinner' by eating with him in order that Zacchaeus might become 'a son of Abraham'; just as Jesus touched those from whom he ought to have contracted uncleanness, but instead healed them; so now he becomes a zealot, a rebel against Rome, identifying himself with the national disease he had himself diagnosed, in order that it may be healed. In doing so, it was inevitable that he should put himself outside the pale of Judaism, as he had done ritually by touching the leper and socially by eating with Zacchaeus and his like. In each case – and if this is a construction of the evangelists or their sources it is not only a very sophisticated one but one that has found its way into most types and layers of tradition – the drama plays itself out as Jesus apparently contracts the uncleanness (or whatever) and somehow exhausts its power. The stigma leaves the leper or the sinner on contact with Jesus, though Jesus emerges at the end apparently unscathed. The thieves (or are they freedom-fighters?) on either side of him are thus the last in the long line of outcasts with whom he is associated and who, by this association, are invited into the kingdom of God. On the cross it becomes clear that Israel's real problem is not external (the Roman occupation) merely, but internal also: he shares the ultimate form of its political and social predic-ament and hence reveals, in his last great symbolic act, that the nationalist rebellion whose bloody logical outcome he now shared was something for which Israel was being judged by God, and from which it needed to be saved – by him.

Hence, the irony: claiming to represent Israel, he is cast out by those who themselves claim to represent Israel; in urging Israel to forswear rebellion, he is himself executed as [90] a rebel by the Romans. The death he dies is Israel's death, and the pattern of healings and welcomes that make up so much of the gospel narratives indicates the motive: he dies Israel's death in order that Israel may not die it. He takes the wrath of Rome (which is, like the wrath of Assyria or Babylon, the historical embodiment of the wrath of God) on himself so that, in his vindication, Israel may find itself brought through the judgment and into the true kingdom, may see at last the way to life and follow it while there is yet time. This, to my mind, is where the current 'Quest', if it is followed to its logical conclusion, ought to lead.

V

The syllogism is complete, within the limits imposed by this paper – though each stage of the argument cries out for the further substantiation that space alone denies. But there are a few points that ought to be noted by way of conclusion.

First, it is high time that scholarship recognized that the theology of the evangelists is not something superimposed on to the history they narrate, but something to be discovered within it. This point applies at both the general and the specific levels. To imagine that, because Mark and the others were inter-ested in theology (the much vaunted 'discovery' of redaction-criticism), they were uninterested in history is to allow the anachronistic distinction of fact and value, of event and interpretation, of politics and theology, to determine historical enquiry. More to the point of this paper, it is absurd to imagine that Luke (for instance) has no theology of the cross just because he does not reproduce Mark 10.45 at the expected point. Luke's gospel is full of the *theologia crucis*: at every point Jesus is identified with sinners so that, in the purposes of God which are made explicit after the resurrection, he can open the way for Israel to become a worldwide family.

Second, and closely related, if this integration of theology and history is not taken into account there is a risk that a reaction will set in, which could undo the splendid work presently being done within what I have called the 'Third Quest'. Ironically, the earlier 'quests' allied historical consciousness with idealism: we find out what happened in the past in order to be able properly to distance ourselves from it, retaining only the 'real', namely the ideal, meaning or 'message'. I regard the present reaction against idealism, and the return to genuine realism in many matters philosophical, theological and historical, as a very positive development, but I am concerned lest the present swing become excessive, resulting in sheer materialism (which in this context would mean 'mere history' without implications or interpretations: this, in fact, is a figment of over-realist imagination). What would be regrettable would be the provocation of another, Kähler-like, reaction: if this is all that historical study of Jesus can provide, we must get away from history and rediscover the Christ of faith.[45] As I shall make clear below, this is not a plea to let theological interest or 'relevance' become the yardstick for historical study, but simply a request that we not put asunder matters which are in fact inseparable.

Third, and again related to this, it should be clear that the hypothesis I have offered has an extra strength in addition to proposing an essentially simple account of the matter which manages to retain a good deal of the data: it provides an explanation, otherwise hard to come by, for why, within twenty years of Jesus' death, Paul could quote statements about 'Christ dying for our sins' as already commonplace.[46] The theological [91] interpretation is to be found within the historical events: it is because he died, quite literally, the death of rebellious Israel that his death could be seen as representative for the whole world. Underneath this sequence of thought, of course, we have

---

45 [44] Not that Kähler himself would have said such a thing; see Meyer 1979, 48f.

46 [45] This question, though Sanders never raises it in this form, has an analogous importance to those he does raise frequently, the questions of how Jesus' attitude to the law is [91] related to that of the early church. Historical explanation requires that some account be given; my suggestion would supplement that given by (for instance) Hengel 1981a, giving extra significance in particular to the idea of martyrdom.

to supply the characteristic Jewish presupposition that Israel is somehow paradigmatic or representative of the whole world:[47] Jesus, as Israel's representative, does for Israel and the world what Israel was called to do but could not do. From here there is a straight line into Pauline theology, though that is another story. There is also a comprehensible link with the preaching put into the mouths of the early apostles in Acts: because of the death and resurrection of Jesus, not yet accredited with any sophisticated theological formulae, the people have a chance to 'save themselves from this crooked generation', that is, to take advantage of the breathing space thus offered to join the true family of God before the cataclysm comes in which Israel as then constituted would be swept away.

Fourth, and of considerable importance in the total historical reconstruction of the aims of Jesus, the line of thought I have suggested makes it possible to suggest that Jesus went to Jerusalem with the intention of doing and saying things which he knew were, even humanly speaking, likely to result in his own death. My position has some similarities (but only some) with that of Schweitzer,[48] who (as is well known) saw Jesus as trying to force God's hand, throwing himself on to the wheel of history and, though himself being broken by it, causing it to change direction. He too envisaged Jesus going deliberately to die in Jerusalem,[49] though his scheme rested (as Sanders has shown) on several points that can be quite easily challenged in terms of synoptic studies.

Fifth, and finally, Sanders (1985, 330–4) has criticized fairly devastatingly those who first set up their theology and then suggest that Jesus died for it. This is, of course, a dangerous card to play, and I am not entirely convinced that Sanders, despite his disclaimer, is not open to an analogous charge. In my own defence it should be said that I could not belong to a tradition which believes that Jesus died the death he had predicted for Israel, because as far as I know no such tradition has ever existed. I have come to this view after a fair amount of genuine puzzlement over the question of the connection between the historical circumstances and meaning of Jesus' ministry on the one hand and his death on the other, during which time I have frequently been asked, sometimes with some suspicion, what relevance this historical picture of Jesus

---

47 [46] See Caird 1965, 22; Meyer 1979, 217.

48 [47] Esp. 1925, 229ff., 234f.

49 [48] He even suggests that 'one might use it as a principle of division by which to classify the lives of Jesus, whether they make Him go to Jerusalem to work or to die'; Schweitzer 1954, 389. His use of the 'Messianic Woes' idea (1925, 265f.) is not easy to copy owing to the problem of the date of the emergence of this idea.

might have for contemporary Christianity. This is the point I made above, that the demand for relevance may produce a Kähler-like reaction among the faithful. The question has not been an easy one to answer, though I think my present position offers at least some starting-points.[50] The clue that pointed me in (what I believe to be) the right direction was the following paragraph, which concludes Caird's brilliant lecture on 'Jesus and the Jewish Nation': [92]

> He goes to his death at the hands of a Roman judge on a charge of which he was innocent and his accusers, as the event proved, were guilty. And so, not only in theological truth but in historic fact, the one bore the sins of the many, confident that in him the whole Jewish nation was being nailed to the cross, only to come to life again in a better resurrection, and that the Day of the Son of Man which would see the end of the old Israel would see also the vindication of the new.[51]

I have indicated that I think this view opens up a way to the more usual 'atonement' statements in the New Testament, but it cannot be reduced to 'atonement-theology' of a sort which would allow for the argument (Sanders 1985, 332) that it must therefore be a creation of the early church. On the contrary. It fits exactly with (my version of) what Sanders calls 'Jewish restoration eschatology'. It also has the support that Caird claimed for his overall view, namely that of the faithful old criterion of dissimilarity, which (like Gollum) may yet after all have its uses. After the very early days of the church the question of Israel was not at issue in the way it clearly was in the ministry of Jesus: nor was the announcement (by a soi-disant faithful Jew) of Israel's imminent judgment exactly a commonplace in the last two centuries BC – until John the Baptist, which is the point at which we, and for that matter Jesus, came in. I am not, then, claiming that Jesus died for an abstract doctrine, whether of atonement, justification or whatever, but for a concrete reality: Israel.[52]

---

50 [49] Schweitzer (1925, 250f.) got around the equivalent problem, quite acute in his case, by making Jesus' 'personality' the point of relevance (this, of course, was what Bultmann was reacting to in his polemic against that word. He faced the same problem himself, but found, as is well known, a different way: through demythologization), though by the third edition of the book Schweitzer was emphasizing 'the Spirit of Jesus' as the universalizable factor (1954, xv).

51 [50] Caird 1965, 22. This point is not usually picked up by those who have discussed this work; I am not aware that Caird elaborated it anywhere else. I once had a brief exchange of letters with him on the subject, in which he indicated that he agreed entirely with the way I was developing his idea.

52 [51] There is a brief statement of a similar-sounding point in Lohfink 1984, 25, and indeed Lohfink's book has several analogies to my case. He does not, however, develop this line of thought very far.

To sum up. The large historical question to be faced by all students of the life of Jesus is: why did Jesus die? My answer is that at the heart of his many controversies with his contemporaries stood his proclamation, and symbolic enactment, of God's imminent judgment against Israel, and that this precipitated his being handed over, by the Jewish leaders, for execution by the Romans. This answer, so far, is similar to, though in one respect more sharply defined than, that of Sanders. Mine, however, opens the way directly, and without a change of gear, to the 'other' way of hearing the question 'Why did Jesus die?', namely the 'theological' way. And my suggestion is that the evangelists, wanting to give the 'theological' answer, believed that the best way to do so was simply to tell the story and allow its overtones to ring for themselves.

If this argument is even more or less along the right lines, it suggests that, precisely because Jesus is (as Sanders, Borg and the others have argued so well) to be fitted in to his Jewish milieu and made comprehensible in terms of first-century history, theology and politics, his death, and his attitude to that death as he saw it approaching, can be understood in a way which does not make him 'weird',[53] but historically and theologically comprehensible. He did not have to force the authorities' hands: merely to bring his ministry of warning and invitation to a fitting climax in the Entry and the action against the Temple. If it is asked at this point whether Jesus regarded his death as the proper and intended climax to his ministry, it will now be apparent that this is a very similar question to the one we postponed earlier, whether he believed the judgment on Israel to be [93] inevitable or merely contingent on a failure to heed his message. Schweitzer answered both questions in the affirmative, rejecting the ever-popular idea of a 'Galilean springtime', an early period when it looked as though Jesus' mission would be a 'success', followed by rejection, withdrawal from the crowds, and the embracing of a 'plan B', namely the cross as a second best. This is certainly not how the evangelists see the matter. To what extent hindsight, and the desire to make it look as though Jesus, and perhaps God, had had the cross in mind all along, have influenced their presentation, it is unfortunately impossible to discuss here.

Jesus, then, believed himself called by God to announce Israel's imminent judgment and to inaugurate in and around himself Israel's reconstitution. He continued to pursue his vocation even when it was more than apparent

---

53 [52] So Sanders 1985, 333, as his summary of the view which suggests that 'Jesus determined in his own mind to be killed and to have his death understood as sacrificial for others, and . . . that he pulled this off by provoking the authorities'.

where it would lead, believing that if Israel's death could be died by its representative, it might not need to die this death itself. This was not out of line, as we have seen, with the pattern of significant actions that marked his public career as a whole, in which he constantly shared the uncleanness or stigma of the physically or socially handicapped, in order to heal and restore (or, as the evangelists often say, 'save') them. Though this view cannot be subsumed within the pre-packaged theologies of atonement or justification normally on offer, it can take up their strong points within itself, giving them back the flesh and blood of which, as abstract ideas, they are all too often bereft. By putting Jesus back into his social and political context we do not capitulate to Brandon's theory, any more than by suggesting that he may have had theological reasons for going to his death we make him historically incomprehensible. History is not the handmaid of theology, nor theology of history. If we understand Jesus in the way I have suggested, history and theology turn out to be mutually interdependent ways of talking about the same thing.

3

'Constraints' and the Jesus of History

Anthony Harvey, originally a classicist, taught New Testament Studies at Oxford during my time as a graduate student. We then served together on the Church of England Doctrine Commission from 1978 to 1981, during which time (not without some awkwardness on both sides) he was appointed as the internal examiner for my doctoral thesis. He had also given the Bampton Lectures in Oxford in 1980; I didn't hear them, since we were living in Cambridge, but they were then published (as *Jesus and the Constraints of History*) around the time I moved to Montreal. They were fresh, original, and played right in to the work I had already begun to do but with several stimulating points of continuing disagreement. His work, and these comments on it, were then bubbling away in the back of my mind as I was working out my own tentative solutions to similar questions, and the moment arrived when I thought it would make sense to write the present article, which the *Scottish Journal of Theology* did me the honour of publishing. It is fascinating to look back over thirty years and see how themes that have more recently been developed in new ways in my work (particularly in my own Gifford Lectures) were here in embryo, not least the reflections on 'history', what it is and how it should be done. The christological reflections towards the end of the piece are now common coin in New Testament studies; in the early 1980s this was not the case.

The opening scene, drawing on one of Chaim Potok's novels, came at a time when I had been trying to soak myself in the study of the Jewish world both ancient and modern. This was my first attempt to weave together themes from quite other areas with the exposition of historical and theological material. Working in Montreal, where the sharp French–English divide had a dark undertone of difficult catholic–Jewish relationships (with us 'Protestants' poised awkwardly between the two!), the question of what it might mean to be a loyal Jew with a strong and perplexing vocation – a theme to which I returned recently in my biography of Paul (Wright 2018b) – had a powerful resonance.

I notice in the footnotes that I, like Harvey himself, was interacting quite a bit with the remarkable work of John Bowker, another member of the same Doctrine Commission in the late 1970s. Bowker, like Harvey only a few years later, had originally studied at Worcester College, Oxford, to which I had moved, as Chaplain and Fellow in Theology, by the time this article appeared.

[189] What sort of a thing is a 'constraint'?

In Chaim Potok's novel *My Name Is Asher Lev*, the young Jewish painter learns the answer after the exhibition of his sensational *Brooklyn Crucifixion*:

> 'Papa—'
> But he was not listening. He stood on the kerb; hailing a cab.
> 'Mama—'
> 'There are limits, Asher.' Her voice trembled and her eyes were wet. 'Everything has a limit. I don't know what to tell you. I don't want to talk to you now.'
> . . . 'Asher Lev,' the Rebbe said softly. 'You have crossed a boundary. I cannot help you. You are alone now. I give you my blessings.'
> . . . Asher Lev paints good pictures and hurts people he loves. Then be a great painter, Asher Lev; that will be the only justification for all the pain you will cause. But as a great painter I will cause pain again if I must. Then become a greater painter. But I will cause pain again. Then become a still greater painter. Master of the Universe, will I live this way all the rest of my life? Yes, came the whisper from the branches of the trees. Now journey with me, my Asher. Paint the anguish of all the world. Let people see the pain. But create your own moulds and your own play of forms for the pain. We must give a balance to the universe.
> Yes, I said. Yes. My own play of forms for the pain.[1]

Asher Lev, caught between the 'constraints' of Hasidism and art, finds the resolution in a new and paradoxical obedience to both. In the exile he suffers because of his work, he hears the [190] summons of his mythical ancestor, calling him to embrace the underlying family tradition, to become 'a weary Jew travelling to balance the world', to make 'an act of eternal atonement'.[2]

It is through the attempt to understand the 'constraints' operating on a troublesome Jew of an earlier day that Anthony Harvey has sought, in his

---

1 Potok 1974, 314, 318–19.
2 Potok 1974, 282–3.

1980 Bampton Lectures, a way forward in the current debate about Jesus.[3] Harvey's book is part of a new trend in studies of Jesus. After the failure of the old nineteenth-century 'Quest of the Historical Jesus', so brilliantly described, and demolished, by Albert Schweitzer, it was generally held, particularly in Germany, that little of value could be known, historically speaking, about Jesus. Schweitzer's alternative to the liberal lives of Jesus was his picture of Jesus the apocalyptic visionary whose dreams ended in disaster. Many scholars, perhaps not surprisingly, thought that if that was the result of historical study, theology would be better off without it. With the so-called 'New Quest' initiated by Ernst Käsemann and others a partial return to history occurred, but this movement too has had its limitations.[4] What we are now witnessing is a third 'Quest' – not that it is a coordinated effort or the product of a single group; rather, scholars have at last begun to face the challenge posed by Schweitzer, and to renew the attempt to understand Jesus historically, that is in the context of his first-century Jewish social, cultural and political background.[5] The question of what significance this has for Christian theology is sometimes left to one side (Sanders), sometimes assumed to be negative (Vermes), sometimes cautiously argued to be positive (Meyer): the whole issue is fraught with all kinds of difficulties, not to be easily resolved.[6] Harvey's book is itself a brilliant [191] attempt to operate within the constraints of current scholarly debate while retaining a good deal of individuality in both content and method, enabling him to bring fresh light to several well-worn problems.

At the heart of the book, as the title implies, is the notion of 'historical constraint', and the aim of this article is to examine this concept and to attempt to clarify its meaning. Thus, although questions of content will inevitably arise, especially towards the end, I am here mostly concerned with method.

We must begin with Harvey's own statement of what 'historical constraints' are.[7] 'No individual', he writes,

---

3 Harvey 1982.

4 See Robinson 1959; Käsemann 1964. For criticism of the 'New Quest' see e.g. Meyer 1979 (see the new edn of Meyer (2002) with my new introduction, the latter of which is reprinted below, ch. 8).

5 I am thinking particularly of such works as Meyer 1979; Borg 1984; Sanders 1985; Vermes 1973; Riches 1980.

6 See Morgan 1987 (this was forthcoming at the time the present article was published, but as the editor of the relevant volume I had already seen it).

7 Harvey 1982, 6–7. In a note, Harvey explains that his use of the term is 'arbitrary and nontechnical', and acknowledges indebtedness to Bowker 1973b.

if he wishes to influence others, is totally free to choose his own style of action and persuasion: he is subject to constraints imposed by the culture in which he finds himself. If communication is to take place, there must be constraints which are recognised by both the speaker and his listeners, the artist and his public, the leader and his followers.

Harvey then applies this to Jesus. In order to communicate,

he had to speak a language [his hearers] could understand, perform actions they would find intelligible, and conduct his life and undergo his death in a manner of which they could make some sense. This is not to say, of course, that he must have been totally subject to these constraints. Like any truly creative person, he could doubtless bend them to his purpose. But had he not worked from within them, he would have seemed a mere freak, a person too unrelated to the normal rhythm of society to have anything meaningful to say.

He then suggests that it is possible, working from sources both within and outside the New Testament, 'to give definition to the historical constraints within which Jesus *must have* lived, worked and died' (my italics) and to see that, within those constraints, 'only a certain number of options, a relatively small range of [192] styles of action, was open to Jesus'. Careful use of New Testament evidence will then enable the scholar 'to make a well-founded judgment on the question of which of these options was actually adopted by him'.[8]

On this foundation the bulk of Harvey's book is built. After two introductory chapters, in which the notion of 'constraint' is introduced and the historical significance of the indubitable fact of the crucifixion is drawn out, there are five full discussions of different 'constraints' within which Jesus, according to Harvey, must have lived and worked. The first is Law: within the legal constraints of first-century Palestine, it can be deduced (so the argument runs) that Jesus' teaching must be regarded as that of somebody claiming that the urgency of the moment overrides the particular claims of some of the law's provisions.[9] The second is Time: the current expectation of God's inbreaking rule in history sets the stage for Jesus' eschatological message.[10] The third is

---

8 Harvey 1982, 7, 9.
9 Harvey 1982, 36–65.
10 Harvey 1982, 66–97.

Miracle: granted the understanding of the miraculous current in the ancient world in general and Palestine in particular, it can be seen that Jesus refused certain well-known styles of operation (for example the 'charismatic', p. 107) and that in fact he fits none of the regular available categories.[11] The fourth and fifth chapters, on Messiahship and monotheism respectively, explore the expectations and beliefs of Judaism at the time and attempt to describe Jesus' self-understanding in terms of them.[12] This thin summary does not of course do justice to the rich material in these chapters, and is merely intended to show any who have not yet read the book how the central idea of historical constraint is developed, and on what sort of material it may be used. To this central idea we now return.

'Constraints', then, are factors that limit the potential actions of a subject. They are, if you like, the sensibilities of Asher Lev's parents on the one hand and the demands of his art on the other. So far, this is fairly uncontroversial, and in line [193] with John Bowker's detailed and technical use of the term.[13] But what, precisely, is the connection between 'constraints' and 'history'? In what sense, if any, is an *historical* constraint different from any other sort? I confess that when I came to Harvey's book, having already heard an earlier version of the second chapter, I assumed that the title-phrase meant that 'history' should be seen as the empirical evidence which imposes certain constraints on the *historian*, limiting the choices *we* face, as students of history, in reconstructing probable hypotheses about the past. The second chapter, indeed ('Political constraints: the crucifixion', pp. 11–35), can and perhaps should be read in that way: the unquestionable fact of Jesus' crucifixion, seen in the light of certain fixed points in Roman and Jewish law and politics, limits the historian to a particular reconstruction of the character of Jesus' ministry. But this meaning of the phrase 'the constraints of history' is subtly different from the way in which the idea of 'constraint' is used in the definition set out above, in which the 'constraints' are exercising their limiting force not on the historian but on the figure under investigation – in this case, Jesus of Nazareth. It is clear, of course, that the two are related: in working out what choices were open to Jesus, the historian will work within the limits apparently set by his or her hypothetical reconstruction. But they are certainly not identical. Ambiguity between the two is reflected in the italicized phrase

---

11   Harvey 1982, 98–119.

12   Harvey 1982, 120–53, 154–73.

13   See Bowker 1973b, 60–1, 87–9 (cited by Harvey 1982, 6) and frequently (see index s.v. 'Constraints'); also Bowker 1978, e.g. 17, 74 and especially (on the present subject, i.e. the 'constraints' operating on Jesus) 126, 170, 179–88, 190–1.

in the quotation above ('the historical constraints within which Jesus *must have* lived . . .'): this seems to be the 'must' of historical inference ('it *must have* been raining, because the streets are wet') but it carries the further implication of the 'must' of human necessity (Jesus himself *had to* stay within certain limits), albeit with the caveat entered earlier ('he could doubtless bend them to his purpose'). The one method charts the constraints that history places on the historian; the other, the constraints that the contemporary environment placed on the subject – and through which, like Asher Lev, he or she might consciously break. The [194] former seems, in principle, clear and beyond controversy, although Harvey's application of it in chapter 2 reaches conclusions that go a long way beyond what some of his predecessors in writing about Jesus have felt able confidently to assert. The latter is perhaps not so much the 'constraints of history' as the 'history of constraints'. About this method – which seems to be the one Harvey intends to use, and certainly does use in his last (and inevitably controversial) chapter, on Monotheism – there are various comments to be made.

The first point is fairly obvious. We are seldom if ever, as historians, in the happy position of being able to chart so well the 'constraints' acting on a person that we can draw an initial map of them and then simply fill in the blank in the middle. Such an accomplishment – the El Dorado of deterministic behaviourism, applied to historiography[14] – would be unthinkable even for a figure of the recent past for whose life and environment we have a mountain of evidence (for example Churchill). When we move back to the comparatively scanty sources for the ancient world, we are in a much worse state – although the resultant absence of controls ('constraints' in the first sense, namely those that operate on the historian), and the consequent difficulty of falsification, frequently disguise the fact. But if this is so, we cannot entirely escape circularity in the historical method that employs the notion of 'constraint'; for among the pieces of evidence used to reconstruct the constraints on Jesus are the documents which, prima facie, purport to tell us 'which of these options was actually adopted by him'. In other words, we are not in the situation of possessing all the bits round the edge of the jigsaw and using them to determine in advance what shape the central figure must be. We have *some* bits from *all over* the jigsaw, and part of the basis for reconstructing the margin itself will be the shape of some of the more central pieces. The two sorts of constraint are in fact inseparable.

---

14   See Bowker 1973b, *passim.*

Sometimes, in fact, the historian operating with the notion of 'constraint' is working in exactly the opposite direction from that which Harvey describes. In Bowker's example of Queen Elizabeth I,[15] the problem is not that of determining whether or [195] not, granted the constraints on her, she ever married, but rather that of assessing, granted the fact that she did not, what the constraints might have been that kept her single. Here the central person and event is the datum, and the constraints themselves are the object of (extremely hypothetical) investigation. The same is true of Asher Lev in my earlier example: the novel invites the reader to ponder the balance of constraints that made him what he was. This is, in fact, closer to Harvey's method in the second chapter: granted the fact of the crucifixion, what were the 'constraints' – the 'outer' framework of Jewish and Roman law and politics, and the 'inner' framework of the conduct and self-understanding of Jesus – that led to it? For most investigations, in fact, a movement to and fro is apparently appropriate, from periphery to centre and back again or vice versa: in the chapter on miracles, we begin with the indubitable fact that Jesus was known as a miracle-worker (pp. 98–101), move outwards to assess the constraints operating in that area (pp. 101–13), and then inwards again to the gospels (pp. 113–19), though with 'the remarkable conclusion that the miraculous activity of Jesus conforms to no known pattern' (p. 113). This in turn suggests that the constraints operating on Jesus were *not* those of standard contemporary wonder-working, and these constraints therefore themselves become, like the reasons for Elizabeth's lifelong spinsterhood, the elusive object of historical research.

All this would suggest that the notion of 'constraint' is, to say the least, a much more complicated historical tool to work with than one might have thought at first sight. It also points up one very necessary warning: that, however well we can plot the 'constraints' that might apparently limit the actions of an individual, we can never, historically speaking, 'predict' the rebel, the genius or the radical innovator. Unless we bring a deterministic presupposition to our work, we will be cautious even about suggesting a complete *ex post facto* explanation of them; determinist historiography is an ambitious statement of intent, a means of setting puzzles rather than of solving them.[16] Any attempt at total explanation would need to include so many all-but-unknowable factors, psychological and genetic as well as [196] sociological, cultural and political,

---

15 Bowker 1973b, 61–3.
16 See Bowker 1973b, chs. 3, 6, 7.

that solutions would recede from research like a rainbow's end. We still cannot decide why Elizabeth remained unmarried when so many 'constraints' might have urged her to find a husband, any more than Asher Lev's parents could understand why he *had* to paint nudes and crucifixions despite the crushing constraint of his Jewish orthodoxy.

This means that our plotting of 'constraints' must always be accompanied by a saving clause, must carry an 'if . . .' about with them. To borrow another of Bowker's examples, and one not without significance both for Asher Lev and for Jesus, the Sinai covenant exerted a powerful and yet flexible constraint on Jews – *if* they wished to remain acceptable as Jews.[17] The history of assimilation (and the constant warnings against it) are powerful evidence that there have been other competing constraints exercising a pull on the children of Israel, no less powerful for being less easy to describe. Within Judaism itself there were those who understood themselves to be under the compelling constraint of a God-given vocation to challenge, precisely from within, the current interpretation of the covenant constraint itself. Jeremiah and John the Baptist, both seen in the New Testament as somehow prototypical of Jesus (Matthew 16.14 and parallels), are obvious examples. If we were studying that sort of person, it would hardly do to set up as a 'constraint' the contemporary Jewish view of God and the world, and then insist that the person be simply fitted into it. The only sense in which contemporary belief in the inviolability of Jerusalem limited the options open to Jeremiah was that it was *that* misunderstanding of the covenant, and not another one, that he found himself called to attack. And, most significantly, in his case (as in that of John the Baptist, or for that matter Asher Lev) the result was an explosion of the existing constraints. There are limits, and, when prophets are constrained to break them, their own existence and that of their people can never be the same again. As a result, the historian is often faced with the problem of new wine and old bottles. Examining the bottles after the explosion tells us little about the wine except that it was indeed new.

This chimes in, up to a point, with Harvey's warnings, and [197] some of his conclusions, about Jesus: he fits no known category.[18] As Bowker says, the constraint of intelligibility does not rule out utter novelty.[19] But this means that, strictly speaking, the use of the 'constraint' idea is less applicable in some areas than in others. It is more use, for instance, in establishing the

---

17 Bowker 1978, 61–76, esp. 74–5.
18 E.g. Harvey 1982, 7, 59.
19 Bowker 1973b, 97.

language that Jesus 'must have' spoken, though even that is by no means a closed question, than in working out what, say, 'the kingdom of God' might (let alone 'must') have meant on his lips. He and his hearers must have had an initial component or nucleus of shared meaning for the term if his use of it was to be to any degree comprehensible, but much of his teaching seems to have emphasized that this 'kingdom of God' was *not* like what they had imagined after all.[20] At a wider level, the whole history-of-religions method (which grew up precisely in the period when hopes for complete 'explanations' of all religious phenomena were running high) is called into question. Designed to demonstrate orderly development or evolution, it is unhappy with just that sort of irregularity which real history is constantly unearthing.[21]

This is particularly important when we come to assess the fashionable 'criterion of dissimilarity' used, particularly within the so-called 'New Quest', for assessing the authenticity of specific sayings of Jesus. This 'criterion' is frequently stated in some such form as this: whatever material can be shown to be in line with the Judaism of the period, or to fit in with the later interests of the post-Easter church, cannot for that reason be ascribed with any certainty to Jesus. This criterion has the apparent virtue of being neutral and 'objective', seeking to build on solid foundations by isolating only those sayings that 'must' have come from Jesus himself. But it too has its own agenda. The (post-Bultmannian) movement of scholarship out of which this 'criterion' comes seems to favour, as Bultmann did, a picture of Jesus as the teacher of timeless truths, or at least as the preacher of the timeless call for decision, far removed from the real life of either Judaism or the early church. Judaism (it is thought) was **[198]** bound by the law and its history; the early church fitted Jesus into its Jewish framework: post-Pauline Christianity made him the founder of the catholic church. The 'criterion of dissimilarity' is a means of ensuring that the 'right' Jesus – the Jesus who is different from all these, who is more like the Jesus desired by modern existentialism – emerges from the shadows of history. Objecting to this 'criterion' on the grounds that it isolates the merely idiosyncratic[22] is proper and necessary, but does not quite touch the heart of the matter. What is at stake is a particular arrangement of the five all-important pieces of the New Testament jigsaw – Judaism, Jesus, the early church, Paul, post-Pauline Christianity. The 'criterion of dissimilarity' is not neutral: it already has a particular solution in view, and is a means of arriving

---

20 See Caird 1980, 11–12.
21 Bowker 1973b; 1978, *passim*; see Neill 1964, 281.
22 E.g. Hooker 1972.

at it. That solution – Jesus in isolation from Judaism and the early church, with Paul as his lone ally – was of course a reaction to the older pre-critical account of Jesus which separated him entirely from his Jewish background (except for the negative backdrop provided by a caricatured Pharisaism) and made him the inaugurator, or first great teacher, of the church as a whole. We have more recently been faced with the diametrically opposite point of view, expressed for instance (though in very different ways) by Vermes and Cupitt:[23] Jesus was a Jewish teacher first and last, and the church from (at least) Paul to the present day has misunderstood him and corrupted his message. Harvey's position, it seems to me, leans towards a modified version of the last one. The 'constraints' of the Jewish background meant (for instance) that neither Jesus nor his first followers could have used language about him in the way that later gentile Christians, 'released from the constraint of Jewish monotheism', were able to do. We will have to return to this argument. For the moment, we must make three methodological points.

1 Harvey's developed notion of 'historical constraint' cuts clean across the 'criterion of dissimilarity', and is right to do so. An historical method that attempts to fit its subjects into their background, instead of carefully divorcing them **[199]** from it, must be accounted the more actually 'objective'. Once Jesus is separated from his milieu, he can be made to say almost anything.

2 Although, however, Jesus was and is only comprehensible in terms of his Jewish background, he nevertheless consciously and deliberately broke through the constraints, or at least some of them, that were thus laid on him. Without this, the crucifixion is historically inexplicable. This is the grain of truth seized on by the inventors of the 'criterion of dissimilarity'. We cannot, however, start here. We must first plot the constraints, and then see how they were broken.

3 It is highly probable, historically speaking, that the early Christians under-stood Jesus at least as well as we can. Indeed, one recent and important writer has drawn on studies of the early Palestinian church to draw infer-ences about Jesus himself.[24] Here again historical constraint, though of a different sort from that described by Harvey, calls the criterion of dissimilarity into question. Again there are distinctions to be drawn as well: the differences between the circumstances of the church after Easter

---

23 E.g. Vermes 1973; Cupitt 1979.
24 Borg 1984, e.g. 132–3, 135.

and those of Jesus prior to Calvary strongly imply a difference in aims and message.

We should therefore look in the gospels for points of both continuity and discontinuity between Jesus and his Jewish background on the one hand, and his Christian successors on the other. Not just any points of continuity and discontinuity, either, but such points as will help to account, as 'historical constraints', for two major historical events of the period, the crucifixion and the rise of the early church (as well as for that mass of detailed evidence that we call the New Testament[25]). We must, in other words, put the historical question thus: granted the crucifixion and the rise of the early church, what is the historian constrained to infer about the central actors in the drama, their motives, sayings and achievements?

Despite the cautions I have voiced above about his use of the [200] notion of 'constraint', Anthony Harvey's book is clearly an important step in this direction. In what follows I want to suggest some other steps that seem to me equally worth taking.

To begin with, there is the constraint of *Israel's hope*. Harvey frequently touches on this point, but never (it seems to me) exploits it anything like to the full. Like many other writers, including most Bultmannian and post-Bultmannian scholars, he universalizes the hope for the coming age, seeing it as the time of restoration for humanity and the world in general. But there was nothing generalized about the new age for which Jesus' contemporaries were longing. The fact that gentiles were often included in the vision of the age to come did not mean that the Jew–gentile distinction had been abolished, that in the cosmic scope of 'apocalyptic' the category of the chosen people had ceased to matter.[26] The new age was to be the restoration of the kingdom to *Israel*. It was within *that* context that some Jews hoped for a Messiah,[27] some for the resurrection of the dead, and some for the ingathering of the gentiles. For too long, as Harvey rightly emphasizes, scholars have attempted to catalogue Jewish messianic expectations without reference to the hope of the people as a whole, and have then asked, prematurely, whether Jesus fulfilled them. It is much more to the point to ask whether, or in what sense, Jesus fulfilled, or saw himself as fulfilling, or was seen by some

---

25 See Moule 1967.

26 This cosmic scope of apocalyptic is often used as just such an excuse for generalizing what should remain particular, in, for instance, the work of E. Käsemann.

27 Rightly, Harvey 1982, 77.

as fulfilling, the great all-embracing hope that *God would now at last act in history to restore the fortunes of his chosen people*. Apocalyptic, born out of the unbearable tension between covenant promises and contemporary politics, did not look for a new world in which Israel was no longer a significant entity but for a new *world order* in which Israel, God's people, would be exalted to its rightful position.[28]

Since Albert Schweitzer, people have shied away from the idea [201] that Jesus really was an apocalyptic prophet. Schweitzer went down that road and seems to have ended in a cul-de-sac.[29] Believing (rightly) that Jesus can only be understood against his apocalyptic Jewish background, Schweitzer thought (like the disciples on the road to Emmaus) that the crucifixion had falsified Jesus' claims (Luke 24.21: 'we *had hoped* that he was the one to redeem Israel'). But there is within the gospels, with a strong claim to go back to Jesus himself,[30] a consistent *redefinition* of the Jewish hope. The hope is being neither denied, nor universalized, nor yet simply underwritten: it is being fulfilled *in Jesus himself*, the Jew, the Man. God is establishing his kingdom through one who is taking the role of Israel on himself.[31] In the midst of the constraints imposed by his background, Jesus journeyed to Jerusalem to bring a new balance to Israel and the world. As a result, he was of course rejected by the orthodoxy that did not understand the 'constraint' of his vocation ('the son of man *must* suffer . . .'). But this rejection was itself taken up into the vocation, completing in one act the mission of Jesus and the destiny of Israel. The multiple constraints on the troublesome young Jew worked their way out in a new and paradoxical obedience unto death, an act of eternal atonement.

Within this context we can move towards a more truly historical account of Jesus' understanding of his own vocation. Heaven forbid that we should embark once more on pseudoscientific psychological analyses or 'personality' studies: the Old Quest of nineteenth-century liberalism is (one may hope) gone for ever. But if we can know – as we surely can – that (say) Jeremiah, John the

---

28 The phrase 'a new world order' has now been used, with a slightly different sense, by Sanders 1985. I use it in order to indicate the continuity of the hoped-for state with present space-time events. I have discussed the issues involved here in Wright 1985 (ch. 2, above, in the present volume). If 'apocalyptic' is thus understood as a complex, and theologically charged, metaphor-system for referring to future space-time events, a different perspective is introduced to Harvey's fourth chapter ('Jesus and time: the constraint of an ending').

29 Schweitzer 1954; see the account in Neill 1964, 191–200.

30 See Caird 1965.

31 This shows that to make a split between Jesus' expectation of the kingdom and his expectations concerning his own fate is to create a false antithesis, contra e.g. Watson 1985.

Baptist and the apostle Paul each firmly believed himself to have a unique role to play in the purposes of the God of Abraham, Isaac and Jacob, it hardly makes sense to say less than this of Jesus. And when we then ask how Jesus conceived of this unique role, we find – as Harvey has shown so well – that the old categories will not fit. The oblique hints are more evocative by far than direct claims could have been. The [202] 'least in the kingdom' is greater than the one whom he styled 'more than a prophet'; selling up and following him will attain what Torah by itself could not; something greater than Israel's greatest king is here.[32] The obvious probability that the proclamation of God's imminent judgment on Israel, and the taking of Israel's role on to himself, would end in a violent death[33] is merely part of Jesus' whole understanding of his role and purpose. In faith, he could comprehend that death as the accomplishment of God's strange purposes for Israel, and hence could believe also that God would vindicate him, as Israel itself hoped to be vindicated, on the other side of a death undergone in obedience to God's will. Thus there would be fulfilled, in him, the great apocalyptic metaphors of Israel's resurrection and of the vindication 'on the clouds of heaven' of the one 'like a son of man'. It is a matter of history, not of uncritical piety or spurious psychologizing, to ask: who did he think he was?

If the first answer to that question is, as I believe it must be, 'the one in and through whom Israel's God was fulfilling his purposes, transforming Israel in the process' (which is so very nearly equivalent to 'Israel's Messiah' as to make very little difference), a supplementary question needs to be asked, about the *appropriateness* of such a fulfilment. Is it conceivable that Jesus, the Jew, the Man, could have asked himself how it was that he came to be performing a task which, at various crucial points in the prophetic writings, YHWH had reserved for himself precisely on the grounds that nobody else could do it?[34] It is well beyond the scope of this paper to answer that question. But, as a preliminary ground-clearing exercise, we must make some comments on the 'constraint of monotheism' within which, according to Harvey's final chapter, such questionings must be set.

Harvey begins this final chapter with an account of Jewish monotheism itself. Expressed in the *Shema*, the belief that God is one stood at the heart of Jewish thought and piety. It is admittedly not always easy to assess what precisely this confession means. Sometimes it appears to be a declaration of

---

32   Mt. 11.11; 19.21; 12.42, and parallels.

33   See Harvey 1982, 147ff.; and cp. Schillebeeckx 1979, 298–312.

34   See e.g. Isa. 59.15–21; 63.3–6; Ezek. 34.11–16, 20–24.

[203] YHWH's supremacy over all other 'gods', sometimes a denial that such other beings even exist. It comes into sharpest focus when contrasted with pagan polytheism, which was capable of adding more 'gods', almost at will, to the pantheon (pp. 154–6). Since, Harvey continues, even those Jewish writers who use 'divine' language of (for example) Moses are not intending thereby to compromise the creator's unique divinity, it is not surprising that the New Testament writers too avoid direct ascriptions of divinity to Jesus (p. 157), a step only taken when 'the new religion had spread well beyond the confines of its parent Judaism' (pp. 157–8). Instead, the New Testament speaks of Jesus as 'son of God', which, devoid of the associations placed on this phrase either by patristic or Romantic thought, may be construed in three ways: the son as obedient, the son as apprentice, the son as agent (pp. 158–65).[35] From this it is clear, according to Harvey, that the phrase 'son of God' could hardly have been a regular designation of Jesus during his lifetime, although he does not rule out the idea that the acknowledgment of Jesus' sonship after the resurrection was intended to express a truth which had always been present, though hidden (pp. 165–8). Jesus nevertheless seems to have described himself thus, either directly or by implication, as 'a way – perhaps the only way – of claiming such unprecedented divine authorisation, at the same time preserving intact that respect for the indivisible oneness of God which was the instinctive possession of any religious Jew' (p. 168). The evidence for this is found in the 'abba'-form of address to God, and in various parables (for example the wicked tenants), and in the charge of blasphemy, which Harvey, unlike some other recent scholars, regards as 'one of the most securely attested facts' about Jesus (p. 171). There is thus a tension set up between the constraint of monotheism on the one hand and, on the other, 'the necessity felt by Jesus to assume a unique and God-given authority for his words and deeds' (p. 172). Recognizing this, the disciples were on occasion moved to acknowledge Jesus as one 'to speak to whom was as if to speak to God himself', or to prostrate themselves before him 'as if in the presence of God himself' (p. 172). This was as far as one could go within the [204] existing constraints. But later, 'released from the constraint of Jewish monotheism, gentile Christians began to think of Jesus as also, in some sense, God' (p. 173). It is to the earlier formulation, however, that we should return, since, according to Harvey, it says all that needs to be said to demonstrate the challenge of Jesus not only in his own generation but also today.

---

35 See further Harvey [1987], in which he discusses more fully the Jewish background to the idea of 'agency'.

This chapter is a worthwhile and stimulating contribution in many respects. The analysis of 'son of God' is particularly interesting, and the concept of 'agency' clearly one worth pursuing further. But there is a basic problem about the 'constraint of monotheism' itself that must be faced. It has become a standard view, almost a commonplace of New Testament scholarship, that the idea of incarnation was, almost literally, unthinkable to a Jewish mind. Many Christian scholars have finally accepted what Jews since (at least) the time of Trypho have been urging: that a 'God-Man' is a pagan idea that has corrupted the pure Jewish religion. Trinitarianism, on this view, can in the last resort mean only tritheism.[36] But this position is beset with difficulties, of which we may here outline five.

(1) It has been shown often enough that the Jew–Greek distinction is, in terms of religious ideas, thoroughly anachronistic at this point in history.[37] We cannot presume to be able to split the two apart and set up a rigid and unbreakable 'constraint' based on one or the other. Previous attempts to do this within the field of New Testament Christology have not been notably successful.

(2) It could, indeed, be argued that the rigid numerical monotheism of the rabbis itself owed more to Greek interpretations of their tradition, and to the desire to combat early Christianity, than to the somewhat more flexible Old Testament background. At the period in question, the assertion of monotheism was not a matter of speculative theology such as would lend itself to discussions of whether there might be plurality within the unity of God. It was a matter of asserting, [205] often in the teeth of contemporary circumstances and at the risk of life and limb, that the God of Israel was the God of the whole world, and vice versa. It was this belief that enabled Israel to hold up its head and to hope for God's eventual victory over the forces of evil (in other words, for Israel's eventual triumph over its oppressors). And, so far from Jesus being bound by this constraint, it seems to have been just this interpretation of Israel's role within the purposes of God that he attacked.[38] God's kingdom would not come in military victory over the Romans, but in turning the other cheek. The cross symbolizes the paradoxical announcement of this alternative

---

36   See Cupitt 1979; Hick 1977; Schoeps 1959; Epstein 1959, 134.
37   See particularly the work of Martin Hengel, e.g. his Hengel 1974. Note also the preface to the 4th edn. of Davies 1980, xxiii–xxv.
38   See particularly Borg 1984.

'kingdom': instead of defeating the Romans, the king of the Jews dies at their hands. It thus appears (a) that the real meaning of monotheism at the time of Jesus was more political and less speculative than Harvey makes out, and (b) that Jesus in any case did not see himself as bound by it as a 'constraint'. To suggest that God's kingdom would come through death at Roman hands was just as unthinkable then as incarnation was held to be subsequently in anti-Christian Jewish polemic. That, in a further twist of the paradox, is precisely why Jesus was crucified.

(3) The twentieth-century debate on incarnational theology and the New Testament has all too readily followed the change in fashion within the history-of-religions movement. In the first forty years or so of this century the history-of-religions school, with names like Reitzenstein and Bousset to the fore, was zealously promoting the idea that Christianity was a Hellenized movement which had, thankfully, broken away from the shackles and 'constraints' of Judaism. Gnostic writings, mystery-religions, descending and re-ascending gods or divine figures – all formed the stock concepts out of which the early Christians (and particularly Paul) had fashioned their theological ideas. Jesus himself, of course (insofar as anything could be known about him after Schweitzer's demolition job, and in the light of the needs of this religio-historical interpretation), preached the timeless truths that related to all human beings; the earliest church Judaized his memory, but Paul broke loose and, as the missionary to the gentiles, created Christianity as a non-Jewish religion. All this, of course, at a time when, with Hegel and [206] Nietzsche in the background and the Luther revival and dialectical theology in full swing (not to mention other non-theological factors in the Europe of the 1920s and 1930s), the drive was on to rescue essential Christianity – Jesus, Paul, Luther and their apparent heirs and successors – from all things Jewish. The result is with us still, as evident in Harvey's final chapter as anywhere. *The idea that the Incarnation is a fundamentally non-Jewish concept owes a good deal of its power in this century to the fact that it was propagated by those who wanted to rescue Christianity from Judaism.*

But, while a good deal of scholarship still reads the New Testament in this way, a great change has come since the Second World War, heralded by W. D. Davies's two brilliant books on Paul and Jesus.[39] In line with both the neo-orthodox 'Biblical Theology' movement and with the post-war rejection of anti-semitism, Jewish concepts suddenly became 'good' and pagan ones

---

39 Davies 1948 (4th edn, with new introduction, 1980); Davies 1964.

'bad'. Jesus became a great Jewish teacher misunderstood by the politicans (a role he still enjoys in many works); Paul, a rabbi who believed simply that the Messiah had come. Incarnational theology, for so long believed to be a Greek idea and therefore good, was suddenly regarded as a non-Jewish idea and therefore bad. Not only is this Jew–Greek distinction anachronistic for the period in question, as we have seen, but the modern statements of supposedly 'incarnational' doctrine now being regarded as non-Jewish and therefore unacceptable may not be what early incarnational theologians believed at all, but twentieth-century constructs *originally designed precisely in order to be non-Jewish and therefore acceptable*. There are three historical considerations which suggest that this is in fact the case.

(a) There are hints that some Jews of this period were not, in fact, so scrupulous about strict numerical monotheism as has been suggested. Whatever we may conclude about the speculative and metaphorical language used of God's 'Word' or his 'Wisdom', the fact that the suggestion of 'two powers in heaven' needed to be firmly anathematized shows that the 'Jewish mind' was not, after all, incapable of thinking such new [207] and daring theological thoughts.[40] The sharpening of monotheistic doctrine in this period may have had more to do with opposition to Persian dualism (to which Christianity would of course also be opposed) than with speculation about the singularity or plurality of God himself. It is arguable, too, that a good deal of the strictness attaching to monotheism in Judaism after AD 70 owes its force both to the rise of Christianity itself and to the threat of assimilation. To what extent Jews attacked polytheism because it was pagan or pagans because they were polytheists it is impossible to say.[41]

(b) When the early Fathers were exploring what precisely it was that they felt constrained to say about Jesus, they never for a moment talked in terms reminiscent of a pagan religion adding a new god to its pantheon. Nor, in thinking of Jesus 'as also, in some sense, God', did they for a moment imagine themselves to be 'released from the constraint of Jewish monotheism'.[42] On the contrary. They continued to assert that the one God who had now made himself known in Jesus was to be identified as the sole creator of the world. They refused to lapse into the dualism offered by Persian thought from without or Marcion and the Gnostics from within. They transferred to the church the doctrine of election that had been the essential corollary

---

40   See Harvey himself (1982), 155–6; Segal 1977.
41   See e.g. Epstein 1959, 134, 198.
42   Harvey 1982, 173.

of monotheism within the Jewish scheme of thought. All the essentials of Jewish monotheism remained – transposed, of course, into the new key: instead of 'There is one God, and Israel is his people', the church declared 'There is one God, and Jesus is his son'. Again, the reason why the (apparently bewildering) doctrine of the Trinity was propagated was precisely that the constraint of monotheism in its essentials still obtained. It is important to distinguish between the Greek and Latin philosophical language in which the debates were conducted and the basic constraints that determined what it was they were trying to say. The Fathers were after all 'constrained' to use such language in the interests of mutual intelligibility, and since James Barr's *Semantics of Biblical Language*[43] no-one should be allowed [208] to suggest that the pedigree of the words used is the only, or even the most important, clue to their meaning. Whether the great Trinitarian theologians were wrong in believing that they could talk in the way they did without self-contradiction is quite another matter. That they believed it is not in doubt. This alone should make us cautious about equating incarnational or Trinitarian ideas with non- or anti-Jewish ones. The main things monotheism was designed to combat are combated also by Trinitarianism, the 'Christian form of monotheism'.[44]

(c) At certain key points in the New Testament we can, I believe, see the beginnings of incarnational theology, and *it is set within an explicitly monotheistic framework*. One of the best examples is 1 Corinthians 8.4–6, whose line of thought is as follows. Paul, faced with the question of meat offered to idols, lays down as a basis the Jewish principle enshrined in the *Shema*: no idol has real existence, there being 'no God but One' (v. 4).[45] He then acknowledges that there are many so-called 'gods' and 'lords' in the world – he is far from unfamiliar with the pagan pantheon (v. 5) – but, he says, we Christians are monotheists, not polytheists, and again (v. 6) he quotes the *Shema* to prove his point. Or rather, he *adapts* the *Shema*: *kyrios ho theos hēmōn, kyrios heis estin* (Deuteronomy 6.4 LXX) has become *all' hēmin heis theos . . . kai heis kyrios*. And Paul, not only within this monotheistic *formula* but as the climax of his monotheistic *argument*, glosses *theos* with 'the father, from whom are all things and we unto him' and *kyrios* with 'Jesus Christ, through whom are all things and we through him'. It misses the point to suggest that Paul is not necessarily referring to Jesus' mediatorial activity in the creation

---

43 Barr 1961.

44 *Pace* e.g. Ruether 1974, esp. 246–51.

45 See too the motif of 'loving God' in v. 3 (cp. Dt. 6.5 etc.).

of the world.[46] The crucial question is not whether Jesus is identified with a hypothetical pre-existent figure. Within Paul's argument – and within the context of his Corinthian audience's background – the main point is that, for Christians, monotheism has not been abandoned, but simply reinterpreted *to include Jesus within it*. What we are thus faced with is the [209] category so carefully excluded a priori from twentieth-century history-of-religions research: a Jewish incarnational theology.

(4) If the 'constraint of monotheism' functioned as Harvey has suggested, with the result that Jesus simply believed himself to be the uniquely authorized agent of God, it seems to me very difficult to envisage the state of affairs where he would accept without rebuke worship offered to God himself (see Harvey, p. 172). The parallels with other figures in the New Testament who seem to have believed themselves to be fully accredited representatives and agents of God – Paul and Barnabas in Acts 14.14–18, and the angel in Revelation 19.10; 22.8–9 – suggest that either the events (Thomas's confession in John 20.28, the disciples' prostration in Matthew 14.33, and so on) did not happen at all, or that Jesus was, as part of his human faith-awareness of the particular role to which he was called in the divine purpose, aware also of an appropriateness in the offering of such worship to him. Without this, I question whether the scene proposed is even credible. A mere man, a Jew at that, calmly accepting divine worship without pride or scandal is not easy to envisage.[47]

(5) All of this brings us back to our question. Is it possible, after all, to imagine a young Jew bound simultaneously, and paradoxically, *both* by the constraints of orthodoxy *and* by those of his own peculiar vocation? If it is, it may also be possible that the 'blasphemy' charge at Jesus' trial really may have been intended in the sense implied by John 10.33 ('because you, being a man, make yourself God'). This preserves both the fact of the constraint of monotheism (in some sense) and the possibility that here Jesus may have 'bent' that constraint to his own purpose – or rather, from his point of view, straightened it to fit the truth and purpose of God. What Jesus was saying and doing was rightly perceived as a threat to the established order of Judaism, at every level. He was, we could suggest, the classic type of rebel-from-within, the one who is so disturbing precisely because he *is* intelligible, he *is* communicating, he *is* operating within the constraints in some senses, while at the same time

---

46 Contra e.g. Dunn 1980, 179–83.
47 See the similar arguments now advanced by Bauckham 1981; France 1982.

bursting [210] through them, perhaps even through a rigidly conceived anti-incarnational monotheism. He is challenging Israel's right to go on living as it has been doing, just as John the Baptist did, and Elijah and Jeremiah before him. He comes as the owner's son to the vineyard, to demand that the tenants shall cease regarding it as their own. The outcome is predictable: 'This is the heir: come, let us kill him, and the inheritance will be ours' (Mark 12.7 and parallels). If Jesus, coming as the Owner's son, is somehow taking on himself the role of Israel, then he is indeed a threat. Everything has a limit. He has crossed a boundary. And paradoxically, in doing so and suffering the consequences, he is fulfilling his own vocation *and that of Judaism as a whole*: called to share and bear the anguish of the world, he has created his own moulds, his own play of forms for the pain.

4

Taking the Text with Her Pleasure: A Post-Post-Modernist Response to J. Dominic Crossan, *The Historical Jesus*

(With apologies to A. A. Milne, St Paul and James Joyce)

This piece was, and is, a *jeu d'esprit*, and as such it took quite a risk. Dom Crossan's big book *The Historical Jesus* was in all sorts of ways a landmark: Crossan, one of the most brilliant writers of the time, had been building up to this volume for some while, not least through the work of the 'Jesus Seminar', of which he was the co-chair, along with the late Robert Funk. I had worked carefully through the book when it appeared, and when I was asked to sit on the panel to discuss it at the Annual Meeting of the Society of Biblical Literature, in San Francisco in 1992, I was keen to have a go. (This was also the meeting at which my first two big monographs, *The Climax of the Covenant* (Wright 1991) and *The New Testament and the People of God* (Wright 1992a), were launched, as some readers may perceive.)

The problem was: how? Crossan was well on top of postmodern literary theory, and any attempt to give an old-fashioned modernist exposition and refutation would have been, I reckoned, beside the point. One might as well set a bulldog to catch a butterfly. So, since Crossan had made much of 'story' in his work (quite rightly in my view), I thought a story would be the right way to approach things. I was greatly helped in this, in two quite different ways, by my old friends Canon Douglas Holt, who had preached a 'narrative' sermon in Worcester College a few weeks before and had thereby given me some ideas on how to go about it, and Dr Andrew Moore, who sat me down late one night before I was due to fly to San Francisco, talked me through what I was going to do (I had copious notes but hadn't yet written the piece), and prayed with and for me. That night, and the next day on the plane, all kinds of ideas kept bouncing into my head, and I jotted them down and tried to work out the necessary narrative. The morning after the long flight, thoroughly jet-lagged, I sneaked out of the hotel around 3 a.m. and found breakfast in an all-night diner around the corner, where I had a close-up view of San Francisco nightlife on the one hand and an uninterrupted four hours of scribbling on the other. Returning to the hotel, I asked my roommates if I could get away with it, and they – particularly, I recall, Dr Grant LeMarquand – were eager that I should. So the next morning I repeated the process, finished the scribbled text and went to the session.

The piece succeeded better than I had dared to hope. The large audience got the point and enjoyed the different approach. The members of Crossan's sizeable fan-club were furious (some never spoke to me again); but Crossan himself, a master of the tease, saw what I was doing, and we became, I'm glad to say, good friends. He did complain about the opening italicized lines where I place him in the neo-Bultmannian 'New Quest', because, as he said, he is Irish and catholic, not German and protestant. But I am unrepentant, for reasons apparent in chapter 2 of *Jesus and the Victory of God*.

I did also hear that Elisabeth Schüssler Fiorenza had objected to the closing scene as being stereotypically sexist. She seemed to have missed the point that the final pages were all aiming for the Joycean denouement, which was itself a hinted tribute to Crossan's brilliant Irish literary pedigree . . .

[303] *Crossan's newest book bases its reconstruction of Jesus on sources such as the* Gospel of Thomas, *a hypothetically reconstructed 'Early Q', and a hypothetical 'Cross gospel' reconstructed out of the* Gospel of Peter. *Crossan argues that, faced with the 'brokered empire' of the Roman world, Jesus initiated a 'brokerless kingdom' in which all had equal access to God. Crossan's work in one way, and that of scholars like Helmut Koester and Burton Mack in other ways, form a serious revival of the until-recently moribund Bultmann school of gospel interpretation.*

Once upon a time there was a book. We do not know where she came from, or how she grew to be what she was; one doesn't know that about books, only that, well, there they are – or at least, that we find ourselves confronted in what we feel to be a bookish way when we are in their presence. And the sense of being so confronted is so strong in this case that we will skip Stanley Fish and say, again but with more conviction, once upon a time *there was a book*.

Her name – well, we can't be sure about her name. But the words 'Mediterranean Jewish Peasant' on her jacket are pretty obviously a secondary, modernist and historicizing addition. It may well be that it derives from her initials, M. J. P. We shall call her Michelle.

If we can't know where Michelle came from, since of course real authors are notoriously elusive, at least we can know her *implied* author. An adopted parent, she knew, could be almost as satisfying as a real one. Michelle felt good about her implied author, as indeed she had every right to; for her implied author, clearly, was a serious postmodernist. She glowed with pride at the thought. She had heard that there were other, um, books, even of her own age, that continued to press the old modernist distinction between *fact* and *interpretation*. Facts, they said, were things you discovered by objective research in places like the basement of the Harvard Divinity School; interpretations were what humans did with facts. Michelle knew that this was a decidedly false dichotomy, and preened herself on the fact – or at least the impression – that her implied author had no time for such nonsense. Reconstruction is [304] everything. All we can do is to tell stories, and see what happens. 'There is only reconstruction.' She repeated the sentence lovingly. She thanked her implied author that she was not as other books: positivist, objectivist, dispassionate, and all the time hiding social power and imperialist control. Her vocation, she felt in her bones, or at least her spine, was to challenge the reader on the level of formal method, material investment and historical interpretation. Her implied author, in short, was savvy, courageous, a brilliant wordsmith, subverting current ideologies with his shafts of wit, his subtle irony, his shrewd aphorisms. A shadow of doubt crossed Michelle's mind as she reflected on this implied author. He was beginning to look disturbingly like her implied *subject*. Was that inevitable, she wondered, and if so did it matter?

Michelle turned her attention to her implied readers. There were lots of them, she thought with pride. The *New York Times* review had done its work well. But who were they? The natural assumption might have been that a book with a postmodernist implied author would have a postmodernist implied reader. So, indeed, it seemed. 'In the end, as in the beginning, now as then, there is only the performance.' 'These words are not a list to be read . . . they are a score to be played and a programme to be enacted.' Did this not send a signal to all implied readers that, if they weren't already postmodernists, they had better become such at once? Michelle sighed with content. It is a comforting thing for a book to feel integrated, to have implied author and implied reader shaking hands with each other across the intertextual void.

No sooner had Michelle decided that this question was settled, however, than her eye was caught by the clothes she was wearing. It was a fine jacket, to be sure: sophisticated with the merest hint of seductiveness. But what was this? There, on the jacket, were words that appeared to subvert the whole identity she had just decided she possessed. 'The first comprehensive determination of who Jesus was, what he did, what he said'. It was the word *determination* that really worried her. It sat uneasily in her mind beside all her resolute implicit postmodernism, like a large Scotch sitting uneasily in the stomach alongside half a bottle of red wine. It surely couldn't be the case, could it, that, though her implied author was a postmodernist, her implied reader was after all an arrant, unreconstructed, old-fashioned *modernist*? A way out offered itself. A jacket is only a jacket, and when you get indoors – into a library, say – you usually take it off, revealing a truer self underneath. Perhaps after all it wasn't the implied *reader*, but only the implied *purchaser* (a category strangely absent from recent literary theory) who was a dyed-in-the-wool modernist. She felt somehow that this was a bit of a cop-out, but all this auto-analysis had wearied her. She resolved to return to [305] the question in the morning, and, slipping somewhat guiltily out of the jacket, fell into a deep postmodernist sleep.

As she slept, she dreamed. She found herself standing in the old library at Alexandria, some time in the middle of the second century. The librarian, an ageless man with a long, white beard and sad eyes, was sending his assistants back to the market one more time in search of the most elusive of books.

'We already have the combined texts,' he was saying. 'I want the early one – the pure one – the unadorned one, the one that looks just like our beloved *Thomas*.'

'Master,' they replied, 'we have toiled all night and taken nothing. The booksellers say they've never heard of it. They think you're just imagining it. They've looked in the catalogues for codices in print, papyri in print, and scrolls in print for the last hundred years and there's just nothing listed under Early Q. Are you *sure* it's not just a figment of your imagination?'

The old man leaned back in his chair, closed his eyes, and looked sadder and wiser than ever.

'Ah,' he said as though in a trance, 'I can see how it will turn out. We will never find it. Nobody will ever find it. But I will tell you how it will be in the last days. There will be no agreement. There will be a man called Dominic who will claim that most Jesus-material comes from Thomas; and he will be opposed by a man called Thomas who will claim that most Jesus-material is Dominical.'

Michelle woke up with a start. It was like an apocalyptic vision, she thought. Her implied author didn't approve of them; they weren't in *Thomas*, and one of the ways you knew what was in Early Q was that it was non-apocalyptic. Was this, perhaps, her subconcious telling her something that her own pages hadn't allowed for? She fell asleep again, and dreamed one more time. She saw an old, old man, with the preaching-gown of a Lutheran, the mind of a neo-Kantian and the sad smile of a Heideggerian existentialist. His Jesus had been a man of words, aloof from the real concerns of first-century Judaism. And now the old man was dying. The 'New Quest' that his followers had invented to try to keep him alive in changing times had itself become old and tired. Finally, a Third Quest had arisen: it had rejected the old man and spurned his methods and his followers. It had reinstated apocalyptic Judaism as the true matrix of Jesus, and had focused as much on his actions as on his words. It had even begun to explore the historical reasons for his death, instead of regarding the Passion narratives as simply historicizing accounts of primitive theology. It finally starved the old man to death (Michelle had a feeling, she didn't know why, that this had happened in 1985), and he was buried unceremoniously in a pauper's grave. Three years passed, and the watchers at the tomb – the sorrowing followers of the old man – sat there still, playing with coloured billiard-balls and recounting aphorisms. Then, suddenly, there was an earthquake. The **[306]** tomb opened, and there came out three men, followed by a large book. The first man was himself a German, with an accent not unlike the original old man; he carried under his arm two volumes dedicated to the old man's memory. The second was an American, with a beard like a lion, and a sword in his right hand with which he had slain innocent myths ancient and modern. The third was an Irishman with a tongue of silver. And behind them came the Book. As Michelle looked in her dream, a loud voice was heard, saying, 'Have you reconstructed the Quest?' And an answer came from the Book – and Michelle recognized her own voice – 'Wait and See'. [I should say at this point that the answer 'Yes', found in some sources of the Crossan gospel, is clearly secondary, being a naive doublet of the end of this story.]

Michelle awoke, sweating all over – not a good thing for a book to do at the best of times. She put on her jacket, resolved to get to the bottom of it. But to whom could she turn? If she went to a modernist psychiatrist for a methodological critique, he or she would tell her she had been hallucinating not only at night but all her life. If she went to a postmodernist psychiatrist for a methodological critique, she would be told some more stories that might or might not help. A wave of hermeneutical sea-sickness swept over her, as she longed for a fixed point on which to rest her eyes, and simultaneously felt guilty for wanting it. She resolved, in the best postmodern fashion, to try self-analysis in the first instance.

Let's take the matter of *criteria*, she thought. I suppose that's important; but, strictly speaking, modernists have holes, and positivists have nests, but the son of postmodernism ought to have nowhere to lay his head. Where, then, do these criteria come from? Double or multiple attestation appear fine – or do they? How do we know that a single one-off story might not be the pearl of great price for which one should sell all the lesser pearls of frequently repeated aphorisms? Michelle felt through her pages to see how rigidly the 'criteria' were applied. With a sense of guilty relief, she came to the passage on the Lord's Prayer. It met all the criteria; there could be no question about it. There were probably, she recalled, three independent versions. But, her implied author had said, 'I do not think . . . ', 'I do not believe . . . ' 'that such a coordinated prayer was ever taught by Jesus to his followers'. Maybe, thought Michelle, maybe these neo-modernist criteria are only a surface noise. When push comes to shove, they can be dispensed with, leaving a purer, more personal storytelling underneath. She wasn't quite happy about this, but it would do for the moment, she thought.

And what about sources? Michelle felt decidedly uneasy about the chronological list of supposed Jesus-sources that nestled so impressively inside her back cover. Why was she uneasy? After all, surely it [307] was an excellent thing to set the material out so that one could see where one was. The fact that a modernist would want to do that as well was surely just a superficial coincidence. But the order itself – the way in which the sources were listed chronologically – she still found deeply puzzling. Her implied author, of course, would never have made the naive mistake of thinking that because Matthew's gospel highlights the conversion of Matthew it was therefore written by Matthew, or that because John's gospel highlights the role of the Beloved Disciple it was therefore written by him. Why was it, then, that *Thomas* 12 could be invoked so straightforwardly as evidence that the first layer at least of the book was 'composed by the fifties CE, possibly in Jerusalem, under the aegis of James' authority', or that *Thomas* 13 could be pressed into service to support a second layer being written in the 60s or 70s 'under the aegis of the Thomas authority'? It was, of course, a happy thing to be under someone's 'aegis' rather than simply the product of someone's pen; perhaps the notion of 'implied aegis' should be added to those of implied author, reader and purchaser. And it was, of course, much more satisfactory to speak of 'the Thomas authority' than of Thomas himself, even if it did sound a bit like

62

a local government department. Yet doubts remained, as they did with the Cross gospel itself; Michelle had heard it whispered in the library that even her implied author's closest implied colleagues weren't happy with his extraction of a section from the *Gospel of Peter*, his firm dating of it in the 50s, his placing of it in Galilee, and his declaration that it was the single source of all the canonical Passion narratives. The whole construct, of course, was a quite brilliant fiction (in the postmodern sense) about the early church, despite the tactical disclaimer which, no doubt due to implicit modesty, stated that the book was about Jesus, not about the earliest church. But did it really work, even on that level?

As Michelle pondered this, she was reminded of Winnie-the-Pooh who, in his search for Woozles, went round and round the same clump of trees following his own footprints in the snow, and using the extra sets of tracks, each time round, as evidence that the quarry was more real and numerous than before. How did it go? Early *Thomas* and Early Q give a 'sapiental' portrait of Jesus the Cynic or Jesus the early Gnostic; these are the earliest sources, therefore that's what Jesus was probably like. Once round the trees. Why are Early *Thomas* and Early Q early? Because they contain no apocalyptic and are sapiental, or Cynic, or gnostic. Twice round the trees. Why is the absence of apocalyptic a sign of earliness? Because Jesus and the earliest church weren't into that stuff. Three times round the trees. How do we know Jesus and the earliest church weren't into that stuff? Because of Early *Thomas* and Early Q. As Michelle thought of [308] the ever-increasing footprints in the hermeneutical snow, she didn't exactly feel that the circle was *vicious*. That wasn't a nice thing to think about one's implied author. She did, however, have an uncomfortable feeling that the circle was *shy*: that is to say, that any *virtue* it might possess remained well hidden behind a thick veil of hermeneutical modesty.

Keeping her jacket on, Michelle sat in the library, pondering deeply. Then, ignoring the regulations, she began to whisper to the books on either side of her. How did the analysis of Jesus' social world square with what the others had been saying? It was now her turn to be shy, as she could see glances being exchanged by a couple of paperbacks further down the shelf. Yes, they'd all heard of Social Banditry. Hadn't that rather forbidding book on Spirals of Violence been going on about it a few years ago? But wasn't there a danger of replacing the now-unfashionable pan-Zealot hypothesis with a pan-Bandit hypothesis? Surely a good postmodernist would want to insist on a much looser, more varied and storied, world. Michelle got even more worried, and went back to her own thoughts. It was all very well, she thought, for her implied author to tell stories about the first century based on studies of the twentieth century, or to tell stories about the Middle East based on studies of South American Indians. But would her modernist implied readers like it? She wasn't at all convinced. How could she reassure them? She remembered with a glow of relief the quote, from a distinguished figure, on the back of her jacket. 'The book', it said, 'avoids projecting current ideologies.' That was a fine thing. Nobody, modern or postmodern, wanted mere projection. But, she thought with a start, supposing I'm projecting *non*-current ideologies? Michelle felt through her pages again, and came upon the phrase that the publishers had so gladly highlighted in their press release: Jesus and his followers fitted into the mould of being 'hippies in a world of Augustan yuppies'. Where did *that* come from? It was quite true that the hippy culture wasn't a current ideology. It belonged, she well knew, in the 1960s, not the 1990s. Back to the implied purchaser again, she thought. The quote on the jacket was true, but it wasn't comforting.

Michelle was by this time thoroughly nonplussed. The more she longed for integration, the more disintegration seemed to lie close at hand. The sense of *Sturm und Drang*, so deeply beloved of postmodernists, was all very well for *them*, she thought bitterly. *They* didn't have to live with it day by day. They projected it on to their existentialist forebears, and simply basked in reflected *Angst* from the safety of implicit authorship. Where could *she* turn for help? A vision came into her mind of a book that would understand; a book that would reassure her; a book that would appreciate the problems she'd been through, and would bring comfort and warmth into her life. [309]

In her mind's eye she could see him now. He wouldn't be a modernist or positivist, of course. She could never go with someone like that. And he'd have to understand her wayward side, her delight in the free play of deconstruction and reconstruction. But he would also give her an inner reconciliation, a sense of being at peace with herself. He would help her to work out the tension between her implied author and her implied readers. He would help her out of the introverted world of postmodernism, with its tendency to neurotic self-examination – wasn't that what she'd been doing all day so far? – and into the hermeneutically risky but ultimately more satisfying world of public discourse. She would find herself in a brand-new way.

She could see him now in her mind's eye. She wandered back to the study and sat shyly on the desk, hoping, waiting. And as she waited, it came to her.

If all there is is reconstruction, she thought, then all there is is *somebody's* reconstruction. Every reconstructor then becomes a broker – which, throughout her pages, was a word that seemed to carry all kinds of negative overtones, not least (she supposed) through its implicit association with those yuppies, whether Augustan or otherwise, of whom her implicit author so deeply disapproved. How could we ever make progress, she wondered, away from this brokered hermeneutical empire? The embattled brokerage that had constituted her inner *Angst* all day longed for the brokerless kingdom of public truth; who would help her find it?

A soft voice behind her (he'd been reading the back of her jacket) made her turn in surprise. She found herself looking into the eyes of a critical realist.

They gazed at one another with unspoken questions and answers. He needed her, his eyes said, as much as she needed him. From somewhere there came a voice, which she dimly recognized:

There is therefore now no solipsism for those who engage in critical realism;
For the law of the freshly storied world has set you free from the law of private worlds and inner tension between modern and postmodern.
For what positivist historiography could not achieve, in that it was weak through the postmodern critique, critical realism can achieve.
Offering itself in the likeness of postmodernism's stories, it condemns postmodernism's collapse into *mere* story,
In order that the brokerless kingdom of public truth may be available to all who walk not according to positivism, nor [310] according to relativism, but according to a newly storied public world.

A covenant, she thought. A new covenant. A covenant that might reach . . . but modesty forbade her from completing the sentence. She looked steadily at him. Ask me, she said with her eyes. He asked her, but she couldn't speak. She felt the negations of postmodernism melting away inside her. He softly removed her modernist jacket. Ask me again, she said with her eyes. He asked her again, and now she found her voice. Yes, she said. Yes. Yes.

5

Jesus

When I was invited to contribute to the Festschrift for Professor Morna Hooker, I was delighted and honoured. I had attended Professor Hooker's lectures on Romans when reading Theology in Oxford in the early 1970s, and had then followed her to Cambridge and been a member of her seminar. She was unfailingly kind and supportive to me, even though our ecclesial differences (she being a Methodist) and our various theological and exegetical differences remained not far from the surface in our discussions.

The topic of the volume was to be early Christian thought within its Jewish context, drawing together various aspects of what was a whole new venture for much post-war scholarship. Writers in earlier years had often assumed, as some still do today, that since Paul's doctrine of justification was opposed to 'works of the Jewish law', and since Jesus engaged in controversy with the Pharisees, they must both have been opposing something called 'Judaism', and that one would then be wrong to look to the Jewish world for clues as to the nature of early Christianity, the thought of its early figures and the nature of its first writings. As a historian, committed to the attempt to get inside the mind of the people I was studying, I was naturally eager to join in this venture, and honoured to be asked to write about Jesus himself.

This was the time at which, in the USA and some other places, regular attempts were being made to separate out different strands or styles of ancient teaching. In particular, the 'Jesus Seminar' was picking up the then fashionable antithesis between 'wisdom' and 'apocalyptic'. This was part of the reaction to twentieth-century 'apocalyptic' such as that of the dispensationalist and fundamentalist teachings from which some of the Jesus Seminar had themselves escaped: by making Jesus a teacher of 'wisdom' they supposed themselves to be rescuing him from 'apocalyptic'. It is ironic that at the same time, in another part of the American biblical studies world, J. Louis Martyn was writing his large commentary on Galatians, insisting on making Paul the teacher of something he called 'apocalyptic', which was designed to mark out Paul from teachings that reminded Martyn and his followers of those same American fundamentalists.

The only cure for this kind of puzzle is history. I was, at the time of writing, engaged in my large historical project on Jesus, and the present article drew out some significant strands from that work (*Jesus and the Victory of God*, 1996) and tried to display them in relation to some of the current debates.

[43] Introduction

When, in 1973, Geza Vermes published the first of his three major books about Jesus, its title sent shock waves through certain sections of the reading public. *Jesus the Jew*: the very phrase was polemical, summing up, as only the best titles succeed in doing, the book's content and thrust. Vermes, like a few writers before and a great many since, attempted, by arguing for the essential Jewishness of Jesus, to undermine certain commonplace Christian affirmations. The debate continues.

But, as it continues, it broadens out. We have learned – not least through the other labours of Vermes himself – just how many-sided was the Judaism of the first century. The present writer, having in a recent work expanded what had been a single chapter on first-century Judaism into five chapters totalling some two hundred pages, was taken to task by a reviewer for making things too simple, for missing out too much data.[1] The more we learn about the Jewish world of the first century, the more we are aware of its multiple diversities.

Nevertheless, there is still clearly something we can call 'first-century Judaism'. We would not know, otherwise, what this thing was whose multiple diversity we were so firmly asserting. This is, of course, yet another low-grade re-run of the old debate between Platonists and Aristotelians, which emerges in all sorts of contexts. Some people see things as large wholes, albeit containing many different parts; others see things as collections of diverse parts, albeit still retaining some semblance of family relationship. This, we may suspect, is more a matter of personality than of scholarship. In the [44] case in question, the diversity of first-century Judaism has been emphasized all the more as we have become aware, not least through the work of E. P. Sanders, that past generations have operated with a simplistic caricature of Judaism, which has then been used as a foil for Christianity.

Awareness of past caricatures does not, of course, constitute of itself an argument for diversity. This point needs to be asserted, perhaps, over against

---

1 Johnson 1994, commenting on Wright 1992a, Part III. At several points in what follows I shall depend, without further note, on the relevant discussion in the latter work.

those who are tempted to reject any global description of first-century Judaism on the grounds that previous global descriptions have been caricatures. Nor does recognition of diversity prevent fresh caricatures being propounded, carrying in their wake further false antitheses between some particular form of 'Judaism' and early Christianity. The historical task must proceed, as all history proceeds, both by detailed examination of specific points and by attempts at drawing larger pictures, and by the incessant dialogue between those two activities. This essay is necessarily concerned with the larger picture; space forbids discussion of the details. (In addition, space prohibits any attempt to justify the inclusion of the passages on which I shall draw as material representing, more or less, what Jesus said or thought. I am as well aware as anyone of the enormous volume of discussion on this topic; what follows is in the nature of a hypothesis, to stand alongside all those other hypotheses by which, in fact, scholars judge the questions of authenticity.)

With these provisos and caveats, we turn to some questions about Jesus within his Jewish context. Or rather, as the preceding paragraphs justify, within just some Jewish contexts. No doubt Professor Morna Hooker, to whom these remarks are dedicated with gratitude and respect, will be able to think of several more that could, and perhaps should, have been included. But these will serve, I trust, as an indication of the perpetual fascination of the topic, a fascination which, in my own case, was nurtured in its early stages by the lectures and writings of Professor Hooker herself.

Jesus and Politics

As soon as we look at the first of these contexts, we discover that complexity is indeed the order of the day. Our brightest spotlight on first-century Jewish politics is provided by Josephus's account of the Jewish War of 66–70. Anyone who has tried to work out the [45] details of who was in league with whom, against whom, for what ends, for how long and with what effect, will bear witness to the extraordinary problems involved. This complexity should remind us of the problem we face when we ask the deceptively simple question: was Jesus, or was he not, involved in the Jewish politics of his day?

This question has been part of the 'Quest for the Historical Jesus' ever since the posthumous publication, in 1778, of the thesis set out by H. S. Reimarus. Jesus, he suggested, was a failed Jewish revolutionary, whose followers invented Christianity as a different sort of movement entirely. This proposal, in some form or other, has been put forth by several subsequent writers, and, though it has frequently received damaging criticism, continues to exercise a powerful attraction for some.[2] Popular as well as scholarly writers have often assumed that for Jesus to be involved in such a messy business as political, or revolutionary, activity would somehow diminish him theologically:

> Was Jesus. . . more deeply involved in a struggle to help the oppressed people of Israel than we have hitherto been told . . . ?
> This, to the devout Christian, will seem blasphemy . . . reducing the Son of God to the Son of Man.[3]

Further, it has often been assumed that, if Jesus was involved in 'political', especially revolutionary, activity, this sets him apart from other styles of action, and indeed of speech. Revolutionaries, it is often assumed, do not go in for such esoteric activities as the writing, or the reading, of 'apocalypses'; they would not be likely to engage in the spinning of proverbs and the teaching of wisdom. They would not willingly give up their lives; thus, if Jesus intended to die in something like the way he did, that too would prove that he was not 'revolutionary', and perhaps not 'political'.

I shall argue presently that these antitheses are mostly false. But we must notice at once, simply at the level of 'politics', that revolution was by no means the only 'political' option open to first-century Jews. Caiaphas and his family were thoroughly 'political'. The Temple, where that family operated, was the centre of political, as well as of religious, life for first-century Jews. The Pharisees, though split between the rigorous Shammaites and the lenient and (at this stage) [46] less powerful Hillelites, formed a popular political pressure-group, whose voice had to be listened to. Those who supported Herod were inescapably involved in politics. Even the Essenes, if indeed it was they who inhabited Qumran, were making a definite political statement simply by living quietly in the desert. Their future plans were decidedly 'political', as one would expect from a group claiming to be the true Israelites.

Thus, anyone who called Herod 'that fox' (Luke 13.32), or who, in Herod's territory, challenged the permissibility of divorce (Mark 10.1–12), would (in today's language) be perceived to be making 'political' statements. Anyone who challenged the Pharisees at the point of the crucial symbols of national identity (sabbaths, food laws) would be acting just as 'politically' as someone

---

2 Brandon 1967; cf. Hengel 1971; 1973; Bammel and Moule 1984. On this whole topic there is a helpful discussion in Borg 1994a, ch. 5, to which the following is in part indebted.
3 Du Maurier 1966, 94.

who, in today's culture, burns a national flag – or as someone who, in the first century, pulled down a Roman eagle from outside the Temple. Anyone who, by baptizing people in the Jordan, or by undertaking an itinerant renewal ministry, seemed to be offering people blessings they would normally receive through the official channels – namely the Temple in Jerusalem – would be acting 'politically'. Anyone who entered Jerusalem on a donkey, surrounded by chanting followers, and who proceeded to enact a symbolic cleansing, let alone a symbolic destruction of the Temple (deciding between those interpretations is not the point at issue here), was very definitely acting 'politically'. Anyone who was executed with the charge of 'King of the Jews' above his head was perceived by someone, including most likely some of his accusers, judges and executioners, to have made 'political' claims. Thus if we are to be serious about the overall complexity of first-century Judaism(s), we either have to say that all the above incidents and sayings are creations (highly political ones, at that) of the later church, or that Jesus was an inescapably 'political' figure – even though, with most scholars, we may deny that he was involved in, or intended to be identified with, a specifically revolutionary tendency or movement. Within the Jewish political context of his day, Jesus was most likely thoroughly 'political', but also thoroughly opposed to violent revolution.

This conclusion, however, cannot be used as a Procrustean bed. Everything has a political dimension, but politics is not everything. How does Jesus fit within other Jewish contexts, and how do they intersect with the political one? [47]

Jesus and 'Apocalyptic'

Modern scholarship has often found 'apocalyptic' decidedly distasteful. (I say 'modern' somewhat carefully; postmodern scholarship has been much more open to the phenomenon.) Indeed, one German scholar pointed out what he called 'the agonised attempts to rescue Jesus from apocalyptic': a whole range of scholars, embarrassed by the lurid style and shocking content of so much 'apocalyptic' writing, did their best to screen Jesus off from it. Mark 13 and its parallels were the obvious casualty (wished on to the Jesus-tradition, according to this interpretation, by early Christians who quickly reverted to apocalyptic speculation); but several other passages were excluded as well, mostly those issuing warnings of imminent judgment. This anti-apocalyptic mood has recently received fresh impetus from the 'Jesus Seminar' in the United States, whose members voted fairly consistently against the authenticity of most 'apocalyptic' passages.[4] In particular, anything to do with the future activity of a 'son of man' figure has been taboo in such circles, whether that figure be thought of as Jesus himself or someone else.

Part of the trouble has been, of course, that 'apocalyptic' has regularly been supposed to mean 'end-of-the-world', with that last phrase taken in a very literal, physical sense. If Jesus had an 'apocalyptic' message, on this reading, he believed that the space-time universe would shortly come to a stop. He was therefore, crudely and obviously, wrong. This unwelcome conclusion formed the backdrop to earlier rejections of an apocalyptic Jesus. More recently, political considerations have played a much stronger role. The members of the Jesus Seminar, or at least their spokespersons, do not give the impression that they would be very perturbed to discover Jesus to have been wrong about something; but they do mind very much his giving apparent legitimation to contemporary 'apocalyptic' theories, especially those in which the imminent end of the world justifies certain forms of right-wing activity. Why worry about nuclear disasters if the world will end next week?

Attempts to locate Jesus within this Jewish context thus divide, between advocates of an 'end-of-the-world' Jesus and supporters of a 'non-apocalyptic', or even a 'non-eschatological', one. (We should [48] note that some who propose the 'apocalyptic' Jesus do so in order to reduce his theological significance; others, in order to emphasize a supposedly 'apocalyptic' Christian message. This parallels the two positions on 'Jesus the revolutionary': for Reimarus, Jesus was 'merely' a revolutionary, but for the ardent liberation theologian this is the key to his continuing significance.) But these two extreme positions are by no means the only ways of construing the 'apocalyptic' material in the gospels. As with politics, we shall do well to consider a more nuanced approach.

Much recent work on apocalyptic has emphasized its rootedness in the struggle of oppressed peoples for justice and liberty. Apocalyptic imagery caricatures military and political oppressors as monsters, from whom the faithful will be rescued by (perhaps) angels of light. There should be no doubt that a good deal of Jewish 'apocalyptic' writing, not least in the first century, comes into roughly this category. One need only read *4 Ezra* (2 Esdras) 11—12, with its vision of the eagle and the lion, to see this quite clearly. But, when this point is fully grasped, it becomes quite clear that those who wrote

---

4 The Seminar's process is explained, and the results set out and explained, in Funk and Hoover 1993. The earlier German work is Koch 1972.

such material were by no means hoping for the actual end of the space-time universe. What they wanted was a great reversal in fortunes, such as would merit the *metaphorical* use of 'end-of-the-world' language.

A much more subtle sliding-scale of meaning then emerges. At one end, 'apocalyptic' is simply a way of saying 'We, the oppressed, are longing for freedom', and of saying it with great poetic power and passion. This could be said at any time, without any particular thought that the act of liberation, when it came, would be unique, or historically climactic. At the other end, the language of 'apocalyptic', though referring to events (as we would say) *within* time and space, could still refer to a great single happening that would liberate Israel once and for all, and so at last bring about the creator's plan to restore justice and peace to the entire cosmos. Jesus could have used 'apocalyptic' in either of these ways – either, that is, illustratively or climactically – without in either case intending to refer to the end of the space-time universe.[5]

Locating Jesus within his 'apocalyptic' Jewish context, therefore, is not as simple as it once appeared. The breakthrough achieved by Weiss and Schweitzer nearly a hundred years ago was, in fact, a case **[49]** of four steps forward and two back. It was a real advance, not (in my view) to be lost, to show that Jesus conceived of his work within the framework of Jewish apocalyptic expectation. But it was a real mistake, not (in my view) to be perpetuated, to suppose that he thought of that expectation as meaning the end of the space-time world. Rather, like other readers of Daniel 7 in the first century (Josephus and *4 Ezra* are obvious examples), he saw that text as referring to the moment when the great drama of Israel's long history would reach its peak. He read it and re-used it, in other words, climactically, not merely illustratively. He was not simply using 'apocalyptic' language to give colour and force to a message that was, in itself, ahistorical (the teaching of a new wisdom, for example, or a new spirituality, or the launching of a particular social or political movement). Rather, he was claiming, as indeed others had done before and would do again, that in his own work the long night of Israel's exile was coming to an end, and the new age was dawning – the new age in which, when Israel's mission was accomplished, the whole world would be put to rights. And, as we suggested earlier, there was no reason why this message should not grow out of, and appeal to people within, a situation of real or supposed political oppression. The hope for

---

5 Marcus Borg (1994b) chronicles his own subtle shift of emphasis from 'climactic' to 'illustrative' (my terms for his distinction) between 1984 and 1994.

Israel's God to act at last within history to liberate his people was the perfect setting for such a message; apocalyptic language was, at that time, a natural medium for it.

The debate today between those who push Jesus into the 'end-of-the-world' model and those who try to extricate him from it has close analogies with earlier debates between the followers of Schweitzer and those who, like C. H. Dodd, tended to make Jesus into some sort of moralist. Indeed, the debate today often uses (somewhat unhelpfully) the Schweitzer–Dodd categories of 'futurist eschatology' and 'realized eschatology', though under the latter title the Jesus Seminar, at least, has smuggled in all kinds of material, including some frankly gnostic ideas, which Dodd would have found quite unacceptable. The older form of the question ('If Jesus expected the end of the world, why would he have taught such wonderful ethics?' or 'Granted that Jesus taught such wonderful ethics, why would he have predicted the imminent end?') has given way to a newer formulation, with the new code-word 'sapiential' set over against 'eschatological'. If Jesus was a sapiential teacher, he cannot have had an eschatological message. If he spoke in teasing aphorisms, he [50] cannot also have spoken of the son of man coming on the clouds. Or so it is widely supposed today.

The viewpoint I have proposed, however, strongly suggests that these are false antitheses. I have argued in this section that, if Jesus believed that his own work was in some way bringing about the climactic moment of Israel's history, so that it could be described appropriately in 'apocalyptic' language (though no doubt in other ways as well), this locates him believably within the actual worldview and belief-system of a good many first-century Jews. I have also suggested that this 'apocalyptic' perspective is not to be set over against the 'political' one, but rather belongs closely with it. As we shall now observe, it also belongs closely with 'wisdom'. At least, it does so once we have grasped what that 'wisdom' is all about.

Jesus and 'Wisdom'

Where, in the first century, shall 'wisdom' be found? What is the Jewish 'wisdom' context within which we might locate Jesus? How might 'wisdom' teaching in the first century relate to other types or styles of teaching or message?

'Wisdom', as a context for understanding Jesus, is perhaps more fashionable today than ever before, not least (but not only) among the members of the Jesus Seminar. Jesus' pithy aphorisms, telling sayings and subversive stories have all been seen as evidence that this was his basic mode of teaching and discourse. But, even within this, the ways divide. According to a strong current of contemporary opinion, Jesus' teaching was only marginally Jewish; the real background and context within which he makes sense is that of the aphoristic, Cynic-style wisdom that he might conceivably have met in the towns and cities of Galilee.[6] Many, however, have backed off from this conclusion, and have argued for a far more Jewish context, while still placing their major emphasis on Jesus as a 'sage', or teacher of subversive wisdom.[7] [51]

In fact, once we place Jesus' sayings into the context of even those books of Jewish wisdom that have come down to us, notably Ben-Sirach and the Wisdom of Solomon, the hypothesis of a non-Jewish wisdom source for his teaching looks simply unnecessary. In a good many sayings whose authenticity it is presently quite fashionable to assert, the most obvious roots for the tone and content of the material are in these Jewish works, not in the more distant, and in any case historically difficult, Cynic semi-parallels. But how do such sayings – the camel and the needle's eye, the old wine and the new bottles, and the like – relate to the other categories we are considering?

It is again becoming increasingly common, in my view rightly, to say that such sayings belong with a subversive political stance, though not an overtly revolutionary one. Some wisdom sayings in the tradition merely express *conventional* wisdom, the sort of thing that people tell one another to reinforce stereotypes and maintain a status quo. Other sayings are designed to break open such ways of thinking and create the possibilities of new ones, and such were many of Jesus' sayings. They are not the language of the zealous hothead, for whom nothing short of a direct call to arms would do. They are the language of the subversive sage, convinced that there is a different way of being human, and (more especially, in this context) a different way of being *Israel*, and that, if people refuse to be led blindly along by blind guides, they might open their eyes and see, and embrace, this different way. Jesus' wisdom-teaching, precisely within its Jewish context, keeps open the possibility of his political significance.

But, despite current fashion, wisdom also belongs closely with apocalyptic.

---

6 Among those arguing this case most strongly are Mack 1988; 1993; Downing 1988; 1992. Crossan 1991 is more nuanced and subtle; his portrait of Jesus, though similar to Mack's in many ways, does not depend on the identification of Jesus as a Cynic.

7 E.g. Borg in several works, rejecting the 'Cynic' interpretation and aligning Jesus' wisdom-teaching with the Jewish prophetic strand; Witherington 1994, arguing (as I shall presently) for a connection between 'wisdom' and various Jewish strands of thought, including eschatology.

Not only is it the case that the apocalyptist, just as the teacher of wisdom, is attempting to open people's eyes to see another dimension of reality which had previously been opaque, or simply ignored. Not only is it the case that apocalyptic, like subversive wisdom, functions as a way of asserting a different social, cultural or political possibility. More importantly, in a good deal of Jewish wisdom-teaching such as we may suppose to have provided the broad background of Jesus' teaching, wisdom and apocalyptic go hand in hand. Thus, for instance, the Wisdom of Solomon sets its praise of Wisdom within the story of Israel from creation to exodus, with the strong implication for its own day: those who hold to the divine wisdom will be rescued, like Israel from Egypt, when God finally [52] acts. Even Ben-Sirach implies the same, when in chapter 24 he weaves into his wisdom-poem his belief that Israel, and the Temple, is the place where Wisdom has decided to dwell. Daniel, at the very moment when declaring ('apocalyptically') that the dead shall rise and be judged, goes on to designate the righteous, who 'shall shine like the brightness of the sun', precisely as the *wise* (12.3). The Qumran Community Rule, which is foundational for (one version at least of) the community's apocalyptic eschatology, sets out in that context the typically 'wisdom' motif of the Two Ways, wisdom and folly (1QS 3—4). Possessing and teaching wisdom, within all the varied traditions represented in this quick survey, does not mean embracing or advocating a private, esoteric or ahistorical knowledge, but rather living by the true interpretation of Israel's law, and, most important, being among the people who will be vindicated when God acts within history, as he surely will.

We find exactly this emphasis in the teaching of Jesus. Witherington has argued that Jesus' subversive wisdom sayings were 'very likely grounded in Jesus' conviction that God's eschatological reign was breaking into the midst of Israel through his ministry'.[8] The antithesis between wisdom and apocalyptic is unwarranted, whether we look at the Jewish context, at Jesus himself or (though space forbids this here) the early church.

An obvious example is the parable of the wise and foolish maidens in Matthew 25.1–13. Here we find exactly that contrast of wisdom and folly which goes back to such early forms of the wisdom tradition as the book of Proverbs itself. But the context is of course that of apocalyptic eschatology. The critical insight is this: Jesus is urging his hearers to grasp the true wisdom, since only those who do so will be ready for the great day that is shortly to arrive. This true wisdom is deeply subversive, and yet deeply

---

8   1994, 172.

affirming of Israel's highest and best traditions. Whatever arguments may be mounted against the authenticity of this or that saying or parable, there runs through every strand of material the same collocation of wisdom and apocalyptic which, I suggest, characterized the teaching of Jesus at point after point. 'Jesus the sage' is also Jesus the prophet. 'Sapiential' teaching is to be understood in the setting of Jesus' 'apocalyptic' message. God is bringing in the kingdom for which Israel longed; but only those who discover the true wisdom will inherit it. [53]

Jesus and Martyrdom

But how will the kingdom come? And what is this true, subversive wisdom? What is the Jewish context that best explains how Jesus saw the immediate future? What was his own role to be? Did he foresee his own death, and if so what interpretation did he give to it? At each of these questions, opinions once again sharply diverge. We cannot here do more than take one particular bull by the horns. I propose that the correct context, or at any rate a correct context, for understanding Jesus' attitude to his own death is found in the Jewish martyr-literature of the time.[9] The subversive wisdom that Jesus' followers would have to grasp, if they were to inherit the kingdom of God, was the secret, far more subversive than anything the Cynics ever dreamed of, that new life, God's life, springs out of sacrificial death. And, just as Jesus exemplified and embodied the true wisdom in so many other ways, he believed he would embody it also in this – and at the same time fulfil the dreams of the earlier martyrs. The kingdom would come not least by means of his own death, through which Israel would at last be redeemed.

This claim is of course itself subversive within the present state of the discipline. Scholars divide over the question of Jesus' attitude to his own death. Those who think of Jesus as a Cynic sage can make nothing of the idea, and hold (along with others, such as Vermes) that Jesus did not intend to die, and that, in terms of his own intention, the event was strictly speaking an accident. (Crossan goes so far as to deny the historical nature of the four canonical Passion accounts altogether, but so far the energy and enterprise with which he has promoted this extreme view have not succeeded in persuading many others.[10]) Even those who see Jesus' mission in far more Jewish terms have sometimes had difficulty imagining him going deliberately to his death: for

9   This is suggested quite strongly by Bockmuehl 1994, ch. 4.
10   Crossan 1988; 1991; 1995.

E. P. Sanders, such an attitude would just make him 'weird', and 'strange in any century'.[11] A more moderate position would suggest that, though Jesus may well have had a pretty shrewd idea where his mission would lead him eventually, death was a strong possibility with which he constantly reckoned, rather than, in itself, a vocation he felt bound to [54] pursue.[12] Those who, despite such challenges, have continued to believe that Jesus envisaged his own death, and interpreted it in advance, have often done so in ways which make it look as though Jesus held some complicated early version of later Christian atonement-theology, and realized that he had to engineer his own death in order to set the celestial mechanics of the scheme into operation.

I suggest that the Jewish contexts we have already begun to explore offer a way through this central historical, and also theological, dilemma. Jesus' forebears in subversive Jewish politics, in apocalyptic eschatology and in subversive wisdom included the heroes of the Maccabaean period, whose memory was kept green by the annual retelling of their story at Hanukkah, and by contemporary rewritings of it such as 4 Maccabees. In these stories we find tales of people who – at least within the story, which is after all where Jesus and his contemporaries would have met them – faced death in the belief that God's will, not theirs, should be done,[13] and that their loyalty to God and his cause overrode their own natural desire for survival. Further, we find the most interesting idea that somehow, when such deaths did occur, those who suffered them were somehow *drawing the wrath of God on themselves*, suffering in the place of Israel.[14] ('Wrath' here, of course, is a very concrete, historical thing, as for instance in 2 Kings 3.27, where 'great wrath came upon Israel' means, basically, 'Israel was heavily defeated in battle'.) Nor does this make the martyrs, or those who wrote their stories, 'weird' within their own contexts; there is a persistent suggestion, both in ancient Jewish texts and in continuing post-Christian Jewish reflection, that obedient suffering and death might actually atone for the sins of the people.[15] There is, I hasten to add, no evidence to suggest that a large number of Jews in Jesus' day held this tradition in high esteem, or actively attempted to put it into operation. But there is good reason to draw on it as the vital clue to understand why Jesus went up

---

11 Sanders 1985, 333. The whole discussion (331–4) is a very interesting survey of possibilities on this question.

12 See the sensitive and careful discussion in Moule 1977, 108f.

13 E.g. 1 Macc. 3.58–60, with its interesting parallel to e.g. Mt. 26.39, 42.

14 2 Macc. 7.32–38; 4 Macc. 6.27–29; 17.20–22; cf. Sir. 45.23; 48.10.

15 Notably, of course, Gen. 22 and Isa. 53, and subsequent Jewish traditions that make fresh use of those passages. Cf. Bockmuehl 1994, 90, with refs. to other discussions.

to Jerusalem and, as it seems, deliberately provoked a confrontation with the authorities. Just as Judas Maccabaeus led his forces against the pagans, and against those compromised Jews who had sided with them, Jesus went up to Jerusalem to challenge its [55] rulers in prophetic word and action with his alternative vision of Israel, his apocalyptic warnings of judgment, his deeply subversive wisdom. Granted his vision and vocation, he could do no other. But he knew where it would end, and embraced that end as itself integral to, and indeed climactic within, the vision itself.

Albert Schweitzer is still, after nearly a century, as close to the truth as anyone at this point. Jesus, he argued, believed in the 'messianic woes', that is, in the Jewish idea that the great divine action would come about through, and immediately after, a period of intense suffering. Jesus went to his death to take this great suffering on to himself, so as to carve a way through on behalf of his people. (Where Schweitzer went wrong, I think, was in his suggestion that this intention was a second best, a plan which Jesus embraced after the failure of the early Galilean mission. If I am right, Jesus' vision of the kingdom always included this strange and dark vocation.) Messianic woes combine easily enough with Maccabaean-style martyrdom to give a plausible setting for Jesus' self-understanding.

Taken together, these beliefs point beyond themselves to another highly Jewish idea, which sets these two firmly in their unique eschatological context. In line with several other scholars, I have argued elsewhere that those first-century Jews who were eager for their God to act on their behalf interpreted that forthcoming action as the real end of exile.[16] Babylon had been followed by a succession of other pagan empires. Until the last and greatest of these, namely Rome, was finally defeated, and Israel vindicated, the great prophecies of return from exile had not been fulfilled. As Isaiah 52 makes crystal clear, Israel's deliverance from Babylon is an intrinsic part of the meaning of 'kingdom of God'. Jesus, I suggest, did not envisage the coming of that kingdom as the end of the space-time universe. Nor did he see it as an instant, one-off, transformation of the entire cosmos into its God-ordained eventual state of peace, justice and new life. He saw it as *the end of Israel's exile* and consequently the launching (not in itself the completion) of the final stage of the divine plan for the world. I suggest that Jesus envisaged his own death as the culminating and climactic moment in Israel's exile, through which the great redemption would occur.

Martyrdom; messianic woes; end of exile. These ideas do not, of course,

---

16   Wright 1992a, 268–72.

exhaust the remarkable store of images and ideas that seem [56] to have gathered around the crucifixion of Jesus from the earliest days of Christianity. I have not even mentioned the Last Supper, with all its rich associations of history, prophetic symbol and kingdom-expectation. I have not attempted to draw out the vexed notion of sacrifice. But I have attempted to show that, within the complex Jewish contexts which surrounded him, Jesus had available to him various interlocking beliefs that could have informed his own sense of vocation, and pointed him to his own execution at the hand of pagan rulers as the necessary mode and means of Israel's redemption.

This, then, was the ultimately subversive wisdom. The new life of the kingdom would come through, by means of, on the other side of, suffering and death. Hence the cryptic call to take up the cross, itself as much a part of the call to true wisdom as anything else in the gospels. All other wisdom, be it never so politically or socially subversive, ends up with a rearrangement of the present order of things. Only this wisdom, held as it is within a truly apocalyptic frame of reference, challenges all the powers and systems of the world at their root. Politics, apocalyptic, wisdom and martyrdom meet together as Jesus goes to Jerusalem. It is not only first-century categories that are drawn together, and fused into a new whole, in the crucifixion.

Conclusion

I have chosen four categories from current debate as the starting-point for this exploration of Jesus within his Jewish contexts. But there are other themes crying out for attention, which we can only indicate by way of conclusion. The most obvious is the Temple. Jesus' action in the Temple was his most overtly political act; his prediction of its destruction was the negative focal point of his apocalyptic warnings; his claims to speak for, and perhaps to embody, true wisdom challenged Ben-Sirach's belief that Wisdom resided in the Temple; and it was, most likely, his Temple-action that led to his death. One of the solid advances in recent Jesus-scholarship (Vermes is an exception here) is the increasing focus on the Temple as the key to a good deal of Jesus' mission and self-understanding.[17] [57]

But this points us to the most important missing theme: Christology – to which, indeed, the Temple may well provide one of the vital (and often ignored) clues. If my placing of Jesus in his Jewish contexts is anywhere near the mark, the two categories that present themselves as most obviously

17   Cf. e.g. Chilton 1992.

relevant are Prophet and Messiah. Jesus' passion for putting wrongs to right, the challenge of his subversive wisdom, his apocalyptic denunciation of the present Jerusalem, and his Jeremiah-like readiness to suffer the woes that were befalling his people – all these, and much more besides, mark him out as a prophetic figure, and suggest strongly that he saw himself in this way. (After the section 'Jesus and "Wisdom"' above, it should be clear, against much current writing, that 'prophetic' cannot be played off against 'sapiential'.) But Jesus' sense that God would act through his own work; his drawing of Israel's destiny on to himself; his leadership of the little group that, half-understanding, attempted to grasp his subversive wisdom; his quasi-royal action in the Temple: these, and much more, mark him out as a would-be Messiah. Of course, there were prophets and Messiahs in plenty in the first century. One aspect of Jesus' Jewish contexts, often ignored, is the fact that, largely through Josephus, we know of at least a dozen such in the period from Herod to Bar-Kochba. What makes Jesus different?

The answer cannot simply be the slant of his politics, the target of his apocalyptic, the doubly subversive nature of his wisdom, or the breathtaking gamble of his martyrdom. These are all, I think, unique combinations and reappropriations of elements of Jewish thought, lore and tradition. No: by themselves, these would simply make Jesus a quite remarkable would-be prophet, a truly outstanding would-be Messiah. But ultimately he would join Simon, Athronges, and all the others, including Bar-Kochba himself, as a noble failure.

What makes Jesus different is the resurrection.

6

Five Gospels but No Gospel:
Jesus and the Seminar

My own work on Jesus in his historical context, particularly in the late 1980s and early 1990s, coincided with the time when the 'Jesus Seminar' was in full cry. I was myself a 'corresponding Fellow' of this movement when it was founded in the mid-1980s, since I was still then teaching in Montreal and realized that this was a North American enterprise to which I, as myself a Jesus-researcher, might well need to belong. In retrospect, as the present article makes clear, it is probably just as well that at that point I returned to Oxford and cut many American links, including this one.

I have written about the Jesus Seminar elsewhere, notably in chapter 2 of *Jesus and the Victory of God* (Wright 1996b). But when I was asked to write the present article, a year before my book was complete, I decided to set out my critique, in the form of a book review of the Seminar's flagship volume, more fully than was going to be possible in my own forthcoming volume.

Among the other ironies which a rereading of this piece highlights is that certain theologians have used the work of the Seminar as an excuse for pouring scorn, or at least severe health-warnings, on any attempt to 'do history' in relation to Jesus himself. There you are, they say: try to study the history of Jesus and look what you will end up with! But, as the present article makes clear, what the Seminar was doing was not real 'history' at all. Criticizing 'history' because of the Seminar is like warning against air-travel because of Icarus.

[83] Looking for Jesus

People have been looking for Jesus for a long time, but never quite like this. The 'Quest of the Historical Jesus' has been proceeding, in fits and starts, for two hundred years. Its story has often been told;[1] in recent years there has

---

1 Wright 1992b.

been a flurry, not to say a flood, of writing about Jesus, and debates of all sorts, about every aspect of the evidence, and every conceivable reconstruction of Jesus' life, teaching, work and death, have been running to and fro.[2]

Most of [84] this writing has been produced by individual scholars, working independently. But in the last few years a new corporate venture has emerged, attempting by a process of discussion and voting to arrive at an answer to the question, 'What did Jesus really say?' This group has called itself 'The Jesus Seminar', and among its many recent publications one stands out as a kind of flagship: *The Five Gospels*, published late in 1993 by Macmillan (though emanating from the Seminar's own publishing house, Polebridge Press). This is the subject of the present chapter.

No doubt there are at least as many opinions about 'The Jesus Seminar' as the Seminar itself holds about Jesus. Passions, in fact, already run high on the subject, and may run higher yet before the storm abates. Some of the Seminar's members treat any questioning of its work like a slap in the face – though not with the turning of the other cheek, as one might have thought considering that that saying received the rare accolade of a red vote (meaning authentic; see below).[3] In other quarters, one only has to mention the Seminar to provoke a wry smile, or even guffaws of laughter. At a packed and high-profile meeting of the Society of Biblical Literature's 'Pauline Theology' seminar in 1991, the person in the chair – one of the most senior and respected of North American biblical scholars – rejected a call for a vote on the subject that had been under discussion by simply saying, 'This ain't the Jesus Seminar.' This was greeted with laughter and applause in about equal measure.

So what is the Jesus Seminar up to, and what should we think about it? It has now completed many years of detailed and painstaking work, and, though it may well all deserve discussing, there is no [85] space here to go into its many products, with all their presuppositions, methods, decisions and results.[4] I have, in any case, written about all that elsewhere.[5] I want in this essay to concentrate on *The Five Gospels*, the book towards which all else was preliminary.

---

2 We may note, for instance, Farmer 1956; Caird 1965; Vermes 1973; 1983; 1993; Meyer 1979; 1992a; 1992b; Harvey 1982; Borg 1984; 1987b; Sanders, 1985; 1993; Theissen 1986; Horsley 1987; Freyne 1988; Charlesworth 1988; Witherington 1990; Meier 1991; [84] 1994; Crossan 1991; Chilton 1992; Chilton and Evans 1997; Evans 1995.

3 Mt. 5.39; cf. Funk and Hoover 1993, 143–5.

4 See e.g. Funk, Scott and Butts 1988; Miller 1992; and the Seminar's journal *Forum: Foundations and Facets*.

5 Wright 1996b, 28–82.

The 'Five Gospels' in question are (in case there was any doubt) Mark, Matthew, Luke, John and *Thomas*. The inclusion of the last of these will still raise one or two eyebrows, though it is by now well known that the Seminar takes kindly to *Thomas*, not least because of its apparent similarity with (some reconstructions of) the hypothetical source 'Q' – and, as we shall see, the portrait of Jesus that it appears to support. More striking is the technique with which the Seminar's results are displayed. The old 'red-letter testaments' picked out all the words of Jesus in red; this one accords that status to the favoured few among the sayings, those which the Seminar voted as highly likely to emanate from Jesus himself. The rest of Jesus' sayings are set in pink, grey and black, on a rough sliding-scale of the probability and improbability of their coming from Jesus; I shall discuss the precise nuances of the colours presently. Each saying, story or group of sayings/stories is then commented on, and the reasons for the voting are explained, sometimes briefly, sometimes up to a few pages. The text is broken up from time to time by 'cameo essays' on key topics (the kingdom of God, the son of man, and so forth). The text is attractively laid out, with diagrams and occasional pictures. Everything is presented about as clearly as it could be; nobody, from high-school student upwards, could fail to see what was being said. All in all, it is a substantial product, and whatever one thinks of the actual results, it clearly represents a great deal of hard labour.

A New Translation

Six features of the book call for general comment right from the start. First, it uses what the Seminar has called 'The Scholars Version' (*sic*) (SV) – its own translation of the four canonical gospels and [86] *Thomas*. This is an attempt to represent, in colloquial American English, the original flavour of the Greek. Now it is our turn to be slapped in the face:

> Although Jesus was indignant, he stretched out his hand, touched him, and says to him, 'Okay – you're clean!'[6]

> The king came in to see the guests for himself and noticed this man not properly attired. And he says to him, 'Look, pal, how'd you get in here without dressing for the occasion?'[7]

---

6   Mk. 1.41; Funk and Hoover 1993, 43. There is a hint here that the transaction between Jesus and the leper was not a healing, but simply Jesus' declaration that he should no longer be treated as an outcast.
7   Mt. 22.12; Funk and Hoover 1993, 234.

When Jesus noticed their trust, he said, 'Mister, your sins have been forgiven you.'[8]

I have no objection to colloquial translations – though one might have thought this would be the People's Version, not the Scholars'. What I do find somewhat objectionable is the dismissive tone of the introduction, which explains that other versions are 'faintly Victorian' and set a context of 'polite religious discourse suitable for a Puritan parlor'.[9] The New Revised Standard Version (NRSV) comes in for particular criticism; one suspects that its main fault in the eyes of the SV translators is that it is a lineal descendant, on one side of the family at any rate, of the old King James Version, which, as we shall see, represents all that the Seminar abominates by way of American religion. The authors make great play of the fact that, unlike most Bible translations, this one both includes the non-canonical *Thomas* and is not authorized by any ecclesiastical or religious bodies. Instead, pompously, 'The Scholars Version is authorized by scholars'.[10]

Present and Absent Friends

But, second, which scholars? Seventy-four names are listed in the back of the book, and there have been other members, quite influential in earlier stages of the debate, who are not explicitly mentioned here.[11] Some of them are household names in the world of New [87] Testament studies: Robert Funk himself, the driving force behind the entire enterprise, whose earlier work on the Greek grammar of the New Testament is universally recognized as authoritative; Dominic Crossan, whose combination of enormous erudition, subtlety of thought and felicitous writing style have rightly ensured him widespread respect; James Robinson, whose work on the Nag Hammadi texts has placed the entire discipline in his debt; Marcus Borg, Bruce Chilton and Walter Wink, all of whom have made distinguished and distinctive contributions to the study of Jesus in his context (and to much else besides); Ron Cameron, whose forthright and provocative writings on *Thomas* and related topics are rightly famous; John Kloppenborg, one of the leading specialists

---

8   Lk. 5.20; Funk and Hoover 1993, 283.
9   Funk and Hoover 1993, xiii–xviii, here at xiv.
10 Funk and Hoover 1993, xviii.
11 For example, Burton Mack, author of *A Myth of Innocence: Mark and Christian origins* (1988) and other works that have had a profound impact on the work of the Jesus Seminar. Over 200 members are reported [87] to have belonged at one stage or another; Funk and Hoover 1993, 34.

on the hypothetical source 'Q'. In any list of contemporary North American biblical scholars, all these would find a place of honour.

But one could compile a very long list of North American New Testament scholars, including several who have written importantly about Jesus, who are not among those present, and whose work has had no visible impact on the Seminar at all. The most obvious is Ed Sanders, whose work, massive in its learning, and almost unique in its influence over the present state of scholarship worldwide, seems to have been ignored by the Seminar – except for one tiny particular, and that precisely where Sanders is at his weakest.[12] Another figure whose work has been totally ignored is Ben F. Meyer, who has more understanding of how ancient texts work in his little finger than many of the Jesus Seminar seem to have in their entire word-processors, and whose writing on Jesus is utterly rigorous, utterly scholarly and utterly different in its results from anything in the volume we are considering.[13] So, too, one looks in vain for members of the teaching faculties of many of the leading North American colleges and universities. There is nobody currently teaching at [88] Harvard, Yale, Princeton, Duke, McGill or Stanford. Toronto is well represented; so is Claremont (not least by its graduates); several Fellows of the Seminar have doctorates from Harvard. But where is the rest of the guild – those who, for instance, flock to the 'Historical Jesus' sessions of the Annual Meeting of the Society of Biblical Literature? They are conspicuous by their absence.

No doubt some within the Seminar would suggest that this comment is academic snobbery, but they cannot have it both ways. The Jesus Seminar is in something of a cleft stick at this point. On the one hand, the members are determined to present to the general public the findings that 'scholars' have come up with. Away with secrecy, and hole-in-a-corner scholarship, they say: it is time for scholars to come out of their closets, to boldly say what no-one has said before. They must, therefore, present themselves as the pundits, the ones in the know, the ones the public can trust as the reputable, even the authorized, spokespersons for the serious tradition of biblical scholarship.[14]

---

12 Cf. Sanders 1985, remarkably absent from the bibliography of *The Five Gospels*; cf. too Sanders 1993. Sanders and Davies 1989 is listed in the bibliography of *The Five Gospels* as 'an excellent guide', though anyone taking it seriously would be forced to reject a good deal of the Jesus Seminar's methods and results. See below.

13 Cf. esp. Meyer 1979; 1992a; 1992b.

14 For example, see Funk and Hoover 1993, 34–5, whose triumphalism is as breathtaking as it is unwarranted: 'Critical scholars practice their craft by submitting their work to the judgment of peers. Untested work is not highly regarded. The scholarship represented by the Fellows of the Jesus Seminar is the kind that has come to prevail in all the great universities of the world.' Only in the most general terms is the last sentence true; the present essay is a response to the invitation of the previous sentences.

But, on the other hand, they lash out at the 'elitism' of their critics within the broader academic world[15] – while saying on the next page that attacks on members of the Seminar have tended to come from 'those who lack academic credentials'. Sauce for the goose and sauce for the gander: either academic credentials matter, in which case the Seminar should listen to those who possess them in abundance and are deeply critical of their work, or they don't matter, in which case the Seminar should stop priding itself on its own, over against the common herd. The attitude to critics expressed in this book reminds me of John 7.49: in the Scholars Version, it reads: 'As for this rabble, they are ignorant of the Law! Damn them!' It becomes apparent that the work we have here does [89] not represent 'scholars', as simply as that; it represents some scholars, and those mostly (with some interesting exceptions) from a very narrow band among serious contemporary readers of the gospels worldwide.[16]

These comments about the make-up of the Seminar highlight a point that must be clearly made before we go one step further. Though this book claims, on every page, to speak for all the Fellows of the Seminar, it becomes increasingly apparent that it comes from the Seminar's chair, Robert W. Funk (R. W. Hoover is named as co-author, though there is no indication of which author drafted which parts). Dissentient voices are, of course, recorded in the reporting of voting patterns. But it would be a mistake to saddle all, perhaps even most, of the Fellows with the point of view, and the arguments, that we find on page after page. Only occasionally is this really acknowledged. In the bibliography, for instance, one of Marcus Borg's books is listed, with the comment 'It goes almost without saying that he didn't vote with the majority on every issue'.[17] One suspects that that is something of an understatement. In the present essay, therefore, I am discussing the work of Funk and Hoover, not necessarily that of other Fellows; we may note, though, that the whole layout and intent of the book predisposes the reader – not least the non-academic reader, who is clearly in view – to assume that the verdicts reached are those of 'scholars' in a much broader sense.

---

15 For examples, see Funk and Hoover 1993, 1: the present book is 'a dramatic exit from windowless studies'; 34: 'we have been intimidated by promotion and tenure committees . . . It is time for us to quit the library and speak up'; the Seminar's methods have been attacked by 'many elitist academic critics who deplored [its] public face'.

16 There is, for instance, a good deal of important work on Jesus emanating from Latin America; but one would not guess it from reading the Seminar's publications.

17 Funk and Hoover 1993, 540, referring to Borg 1987a.

A Driving Agenda

There is, third, a further agenda involved at this point, which is, one may suspect, the major force that motivates the project in general and several (though by no means all) of its members. They are fundamentally anti-fundamentalist. Listen to these wonderfully objective, value-free, scholarly comments, taken from the book's introduction:

> Once the discrepancy between the Jesus of history and the Christ of faith emerged from under the smothering cloud of the historic creeds, it was only a matter of time before scholars sought to disengage [the two] . . . It is ironic that Roman Catholic scholars are emerging from the dark ages of [90] theological tyranny just as many Protestant scholars are reentering it as a consequence of the dictatorial tactics of the Southern Baptist Convention and other fundamentalisms.[18]

> With the council of Nicea in 325, the orthodox party solidified its hold on the Christian tradition and other wings of the Christian movment [sic] were choked off.[19]

There are only two positions allowed, it seems. One must either be some kind of closed-minded fundamentalist, adhering to some approximation of the historic creeds of the Christian church; one notes that this lumps together Athanasius, Aquinas, Barth, Pannenberg and Moltmann along with the TV evangelists who are among the real targets of the polemic. Or one must be non-judgmentally open to the free-for-all hurly-burly of Gnosis, Cynicism, esoteric wisdom, folklore and so on represented by various groups in the first three centuries – and to the baby-and-bathwater methodological scepticism adopted by the Seminar.[20] The strange thing is that there are several members of the Seminar itself who represent neither point of view; has the author of this introduction forgotten who some of his colleagues are? Unfortunately, as we shall see, this either/or has so dominated the landscape that a great many decisions of the Seminar simply reflect a shallow polarization which has precious little to do with the first century and, one suspects, a great deal

---

18   Funk and Hoover 1993, 7–8.

19   Funk and Hoover 1993, 35.

20   It is interesting to compare the Seminar's work with the comment on the gospels made by a leading secular historian, J. M. Roberts: '[the gospels] need not be rejected; much more inadequate evidence about far more intractable subjects has often to be employed' (1992, 210).

to do with the twentieth, not least in North America. One suspects that several members of the Seminar do not actually *know* very many ordinary, non-fundamentalist, orthodox Christians. Would it be going too far to venture the supposition that more than one leading member of the Jesus Seminar is doing his (or her) best to exorcize the memory of a strict fundamentalist background? Unfortunately, the attempt to escape from one's own past is not a good basis for the attempt to reconstruct someone else's.

This question has another aspect to it that must be noted carefully. It is now endemic in North American biblical studies that very few practitioners have studied philosophy or theology at any depth. [91] Such study, indeed, is sometimes regarded with suspicion, as though it might prejudice the pure, objective, neutral reading of the text. Leave aside for the moment the impossibility of such objectivity (see below). The real problem is that if one is to discuss what are essentially theological and philosophical issues, in terms both of the method required for serious study of Jesus and of the content and implications of Jesus' proclamation, one really requires more sophistication than the Seminar, in this book at least, can offer. This will become apparent as we proceed.

Which Gospels?

The fourth introductory point concerns the treatment of the different 'gospels'. As I said, it is now commonplace to treat the book known as the *Gospel of Thomas* alongside the canonical gospels. If we are studying the entire gospel tradition, this is clearly mandatory. The Seminar is to be congratulated for pushing this fact into the public eye (and for the marvellous work of producing texts of a large number of relevant documents that had not been easily available hitherto). But, when all is said and done, huge questions remain about the relevance of *Thomas* for the study of Jesus. By no means all students of it agree with the majority of the Seminar in placing it early and independent of the canonical gospels.[21] If members of the public are interested in knowing what 'scholars' think, they ought to be told fair and square that diagrams in which a hypothetical first edition of *Thomas* is placed in the 50s of the first century are thoroughly tendentious, and belong out on a limb of current scholarship.[22]

---

21 In favour: Patterson 1993; noted in the bibliography as being influential in the Seminar. Against: Tuckett 1986; 1988.

22 See Funk and Hoover 1993, 18, 128.

In particular, we should not accept without question the assumption that *Thomas*, and for that matter fragments like the Egerton papyrus, are (or belong to) gospels. It all depends on what you mean. *Thomas* does not call itself a 'gospel'. Nor, for that matter, do Matthew, Luke and John; and the opening note in Mark ('The beginning of the gospel of Jesus Christ') may well refer, not to the book which then follows, but to the events which it purports to record. The [92] meaning of the word 'gospel' in the first two centuries of the Christian era is, in fact, quite controversial;[23] sufficient to note here that to call *Thomas*, and for that matter Q, 'gospels' is to make quite a far-reaching decision. It is to say that these works are to be regarded as *proclamations* about Jesus, of the same sort as the four better-known 'gospels', despite the fact that they do not narrate the story of Jesus, do not (for the most part) proclaim him as Messiah, do not tell of his death and resurrection – do not, in fact, do the very things which seem, from the Pauline evidence, to be what the earliest Christians regarded as 'gospel'. Bringing Paul into the picture at this point is of course itself controversial, but not nearly so much as making *Thomas* contemporary with him.[24]

I suggest that nothing would be lost, and a good deal of clarity regained, if, instead of referring to *Thomas*, and indeed Q, as 'gospels', and thereby supposing that they record the theology of an entire group within very early Christianity, we see them as what they are (supposing for the moment that Q ever existed): collections of sayings. Calling them 'gospels' obscures the obvious difference of genre between them and the four ordinarily so called. In an attempt to gain a hearing for different supposed presentations of Jesus, the [93] current fashion distorts precisely that sort of literary analysis that 'scholars' ought to favour.

In fact, although *The Five Gospels* prints all of John as well as the others, it is clear that John is regarded a priori as having little or nothing to do with Jesus himself. This, indeed, is one of the Seminar's vaunted 'seven pillars of

---

23 For example, see Koester 1990; on which see Wright 1992a, 371–443; and, for some comments on Paul's meaning of the term, Wright 1994.

24 The suggestion (Funk and Hoover 1993, 500–1) that the Gnosticism in *Thomas* is very like what we find in John and Paul would be laughable if it did not reveal culpable ignorance of the entire drift of Pauline studies in the last forty years. The brief sketch of how *Thomas* got its name (p. 20) reveals an astonishing naivety, speaking of the apostle being 'revered in the Syrian church as an apostle', and giving as evidence for this Mt. 10.3; Mk. 3.18; Lk. 6.15; Ac. 1.13; Jn. 11.16; 20.24; 21.2. The attribution to Thomas, we are told, 'tells us nothing about the author', but 'may indicate where this gospel was written'. In which of the above texts do we find evidence for Thomas in Syria? If the writers applied the same scepticism to claims about *Thomas* as they do, on the same page, to claims about the other four gospels (the evidence of Papias, for instance), it would quickly become clear how little evidence there is for an early date, or a Syrian provenance, for the *Thomas* collection.

scholarly wisdom'.[25] But here we see, quite sharply, what we shall observe in more detail presently: the Seminar's method has not been to examine each saying all by itself and decide about it, but to start with a fairly clear picture of Jesus and early Christianity, and simply run through the material imposing this picture on the texts.

All Cats Are Grey in the Dark

A note, next, on the colour-coding of the sayings. This is clearly meant to convey a definite and precise meaning. The 'ordinary reader', browsing through *The Five Gospels*, picks up quite quickly that red or pink is a quite rare accolade, that black is common, and that grey, close enough (it seems) to black, also dominates at several points. The book's cover reflects something of this balance, with a small red box on a large black background, and in the small red box the words 'WHAT DID JESUS REALLY SAY?' It seems fairly clear that red denotes what Jesus said, black what he did not, and that pink and grey are softer variants on these two.

Not so simple, however. The voting system was quite complex.[26] There are two cumbersome sets of 'meanings' for the four colours, and an intricate system of numberings for the votes, which were then averaged out. This means that in any given case, especially in relation to pink and grey, the colour on the page does not represent what 'scholars', even the small selection of scholarly opinion represented in the Seminar, actually think. A pink vote almost certainly means that, on the one hand, a sizeable minority believed Jesus actually said these words, while a substantial minority were convinced, or nearly convinced, that he did not. Most, in fact, did not vote pink; yet that is what appears on the page. (I am reminded of the notorious funda-[94]-mentalist attempts to harmonize how many times the rooster crowed when Peter denied Jesus. One of the only ways of doing it is to say that the rooster crowed, not three, but nine times. Thus a supposed doctrine of scriptural inerrancy is 'preserved' – at the enormous cost of saying that what actually happened *is what none of the texts record*.) Thus, the Jesus Seminar could print a text in pink or grey, *even though the great majority of the Seminar voted red or black*. The colours, especially the two middle ones, cannot be taken as more than

---

25 Funk and Hoover 1993, 3. The sayings of Jesus in John are voted almost uniformly black, with 4.43 a solitary pink ('a prophet gets no respect on his own turf'), 12.24–25 and 13.20 a lonely pair of greys ('unless the kernel of wheat falls to the earth and dies . . .' and 'if they welcome the person I send, they welcome me . . .').

26 Described in Funk and Hoover 1993, 34–7.

an averaging out of widely divergent opinion. It is perfectly possible that the colour on the page, if grey or pink, is one for which nobody voted at all.

In particular, the grey sayings conceal a very interesting phenomenon. Spies on the Seminar report that in some cases the grey verdict could be seen as a victory – for those who, against the grain of the Seminar, think Jesus might well have said the words concerned. Take Luke 19.42–44 for an example. This stern warning about the coming destruction of Jerusalem fits with an 'apocalyptic' strand of teaching that, in almost all other cases, the Fellows of the Seminar voted black by a substantial margin. But on this occasion a paper was given arguing that the words could indeed have been spoken by Jesus. Enough Fellows were persuaded by this to pull the vote up to grey – a quite remarkable victory for those who voted red or pink. Seen from within the Seminar, where a good number start with the assumption that virtually no sayings go back to Jesus himself, grey can thus mean 'Well, maybe there is a possibility after all . . .'. Seen from outside, of course – in other words, from the perspective of those for whom the Seminar's products, particularly this book, are designed – it conveys a very different message, namely 'probably not'.

Another example of this occurs in the summary account of the vote on Matthew 18.3 ('If you don't do an about-face and become like children, you'll never enter Heaven's domain'). The following is typical of literally dozens of passages:

The opinion was evenly divided. Some red and a large number of pink votes, in favor of authenticity, were offset by substantial gray and black votes. The result was a compromise gray designation for this version and all its parallels.[27]

Or again, in dealing with the parable of the two sons, and the [95] subsequent saying (Matthew 21.28–31a and 21.31b):

Fifty-eight percent of the Fellows voted red or pink for the parable, 53 percent for the saying in v. 31b. A substantial number of gray and black votes pulled the weighted average into the gray category.[28]

Without using a pocket calculator, I confess I cannot understand how, if a majority in each case thought the saying authentic or probably authentic, the

27 Funk and Hoover 1993, 213.
28 Funk and Hoover 1993, 232.

'weighted average' turned out to be 'probably inauthentic'. A voting system that produces a result like this ought to be scrapped. The average reader, seeing the passage printed as grey, will conclude that 'scholars' think it is probably inauthentic; whereas, even within the small company of the Seminar, the majority would clearly disagree.[29]

In evaluating the colour scheme, therefore, it is important not to think that consensus has been reached. The Seminar's voting methods and results remind one somewhat of Italian politics: with proportional representation, everybody's votes count to some extent, but the result is serious instability. Grey and pink sayings are like the smile on a politician's face when a deal has been struck between minority parties; the informed observer knows that the coalition is a patch-up job, which will not stand the test of time. The reader, particularly the reader outside the scholarly guild, should beware. This volume is only a snapshot of what some scholars think within one particular context and after a certain set of debates. But even the snapshot is out of focus, and the colours have been affected by the process of development. This may be fine if what one wants is an impressionistic idea of the state of play. But the Seminar promises, and claims to offer, much more than that. It claims to tell the unvarnished truth. And therein lies the sixth and final point for comment at this stage.

Jumping on the Bandwagon after the Wheels Came Off

Perhaps the deepest flaw in terms of apparent method is that this book appeals constantly, as does all the literature of the Jesus Seminar, to the possibility that by the application of supposedly scientific or 'scholarly' criteria one will arrive at a definite answer to the question as to what Jesus actually said. This jumps out of the very [96] cover of the book: the subtitle ('The search for the authentic words of Jesus') has the word 'authentic' underlined, and the sub-subtitle, 'What did Jesus really say?' is clearly intended to emphasize the 'really'. The whole enterprise seems to offer the possibility of objective certainty, of methods that will produce results as watertight as $2 + 2 = 4$.

The puzzle about this is that it buys heavily into exactly the sort of positivism that is now routinely abandoned by the great majority of scholars working in the fields of history and texts – including by several members of the Jesus Seminar themselves. The idea that by historical investigation one

29   See also Funk and Hoover 1993, 250, on Mt. 24.32–33: 54 voted either red or pink, but a 35 black vote resulted in a grey compromise (for which, apparently, only the remaining 11 had voted).

might arrive at a position of unbiased objective certainty, of absolute uncon-
ditioned knowledge, about anything, has been shot to pieces by critiques from
a variety of points of view. All knowledge is conditioned by the context and
agenda of the knower; all reconstructions are somebody's reconstructions,
and each 'somebody' sees the world through his or her own eyes and not a
neighbour's. This is so widely acknowledged that one would have thought
it unnecessary to state, let alone to stress. The positivistic bandwagon got
stuck in the mud some time ago, and a succession of critics, looking back to
Marx, Nietzsche and Freud but now loosely gathered under the umbrella of
postmodernism, has cheerfully pulled its wheels off altogether. This, of course,
has not filtered through to the popular media, who still want to know whether
something 'actually happened' or not. The Jesus Seminar, in its desire to go
public with the results of scholarship, has apparently been lured into giving
the public what it wants, rather than what scholarship can in fact provide. As
the previous discussion about voting and colour-coding makes clear, the one
thing this book cannot offer is an answer to the question on its front cover.
All it can do is to report, in a manner that will often mislead the ordinary
reader, what some scholars think Jesus may have said.

At this point some members of the Seminar will want to protest. They know
very well that positivism is a dead-end street. They fully appreciate that most
of the colour-codings, especially the pink and grey, are compromise solutions
hiding a good deal of debate and uncertainty. Unfortunately, such subtleties
were totally lost on whoever wrote the blurb on the back of the book, which
encourages the average reader, for whom the book is designed, to assume that
the colours in the book provide certain, objective, copper-bottomed, positivistic answers: [97]

Did Jesus really give the Sermon on the Mount? Is the Lord's Prayer
composed of his authentic words? *THE FIVE GOSPELS* answers these
questions in a bold, dynamic work that will startle the world of traditional
biblical interpretation . . . In pursuit of the historical Jesus, [the scholars]
used their collective expertise to determine the authenticity of the more
than 1,500 sayings attributed to him. Their remarkable findings appear in
this book . . .

Only those sayings that appear in red type are considered by the Seminar
to be close to what Jesus actually said . . . *According to the Seminar, no more
than 20 percent of the sayings attributed to Jesus were uttered by him* . . .[30]

---

30   The emphasis is in the original.

Underneath the rhetoric about making the results of scholarship generally available, therefore, we find a new form of an old divide between the scholars and the simple folk. The introduction to this book castigates those scholars who 'knew' of the problems about finding the historical Jesus (not to mention the Christ of the church's faith) but who kept these 'findings' from members of the public, who wanted to have their fragile faith confirmed. The Seminar claims to have bridged this divide. But then the Seminar, whose members clearly know that their own work is culture-conditioned, and that the colour-coding system repeatedly hides compromise and serious disagreement, keeps these facts from its own public, which wants to have its *fragile faith in positivism* supported and confirmed. At this meta-level, encouraging the reading public to think that the old Enlightenment bandwagon is still rolling along, when in fact the wheels came off it some time ago, is just as irresponsible as the preacher who hides from the congregation the fact that there are serious questions to be faced about the origin and nature of early Christianity.

This is not to say, of course, that all 'results' of Jesus-scholarship are tenuous and uncertain. There is such a thing as genuine historical knowledge, and it does allow us to make definite claims about Jesus. But it is not to be attained by the route of positivism, still less by the dubious method of vote-taking within a small circle of scholars. It is to be attained by the route of critical realism – a historical method that proceeds, not by atomistic discussion of isolated elements, but by the serious process of hypothesis and verification, during which the perspective of the historian is itself taken into account. I have written about this elsewhere.[31] A good many scholars are pursuing **[98]** this path to a lesser or greater extent. The Jesus Seminar has chosen not to do so.

Towards a New Portrait

The introduction to the book contains a lengthy section (pp. 16–34) setting out the 'rules of written evidence' and 'the rules of oral evidence' that the Seminar formulated and adopted for use in its work. There are thirty-six of these 'rules'. But again and again throughout the book, the 'rules' boil down to three guiding principles that are wheeled out almost ad nauseam as the justification for accepting, or more usually for rejecting, a particular saying or set of sayings.

---

31   Wright 1992a, 81–120.

These three actual guiding principles may be formulated as follows. First, the Seminar in fact presupposes a particular portrait of Jesus. Second, the Seminar adopts a particular, and highly misleading, position about eschatology and apocalyptic, particularly about the kingdom of God; this too was presupposed. Third, the Seminar assumes a particular picture of the early church, especially its interest in and transmission of material about Jesus. In each case there is every reason to reject the principle in question. We must look at each in turn.

I Jesus the Distinctive Sage

As we just saw, the explicit intention of the Seminar was to examine all the sayings and vote on them one by one, allowing a portrait of Jesus to emerge slowly and bit by bit. Thus, for instance, the editors can speak of Matthew 7.16b, which was voted pink, as being placed 'into the red/pink database *for determining who Jesus was*' (p. 157, emphasis added). But what has in fact happened is exactly the reverse. For the majority of Fellows at least, what comes first is an assumption about who Jesus really was, which is then used as the yardstick for measuring, and often ruling out, a good many sayings.

This assumption focuses on the portrait of Jesus as a 'traveling sage and wonder-worker' (p. 128). Sayings can be assessed according to whether they fit with this.[32] The Fellows, or at least their spokespersons in this volume, somehow know that Jesus is a 'reticent sage who does not initiate debate or offer to cast out demons, and [99] who does not speak of himself in the first person' (p. 265). On this basis they feel able to make judgments about sayings that, since they make Jesus do some of these things, cannot be his. As a reticent sage, Jesus 'did not formally enlist followers' (p. 284); he used secular proverbs, having 'perhaps acquired his knowledge of common lore from itinerant philosophers who visited Galilee while he was growing up' (p. 287). He does not, however, quote the Hebrew scriptures very often (pp. 376, 380), so that when we find such quotations attributed to him, they almost certainly come from the early church, which, unlike Jesus, was very concerned to understand his work in the light of the scriptures.

As a reticent sage, Jesus did not, of course, predict his own death (pp. 94, 208 and very frequently); still less did he refer to himself in any way as Messiah or son of God (pp. 75, 312 and regularly). Among the reasons given for this latter assumption is the remarkable argument:

---

32 For example, see Funk and Hoover 1993, 326, on 'daily bread' in the Matthaean and Lukan versions of the Lord's Prayer.

Jesus taught that the last will be first and the first will be last. He admonished his followers to be servants of everyone. He urged humility as the cardinal virtue by both word and example. Given these terms, it is difficult to imagine Jesus making claims for himself... unless, of course, he thought that nothing he said applied to himself.[33]

What the writers seem to ignore is precisely that Jesus taught these things. By what right? Even at the level of teaching, Jesus' words carry an implicit self-reference. When we put even a small amount of his teaching into its first-century Jewish context (see below), it was inevitable that questions should be asked about who he thought he was; and virtually inevitable that he would reflect on such a question himself. Instead of this context, however, the Seminar's spokespersons offer one that may perhaps be thought just a little anachronistic:

Like the cowboy hero of the American West exemplified by Gary Cooper, the sage of the ancient Near East was laconic, slow to speech, a person of few words. The sage does not provoke encounters ... As a rule, the sage is self-effacing, modest, unostentatious.[34]

Jesus, then, was not aware that he had a specific mission to carry out (p. 70). He did not organize 'formal missions' (p. 311). He was not 'given to institution building' (p. 213). The older liberalism was right after all: Jesus' teaching was about being nice to people, not [100] about warning them of punishment in store for the wicked (pp. 170, 181, 289–90, 320 and frequently).[35]

In particular, when Jesus did speak it was almost always in pithy, subversive, disturbing aphorisms. (This, of course, was the presupposition for the Seminar's whole enterprise, of breaking up the text into isolated sayings and voting separately on them.) Thus, in rejecting Luke 22.36–37, the editors comment:

there is nothing in the words attributed to Jesus that cuts against the social grain, that would surprise or shock his friends, or that reflects exaggeration,

---

33 Funk and Hoover 1993, 33.

34 Funk and Hoover 1993, 32.

35 The Seminar nevertheless held, we are told, that the judgmental sayings in Mt. 11.12–14 (for example) were uttered by a Christian prophet 'speaking in the spirit and the name of Jesus' (Funk and Hoover 1993, 181; cf. 320). We are to assume, it seems, that the prophet in question misunderstood that spirit, and misused that name, quite drastically. 'Jesus ... would not have told Capernaum to go to Hell after instructing his disciples to love their enemies' (p. 320). This touching naivety is rightly questioned at 214: 'prophetic anger does not entirely contradict the injunction to love one's enemies. It is possible for the two to be combined in one person.'

humor, or paradox . . . [thus] nothing in this passage commends itself as authentically from Jesus.
(p. 391)

Proverbs that 'are not particularly vivid or provocative' or which 'do not surprise or shock' 'belong to the stock of common lore and so are not of Jesus' invention' (p. 157). It is admitted that Jesus could have used such proverbs, but again and again they attract a grey or black vote.[36]

The Seminar claims, then, that a portrait of Jesus 'begins to emerge' from their work at certain points (p. 340). Not so. The portrait was in the mind all along. It is, for the most part, a shallow and one-dimensional portrait, developed through anachronistic parallels (the laconic cowboy) and ignoring the actual first-century context. Its attractive and indeed sometimes compelling features, of Jesus as the subversive sage, challenging the status quo with teasing epigrams and parables, has been achieved at the huge cost of [101] screening out a whole range of material that several of the leading Jesus-scholars around the world, in major, serious and contemporary works of historical reconstruction, would regard as absolutely central. By far the most important of these is the material often designated 'apocalyptic'; and, within that, Jesus' announcement of the kingdom of God – or, as the Seminar often puts it, 'Heaven's imperial rule'. The rejection of this material is the largest and most central presupposition that the Seminar brings to its entire work, and it deserves a separate section.

2 The Resolutely Non-Apocalyptic Jesus

The most thoroughgoing way in which the Seminar applies the criterion of dissimilarity, according to which Jesus stands out from his surrounding context, is in relation to apocalyptic. Here this reader at least had a strange sense of déjà vu. Nearly three decades ago Klaus Koch wrote a book describing, among other things, what he called 'the agonised attempts to save Jesus from apocalyptic'.[37] Albert Schweitzer, at the turn of the century, had described Jesus as an apocalyptic visionary; many theologians after Schweitzer found

---

36 There seems to be an added confusion at this point. According to all the Seminar's literature, the voting was supposed to be on the question of whether Jesus said things, not on whether he was the first to say them. But frequently the votes seem to have reflected the latter point instead, e.g. Funk and Hoover 1993, 106, 168, 176, 240, 298–9, 337 and elsewhere. This produces a strange heads-I-win /tails-you-lose situation. The secular, non-Jewish sages who (according to the Seminar) may have influenced Jesus in his early days provide us, we are told, with the model for how he spoke. But if a saying looks as though it came from such common stock, it still does not attract a pink or red vote.

37 Koch 1972.

this too much to stomach, and neatly extracted Jesus from his surrounding Jewish, and apocalyptic, context. This was normally done for apologetic motives: if Jesus predicted the end of the world, he was wrong, and this has serious implications for Christology.

The Jesus Seminar, of course, harbours no such motive. Instead, it has a different one, no less all-pervading: Jesus must not in any way appear to give sanction to contemporary apocalyptic preaching, such as that on offer in the fundamentalist movements against which the Seminar is reacting so strongly. Jesus must not, therefore, have supposed that the end of the world was at hand, or that God was about to judge people, or that the son of man (whom the Seminar persists in misleadingly calling the son of Adam) would shortly 'come on the clouds'. All these things form the scriptural basis for much stock-in-trade fundamentalist preaching; the Seminar therefore wishes to rule them out of court.[38] The older flight from apocalyptic was designed [102] to save orthodox Christianity; the newer one is designed to subvert it.

But, though the motive is different, the effect is the same. Although John the Baptist is described as 'the precursor and mentor of Jesus' (p. 128), Jesus' own ministry and message were utterly distinct. John pronounced apocalyptic-style warnings of impending judgment; Jesus did not. Likewise, the very early church (though not the Seminar's hypothetical early Q, and not *Thomas*) reinterpreted Jesus' sayings in an apocalyptic style that distorted Jesus' own intention. Thus Matthew 10.7, in which Jesus tells the disciples to announce that 'Heaven's imperial rule is closing in', is an 'apocalyptically oriented summary', which 'was not, however, the point of view of Jesus' (p. 168). So, too, the warnings of judgment on cities that rejected the disciples are 'alien to Jesus, although not to the early disciples, who may have reverted to John the Baptist's apocalyptic message and threat of judgment, or they may simply have been influenced by apocalyptic ideas that were everywhere in the air' (p. 169).

Stated as baldly as this, the agenda is exposed for what it is: a further agonized attempt to rescue Jesus from contamination with the dreaded 'apocalyptic'. By what means does the Seminar know, a priori, that Jesus so firmly rejected something which was 'everywhere in the air', which was absolutely central to the work of John, who is acknowledged as Jesus' 'precursor and mentor', and which was fundamental, in some shape or form, to all forms of early

38 Any who think this analysis over-suspicious should spend half a day reading through the Seminar's journal *Forum: Foundations and Facets*, and the work of Burton Mack in particular, which was heavily influential on the Seminar's decisions [102] at this point; cf. Mack 1987; 1988.

Christianity known to us – except, of course, to the *Thomas* collection? (We had better leave the doubly hypothetical 'Early Q' out of account, since the only reason for inventing a non-apocalyptic 'Early Q', when so many 'apocalyptic' sayings are in the Matthew/Luke parallels on which the Q hypothesis rests, is the very assumption we are examining, that Jesus and one strand of his followers did not make use of this world of thought.) If almost everyone else thought and spoke like that, how do they know that Jesus did not?[39] The **[103]** answer is that they do not. This 'conclusion' was, in their phrase, 'in the air' from the inception of the Seminar. It was a starting-point, not a result. It may even, we may suspect, have been one of the reasons why the Seminar came into existence in the first place.

But this view of apocalyptic, and of Jesus' participation in it, can be controverted again and again by serious study of the first-century phenomenon which goes by that name. I have argued in detail elsewhere, in line with a fair amount of contemporary scholarship, that 'apocalyptic' is best understood as a complex metaphor-system through which many Jews of the period expressed their aspirations, not for otherworldly bliss, nor for a 'big bang' that would end the space-time world, but for social, political and above all theological liberation.[40] This enables us to affirm that Schweitzer and others were absolutely right to see Jesus as part of apocalyptic Judaism, while denying Schweitzer's unhistorical notion (shared, of course, by fundamentalists) that apocalyptic language was designed to be taken literally. The Seminar is fighting a shadow.

In particular, the language of the kingdom of God has been studied in great detail by scholars with far more awareness of the first-century Jewish context than is evident in the present book.[41] There is no sign that this scholarship has been even noted, let alone taken seriously, by the Seminar. Instead, there is a persistent and muddled repetition of outdated and/or naive points of view:

Mark 13 is an apocalypse (an apocalypse tells of events that are to take place at the end of history. In Mark's version, the end of history will occur when

---

39 See also Funk and Hoover 1993, 112, where the comment (on Mk. 13.14–20) that 'almost anyone could have formulated these warnings' is followed at once by the report of near-unanimity among the Fellows that 'Jesus was not the author of any of these sayings'. In place of the distinctive Jesus of some traditional Christology, who stood out from everyone else because of his divinity, we have the distinctive Jesus of the Seminar, who was certainly **[103]** incapable of saying things that almost anyone else at the time might have said. This is almost a secular version of the docetic heresy.

40 Wright 1992a, 280–338.

41 For details, see e.g. (among a great many) Chilton 1984; 1987; Beasley-Murray 1986; Barbour 1993; and the discussions in the other works about Jesus referred to above in n. 2.

the son of Adam appears on the clouds and gathers God's chosen people from the ends of the earth). This and related themes make Mark 13 sound much like the Book of Revelation . . .

A notable feature of early Christian instruction is that teaching about last [104] things (termed *eschatology*) occurs at the conclusion of the catechism or manual of instruction. Paul tended to put such matters toward the close of his letters, for example, in 1 Thess 5.1–13 and 1 Corinthians 15. In the second-century Christian manual known as the Didache, instruction in eschatology also comes last, in chapter 16.

Mark thus appropriately makes Jesus' discourse on last things his final public discourse . . .[42]

An apocalypse is a form of literature in which a human agent is guided on an otherworldly tour by means of visions. On that tour, the agent learns about a supernatural world unknown to ordinary folk, and the secrets of the future are also revealed . . .

The so-called little apocalypse assembled by Mark in chapter 13, and copied by Matthew and Luke, is not actually an apocalypse in form. But it has the same function . . .[43]

The comment about Paul shows, as clearly as anything else, the shallow and largely spurious level of analysis employed here. Paul is just as capable of talking about (what we call) 'the last things' at other points in his letters (for example 2 Corinthians 5). And the whole statement – it is hardly an argument – is designed to minimize the role of 'apocalyptic' in the gospel accounts, isolating Mark 13 and its parallels from the rest of the text, in a way that, as the last comment quoted tacitly admits, does great violence both to that chapter and to the rest of the synoptic tradition.[44]

It is with discussion of the kingdom of God (or whatever it is to be called; 'Heaven's imperial rule' does have the virtue of jolting or confronting a contemporary reader in a way that 'kingdom of God' has largely ceased to do) that the problem is focused most clearly. The 'cameo essay' on the subject (pp. 136–7) is extremely revealing; and what it reveals is a string of misunderstandings, prejudices and false antitheses.

---

42 Funk and Hoover 1993, 107.
43 Funk and Hoover 1993, 246.
44 See Wright 1992a, 394–5.

The essay sets out four categories. First, there is the preaching of John the Baptist. Second, there are sayings of Jesus that speak of God's rule as future. Third, there are sayings of Jesus that speak of God's rule as present. Fourth, there is a passage from Paul. Already there are problems. (1) The passage quoted from John the Baptist (Matthew 3.7, 10) does not mention the kingdom of God, and in any [105] case would be regarded by many as a later formulation, not necessarily giving us access to John himself. (2) The main passage quoted as an example of sayings of Jesus about God's future rule is Mark 13.24–27 and 30, which again does not mention the kingdom of God, but speaks instead of the son of man coming on the clouds. (3) One of the passages quoted as illustrating sayings of Jesus about God's rule as present is Luke 11.2, which is the petition from the Lord's Prayer, here translated as 'Impose your imperial rule'. If this indicates that the kingdom is already present, why is one commanded to pray for it as though it were not yet here? (4) The single passage quoted from Paul is 1 Thessalonians 4.15–17, which says nothing about the kingdom of God, but speaks of the dead rising, the lord descending and the living Christians being caught up in the air. There are, of course, passages in Paul which speak explicitly about the kingdom of God, and in some that kingdom is a present reality (for example Romans 14.17). The only reason I can imagine for quoting 1 Thessalonians 4 in this context is that the author of the essay is assuming an equation between 'future kingdom of God' and 'end-time apocalyptic events', and taking passages about the latter, which fundamentalists have interpreted in a particular way (for example the 'rapture'), as expressions of this 'apocalyptic' view of the kingdom. But each stage in this line of thought is quite unwarranted. Indeed, the author of the essay more or less agrees with the fundamentalist interpretation of the key texts, in order then to dismiss them as indices of Jesus' mind.

The discussion that follows the citation of these texts poses an utterly spurious either/or:

Does this phrase [kingdom of God] refer to God's direct intervention in the future, something connected with the end of the world and the last judgment, or did Jesus employ the phrase to indicate something already present and of more elusive nature?

The first of these options is usually termed apocalyptic, a view fully expressed in the book of Revelation, which is an apocalypse.[45]

---

45   Funk and Hoover 1993, 37.

Here we have it: 'apocalyptic' is, more or less, 'that which fundamentalists believe about the end of the world'. The author seems to imply that the fundamentalists have actually read some of the texts correctly. So much the worse for the texts; clearly the Seminar is going to take a different view, which will involve ditching those wicked 'apocalyptic' ideas and setting up its own alternative. But if **[106]** this loaded argument functions like a shopkeeper putting extra weights on the scales, what follows is the equivalent of leaning on them with both elbows:

> Did Jesus share this [apocalyptic] view, or was his vision more subtle, less bombastic and threatening?
> The Fellows . . . are inclined to the second option: Jesus conceived of God's rule as all around him but difficult to discern . . . But Jesus' uncommon views were obfuscated by the more pedestrian conceptions of John, on the one hand, and by the equally pedestrian views of the early Christian community, on the other.[46]

As we saw before, Jesus seems to have been radically different from his 'predecessor and mentor', and was radically misunderstood by almost all his followers from the very beginning. In particular, despite the other passages (such as p. 7) in which the authors regard Paul as the great Hellenizer, or Gnosticizer, of the gospel, they wheel him out this time as another representative of Jewish-style apocalyptic:

> The views of John the Baptist and Paul are apocalyptically oriented. The early church aside from Paul shares Paul's view. The only question is whether the set of texts that represent God's rule as present were obfuscated by the pessimistic apocalyptic notions of Jesus' immediate predecessors, contemporaries, and successors.[47]

'Apocalyptic', then, is unsubtle, bombastic, threatening, obfuscatory, pedestrian and pessimistic – and shared by everybody from John the Baptist through to the early church, apart from Jesus himself. This picture is then fitted into the broader old-liberal agenda, as follows: future-kingdom sayings are about judgment and condemnation, while Jesus instead offered forgiveness,

---

46 Funk and Hoover 1993, 137.
47 Funk and Hoover 1993, 137.

mercy and inclusiveness.[48] The evidence adduced to support this astonishing piece of rhetoric – and this remarkably old-fashioned, almost pre-Schweitzer, view of Jesus – is the existence of texts about the kingdom as a present reality, such as Luke 17.20–21; 11.20, and *Thomas* §113. In addition, the parables are supposed to represent the kingdom as a present, rather than a future, reality. The Jesus Seminar therefore voted 'present-kingdom' sayings pink,[49] and 'future-kingdom' sayings black. It was **[107]** as easy as that.

I have to say that if I had been served up this 'cameo essay' by a first-year undergraduate, I would quickly have deduced that the student, while very ingenious, was unfamiliar both with some of the basic secondary discussions of the topic,[50] and, more damaging still, with the meaning of the primary texts in their first-century context. The determination to rule fundamentalism off the map altogether has so dominated the discussion (if not the Seminar itself, at least in this apparently authoritative interpretation of its work) that texts of great subtlety and variety have been forced into a tight and utterly spurious either/or and played off against one another. It would be one thing to find a student doing this. When two senior academics do it, after having gone on record as saying that 'critical scholars practice their craft by submitting their work to the judgment of peers', while 'non-critical scholars are those who put dogmatic considerations first and insist that the factual evidence confirm theological premises',[51] the uncomfortable suspicion is aroused that it is the latter description, not the former, that fits the work we have in our hands. Sadly, this suspicion can only be confirmed by the bombastic, threatening and utterly pedestrian nature of the discussion itself.

There is, of course, a good deal more to be said about the kingdom of God in the teaching of Jesus. There is need for much discussion and careful reconstruction. This, however, cannot be the place for it. We conclude that, when it comes to the central theme of the teaching of Jesus, the Seminar, at least as reported in this volume (and with dissentient voices drowned out by the voting averages and by those who voted black for everything on

48   Funk and Hoover 1993, 157.

49   For example, *Thomas* §113; the explicit reason given for the vote is that this saying provides 'a counter-weight to the view that Jesus espoused popular apocalypticism' (Funk and Hoover 1993, 531). Here, no doubt, is **[107]** one of the real reasons for the Seminar's long-running love-affair with *Thomas*: the collection offers apparent historical grounds for dumping apocalyptic.

50   For example, Ladd 1966; Chilton 1984; 1987; Beasley-Murray 1986; Barbour 1993; and the many recent discussion of the parables, e.g. Boucher 1977; Bailey 1983; Drury 1985. The major earlier discussions, involving such magisterial figures as Dodd and Jeremias, might as well not have happened.

51   Funk and Hoover 1993, 34.

principle), allowed itself to make **[108]** its key decisions on the basis of an ill-informed and ill-advised disjunction between two ill-defined types of kingdom-sayings. The entire history of debate this century on the subject of Jesus and eschatology goes by the board. It is one thing to disagree with the line of thought running, broadly, from Schweitzer to Sanders. It is something else to ignore it altogether. Eschatology and apocalyptic, and 'kingdom of God' within that, have here been misunderstood, misanalysed and wrongly marginalized.

Two tailpieces to this discussion: first, the effect of the Seminar's portrait of Jesus at this point is to minimalize his Jewishness. The authors claim, of course, that Jesus was 'not the first Christian' (p. 24); that is, he does not belong to the Christian movement, but (presumably) to Judaism. But only minimally – if the Seminar's analysis of 'kingdom of God' were to be accepted. Quite unintentionally, of course, the Seminar has reproduced one of the most dubious features of the older liberal picture of Jesus. Judaism only appears as the dark backcloth against which the jewel of Jesus' message – not now as a *Christian* message, but as a subversive, present-kingdom, almost protognostic, possibly Cynic, laconic-cowboy message – shines the more brightly. We do not actually know anything about wandering pagan philosophers whom Jesus might have met in the days of his youth. There is no evidence for them. But they are brought in of necessity; otherwise one might have to admit that Jesus' language about the kingdom of God was thoroughly Jewish, and belonged within the Jewish setting and aspirations of his day.

At the same time, the authors are clearly anxious not to play Jesus off against 'Jews'. They are very much aware that some allegorical readings of Jesus' teaching have produced tragic consequences for Jewish–Christian relations (p. 234). They are so coy about using the word 'Jew' that they insist on saying 'Judean' instead – even, amusingly, when the Jews in question are mostly Galileans, not Judaeans at all (for example p. 168). But they seem unaware that, within our own century, the attempt to paint Judaism as dark, pessimistic, bombastic, pedestrian religion, expecting a great and cataclysmic final judgment, and to paint Jesus as having countered this by offering (the supposedly unJewish message of) mercy and love and forgiveness, has itself generated tragic consequences.

Second, there are all sorts of signs that the authors, representing some but surely not all of the Seminar, simply do not understand how first-century Judaism, in all its plurality, works. The discussion **[109]** of 'hallowed be your name' in Matthew 6.9 implies that there is a paradox in Jesus using the form 'Abba' and then asking 'that the name be regarded as sacred' (p. 149).

There may, no doubt, be a paradox there, but not at that simplistic level. The point of asking that the divine name be hallowed is, as has very often been pointed out, that the name is hallowed when the people of God are vindicated, rescued from their enemies. This discussion is sadly typical of many points where quite basic perspectives on central texts seem to be ignored altogether. Thus, for instance, we read that Luke 23.31 ('if they do this when the wood is green, what will they do when it is dry?') is enigmatic, which is undoubtedly true. But then, when the authors say 'no one knows what it means, although it, too, must have something to do with the fall of Jerusalem' (pp. 395–6), one wonders if they bothered to check any of the major commentaries.

In particular, the authors offer (p. 242) a brief discussion of first-century Pharisaism, in order to substantiate the Seminar's decision to cast black votes for most of the sayings in Matthew 23. They repeat uncritically the line that Sanders took from Morton Smith, though there was never much evidence for it and always plenty against it: the Pharisees were based in Judaea, not Galilee, so Jesus may not have come into contact with them or even known much about them (pp. 242, 244).[52] This is backed up in a way that neither Sanders nor Smith suggests: 'The teachings of the rabbis in Jesus' day were all circulated by word of mouth; it was not until the third century C.E. that rabbinic traditions took written form in the Mishnah.' This last statement is of course true, but totally irrelevant, implying as it does that word-of-mouth circulation would be a casual, inefficient, uncertain thing, so that, lacking written texts, Jesus would not have known much about Pharisaic teaching. As we shall see presently, however, in a substantially oral culture, oral teaching will have circulated far more widely, and far more effectively, than written texts.

The authors further suggest that the Pharisees became the dominant party after the fall of Jerusalem, and that 'at the council of Jamnia, [110] in 90 C.E., the Pharisees laid the foundations for the survival of Judaism in its modern form – rabbinic Judaism'. Meanwhile, even in the last quarter of the first century, the 'emerging church, in its Palestinian and Syrian locales, was still largely a sectarian movement within Judaism'.

All this comprises so many half-truths and inaccuracies that one is tempted to wonder whether it is worth reading further in a book supposedly about the first century.[53] It is highly likely that the Pharisees were already very

52 See Sanders 1985; Smith 1977. Sanders 1993 has toned this right down, perhaps as a result of his further researches reflected in Sanders 1992. For discussion, see Wright 1992a, 181–203; on this point, see esp. 195–6.

53 On all of the following, see Wright 1992a, 145–338.

influential, quite possibly the most influential group, within the pluriform Judaism of the pre-70 period. The group that became dominant after 70 was one variety of Pharisees, namely the Hillelites, over against another variety, the Shammaites. But even this was not achieved overnight; it was only with the collapse of the second revolt, in 135, that the shift of influence was complete. In addition, our knowledge of the council of Jamnia is very nebulous; its date and achievements are very uncertain. The later rabbinic traditions about it are, most likely, far more heavily overlaid with subsequent reinterpretations than almost anything we find in the gospels. To use it as a fixed point for establishing early Christian material is like a hiker taking a compass-bearing on a sheep. Finally, we do not actually know very much at all about the church in Palestine and Syria in the last quarter of the century. What we do know is that a sharp division between the church, precisely in Palestine and Syria, and Pharisaic Judaism of the more zealous (that is, Shammaite) variety had already taken place *in the first five years after Jesus' death*. We know this because of Saul of Tarsus, alias the apostle Paul, who, for neither the first nor the last time, puts a spoke in the wheel of the Jesus Seminar's speculative reconstructions of early Christianity.

Lest all these criticisms be misunderstood, I should stress: there is nothing wrong with trying to popularize the results of scholarship. Quick overviews of complex issues are necessary in such work. But popularization sometimes reveals crucial weaknesses that a more high-flown and abstract language would have masked. So it is in this case. Serious contemporary research on first-century Judaisms by no means rules out the possibility, which must then be decided (and interpreted) on quite other grounds, that Jesus did come into sharp [111] confrontation with the Pharisees. What the discussion tells us is that the members of the Seminar, or at least their spokespersons in this book, are not to be trusted to know their way around the details of the first century, which they are supposed to be describing.[54]

3 Oral Culture, Storytelling and Isolated Sayings

The third driving principle behind a great many of the Seminar's decisions can be stated quite baldly.[55] It is assumed that only isolated sayings of Jesus

---

54 Compare Funk and Hoover 1993, 362–3, where we are blithely told that 'people in the ancient world' (which people? all people? Jews?) 'thought that the sky was held up by mountains that serve as pillars at the edge of the world'. No doubt some people thought that. To offer it as an interpretative grid for a text in the gospels (Lk. 17.6, which is in any case about trees, not mountains) is rather like trying to interpret a Mozart opera by means of nuclear physics.

55 See Funk and Hoover 1993, 25–9, discussed below.

circulated in the earliest post-Easter period. Unless a saying can be conceived as having enough intrinsic interest and, as it were, staying power to survive being passed on by word of mouth, all by itself and without any context, we can assume that it cannot be original to Jesus. Words of Jesus that fail this test, and which occur within more extended narratives, are simply part of the storyteller's art, or of the evangelist's theology.[56] This is, at its heart, an assumption about the nature of early Christianity.

Examples of this principle in operation could be picked from almost anywhere in the book's 500 and more pages. Here are some taken at random:

> The words ascribed to Jesus in this story [rebuking wind and waves, Mark 4.35–41] would not have circulated independently during the oral period; they reflect what the storyteller imagined Jesus would have said on such an occasion.[57]

> The stories Mark has collected in chapter five of his gospel contain words [112] ascribed to Jesus that are suitable only for the occasion. They are not particularly memorable, are not aphorisms or parables, and would not have circulated independently during the oral period. They cannot, therefore, be traced back to Jesus.[58]

> The words ascribed to Jesus [during the healing of the blind man in Mark 8.22–26] are the invention of the evangelist. Because they are incidental dialogue and not memorable pronouncements, they would not have been remembered as exact words of Jesus.[59]

> Jesus' public discourse is remembered to have consisted primarily of aphorisms, parables, or a challenge followed by a verbal retort. Matt 4:17 does not fall into any of these categories.[60]

---

56 Even at the level of reporting what is in the text, the Seminar's spokespersons here leave much to be desired. In Funk and Hoover 1993, 210, commenting on Matthew's transfiguration narrative (17.1–9), they declare that, by contrast with Matthew, 'in Mark's version, Jesus says nothing at all', and say that in this respect Luke has followed Mark. However, in Mk. 9.9 we find a saying of Jesus, parallel to that in Mt. 17.9, but simply in indirect speech: 'He instructed them not to describe what they had seen to anyone, until the son of Adam rise from the dead.' Funk, as a grammarian, would surely acknowledge that *oratio obliqua* is still *oratio*.

57 Funk and Hoover 1993, 60.

58 Funk and Hoover 1993, 62.

59 Funk and Hoover 1993, 75.

60 Funk and Hoover 1993, 134. Procrustes would have been proud of this one.

The remarks quoted from Jesus [in Matthew 8.5–13] are intelligible only as part of the narrative and could not have circulated as a separate saying apart from this narrative context. They were accordingly voted black.[61]

The words attributed to Jesus in the story of the feeding of the crowd all belong to the narrative texture of the story. They cannot be classified as aphorisms or parables and so could not have circulated independently during the oral period, 30–50 C.E. As a consequence, they cannot be traced back to Jesus, but must have been created by the storyteller.[62]

The basis for these judgments is found in the extended discussion of oral memory and tradition in the introduction (pp. 25–9). It is impossible, without quoting the entire section and discussing it line by line, to show the extent of the misunderstandings it reveals. Though the authors regularly refer to oral cultures, the only actual examples they give come from a very non-oral culture, that of their own modern western world.[63] Referring to what Thucydides says [113] about making up speeches to suit the occasion (p. 27) is not to the point; the speeches in question tend to be longer by far than any of Jesus' reported discourses, even the Sermon on the Mount and the Johannine 'farewell discourses'. In any case, Thucydides was a man of learning and letters, and to that extent less representative of a genuinely oral culture.

The theory that sayings, aphorisms, memorable one-liners and sometimes parables are the things that survive, whereas *stories* about Jesus, with his words embedded within them, do not, is clearly promulgated with one eye on the results. 'It is highly probable', we are told – this, recall, at the introductory level, before we have examined a single saying! – that the earliest layer of the gospel tradition was made up almost entirely of single aphorisms and parables that circulated by word of mouth, without narrative context – precisely as that tradition is recorded in Q and *Thomas*.[64]

---

61 Funk and Hoover 1993, 160.

62 Funk and Hoover 1993, 205; compare with 199–200.

63 'We' rephrase jokes and witticisms, such as those of Oscar Wilde (Funk and Hoover 1993, 27); 'we know' that oral memory 'retains little else' other than sayings and anecdotes that are short, provocative and memorable (p. 28); 'recent experiments with memory' have reached various conclusions about the capacity of memory, emphasizing that, though people remember the gist of what was said, they do not recall the exact phrases. All of these examples are 100 per cent irrelevant when we are considering a genuinely oral culture, such as still exists in certain parts of the world, not least among peasant communities in the Middle East. On the whole topic, see Bailey 1991.

64 Funk and Hoover 1993, 28.

With the evidence thus well and truly cooked in advance, it is not surprising that the portrait of Jesus-the-quizzical-sage 'emerges' from the subsequent discussion. It could not help doing so. The theory about what sort of material survives in oral tradition, I suggest, was designed to produce exactly this result.

Against this whole line of thought we must set the serious study of genuinely oral traditions that has gone on in various quarters recently.[65] Communities with an oral culture tend to be *storytelling* communities. They sit around in long evenings telling and listening to stories – the same stories, over and over again. Such stories, especially when they are involved with memorable happenings that have determined in some way the existence and life of the particular group in question, acquire a fairly fixed form, down to precise phraseology (in narrative as well as in recorded speech), extremely early in their life – often within a day or so of the original incident taking place. They retain that form, and phraseology, as long as they are told. Each village and community has its recognized [114] storytellers, the accredited bearers of its traditions; but the whole community knows the stories by heart, and if the teller varies them even slightly they will let him or her know in no uncertain terms. This matters quite a lot in cultures where, to this day, the desire to avoid 'shame' is a powerful motivation.

Such cultures do also repeat, and hence transmit, proverbs and pithy sayings. Indeed, they tend to know far more proverbs than the orally starved modern western world. But the circulation of such individual sayings is only the tip of the iceberg; the rest is narrative, narrative with embedded dialogue, heard, repeated again and again within minutes, hours and days of the original incident, and fixed in memories the like of which few in the modern western world can imagine. The storyteller in such a culture has no licence to invent or adapt at will. The less important the story, the more adaptation may be possible; but the more important the story, the more the entire community, in a process that is informal but very effective, will keep a close watch on the precise form and wording with which the story is told.

And the stories about Jesus were nothing if not important. Even the Jesus Seminar admits that Jesus was an itinerant wonder-worker. Very well. Supposing a woman in a village is suddenly healed after a lengthy illness. Even today, even in a non-oral culture, the story of such an event would quickly

---

65 For example, see Wansbrough 1991, referring to a large amount of earlier work; Bailey 1991. The following discussion depends on these and similar studies, and builds on Wright 1992a, 418–43; 1996a, 133–7.

spread among friends, neighbours and relatives, acquiring a fixed form within the first two or three retellings and retaining it, other things being equal, thereafter. In a culture where storytelling was and is an art-form, a memorable event such as this, especially if it were also seen as a sign that Israel's God was now at last at work to do what he had always promised, would be told at once in specific ways, told so as to be not just a celebration of a healing but also a celebration of the kingdom of God. Events and stories of this order are community-forming, and the stories that form communities do not get freely or loosely adapted. One does not disturb the foundations of the house in which one is living.

What about detached aphorisms, then? Clearly, a memorable saying is a memorable saying, and could circulate independently. But what about sayings that sometimes have a context and sometimes not? I suggest that the following hypothesis is far more likely than [115] that proposed by the Seminar.[66] It was only later, when the communities had been scattered through external circumstances (such as sundry persecutions, and the disastrous Jewish War of 66–70), that individual memorable sayings, which might very well have enjoyed a flourishing earlier life *within various narrative settings*, would become detached from those settings and become *chreiai*, isolated pithy sayings with minimal narrative context, such as we find (of course) in *Thomas*, and also to some extent in Luke. It is heavily ironic that the reason often given for supposing Luke's version of Q to be earlier than Matthew's is that Luke's versions of Q sayings are more *chreia*-like, while Matthew's are more embedded in Jewish, and often in narrative, contexts. Unless one had been fairly well brainwashed by the idea that Jesus-traditions consisted originally of non-Jewish, detached sayings, and only in the second generation acquired a Jewish setting, complete with scriptural overtones and so forth, the most natural historical hypothesis here would have been this: that Jesus' earliest hearers, being Jews, eager for their God to act in their present circumstances, would have told stories about Jesus in a thoroughly Jewish way, with scriptural echoes both deliberate and accidental. Then, later on, the church, which was leaving the tight storytelling communities, and going out into the wider hellenistic world, would find it easier to detach sayings from their original

---

66 Sometimes the absence of narrative context in the *Thomas* collection is remarked on (e.g. Funk and Hoover 1993, 122) as though this were of great significance – which it clearly is not, since *Thomas* never has any such contexts. Waving *Thomas* around (e.g. p. 102), as though its detached sayings somehow prove that the saying first circulated independently and only subsequently acquired its synoptic context, constitutes an empty celebration of a circular argument.

narrative context and present them, like the sayings of wise teachers in the greco-roman world, as isolated nuggets of wisdom.

The Jesus Seminar's view of oral tradition is thus based, not on the most likely historical hypothesis, but on the same view of the distinctive Jesus that has been seen to dominate the whole picture. Jesus would not have quoted scripture;[67] he did not share, or address, the [116] aspirations of his contemporary Jews; he did not even follow the line taken by his 'precursor and mentor'. Nothing much memorable ever happened to him, or if it did we do not know about it. He was not involved in incidents that made a deep impression on the onlookers, causing them to go at once and tell what they had seen over and over again, with the anecdote quickly fixing itself into a pattern, and the words of Jesus, including incidental words, becoming part of that regularly repeated story. He never spoke about himself (the more one thinks about this suggestion, the more absurd it becomes); his conversation consisted only of subversive, teasing aphorisms. He must, in short, have been a very peculiar human being (as one Fellow of the Seminar pointed out to me, a Jesus who always and only uttered pithy aphorisms would start to look like some of the less credible cinematic Jesuses). Such a person would in fact be quite maddening. More importantly, as a historian I find it incredible that such a Jesus could have been a significant historical figure. It is not at all clear why people would have followed him, died for him, loved him, invented rich and powerful stories about him, and (within an almost incredibly short time, and within a context of continuing Jewish monotheism) worshipped him.[68]

Perhaps the greatest weakness of the whole construct lies just here. In order to sustain their home-made view of Jesus, the authors of this book, and presumably a fair number at least of Fellows of the Jesus Seminar, have had to invent, as well, an entire picture of the early church out of not much more than thin air. Sometimes they have borrowed other people's inventions, but they, too, are based on little or nothing. Paul, as we have seen, is the one major fixed point in early Christianity; we know that he was active, travelling, preaching and writing in the 40s and 50s, but we do not know anything at all, with the same certainty, about almost anyone else. We do not know that Q even existed; notoriously, there is a growing body of opinion that it did

---

67 For example, Funk and Hoover 1993, 174, where the reference to Micah in Mt. 10.34–36 is given as a reason for inauthenticity. Compare p. 201, where we are told that 'scholars believe that most, perhaps all, quotations from scripture attributed to Jesus are secondary accretions'. This is quite breathtaking, both in its ignoring of serious and well-known scholarly traditions [116] in which Jesus is seen as a major expositor of scripture, and in the extraordinary non-Jewishness of the portrait that emerges.

68 On the worship of Jesus and Jewish monotheism, see Wright 1991, 18–136; 1992a, 457.

not (though one would never guess this from reading *The Five Gospels*), even as there is a growing body of opinion, [117] represented strongly within the Jesus Seminar, that expounds ever more complex theories about its origin, development, historical setting, and theologies.[69] Of course, once scholars are allowed to invent whole communities at will, anything is possible. Any jigsaw puzzle can be solved if we are allowed to create new pieces for it on a whim. But we should not imagine that historical scholarship built on this principle is of any great value.

Conclusion

Let me be quite clear, in bringing the discussion to a close, on several points at which misunderstanding of what I have said might perhaps arise.

First, I have no quarrel with the enterprise of publishing as much of the early Jesus-material as possible, from both the canonical and non-canonical sources, and bringing every scrap of possibly relevant evidence into full play. Indeed, I am deeply grateful for the immense labour and effort that members of the Seminar have expended to enable all of us involved in the search for Jesus to study these texts more easily. But, as with recent controversies about the Dead Sea Scrolls, the Seminar should be wary of suggesting that those who find the canonical material to be more reliable than the non-canonical are part of a conspiracy of silence, inspired by thoroughly non-historical motives, that is, by the desire for some form of closed-minded traditional Christianity. Frankly, *both* the desire to 'prove' orthodoxy *and* the desire to 'disprove' it ought to be anathema to the serious historian. The first of these is, of course, the way to what is normally called fundamentalism; the second, taken by at least some (and they are clearly influential) in the Jesus Seminar, is no less closed-minded, and in fact fundamentalist, in practice. Hatred of orthodoxy is just as unhistorical a starting-point as love of it.

Second, I have no quarrel with popularizaton. I totally agree with Robert Funk that the results of scholarship are far too important, on this of all questions, to be confined to the classroom and library. I will go further. The Jesus Seminar, in this and in several other of its publications, has done as good a job of popularization as any scholarly group or individual I have ever seen. Its charts, diagrams, tables, layout and so forth are exemplary. I am not, in short, in any way [118] a scholarly snob, who wants to keep the discussion

---

69 The problematical nature of this aspect of 'Q studies' is treated by C. A. Evans in his chapter on assumptions and methodology (in *Authenticating the Words of Jesus*); see Evans 1999.

within a charmed circle. My problems lie elsewhere. The thing that is thus being often brilliantly communicated, especially in *The Five Gospels*, is not the assured result of scholarship. It is a compromise of pseudo-democratic scholarship, based on principles we have seen good reason to question, employing methods that many reputable scholars would avoid, ignoring a great deal of very serious (and by no means necessarily conservative) contemporary scholarship, making erroneous and anachronistic assumptions about the early church and its cultural context, and apparently driven by a strong, and strongly distorting, contemporary agenda. There was no point in popularizing all this. One should only popularize scholarship when it has passed the test this book itself suggests: submitting work to the judgment of peers (p. 34). For what it is worth, my judgment is that *The Five Gospels* does not pass the test. Any non-scholar reading this book is likely to be seriously misled, not only about Jesus, but about the state of serious scholarship. This is culpably irresponsible.

Third, I repeat what I said early on: I have no quarrel with the scholarship of many members of the Seminar. Some I am privileged to count as friends, and I trust that what I have said here will not put that friendship in jeopardy. From within the Seminar, as we saw, several of the discussions, not least some of the votes that ended up grey, must appear as highly significant, points of potential advance in understanding. Several Fellows have done sterling work in persuading others within the Seminar to adopt, or at least to allow for, views other than their original ones; pulling votes up from black to grey may indicate, for many, an opening of an otherwise closed mind. From within certain circles in the North American academy, this is quite a significant achievement. From outside the Seminar, however, the present volume cannot but appear as a disaster, for which the individual Fellows cannot and must not be held responsible, since they did not write it. The two authors of this book are men whose work in other fields I admire and have used a good deal: Funk's Greek grammar is always close at hand, and Hoover's work on a key Greek term used once by Paul is foundational, I am persuaded, for the correct understanding of a much controverted and hugely important passage.[70] But they, as the named authors, must unfortunately **[119]** bear responsibility for this, the flagship work of the Jesus Seminar. It does them no credit. Indeed, it obscures any good work that the Seminar itself may have done.

Fourth, and perhaps most importantly of all: I agree completely with the Seminar that the search for Jesus in his historical context is possible, vital

---

70   Funk 1973; **[119]** Hoover 1971; see Wright 1991, 56–98.

and urgent. I am as convinced as it is that if the church ignores such a search it is living in a fool's paradise. What is more, my own study of Jesus leads me to think that 'conservative' and 'orthodox' Christianity, in the twentieth century at least, has often, indeed quite regularly, missed the point of Jesus' sayings and deeds almost entirely. But the way to address this problem is not, and cannot be, the way taken by the Jesus Seminar. One cannot tackle serious historical problems by taking them to bits and voting on the bits one by one. The only way forward must be the way of genuine historiography; and one may search *The Five Gospels* from cover to cover in vain for such a thing. There are a good many people engaged in serious historical study of Jesus at the moment, but the Seminar in its corporate identity (as opposed to some of its individual members) cannot be reckoned among their number.

Fifth, in conclusion, I question whether the Jesus proposed by *The Five Gospels* constitutes, or offers, good news, that is, 'gospel', at all. The main thing this Jesus has to offer, it sometimes appears, is the news that the fundamentalists are wrong. Some of us believed that anyway, on quite other grounds. Aside from that, Jesus becomes a quizzical teacher of wisdom, to be ranged alongside other quizzical teachers of wisdom, from many traditions. No reason emerges as to why we should take this teacher any more or less seriously than any other. It is not clear why even a sustained attempt to follow his maxims, his isolated aphorisms, should offer hope in a world threatened by ecological disasters, nuclear holocausts, resurgent tribalisms – and, for those insulated from such things in certain parts of the western world, the moral and spiritual bankruptcy of materialism. The whole point of calling gospels 'gospels' was, I suggest, that they did contain reason for hope, good news to a world that badly needed it.

The Five Gospels, in other words, systematically deconstructs its own title. If this book gives us the truth about Jesus, about the early church, and about the writing of the five books here studied, there is [120] no gospel, no good news. There is only good advice, and we have no reason for thinking that it will have any effect. Many members of the Jesus Seminar would disagree strongly with this conclusion, but this book does not give us any means of seeing why. In any case, those who persist in seeing the Seminar's portrait of Jesus as somehow good news are bound to say, as the book does on almost every page, that Matthew, Mark, Luke and John got it all wrong, producing their own variations on the pedestrian, bombastic, apocalyptic and essentially fundamentalist worldview. If the Seminar insists on retaining the word 'gospels' in the title, then, it is the word 'five' that is deconstructed: all one is left with is *Thomas* and, of course, the doubly hypothetical 'Early Q'.

From a historical point of view it might of course be true that there is no good news to be had. Christianity as a whole might simply have been whistling in the dark for two thousand years. Subversive aphorisms may be the only comfort, the only hope, we have. But this question must be addressed precisely *from a historical point of view.* And, when all is said and done, *The Five Gospels* is of no help whatever in that task. There is such a thing as the serious contemporary search for Jesus in his historical context. This particular book makes no contribution to it.

7

Resurrection in Q?

When I was invited to contribute to a Festschrift for my old friend and colleague David Catchpole I was initially puzzled as to what I should write about. David's brilliant work, probing into the early Christian texts with a microscope and sharp scalpel, has taken him down paths where I was not always able to follow him, no doubt because our minds simply don't work in the same ways at certain points. But the questions he has investigated remain close to the centre of attention in New Testament studies, even if fashions come and go on the various theories about the origin of the synoptic gospels.

So it was with some relief that I realized – since I was in any case working on the question of the resurrection at the time – that there was one area of 'Q studies' in which I might perhaps have a contribution to make. I was glad to be able to investigate this paradoxical question – whether or not Q had anything much to say about the resurrection – in such a way that I could then draw on this at the appropriate point when completing *The Resurrection of the Son of God* (Wright 2003) a couple of years later.

[85] Introduction: Multiple Agnosticisms

New Testament scholars working in different fields often appear to live in parallel universes with little contact between them. We need to specialize if we are to go deeper into our chosen areas; and the multiple non-academic pressures on scholars, not least those who, like David Catchpole, have given of themselves generously to the wider concerns of both academy and church, mean that most of us can scarcely keep up in a small field, let alone across the whole spectrum of early Christianity and related topics. Scholars who, like the present writer, spend much of their lives working on Paul rarely venture across the street to visit those who work on Q, and vice versa.

All this may be inevitable, but I find it regrettable; and there are times when to cross the street, if only as a gesture of interest and support, may be worthwhile. It is, of course, risky. The book of Proverbs (26.17) warns that to meddle in someone else's quarrel is to take a stray dog by the ears. The high degree of current specialization means that one may expect, as the least reward for one's pains, to be told to stick to one's own last, to mind one's own business.

But of course it *is* our business. By comparison with other academic fields – second-Temple Judaism, for instance – the study of the early church and its writings is a small field, with few primary sources and a small geographical and chronological framework. If it is true that a document or tradition existed that corresponds to what people today call Q, and if it is claimed that this document reflects the religious and theological interests and hopes of a community in the middle of the first century, those of us who have worked on documents that we actually possess and communities for which we have first-hand evidence are bound to take notice, especially if these hypothetical documents and communities are claimed to hold significantly different views from those commonly ascribed to early Christians. The large and often high-profile growth of Q studies in recent years, [86] especially in America, has gained much of its energy from the underlying hypothesis that Q, or some form of Q, represents and embodies not only an *earlier* version of Christianity than that which we find in the written gospels from which we deduce its existence, maybe even an earlier version than that of Paul, but a significantly *different* one. In this different version, that which is emphasized in what are now the canonical texts of the New Testament plays little role, and that which is downplayed in the canon plays a greater role. Thus, as in the triple tradition, and perhaps in Q itself, so in contemporary scholarship, the privileged are to be overthrown and the humble exalted, the orthodox to be confuted and the heretics vindicated, the first to be last and the last first.[1]

Just as many scholars (including, perhaps, David Catchpole himself) remain unaccountably agnostic about some things of which I am quite convinced, so I find myself wanting to return the compliment on this particular subject. I have never been fully convinced that the Q hypothesis does justice to the evidence, but nor have I been convinced that any of its rivals succeeds notably better.[2] More particularly, in company with several who do believe in the existence of some kind of documentary Q, I find it impossible to believe that

---

1 Lk. 13.30; Mt. 19.30; 20.16; Mk. 10.31; *Barn.* 6.13. I have written briefly about some recent work on Q in Wright 1992a, 435–43; 1996b, 35–44. Among the key works, from different points of view, are Kloppenborg 1987; Tuckett 1996; and, of course, Catchpole 1993. Perhaps the most strident exponent of the new American Q school is Mack 1993; cf. too Vaage 1994.

2 The work of W. R. Farmer remains seminal, though inevitably controversial; see Farmer 1964. More recently, but equally controversially, see, for instance, Goulder 1989; McNicol 1996. On recent alternatives to Q see the discussion in Tuckett 1996, ch. 1, and the other works referred to there.

we can now discern developmental layers within it which involve significant theological shifts and transformations. In part, I confess, my scepticism at this point arises from an obvious hermeneutic of suspicion. When, a generation ago, Siegfried Schulz proposed a development from an early Q with a low Christology to a later one [87] with a high Christology – a proposal eagerly picked up by Eduard Schillebeeckx – the coherence between the literary theory and the theologically desired result was too close for comfort.[3] When, today, we find scholars passionately advocating the wholesale revision of our picture of early Christianity, and our agendas for contemporary Christianity, so as to minimize supposedly 'apocalyptic' elements in favour of 'sapiential' ones, and 'discovering' in the process that 'Early Q' just happens to fit that agenda, similar scepticism is in my view quite justified.[4]

I do not think, in fact, that within the history of first-century Judaism – and that, if anywhere, is where earliest Christianity belongs, and with it, *ex hypothesi*, Q – it is possible to separate out what we loosely call 'apocalyptic' and 'sapiential' streams of thought and play them off against one another. Too many counter-examples, from 1QS through the Wisdom of Solomon to the *Didache*, taking in books like Matthew and James en route, stand in the way of such a facile analysis, though that is a topic for another day.[5] Thus, though the subject to which I now turn may properly belong within what is sometimes labelled 'apocalyptic', it should not be supposed to be the property of only one narrowly defined group within either Judaism or early Christianity. I propose to consider Q and Resurrection.

This is of course nicely ironic. Many New Testament scholars, including many for whom Q's existence and demonstrability have become an article of personal faith and academic orthodoxy, are at least as agnostic about the resurrection of Jesus as I am about Q. Indeed, one of the attractions of Q in some quarters today is that it seems to say nothing about Jesus' death or resurrection, thus apparently providing evidence of a flourishing type of early Christianity for which those (Pauline?) emphases, so strikingly reinforced in the canonical gospels, were unimportant.

There are, of course, mediating positions here as elsewhere. I think, for instance, of Marcus Borg's insistence that Jesus really was [88] raised from the

---

3   Schulz 1972; Schillebeeckx 1979.

4   The most sophisticated attempt in this genre is that of Crossan 1998; see my article review, Wright 2000.

5   See, briefly, Wright 1996a.

dead even though nothing happened to his body.[6] Perhaps this is rather like saying that though Q may have existed, it was never a document but rather a loose collection of oral traditions, or even of ideas in people's heads. Nobody, after all, has ever seen Q; we only deduce it from its apparent effects. It only appears, one might argue, to those who believe in it, and perhaps it takes a special literary-critical grace to have that sort of faith or experience. But somewhere amid these multiple agnosticisms the question should, I think, be posed: is it really true that Q, as it stands (insofar as it does), has no interest in the resurrection?[7]

The question is seldom raised, and, when raised, normally answered quite swiftly. Two leading Q scholars dismiss the possibility;[8] one recent writer makes a brief case in favour.[9] Q, of course, notoriously lacks both a resurrection narrative as such and the specific predictions of resurrection that are prominent in the Markan tradition.[10] It seems to me that there is more to be said – even though, of course, as with the gospel tradition as a whole, so with Q material in particular, the resurrection, whether of people in general or of Jesus in particular, is not a prominent theme. If, in investigating this possibility, crossing the street as I do so to where the Q specialists live, I may seem like a neighbour giving unwanted and unnecessary advice on how to dig the garden, I trust that David Catchpole at least will take this contribution to ongoing controversy, not least in relation to Christology and community, in the spirit in which it is meant.

I Future Hope in Q

As is well known, several of the sayings in which Matthew and Luke overlap warn of imminent judgment.[11] These passages fit naturally [89] into the world of first-century Judaism, with its prevailing sense that history, particularly Israel's history, was accelerating towards a moment when Israel's God would judge the nations, and the wicked within Israel, in order finally to right the

---

6   See Wright and Borg 1999, ch. 8.

7   In what follows, when I refer to Q, the reader may understand the proviso 'if, that is, it exists'.

8   Kloppenborg 1990, at p. 90 (the 'metaphor' of resurrection is 'fundamentally inappropriate to the genre and theology of Q'); Mack 1992.

9   Meadors 1995, 307–8.

10 Mk. 8.31; 9.9; 9.31; 10.34, with parallels in each case.

11 I follow the convention of referring to Q passages by their Lukan numbering, without thereby implying agreement with the mainstream view in which the Lukan form of the sayings is held to be closer to the original Q.

wrongs with which the world, and Israel in particular, had been plagued.[12] The reasons why there are so many of these warnings in Q cannot be examined here; but we should note that within the worldview where they make sense, namely that of second-Temple Judaism, warnings of this sort would always at least imply, as their correlate, that God's people, the 'righteous', the 'poor', the 'saints', or whoever, would be rescued, saved and vindicated precisely in and through this judgment on their wicked contemporaries. And one of the main ways in which this vindication was conceived was precisely resurrection.[13]

It is not simply a risky argument from silence, therefore, but a safe conclusion to say that where we find stern warnings of judgment we should also hear promises of vindication, salvation and perhaps even resurrection. There are sufficient passages where this implication peeps out for us to be clear on the point. Thus, for instance, the saying about people seeing Abraham, Isaac and Jacob sitting down in the kingdom of God with a great company is designed as a warning, but clearly contains the promise that there will be such an event and that some – presumably including Jesus himself, and those who have faith in him and/or follow him – will share it.[14] And any first-century Jew hearing of a coming feast in which Abraham, Isaac and Jacob would be sharing would understand this in terms of the patriarchs, and presumably a great many others besides, being raised from the dead. This is obviously the case with the references to future resurrection and judgment in Q 11.29–32, which we shall examine in the third section below.

Staying with the patriarchal theme, I think it is likely that the Q saying of John the Baptist about Abraham would also be heard within Judaism and early Christianity as a prediction of resurrection. Q 3.8, a passage whose very close wording makes it a classic [90] example of the evidence on which the Q hypothesis is based, warns against presuming to say 'We have Abraham as our father', and emphasizes the warning with the promise that 'God is able to raise children for Abraham from these stones'. The word for 'raise' here, *egeirai*, was well known in early Christianity as one of the regular words for the resurrection, and would quite likely be seen as an indication that when God raised Abraham himself from the dead a great family would be raised with him from quite unlikely sources – a very similar point, in fact, to that which is being made in Q 13.28–30.[15]

---

12   On the context and content of such sayings see Wright 1992a, ch. 10; Wright 1996b, ch. 8.

13   See Wright 1992a, 32–4. I review this evidence more fully in Wright 2003, and presuppose this review in what follows.

14   Q 13.28–30.

15   Cf. too, interestingly, Rom. 4.16–17. For *egeirein* cf. Lk. 7.14; 9.7, 22; 20.37; 24.6, 34; Paul has more than

This is clearly the meaning, too, of Q 12.4–7 and, in conjunction with that passage, 12.8–9 and even perhaps 12.10. Telling people not to be afraid of those who can kill only the body is clearly telling them that there is a future life beyond the death of the present body – precisely the point to which the martyrs had clung in the Maccabaean period and afterwards.[16] Coupling with this promise the double-edged promise and threat that the son of man (Luke) or Jesus himself (Matthew) will acknowledge and deny those who acknowledge and deny him in the presence of the angels of God (Luke) or the heavenly father (Matthew) likewise clearly implies a future life beyond the grave, since part of the point of the saying is that those who confess Jesus may face death for doing so.

It is possible that the challenge to trust God for clothing (Q 12.28) is also at least a veiled promise of resurrection. The grass in the field is thrown into the furnace, but God can be trusted for future clothing.[17] And the treasure in heaven which Q 12.33 encourages [91] its hearers to seek and store up, a treasure that neither theft nor corruption can spoil, goes well not so much with a notion of a disembodied immortality but with the promise of new creation, stored up at present in the heavenly places, ready to be brought to birth in a new, incorruptible life.[18]

In this context, and granted the second-Temple Jewish setting, the promise about losing one's life in order to gain it (Q 17.33) can only refer to resurrection. Coupling this saying, as Matthew does, with the challenge to take up the cross and follow Jesus (Matthew 10.38; Luke 14.26–27) brings home the force of this: the challenge to martyrdom, to death at the hands of the pagans (which is what taking up the cross meant in the first century), would at once imply the promise of resurrection the other side of death.[19]

---

thirty uses of it. The background includes Dan. 12.2 (Theodotion); LXX Sir. 48.5. This point is valid even though, as Davies and Allison point out, *egeirein ek tinos* is a Semitism meaning 'to come to be born'; Davies and Allison 1988, 308. The question is what a first-century Jewish Christian would have heard in the phrase.

16   See e.g. 2 Macc. 7; Wis. 2.1—3.9. On the Wisdom passage, which despite the popular impression teaches future resurrection for the dead as well as present immortality, see Wright 1992a, 329–30, and the discussion in Wright 2003.

17   Compare and contrast the sayings in *Gos. Thom.* 21 and 37, where, in one interpretation at least, nakedness is a metaphor for the disembodied state (contra e.g. Valantasis 1997, 93–4, 112–3, who suggests that the clothes represent social conditioning). The saying in *Thomas* (36) which precedes the second of these passages is a version of the Q saying that warns against anxiety over clothing. On clothing as a metaphor for resurrection cf. e.g. 1 Cor. 15.53–54; 2 Cor. 5.3. Q 12.28 echoes the promise of new-covenant life in Isa. 40.7–8.

18   Cf. again the contrast of corruption and incorruption in 1 Cor. 15.42–54.

19   The unusual word *zōogonēsei* in Lk. 17.33 should probably be rendered 'bring to life' rather than merely 'keep [one's life]'. *Pace* e.g. Fitzmyer 1985, 1172, 'will give life to it' is not the same as 'will preserve it alive'.

Finally, the last saying in Q arguably envisages the resurrection in a characteristically second-Temple Jewish fashion. In Q 22.30 Jesus promises his followers that they will sit on thrones, judging the twelve tribes of Israel. This is one of those cases where the Matthaean parallel (19.28) appears more primitive, since it specifies twelve thrones, ignoring the embarrassment of Judas;[20] but precisely the Matthaean saying emphasizes that this will take place 'in the regeneration, when the son of man shall sit upon the throne of his glory'.[21] Even if the Lukan version is considered more original, at the time the saying circulated it was obvious that for the prophecy to be fulfilled not only would Jesus need to be alive and present, but the twelve tribes, of whom ten were of course still geographically dispersed, would need to be miraculously gathered. A first-century Jew, faced with that proposal, would naturally, I suggest, assume that this would be accomplished through the resurrection. [92]

2 The Dead Raised Already

Within this broad-based Q theme of future judgment and vindication, with overtones of future resurrection, there are also signs that Q regarded the raising of the dead as something that was happening in the present time as well. Jesus' answer to John the Baptist offers a list of the messianic activities Jesus has been performing, and within the list we find the claim that 'the dead are raised' (Q 7.22).[22]

Within its present gospel contexts, this presumably refers back to previous healings that Q itself does not, of course, relate. For Luke, this means the raising of the widow's son at Nain (7.11–17, immediately preceding this pericope); for Matthew, the obvious reference is to Jairus's daughter (Matthew 9.18–26). The raising of the dead as one of the signs of the Messiah is attested in Qumran as well, in a passage remarkably similar to Q 7.18–23.[23]

In Matthew's version of the 'mission charge', this messianic work is shared with the disciples. Matthew 10.8 commands Jesus' disciples to 'heal the sick, raise the dead, cleanse lepers, exorcise demons', while Luke's parallel charge

---

20 So e.g. Fitzmyer 1985, 1419.

21 In Jos. *Ant.* 11.66, *palingenesia*, 'regeneration', is used in the sense of the rebirth of the Jewish nation after the exile.

22 The phrase echoes the LXX of Isa. 26.19.

23 4Q521.12 (the Messiah will 'heal the badly wounded and will make the dead live, he will proclaim good news to the poor and . . . he will lead the . . . and enrich the hungry'); also frag. 7 1.6, where the Messiah, or perhaps God, 'gives life to the dead of his people'. Text, and short bibliography, in Martinez and Tigchelaar 1998, 2:1045–7.

(10.2–12) merely has 'heal the sick' (Q 10.9). Although this cannot therefore be counted as a Q saying, it seems to be part of a developing Q tradition expanded by either Matthew or an intermediate source (Matthew's version of Q?).

Related to this, but more significant for our purpose, is the striking saying 'Leave the dead to bury their dead' (Q 9.60, with identical wording in Matthew 8.22). I have explored elsewhere the way in which this saying may represent a radical move on Jesus' part, setting the call of the kingdom (in Luke) and following him (in Matthew and Luke) as a higher priority than one of the most sacred duties of family loyalty.[24] Here I want to note the way in which the Q saying resonates with the other material studied above. If those who are not following Jesus are 'dead', it appears that those who are already following him are in some sense 'alive'; Luke at least would presumably comment, in the light of 15.24, 32, that this life, [93] found by those who repent and follow Jesus, is in some sense resurrection life, life from the dead. I think the Q saying as it stands already implies this; the Q context, warning that to follow Jesus is to have nowhere in the present world to lay one's head (Q 9.57–58), indicates that Jesus is offering a future world, to be anticipated in the present, in which a new kind of life has burst on the scene.

A case can be made, therefore, for the following view, granted a reasonably traditional understanding of Q. Q understood the immediate future crisis not just as a moment of terrible judgment, but as the time of vindication and resurrection. This future resurrection, in which the righteous would be vindicated and would share the feast of Abraham, Isaac and Jacob, was already anticipated in the present in two ways: the actual raising back to life of recently dead persons, and the new life, a form of metaphorical life from the dead, enjoyed by Jesus' followers. And all this leads to the harder, but more important, question: does Q after all have anything to say about Jesus' own resurrection?

3 The Sign of Jonah

We return to the passage I postponed earlier.[25] Q 11.31–32 offers an unambiguous statement of the future resurrection. The Queen of the South, and the people of Nineveh, 'will arise at the judgment with this generation and

---

24 Wright 1996b, 401, with reference to the work of Hengel and Sanders.

25 I assume for the purposes of the following that Mt. 16.1–2a, 4 is Matthew's version of Mk. 8.11–12, into which Matthew has inserted in v. 4 the reference to the sign of Jonah, to correspond with his 12.39. On this point see Catchpole 1993, 244, discussing various options.

condemn it'. This is a further instance of the phenomenon examined in section 1 above, where Q affirms the future resurrection – in this case, of non-Jews, which ties in nicely with Q 13.28–30. The implication is that 'this generation' will also arise at the judgment; as frequently in both second-Temple Judaism and the New Testament, there is an implicit tension between the universal resurrection (some to be saved, others to be condemned) and the resurrection seen as the specific gift for those who are saved.[26]

But what about the sign of Jonah itself?[27] Matthew is in no doubt what this sign is: Jonah was three days and nights in the belly of [94] the sea-monster, and in the same way the son of man will be three days and three nights in the heart of the earth (12.40, quoting the LXX of Jonah 2.1). Matthew does not make the point more explicit, but it is clear enough none the less: when the son of man emerges from his three days and three nights of burial, that will be the sign to this generation, the only sign they will be given. During Jesus' ministry, in other words, there will be nothing to compare with the great event which will immediately follow it; and that event, the resurrection of Jesus himself, will function as the sign that will be sufficient to condemn those who do not believe.

Luke's version of the saying (11.30) is briefer and more cryptic: Jonah became a sign to the people of Nineveh, and in the same way the son of man will be a sign to this generation. A case can be made for seeing this as a deliberate abbreviation of the Matthaean text, in line with Luke's insistence elsewhere that Jesus was raised *on* the third day, not after it.[28] Most, however, prefer to see Matthew's version, with its characteristic theme of the fulfilment of scripture, as the more developed, and Luke's as nearer a hypothetical Q original. But does this mean that Luke's saying has a significantly different meaning from Matthew's?

I think not. The immediately following references to the resurrection both of the Queen of the South and of the people of Nineveh create a presumption that this is the theme of the 'sign' as well.[29] Jonah hardly became a 'sign' simply by, or in, his preaching; nor is it likely that the 'sign' refers to the fact of Jonah's being sent from afar, or even from heaven.[30] The 'sign' can only be a reference to Jonah's extraordinary escape from the

---

26 For the former in the NT, cf. e.g. Jn. 5.29.
27 In what follows I am in implicit dialogue with Catchpole 1993, 241–7.
28 So e.g. McNicol 1996, 181, citing Lk. 9.22; 18.31–33; 24.7, 21.
29 Lk. 11.31, 32, using the two regular NT resurrection verbs *egerthēnai* and *anastēnai*.
30 Fitzmyer 1985, 933–6.

sea-monster.[31] The resurrection of the son of man, seen as future from the perspective of the saying in the mouth of the pre-Easter Jesus, will be the equivalent 'sign'. That Luke at least thought like this seems to be clear from the end of the parable of the rich man and Lazarus: if they do not hear Moses and the prophets, neither will they believe even if someone were to rise from the dead (Luke 16.31, coming not long [95] before Luke's discourse in chapter 17 about the coming son of man).

This is not the place to open a new discussion of 'the son of man' either in Q in general or in this text in particular.[32] But certain comments may be made by way (I hope) of further elucidation of the strong hint of resurrection in this passage.

1 There is more evidence than used to be thought for a messianic understanding of 'son of man' in the Jewish world of the first century. To look no further, the rereading of Daniel 7 in *4 Ezra* 11—12 makes it clear that this was how Daniel 7 as a whole (not just as the passage in which a particular 'title' happens to be found) was being understood in at least some circles.
2 The narrative of Daniel 7, seen through the lens of subsequent martyrology, envisages the suffering of God's people being followed by a mighty act of divine judgment on the oppressors and vindication of the righteous sufferers. We know from the Wisdom of Solomon, 2 Maccabees and elsewhere that the Daniel tradition was among the resources drawn on to spur righteous Israelites to resist compromise and to go to their deaths trusting in God's future vindication.
3 The book of Daniel, specifically its twelfth chapter, became in subsequent Judaism the key text predicting the bodily resurrection. Since the underlying narrative of Daniel 11.33–35 and 12.1–3 has much the same underlying shape as that of Daniel 7.2–14, interpreted first in 7.17–18 and then in 7.19–27, and since we know that both passages were used in subsequent Jewish thinking about martyrdom and vindication, we have reason cautiously to link the apocalyptic vision of chapter 7, in which 'one like a son of man' is exalted, with the future resurrection and exaltation of 'the wise' and 'those who lead many to righteousness' in 12.3.

---

31 Catchpole's suggestion that the 'sign' is actually 'no sign at all' (1993, 245–6) seems to me a subtlety that would have passed by a first-century reader, or indeed a hearer of Jesus.
32 On 'son of man' see Wright 1992a, 291–7; 1996b, 513–19, which I presuppose in what follows. These are of course themselves highly abbreviated and preliminary discussions, but indicate the way I think the topic should be tackled and the evidence that might be adduced.

Without texts that make such a link this would remain purely hypothetical (not that purely hypothetical entities have always been frowned on in New Testament scholarship). It is always risky, in any branch of history, to put together two and two and make five. But when such a hypothetical construct opens up new perspectives on existing texts, there is some reason to pursue it further. And I submit [96] that, read within this context of second-Temple Jewish understandings of the Messiah on the one hand and Israel's vindication after suffering on the other, Q 11.30 makes good sense. It can be seen as a reference to the resurrection of Jesus: a future event, from the fictive perspective of Luke's narrative, that will function as a sign to Jesus' contemporaries, and a past event, from the actual perspective of Q, that was already functioning in that way.[33]

Here, then, is an otherwise missing link in Q between the promise of a future general resurrection and the fact of present raisings from the dead both literal and metaphorical. Though, like the rest of the traditions of Jesus' ministry, both canonical and non-canonical, Q has little to say about Jesus' own resurrection, we may claim to have found not only a text that hints at it but also a wider context within which such a hint may be thought to make sense. It may be, after all, fundamentally appropriate to Q. And maybe Q is not, after all, quite so far away in theology and context from the rest of the New Testament as is sometimes suggested.

Reflections

Nothing that I have said here significantly advances an argument for believing today in Jesus' resurrection. If I am on the right lines, though, an argument that is sometimes advanced against, namely the existence of flourishing groups of Jesus' followers who either did not believe in Jesus' resurrection or did not think it important, begins to look thinner. Does my argument, though, encourage us to believe in Q itself?

I do not think so. If I am right, there is no reason why those who wrote, read and preached from Q would have wanted to deny or downplay Jesus' resurrection. If that is so we face once more the old chestnut of possible overlaps between Mark and Q: why should Q not have contained some of the predictions of the Passion and resurrection that we find in Mark, and in

---

33 Cf. Edwards 1971, 56: 'The Q community . . . understands the resurrection of Jesus as *the* sign which is now of crucial significance in bringing people into the renewed fellowship of the coming Son of Man' (italics original).

the traditions that (as we have been taught) flow from him to Matthew and Luke? Of course, [97] the notion of overlaps between Mark and Q requires a remarkable scholarly imagination: all we know really about Q is that it consists of the parts of Matthew and Luke that do *not* overlap with Mark.

Once we have got in our heads the notion of an existing document, however, it is not so difficult to think of it containing more than we realized, and even of Mark knowing it and responding to it in certain ways.[34] But once we extend our imaginations this far, it is not fanciful to suggest other solutions as well: perhaps Q knew Mark, or pre-Markan tradition? Perhaps Q contained all sorts of things that did not fit the theological or editorial purpose of Luke, or of Matthew, or of both? If so, how would we ever know? If (as I think) Luke used Mark, omitting some parts, editing others and adding considerable material of his own, why should he not have done the same with his other sources as well? But have we not then sawn three parts of the way through the branch we were sitting on?

If, in short, the resurrection of humans in general (in the future), and of Jesus in particular (in the recent past), were known to, and referred to by, Q, what theological reason is there for Q not to have had its own resurrection narrative? There is, of course, no literary reason for supposing that it did. But if either Matthew or Luke had access to a different way of telling that particular story, how would we ever know that one of them had preserved the Q narrative and the other had not? I am driven back to supposing that, though Q may have existed, it is beyond our power to know what it contained: in other words, to a puzzled agnosticism comparable to that which some scholars now profess about the resurrection itself (something may have happened, but we cannot now say what).[35] That is not my position, but it demonstrates the right of scholars to remain puzzled about things that some of their colleagues believe in. You cannot, I suggest, take Q seriously and remain agnostic about the place of the resurrection within the earliest forms of Christianity known to us. But you can take the resurrection seriously and still remain agnostic about Q.

---

34   See Catchpole 1993, 70–8.
35   E.g. Wedderburn 1999.

8

Introduction to the Second Edition of B. F. Meyer, *The Aims of Jesus*

I have written before about my debt to Ben Meyer's *The Aims of Jesus*. The present piece explains why it was important to me, and why I believed in 2002, and still believe, it should be taken as seriously today as when it first appeared forty or so years ago. Scholars like Meyer do not come along every year or two, or even every decade or two. The new books that appear every year, clamouring for attention, ought not to stop either the serious student or the seasoned scholar from going deep into the older books that still deserve it.

[9a] The first time I went to a musical, I didn't know how lucky I was. It was the classic production of *My Fair Lady* in London's West End. The singing and dancing were magic, the action sparkled, the emotional parts were touching but not tacky. It was over forty years ago and I remember it still. But I didn't realize just how brilliant it was until I started going to other musicals. Singers can wobble and warble, dancers are sometimes flat-footed; productions try too hard and end up looking silly or affected. I hit the jackpot first time out, but I didn't appreciate it until much later.

I feel like that now on rereading Ben Meyer's masterpiece, *The Aims of Jesus*. I read it when it appeared, nearly a quarter of a century ago. I had been working on Paul; this was the first serious book on Jesus I read. I knew it was exciting, even then, but only now, looking back, do I realize just how important it was and is. Since the late 1970s there have been dozens of books on Jesus. I have read most of them, and even written one or two myself. Ben Meyer's book is shorter than many, partly because with his pithy prose he could pack whole worlds of meaning into short discussions. But it is head and shoulders above most of them. To be frank, if Meyer's arguments had been taken seriously in the academy, much of the nonsense that has been written about Jesus in the last twenty years, not least by the so-called 'Jesus Seminar', could have been avoided. Looking back, I realize now how lucky I was to soak myself in his thought at a formative stage. He gave me courage and hope to move in paths that many had declared no-go areas. Not only my thinking and scholarship but also, I discover, my preaching has been vitally informed by this book.

Ben was a scholar's scholar. His untimely death robbed us not only of a gentle, wise and witty friend but of a razor-sharp mind and an encyclopaedic range of reading and sympathy. He was astonishingly learned, fluent in many languages ancient and modern, at home with an enormous range of ancient and modern sources. He was master of a writing style that made demands on the reader but always rewarded the effort, sometimes with flashes of impish wit. 'Theology like this', he remarked after quoting a summary of the views of Karl [9b] Hase, 'is driven out only by prayer and fasting, neither of which seems to have figured prominently among the resources of liberalism.'[1] Reimarus, he said, brought to his task 'philological erudition and above all, historical imagination, diseased but alive'.[2] For both the methodically credulous and the methodically sceptical, 'method . . . its feet firmly planted in the air, makes up for the lack of knowledge'.[3] I wish we could have had his comments on the scholarship of the last ten years.

Historical Method

This wit regularly had a point: that much of the Quest for Jesus, both before Schweitzer and after, had made tacit assumptions about what it was doing and how to do it which, when laid bare, made nonsense of the repeated claim to 'objectivity' or 'honesty' and revealed the need for a more rigorous method. 'Historical understanding', he writes robustly, 'is in no sense diminished by rejecting Troeltschean relativism or the panoply of biases epitomized in the claim to be dogma-free.'[4] Meyer showed up, back then, the roots of several theories that continue to be hawked around as though they were both up to date and self-evidently true – such as Holtzmann's obsession with discovering the earliest sources, on the assumption that they would be 'plain and undog-matic' and, as such, offer direct access to the Jesus of history.[5] I think it is safe to claim that Ben Meyer was more aware of where western culture has come from and how its assumptions stack up and how they affect historical and

---

1 Meyer 2002, 99. The quote is from Franz Schnabel.

2 Meyer 2002, 29.

3 Meyer 2002, 84f.

4 Meyer 2002, 20f., on the surplus antithesis of 'honesty versus traditional belief', and the importance of recognizing that people can be honestly wrong. Cf. p. 18.

5 Meyer 2002, 37f.

biblical study, than any other practising New Testament scholar of his genera-tion.[6] He was self-aware as an interpreter, as according to his own theories one needs to be.

He showed that from its inception the 'Quest' had had specifically anti-Christian biases and agendas, but (against Kähler a hun-[9c]-dred years ago, and Luke Timothy Johnson more recently) that this did not absolve Christians from the vital importance of the proper historical study of Jesus. 'The quest for most of its history has been fundamentally if unintentionally un-Christian',[7] he wrote, not least because 'for the questers Enlightenment propaganda had become cultural assumption'.[8] At the same time, however, the Quest has, often despite itself, produced an enormous harvest of good and useable historical insight, not least 'the definitively settled fact that the proclamation and ministry of Jesus were totally eschatological'.[9] The Quest must therefore be continued; it is 'indispensable',[10] but it must be pursued by appropriate and thought-out means.

Ben Meyer's first great and (I hope) lasting contribution in this book is both to highlight the need for a fully articulated historical method and to argue himself for one in particular.[11] He drew deeply on the work of the philosopher Bernard Lonergan; while most New Testament scholars never read philosophy and hermeneutics from one year's end to the next (and so condemn themselves to uncritical assumptions about what they are doing and how it relates to other tasks), Meyer knew what the issues were and where to go for help.[12] He drew on great writers about history such as Collingwood to explain what history is and is not, bringing clarity at every point.

As a critic of the Enlightenment – his cheerful polemic sometimes reads more like the 1990s than the 1970s – Ben was not taking the fashionable route away from the unattainable 'objectivity' and into the postmodern morass of feelings and relativity.[13] There was no [9d] question, for him, of abandoning

---

6   The possible exception (depending on how you classify him) must be A. C. Thiselton, who after years of writing about hermeneutics has now produced a major commentary (Thiselton 2000).

7   Meyer 2002, 56.

8   Meyer 2002, 58.

9   Meyer 2002, 58. Would that the 'Jesus Seminar' had recognized this from the outset.

10 Meyer 2002, 58.

11 He followed this up with two remarkable books, both of which repay close study for their insight into historical method and its application to the New Testament – and into the ways in which much current study was going astray: Meyer 1989; 1994.

12 See Meyer 2002, 16–18 and frequently; and cf. McEvenue and Meyer 1991.

13 For his critique, see e.g. Meyer 2002, 58, 102, 207f. (pointing out the Enlightenment's classic meta-narrative: 'passionate outrage at "superstition" . . . and at persecution for dissident belief'), 248.

the search to find out what really happened, and contenting oneself instead with impressions and guesses. Instead, he laid the foundations of an appropriate critical realism. 'The immediate aim', he wrote, in a passage full of programmatic significance both for himself and for many others, including the present writer, 'is to understand the Jesus of ancient Palestine.'[14] Ironically and remarkably, many of the key figures in the Quest – Strauss, Wrede, Bultmann – 'were not deeply interested in this aim'. There was little 'delight in history as such' in the liberalism within which the Quest flourished. History, after all, is not 'merely the minute examination of gospel data with a view to passing judgments of historicity on them' – this was written, remember, ten years before the 'Jesus Seminar' trumpeted its intention to do just this – but is rather 'reconstruction through hypothesis and verification'. And what the historian is really after is 'interacting intentions': the study of who intended to do what, and the consequences (often unintended) that flowed from their actions.[15]

Again and again the judgments Meyer makes about the past Quest resonate with reality in a way that one can perhaps appreciate only after spending half a lifetime studying the books in question. Critical history must not be atomistic, but must aim at full-blown reconstruction. 'Critical history', he declared, 'has been unambitious', while 'ambitious history' has been 'uncritical'.[16] Thus 'scholars of the Straussian cast, like Wrede or Bultmann', [and, he might have added, the Jesus Seminar] 'make no effort to reconstruct history, whereas the fearless hypotheses of a Reimarus or a Schweitzer [and, he might have added, a Crossan] collapse like playing cards'.[17] His central statement on the 'principles of historical criticism' deserves to be engraved on the hearts and minds of all young scholars learning their trade.[18] The four principles are: history is knowledge (not belief); historical knowledge is inferential (not unmediated); the technique of history is the hypothesis; hypotheses require verification. All this may sound obvious, but a moment's reflection will reveal that much that has called itself 'historical criticism' (and has made huge claims for itself and its results on that basis) has ignored one or more of these principles. [9e]

One of the central achievements of this book was thus to map out in advance a programme for the historical study of Jesus that would be quite different

---

14 Meyer 2002, 19.
15 Meyer 2002, 19. The whole passage is highly significant. It plays out in, for instance, Meyer's insistence on studying *aims* where many earlier scholars studied *titles* (175).
16 Meyer 2002, 24.
17 Meyer 2002, 24.
18 Meyer 2002, 87–92.

from the 'New Quest' of the 1960s.[19] From Meyer on there have been two streams of research. On the one hand, there is the renewed New Quest, still doing the same kind of things as J. M. Robinson articulated in his programmatic 1959 work, and now enshrined in the Jesus Seminar and in the books of its chair and co-chair.[20] On the other, there is what I myself labelled the 'Third Quest'. I confess that this idea almost certainly came from Ben Meyer's careful distinction between what he was doing and what the New Quest had done.[21] The key points of differentiation are in *hermeneutical and historical method* on the one hand and *historical focus* on the other. Despite protests from some of the continuing New Questers that this is a tactic aimed at marginalizing them, the distinctions are real and of continuing importance. Clarity is not served by lumping together everyone who has written about Jesus in the last twenty years as belonging to the Third Quest.[22]

The final chapter of Meyer's Part I is entitled 'History and faith' – a topic fraught with continuing significance. Today we are told by one side that the objective results of an 'honest' historiography pose a fatal challenge to Christian faith in any of its traditional or orthodox forms. We are told simultaneously by the other side that to engage in serious historical study of Jesus is itself a capitulation to the scepticism of the Enlightenment, an attempt to find a secure grounding for faith other than in God himself, a suggestion that instead of the Jesus of the God-given gospels we may substitute a Jesus [9f] we have 'reconstructed' for ourselves.[23] In fifteen evocative pages, Meyer offers a way forward out of this sterile either/or.

'From the beginning', he writes, 'Christian faith has been a confession of events in human history',[24] and we must therefore study these events as such. But this does not mean capitulating to the Enlightenment's prejudices; they are not the only basis for doing history. Faith has its own integrity, and it is of course 'God, not historical data', that 'provides the ground and secures the truth of faith'. But history can and must *instruct* faith, showing that many past understandings of what the gospels were saying are inadequate

---

19 See the programmatic statement at Meyer 2002, 20; the brief exposition at pp. 51–4; and the comment at p. 263 n. 117, explaining the need at the time for the 'New Quest' in order to correct previous near-docetic imbalances. This, Meyer implies, is hardly necessary nowadays.

20 Robinson 1959; Funk and Hoover 1993; Funk 1996; Crossan 1991.

21 Meyer 2002, 20. Meyer himself makes reference to H. Schürrmann's phrase, from an article of 1973: 'the newest questioning'. Would that it were so.

22 On the whole issue, see Wright 1996b, chs. 2 and 3. For the misunderstanding, and widening, of the phrase 'Third Quest' see e.g. Witherington 1995.

23 For the first point, see Funk 1996. For the second, cf. e.g. Johnson 1995; 1999.

24 Meyer 2002, 95.

and misleading. We are thus not wedded to the unending scepticism of the Cartesian tradition. But nor are we unable to make real progress in understanding who Jesus actually was, what the gospels intended to say about him, and how faith might be informed, redirected and, through challenge and question, actually strengthened by such historical investigation. For this, and much beside, the first part of this book earns our continuing gratitude and respect.

Historical Reconstruction

Part II of the book offers an outline sketch, with some areas filled in in considerable detail, of what Meyer believed could and should be said about the Jesus of first-century Palestine. At a time when many New Questers were hardly bothering with the detail of the Jewish world, this book drew not least on the Scrolls, and brought out hidden depths to several themes in Jesus' life and teaching.

Searching for Jesus' 'aims', Meyer located him, and his predecessor John the Baptist, fairly and squarely within the first-century Judaism that was looking for the restoration of Israel. This is what he meant by 'eschatological', though without ruling out a future end-of-the-world dimension. Here and elsewhere he stood firmly on the ground cleared by Joachim Jeremias, who though belonging chronologically within the New Quest must be seen in a quite different light. Meyer's refusal to go along with the vilification of Jeremias in some quarters meant the fracturing of at least one friendship. Meyer knew Jeremias's work like the back of his hand, and knew that the slurs against the master (of pseudo-scholarship on the one hand and **[9g]** anti-Judaism on the other) were without foundation.[25] My own criticism of Meyer at this point would be rather different; that he did not allow sufficiently for the *revolutionary* context of Jesus' proclamation, in terms both of what Jesus' audience would have heard when he spoke of God's kingdom and also of the radical redefinition of the revolutionary aim that he articulated. From time to time Meyer's portrait leans more in the direction of a devotional existentialism.[26] But this is not difficult to correct.

Meyer made a major structural and thematic distinction between the public proclamation of Jesus and the private, 'esoteric' teaching reserved for

---

25 See Meyer 1991; Sanders 1991. Let the reader decide.

26 See the brief discussion of the Zealots and their relation to Jesus in Meyer 2002, 235f. For the question, see Wright 1992a, 170–81; Wright 1996b, chs. 6, 7. By 'a devotional existentialism' I mean the kind of understanding found in e.g. Meyer 2002, 162–4.

the disciples. The heart of the public proclamation was of course the reign (or 'kingdom') of God, and Meyer's exposition of this is central to his whole vision. Here the central insight (pp. 132–4) is that 'the reign of God' and 'the restoration of Israel' are intimately and inextricably connected – a correlation that scholarship should never have forgotten, but which was largely ignored through much of the Quest. Within this setting, Meyer expounds Jesus' healings, his parables, and sayings such as the cryptic word about divorce, bringing out their central meaning: something new is happening, Israel is being restored (albeit not in the way many were expecting), Torah is being shown up as belonging to a period now coming to an end, God is beginning to reign.[27] And, within this, the historian must conclude that Jesus was not unreflective, merely a voice talking about God. The hypothesis Meyer formulates, and then tests, is that 'Jesus understood himself to be the unique revealer of the full, final measure of God's will'.[28] And since the point of his proclamation was 'to bring eschatological Israel into being', this confirms that 'Jesus' world of meaning was eschatological' (that is, believing that God was at last doing all that had been promised), 'that the eschatology had an ecclesial character' (envisaged the coming into being of a 'restored Israel' around Jesus himself) 'and a realized element' (that he was not simply talking about something **[9h]** God was about to do but was speaking of what was happening in and through his own work); and, finally, 'that in his own view Jesus himself belonged to the center of the eschaton as its revealer'.[29] Perhaps if Meyer had written this book at twice the length, spelling all this out and rubbing the noses of the New Testament scholarly guild in it, we might have been spared the continuing popularity of a portrait of Jesus as a non-eschatological teacher who would have been shocked at any community coming into being around him, or of Jesus as merely the (mistaken) prophet of a still-future 'end'. In particular, we might have been spared the agonizing attempt to make Jesus unaware of his own significance, a 'proclaimer' who had no thought of ever being himself 'proclaimed'. As it is, we may hope that the small seeds of such powerful sentences may bear fruit in a new generation.

As with teaching, so with actions. Much has been made in subsequent scholarship of Jesus' table-fellowship with sinners, but most of the important points had already been highlighted by Meyer (pp. 158–62). The major advance of

---

27 Meyer 2002, 144f., 290f. (notes).

28 Meyer 2002, 151.

29 Meyer 2002, 153.

the Third Quest, made centrally thematic in E. P. Sanders's brilliant *Jesus and Judaism*,[30] was the significance of Jesus' actions in the Temple, which provide a central picture within which a good deal of the 'esoteric' teaching can be understood. Meyer here drew on second-Temple Jewish traditions about the rebuilding of the Temple, and showed how Jesus' actions fitted into them. Subsequent debate has now advanced these matters a good deal, but when we revisit Meyer we have the feeling that we heard it here first.[31]

When it comes to the 'esoteric' teaching, Meyer stressed particularly the interconnections between Jewish prophecies of the Temple and its 'copestone' with the Messiah and his followers. 'Copestone signified Messiah, Temple, the messianic remnant of believers.'[32] This leads him into an area where few, even of his fellow Roman Catholics, have followed: a subtle and careful defence of the historicity of Jesus' statement to Peter in Matthew 16. Critical of Bultmann in particular, Meyer used the several tools of classic synoptic criticism to argue for the probability that Jesus did indeed refer to Peter as the 'rock' who would be the foundation of the community: 'The Messiah chose the rock and would build the Temple.'[33] Whatever we think of this particular conclusion – and it cannot simply be wished [9i] away by the general protestant consensus – the grounding of the Jewish hope for a rebuilt Temple on such texts as 2 Samuel 7, read in the light of first-century exegesis as seen in the Scrolls and elsewhere, remains vital. What hangs on it is not so much the place of Peter, but rather Jesus' own self-understanding. Here, for once abandoning his usual subtle understatement, Meyer does his best to ensure even a casual reader gets the point: 'The entry into Jerusalem and the cleansing of the Temple constituted a messianic demonstration, a messianic critique, a messianic fulfillment event, and a sign of the messianic restoration of Israel.'[34]

How then would Jesus achieve his goal? Here Meyer is both deeply suggestive and, in my view, less than fully satisfactory. He argues convincingly that Jesus made his talk about the 'coming of the son of man' the equivalent theme, within his secret teaching to the disciples, to the public theme of God's reign.[35] Yet he never explores the way in which such sayings must have related to the immediately future public and politically charged events of the destruction

---

30 Sanders 1985.
31 On the entry and cleansing: Meyer 2002, 168–70; on its secret meaning: 174–202.
32 Meyer 2002, 193.
33 Meyer 2002, 197.
34 Meyer 2002, 199.
35 Meyer 2002, 209.

of Jerusalem and particularly the Temple. This prevents the fuller integration that, I believe, needs to be sought at this point.[36] Jesus looked ahead, Meyer argues, to a coming separation between those in Israel who trusted what God was saying and doing in and through his work ('faith') and those who did not ('unfaith'). And he understood his own task and vocation, his 'messianic destiny', 'to be scheduled for fulfillment only as the outcome and reversal of repudiation, suffering, and death'. Thus far, I am in agreement. But Meyer never worked this out in the integrated way I believe possible. He points in emphatically the right direction: the combination of interpretative motifs in Jesus' sayings about his death being 'for many', and the cup being 'the new covenant in my blood', indicates that he believed that 'the messianic community to be born of the new covenant' would be 'a people whose sins were forgiven'.[37] And he has a deft way of saying both that Jesus knew he would meet a violent end, giving it a scriptural and theological meaning, and that he did not 'intend' this death after the manner of a Kamikaze suicide: 'Jesus did not aim to be repudiated and killed; he aimed to charge with meaning his being repudiated and killed.'[38] I think we can go further, and integrate Jesus' public proclamation still more closely with his death and the meaning he gave to it (though when I put such a pro-[9j]-posal to Ben in the mid-1980s he was not eager to embrace it); but I do not think we can turn back from the point to which *The Aims of Jesus* took us.[39]

However that may be, Meyer's proposed integration of the various themes in the gospel accounts is impressive, being both original and yet profoundly consistent with the overall thrust of the narratives (in other words, it is not a mere novelty that could be rejected as a scholar's fancy). Jesus believed it was his task to be the 'messianic builder of the house of God'.[40] His own rejection and death would intervene, but the 'coming of the son of man' would mean 'the shepherd's return to the head of the reassembled flock' and the successful building of the new Temple, that is, the community.[41] Though Meyer does not discuss it, this seems to presuppose that Jesus' mission depended for its validation not only on the *parousia* but also on the

---

36 See Wright 1996b, ch. 8.
37 Meyer 2002, 219.
38 Meyer 2002, 218.
39 See Wright 1996b, ch. 12.
40 Cf. too Meyer's collection of essays, developing these themes further, entitled *Christus Faber: The master-builder and the house of God* (Meyer 1992a).
41 Meyer 2002, 221.

resurrection – a pairing which he, like his predecessor Jeremias, never (in my view) satisfactorily integrated.

The other strand which is, I believe, missing from Meyer's work is the origin of the early Christians' belief that in Jesus the one God of Israel had been personally present in their midst. It is perhaps too much to ask that such a question could even have been raised, head-on, in the 1970s. As it was, Ben was already doing many things that people had said could or should not be done, and this might have been a step too far for even sympathetic readers. Yet the question will not go away, not least in the light of his own insistence that the deepest meanings of a historical character's intentions and achievements are found not simply in his or her own recorded words and actions but in the traditions they generate. I do not think that Ben himself would have denied that the human being Jesus of Nazareth was mysteriously to be identified with Israel's one true God; but how that identification could be made in terms that a first-century Palestinian Jew could meaningfully think was not a question he even raised, certainly not in this book.[42]

Meyer's conclusion is striking both in method and content. Over against the much-touted 'criterion of dissimilarity' (which he gives its due in its proper place), he finds 'confirmation' of his primary hypothesis (the integration of Jesus' kingdom-proclamation with the [9k] restoration of Israel) in two obvious places: the biblical and second-Temple texts that spoke of the same thing, and the life and work of early Christianity. If Meyer were writing today, with the 'criterion of dissimilarity' not nearly so strongly held, and scholarship far more ready to see continuity as well as discontinuity between Jesus and the Judaism of his day, he might perhaps have put this material at the start of the book. As it is, it leads naturally into his final section entitled 'Reflection'. Here, granted his previous emphasis on the 'coming of the son of man' as a super-natural end-time moment, he must face the question 'Was Jesus mistaken?', and does so with verve, turning the table on Enlightenment scepticism one more time. Prophets have only limited knowledge, but that knowledge is not 'illusion'; rather, '"illusion" may best of all describe the confident supposition of Enlightenment men that unprejudiced reason provided the exactly right vantage point from which to view and weigh and pronounce on prophecy'.[43] The point is well made, but I still think that if Meyer had worked through the second-Temple material yet once more he might have come to see that Jesus' prophecies of an imminent future had more to do with what we now know as

---

42 See Wright 1996b, ch. 13.

43 Meyer 2002, 248. The book was of course written before the word 'men' became politically incorrect.

the events of AD 70 and less with the *parousia* as traditionally conceived. But that remains controversial. Ben Meyer himself relished debate, and I wish he were still with us to continue this one.

The final 'reflection' sums up what Jesus had been about. His whole career 'was a deliberate, sustained question to Israel: "Who do you say that I am?"'[44] Jesus stood outside the normal modes of Jewish self-expression; he must of course be understood as a first-century Jew but he was 'undeducible from, uncontainable in, the religious ecology of his time'. As a result, 'his life was pellucid but unpardonable and accordingly lent itself to many modes of misconstruction' – which, as Meyer himself would agree, has gone on happening ever since. In the end, however, we may cautiously propose an answer to the question, 'What made Jesus operate in this way, what energized his incorporating death into his mission, his facing it and going to meet it?'[45] The answer is found in the tradition that Jesus generated. In four different strands of the New Testament (Galatians, Ephesians, John and Revelation) we find the early Christians saying that Jesus had acted out of love. Since he himself had proposed love for God and neighbour as the defining mark of his restored [91] Israel, we find ourselves in the presence of an 'authenticity' that 'lies in the coherence between word and deed'.[46] This may seem to some a roundabout, indeed downright cryptic, way of saying that the historical Jesus acted out of love, that love generated his deepest aims. But if you compare Meyer's book with the others available at the time, and with most others written since, you will find it a remarkably bold, yet also a remarkably authentic, historical claim.

Conclusion

Ben Meyer would have been the first to insist that neither this book nor his other writings were beyond correction. His notion of critical realism implied continuing public debate, and he would have accepted that with gracious humility – though taking him on, with his massive arsenal of scholarly resources, was not something to be entered into lightly, unadvisedly or wantonly. But the profound scholarship of this book, the many-layered grasp of method, the interaction with scholars of several traditions and languages, the clear central proposals clearly defended, and the striking and often sharply

---

44   Meyer 2002, 250.

45   Meyer 2002, 252.

46   Meyer 2002, 253. See too Wright 1996b, 604–11.

expressed conclusions – all this means that we are dealing with a book that stands out from the crowd. If ever a book deserved a new lease of life after quarter of a century, this one does. Historical scholarship, not least on the New Testament, could do with some clear thinking about method. Scholarship on Jesus, in particular, could do with some fresh attempts to integrate his public and private words and deeds, the major themes of his life, and the reasons for his death, and in particular the correlation between the community that followed him around Palestine and the community that has claimed to follow him ever since. When such attempts are made, wise thinkers will return to Ben Meyer for help.

9

Kingdom Come: The Public Meaning of the Gospels

When I was invited to give an open lecture at the Annual Meeting of the Society of Biblical Literature in November 2007, I decided to attempt an integration of the themes on which I had been working simultaneously during my time as Bishop of Durham. On the one hand, I was increasingly recognizing that the divisions in the church between those who wanted to save souls for heaven and those who wanted to bring God's kingdom here and now reflected only too well the different ways of reading the four canonical gospels. What I could see going on as a biblical scholar and what I was observing as a bishop went closely together. And in both these interlocked movements I could see a failure to glimpse, in theory or in practice, what it might mean to claim (as the evangelists seem to me to have been doing) that Jesus of Nazareth intended to launch, and was successful in launching, God's kingdom on earth as in heaven – *both* in his public career with all its various aspects *and* in his shocking but scripture-fulfilling death.

These reflections were beginning to indicate to me that mainstream gospel scholarship had been led astray from within the post-Enlightenment world that was trying to fulfil the mandate of the gospel with Jesus himself simply as a back-marker, an advance indication, for the brave new world in which the kingdom of heaven and the kingdoms of the world had been held apart. The present essay, covering and trying to integrate several quite different themes in a way one does not normally attempt in the SBL, thus points forward to several projects that emerged over the subsequent decade: the paperback *How God Became King* (Wright 2012), the collection of essays entitled *God in Public: How the Bible speaks truth to power today* (Wright 2016b) and particularly my Gifford Lectures *History and Eschatology: Jesus and the promise of natural theology* (Wright 2019). Biblical scholars often think and write as though their subject occupied a detached silo, pursuing its 'objective' path from one 'assured result' to another. Political theologians – and indeed ordinary politicians! – regularly ignore the Bible, perhaps because if they did happen to look at a selection of recent scholarship they might only see readings that confirm the very split between gospel and culture, theology and politics, church and world with which they were already only too familiar. I was therefore arguing, in ways I have continued to develop, for an integrated approach to all these questions, for a recognition that they are indeed all interlocked, and for a fresh reading of the gospels that might inform and direct the church's witness in a world where the Enlightenment's attempts to upstage and marginalize the work of the gospel are looking increasingly threadbare.

[29] In his new book, *The Great Awakening*, Jim Wallis describes how, as a young man growing up in an evangelical church, he never heard a sermon on the Sermon on the Mount. That telling personal observation reflects a phenomenon about which I have been increasingly concerned: that much evangelical Christianity on both sides of the Atlantic has based itself on the epistles rather than the gospels, though often misunderstanding the epistles themselves.

Indeed, in this respect evangelicalism has simply mirrored a much larger problem: the entire western church, both catholic and protestant, evangelical and liberal, charismatic and social activist, has not actually known what the gospels are there for.

Matthew, Mark, Luke and John are all in their various ways about God in public, about the kingdom of God coming on earth as in heaven through the public career and the death and resurrection of Jesus. The massive concentration on source- and form-criticism, the industrial-scale development of criteria for authenticity (or, more often, inauthenticity), and the extraordinary inverted snobbery of preferring gnostic sayings-sources to the canonical documents – all stem from, and in turn reinforce, the determination of the western world and church to make sure that the four gospels will not be able to say what they want to say, but will be patronized, muzzled, dismembered and eventually eliminated altogether as a force to be reckoned with.

The central message of all four canonical gospels is that the creator God, Israel's God, is at last reclaiming the whole world as his own, in and through Jesus of Nazareth. That, to offer a riskily broad generalization, is the message of the kingdom of God, which is Jesus' answer to the question, 'What would it look like if God were running this show?'

And at once, in the twenty-first century as in the first, we are precipitated into asking the vital question, 'Which God are we talking about, anyway?' It is quite clear if one reads Christopher Hitchens or Friedrich Nietzsche that the image of 'God running the world' against which they are reacting is the image of a celestial tyrant imposing his will on an unwilling world and unwilling human beings, cramping their style, squashing their individuality and their very humanness, requiring them to conform to arbitrary and hurtful laws and threatening them with dire consequences if they resist. This narrative (which contains a fair amount of secularist projection) serves the Enlightenment's deist agenda, as well as the power-interests of those who would move God to a remote heaven so that they can continue to exploit the world.

But the whole point of the gospels is that the coming of God's kingdom on earth as in heaven is precisely not the imposition of an alien and dehumanizing tyranny, but rather the confrontation of alien and dehumanizing tyrannies with the news of a God – the God recognized in Jesus – who is radically different from them all, and whose inbreaking justice aims at rescuing and restoring genuine humanness. The trouble is that in our flat-Earth political philosophies we know only the spectrum which has tyranny at one end and anarchy at the other, with the present democracies our dangerously fragile way of warding off both extremes. The news of God's sovereign rule inevitably strikes democrats, not just anarchists, as a worryingly long step towards tyranny, as we apply to God and to the gospels the hermeneutic of suspicion that we rightly apply to those in power who assure us they have our best interests at heart. But the story that the gospels tell systematically resists this deconstruction – for three reasons having to do with the integration of the gospel stories both internally and externally.

First, the narrative told by each gospel – yes, in different ways, but in this regard the canonical gospels stand shoulder to shoulder over against the *Gospel of Thomas* and the rest – presents itself as an integrated whole in a way that scholarship has found almost impossible to reflect. Attention has been divided, focusing either on Jesus' announcement of the kingdom and the powerful deeds – healings, feastings and so on – in which it is instantiated, or on his death and resurrection. The gospels have thus been seen [30] either as a social project with an unfortunate, accidental and meaningless conclusion, or as Passion narratives with extended introductions. Thus the gospels, in both popular and scholarly readings, have been regarded either as grounding a social gospel whose naive optimism has no place for the radical fact of the cross, still less the resurrection – the kind of naivety that Reinhold Niebuhr regularly attacked – or as merely providing the raw historical background for the developed, and salvific, Pauline gospel of the death of Jesus. If you go the latter route, the only role left for the stories of Jesus' healings and moral teachings is, as for Rudolf Bultmann, as stories witnessing to the church's faith, or, for his fundamentalist doppelgängers, stories that proved Jesus' divinity rather than launching any kind of programme (despite Luke 4, despite the Sermon on the Mount, despite the terrifying warnings about the sheep and the goats!).

Appeals for an integrated reading have met stiff opposition from both sides: those who have emphasized Jesus' social programme lash out wildly at any attempt to highlight his death and resurrection, as though that would simply legitimate a fundamentalist programme, either catholic or protestant, while those who have emphasized his death and resurrection do their best to anathematize any attempt to continue Jesus' work with and for the poor, as though that might result in justification by works, either actually or at the existentialist meta-level of historical method (Bultmann again, and Gerhard Ebeling and others).

The lesson is twofold.

1 Yes, Jesus did indeed launch God's saving sovereignty on earth as in heaven; but this could not be accomplished without his death and resurrection. The problem to which God's kingdom-project was and is the answer is deeper than can be addressed by a social programme alone.
2 Yes, Jesus did, as Paul says, die for our sins, but his whole agenda of dealing with sin and all its effects and consequences was never about rescuing individual souls *from* the world but about saving humans so that they could become part of his project of saving the world. 'My kingdom is not from this world,' he said to Pilate; had it been, he would have led an armed resistance movement like other worldly kingdom-prophets. But the kingdom he brought was emphatically *for* this world, which meant and means that God has arrived on the public stage and is not about to leave it again; he has thus defeated the forces both of tyranny and of chaos – both of shrill modernism and of fluffy postmodernism, if you like – and established in their place a rule of restorative, healing justice, which needs translating into scholarly method if the study of the gospels is to do proper historical, theological and political justice to the subject-matter.

It is in the entire gospel narrative, rather than any of its possible fragmented parts, that we see that complete, many-sided kingdom-work taking shape. And this narrative, read this way, resists deconstruction into power games precisely because of its insistence on the cross. The rulers of the world behave one way, declares Jesus, but you are to behave another way, because the son of man came to give his life as a ransom for many. We discover that so-called atonement-theology within that statement of so-called political theology. To state either without the other is to resist the integration, the God-in-public narrative, that the gospels persist in presenting.

Second, the gospels demand to be read in deep and radical integration with the Old Testament. Recognition of this point has been obscured by perfectly proper post-Holocaust anxiety about apparently anti-Jewish readings. But we do the gospels no service by screening out the fact that each of them in its own way (as opposed, again, to the *Gospel of Thomas* and the rest) affirms the God-givenness and God-directedness of the entire Jewish narrative of creation, fall, Abraham, Moses, David and so on. The Old Testament is the narrative of how the creator God is rescuing creation from its otherwise inevitable fate, and it was this project, rather than some other, that was brought to successful completion in and through Jesus. The gospels, like Paul's gospel, are to that extent folly to pagans, ancient and modern alike, and equally scandalous to Jews. We gain nothing exegetically, historically, theologically or politically by trying to make the gospels less Jewishly foolish (or vice versa) to paganism and hence less scandalous, in their claim of fulfilment, to Judaism. [31]

Third, the gospels thus demonstrate a close integration with the genuine early Christian hope, which is precisely not the hope for heaven in the sense of a blissful disembodied life after death in which creation is abandoned to its fate, but rather the hope, as in Ephesians 1, Romans 8 and Revelation 21, for the renewal and final coming together of heaven and earth, the consummation precisely of God's project to be savingly present in an ultimate public world. And the point of the gospels is that with the public career of Jesus, and with his death and resurrection, this whole project was decisively inaugurated, never to be abandoned.

From the perspective of these three integrations, we can see how mistaken are the readings of both the neo-gnostic movement that is so rampant today and the fundamentalism that is its conservative analogue. Indeed, if an outsider may venture a guess, I think the phenomenon of the religious right in the USA (we really have no parallel in the UK) may be construed as a clumsy attempt to recapture the coming together of God and the world, which remains stubbornly in scripture but which the Enlightenment had repudiated, and which fundamentalism itself continues to repudiate with its dualistic theology of rapture and Armageddon.

It is as though the religious right has known in its bones that God belongs in public, but without understanding either why or how that might make sense; while the political left in the USA, and sometimes the religious left on both sides of the Atlantic, has known in its bones that God would make radical personal moral demands as part of his programme of restorative justice, and has caricatured his public presence as a form of tyranny in order to evoke the cheap and gloomy Enlightenment critique as a way of holding that challenge at bay.

The resurrection of Jesus is to be seen not as the proof of Jesus' uniqueness, let alone his divinity – and certainly not as the proof that there is a life after death, a heaven and a hell (as though Jesus rose again to give prospective validation to Dante or Michelangelo!) – but as the launching within the world of space, time and matter of that God-in-public reality of new creation called God's kingdom, which, within thirty years, would be announced under Caesar's nose openly and unhindered. The reason those who made that announcement were persecuted is, of course, that the fact of God acting in public is deeply threatening to the rulers of the world in a way that Gnosticism in all its forms never is. The Enlightenment's rejection of the bodily resurrection has for too long been allowed to get away with its own rhetoric of historical criticism – as though nobody until Gibbon or Voltaire had realized that dead people always stay dead – when in fact its non-resurrectional narrative clearly served its own claim to power, presented as an alternative eschatology in which world history came to its climax not on Easter Day but with the storming of the Bastille and the American Declaration of Independence.

Near the heart of the early chapters of Acts we find a prayer of the church facing persecution, and the prayer makes decisive use of one of the most obviously political of all the psalms. Psalm 2 declares that though the nations make a great noise and fuss and try to oppose God's kingdom, God will enthrone his appointed king in Zion and thus call the rulers of the earth to learn wisdom from him. This point, which brings into focus a good deal of Old Testament political theology, is sharply reinforced in the early chapters of the Wisdom of Solomon.

Psalm 2 also appears at the start of the gospel narratives, as Jesus is anointed by the spirit at his baptism. Much exegesis has focused on the christological meaning of 'son of God' here; my proposal is that we should focus equally, without marginalizing that Christology, on the political meaning. The gospels constitute a call to the rulers of the world to learn wisdom in service to the messianic son of God, and thus they also provide the impetus for a freshly biblical understanding of the role of the 'rulers of the world' and of the tasks of the church [32] in relation to them. I have three points to make on all this.

First, it is noteworthy that the early church, aware of prevailing tyrannies both Jewish and pagan, and insisting on exalting Jesus as lord over all, did not reject the God-given rule even of pagans. This is a horrible disappointment, of course, to post-Enlightenment liberals, who would much have preferred the early Christians to have embraced some kind of holy anarchy with no place for any rulers at all. But it is quite simply part of a creational view of the world that God wants the world to be ordered, not chaotic, and that human power-structures are the God-given means by which that end is to be accomplished – otherwise those with muscle and money will always win, and the poor and the widows will be trampled on afresh. This is the point at which Colossians 1 makes its decisive contribution over against all dualisms which imagine that earthly rulers are a priori a bad thing (the same dualisms that have dominated both the method and the content of much biblical scholarship). This is the point, as well, at which the notion of the common good has its contribution to make. The New Testament does not encourage the idea of a complete disjunction between the political goods to be pursued by the church and the political goods to be pursued by the world outside the church, precisely for the reason that the church is to be seen as the body through whom God is addressing and reclaiming the world.

To put this first point positively, the New Testament reaffirms the God-given place even of secular rulers, even of deeply flawed, sinful, self-serving, corrupt and idolatrous rulers like Pontius Pilate, Felix, Festus and Herod Agrippa. They get it wrong and they will be judged, but God wants them in place because order, even corrupt order, is better than chaos. Here we find, in the gospels, in Acts and especially in Paul, a tension that cannot be dissolved without great peril. We in the contemporary western world have all but lost the ability conceptually – never mind practically – to affirm that rulers are corrupt and to be confronted yet are God-given and to be obeyed. That sounds to us as though we are simultaneously to affirm anarchy and tyranny. But this merely shows how far our conceptualities have led us again to muzzle the texts in which both stand together. How can that be?

The answer comes – and this is my second point – in such passages as John 19 on the one hand and 1 Corinthians 2 and Colossians 2 on the other. The rulers of this age inevitably twist their God-given vocation – to bring order to the world – into the satanic possibility of tyranny. But the cross of Jesus, enthroned as the true son of God as in Psalm 2, constitutes the paradoxical victory by which the rulers' idolatry and corruption are confronted and overthrown. And the result, as in Colossians 1.18–20, is that the rulers are reconciled, are in some strange sense reinstated as the bringers of God's wise order to the world, whether or not they would see it that way. This is the point at which Romans 13 comes in, not as the validation of every programme that every ruler dreams up, certainly not as the validation of how democratically elected governments of one country decide to act in relation to other countries, but as the strictly limited proposal, in line with Isaiah's recognition of Cyrus, that the creator God uses even those rulers who do not know him personally to bring fresh order and even rescue to the world. This also lies behind the narrative of Acts.

This propels us to a third, perhaps unexpected and certainly challenging reflection that the present political situation is to be understood in terms of the paradoxical lordship of Jesus himself. From Matthew to John to Acts, from Colossians to Revelation, with a good deal else in between, Jesus is hailed as already the lord of both heaven and earth, and in particular as the one through whom the creator God will at last restore and unite all things in heaven and on earth. And this gives sharp focus to the present task of earthly rulers. Until the achievement of Jesus, a biblical view of pagan rulers might have been that they were charged with keeping God's creation in order, preventing it from lapsing into chaos. Now, since Jesus' death and resurrection (though this was of course anticipated in the Psalms and the Prophets), their task is to be seen from the other end of the telescope. Instead of moving forward from creation, they are to look forward (however unwillingly or unwittingly) to the ultimate eschaton. In other words, God will one day right all wrongs through Jesus, and earthly rulers, whether or not they acknowledge this Jesus and [33] this coming kingdom, are entrusted with the task of anticipating that final judgment and that final mercy. They are not merely to stop God's good creation from going utterly to the bad. They are to enact in advance, in a measure, the time when God will make all things new and will once again declare that it is very good.

All this might sound like irrationally idealistic talk – and it is bound to be seen as such by those for whom all human authorities are tyrants by another name – were it not for the fact that along with this vision of God working through earthly rulers comes the church's vocation to be the people through whom the rulers are to be reminded of their task and called to account. We see this happening throughout the book of Acts and on into the witness of the second-century apologists – and, indeed, the witness of the martyrs as well, because martyrdom (which is what happens when the church bears witness to God's call to the rulers and the rulers shoot the messenger because they don't like the message) is an inalienable part of political theology. You can have as high a theology of the God-given calling of rulers as you like, as long as your theology of the church's witness, and of martyrdom, matches it stride for stride.

This witness comes into sharp focus in John 16.8–11. The spirit, declares Jesus, will prove the world wrong about sin, righteousness and judgment – about judgment because the ruler of this world is judged. How is the spirit to do that? Clearly, within Johannine theology, through the witness of the church, in and through which the spirit is at work. The church will do to the rulers of the world what Jesus did to Pilate in John 18 and 19, confronting him with the news of the kingdom and of truth, deeply unwelcome and indeed incomprehensible though both of them were. Part of the way in which the church will do this is by getting on with, and setting forward, those works of justice and mercy, of beauty and relationship, that the rulers know ought to be flourishing but which they seem powerless to bring about. But the church, even when faced with overtly pagan and hostile rulers, must continue to believe that Jesus is the lord before whom they will bow and whose final sovereign judgment they are called to anticipate. Thus the church, in its biblical commitment to 'doing God in public', is called to learn how to collaborate without compromise (hence the vital importance of common-good theory) and to critique without dualism.

In particular, as one sharp focus for all this, it is vital that the church learn to critique the present workings of democracy itself. I don't simply mean that we should scrutinize voting methods, campaign tactics or the use of big money within the electoral process. I mean that we should take seriously the fact that our present glorification of democracy emerged precisely from Enlightenment dualism – the ban-[34]-ishing of God from the public square and the elevation of vox populi to fill the vacuum, which we have seen to be profoundly inadequate when faced with the publicness of the kingdom of God. And we should take very seriously the fact that the early Jews and Christians were not terribly interested in the process by which rulers came to power, but were extremely interested in what rulers did once they had obtained power. The greatest democracies of the ancient world, those of Greece and Rome, had well-developed procedures for assessing their rulers once their term of office was over if not before, and if necessary for putting them on trial. Simply not being re-elected (the main threat to politicians in today's democracies) was nowhere near good enough. When Kofi Annan retired as General Secretary of the United Nations, one of the key points he made was that we urgently need to develop ways of holding governments to account. That is a central part of the church's vocation, which we should never have lost and desperately need to recapture.

All this, of course, demands as well that the church itself be continually called to account, since we in our turn easily get it wrong and become part of the problem instead of part of the solution. That is why the church must be *semper reformanda* as it reads the Bible, especially the gospels. Fortunately, that's what the gospels are there for, and that's what they are good at, despite generations of so-called critical methods which sometimes seem to have been designed to prevent the gospels from being themselves. Part of the underlying aim of this essay is to encourage readings of the Bible which, by highlighting the publicness of God and the gospel, set in motion those reforms that will enable the church to play its part in holding the powers to account and thus advancing God's restorative justice.

10

Whence and Whither Historical Jesus Studies in the Life of the Church?

In the spring of 2010 the annual Theological Conference at Wheaton College, Illinois, was devoted to a discussion of my work, focusing particularly on Jesus and Paul. As well as responding to paper-presenters from various perspectives, I was asked to give two set-piece lectures explaining how I had come into the study of Jesus and Paul and where I saw those studies going. The present paper, on 'historical Jesus studies', was intended not least as a kind of oblique response to the implicit criticism of historical-Jesus work that I had detected in the symposium entitled *Seeking the Identity of Jesus: A pilgrimage*, edited by Beverly R. Gaventa and Richard B. Hays (Grand Rapids, MI: Eerdmans, 2008). I had presented a response to that book at the Society of Biblical Literature Annual Meeting in Boston in November 2008, trying to draw attention to the gulf I had perceived between historical and theological approaches to Jesus, and to the dangers of allowing this split to widen, as it seemed to me the book in question was doing. In particular, I was reacting against the repeated suggestion that to study Jesus historically is to go 'behind the text' in some sense, of which – for whatever reason – we should be suspicious, as though the text itself created its own private world rather than referring to the real, public world and to Jesus within it.

The intention had been that Richard Hays and I would be able to discuss the issues in depth. Sadly, a family funeral meant that he had to leave before that discussion could take place. We have since remedied this with a full joint seminar in St Andrews; but the present statement will, I hope, enable others to see the relevant issues from the point of view that has been foundational to my work for over forty years.

The Wheaton conference had an air of unreality for me, in that, while I was being introduced everywhere as 'Bishop of Durham', only two or three close friends knew that I had, immediately before the conference, submitted my resignation from that office to Her Majesty the Queen, consequent on my appointment at St Andrews.

[115] Introduction

In expressing my gratitude – indeed, amazement – at the favour shown to me in having this conference devoted to discussion of my work, I suppose the best way I can demonstrate that gratitude is by trying to engage with at least some of the issues that have been raised. I am hoping to do so in more specific detail elsewhere, but I want now to speak about where the studies of Jesus in his historical context came from in the last century, how I became involved in that project and where the major problems today seem to me to lie. These are problems both for the academy and for the church, and doubly so therefore for those of us who have tried to straddle the two.

The back story of the historical study of Jesus is by now almost as well known as the story of Jesus himself, but there are none the less one or two things that need to be said by way of reminder. When I was doing historical-Jesus study, it seemed like the natural next thing to be doing in terms of what I'd done to that point. My story may be unusual in some respects, but we all in the western world go back to the great historical works of the last three centuries. You can ignore them if you like, but that means you're going to be reinventing the wheel. Better to engage with them. But when we do engage with the scholarship and church life of the last few centuries, in much of western Protestantism, [116] and indeed Catholicism, we find that the church seemed to operate with a split-level Jesus. When reading the stories in the gospels, everyone knew they referred to an actual man who lived and taught and died in the first century; but then there was this 'Jesus' to whom they prayed, to whom they sang hymns, whom they encountered in the sacraments. But this figure, though known as Jesus, seemed to float free of historical attachment, so much so that when Geza Vermes published his book *Jesus the Jew* in 1973, the very title came as a shock. Faith seemed to be confronted by history in a rather brutal fashion.

When we think of the dominant theological and biblical studies of the first half of the twentieth century, the point is clear: the neo-Kantian Lutheranism that had characterized Bultmann and his successors had set its face against history as such. Bultmann was indeed a great scholar, for all that I, like many others, disagree radically with him. He worked out a remarkably compre-hensive picture of how early Christianity might have been; we need people who have big visions, even if they need to be corrected. In Bultmann's case, we are dealing with a particular kind of Lutheranism, and, while Lutheranism has great strengths, like all traditions it also has blind spots. For Bultmann, right through, history was a dangerous place because it encouraged people to think they could seize control of their own destiny. History thus became antithetical to grace; we must avoid doing too much history, so that grace can still be grace. For Lutherans the framework is often that of the 'two kingdoms' theology: the kingdom of this world and the kingdom of God are separate spheres. For all Bultmann's tradition spoke of its work in terms of historical criticism, its aim was profoundly anti-historical: to use an imagined historical science to keep 'history' well away from 'faith': to keep the two kingdoms of God and the world well apart, to reinforce the perception of a three-decker universe that would keep heaven and earth at a safe distance from one another, and to prevent Christian faith from basing itself on history and so turning itself into a 'work'. It was not, in other words, the neutral, detached historical enterprise that many imagined, designed to discover 'what actually happened'.

There is a particular irony here. The German New Testament scholar-[117]-ship that gave itself to this anti-historical agenda was picked up by many in Britain and America who, despite Bultmann's insistence that presuppositionless exegesis is impossible, hailed his results and indeed his methods as though they were indeed neutral and objective, 'the assured results of criticism'. This was common coin when I was an undergraduate. By the time I was teaching, my own students were expected to know all this, so I had to tell them about the whole tradition of scholarship, even though I was anxious about it from many angles, philosophical and cultural as well as theological and historical. The methods were not, after all, neutral. The source-criticism of the nineteenth and early twentieth centuries, though asking a perfectly fair question (can we trace the route by which literary dependence among the gospels travelled?), was done in such a way as to produce enough 'historical Jesus' to sustain a kind of liberal protestant faith, but to screen out some of the more sharp-edged aspects of the whole portrait. Similarly, Bultmann's method of form-criticism, though asking a perfectly fair question (how did the early traditions of Jesus come to take the shape in which we find them in the gospels?), was not neutral or objective, but was done in such a way as to produce the kind of results Bultmann and others were after within their philosophical, cultural and theological setting. Thus, in Germany after the First World War, there was a strong push to give up the idea of great, heroic leaders such as the Kaiser and Bismarck and to concentrate instead on *die Gemeinde*, 'the community'. The Weimar Republic did not, of course, last long, and indeed it gave rise to the most dangerous of all European 'great, heroic leaders', but it was precisely at that time that Bultmann was arguing his view, that the gospels do not give us a picture of Jesus as the big leader but rather of *die Gemeinde* at prayer, at witness and so on. Thus the Germany of the 1920s left a lasting intellectual legacy, a programme of scholarly reading of the gospels in which the quest was on, precisely not for Jesus himself, but for *die Gemeinde*, the early community of Christian faith. The gospels were therefore to be read as testimony, not to Jesus himself (why would anybody want that?) but to the church's life of faith. As for Jesus himself, it was obvious, from within the two-kingdoms theology, that Jesus could not have been announcing [118] a political message. He was obviously (to them) teaching something existential, something timeless, inculcating a spirituality, a conversion and ultimately a salvation, but not something that would impinge on this-worldly political and social reality. Once we locate Bultmann and his methods within the world of his own day, it all makes sense.

I might comment that this, perhaps, was what Bultmann and others really were called to say in their own day. It is not for us to comment too caustically on tough decisions taken by brave individuals in hard times. But we should not imagine for a moment that this was a neutral, objective, set-in-stone-for-all-time kind of scholarship. Anything but. (Any more than mine or anyone else's is neutral and objective!)

This was a step away from an earlier German scholarship in which serious history had flourished. Ancient historians have always protested against that kind of reading of the period. Ed Sanders, in a recent article, writes that up until the First World War German scholarship (he had Deissmann and others in mind) was producing some splendid and solid work on Jewish and greco-roman history which really did enable one to understand Jesus and early Christianity in its proper historical setting; but that the dominance of Bultmann after the war all but put a stop to that movement. It is now time, says Sanders, to get back to proper history. And I agree. But the legacy of this movement has been a nervous belief among many to this day: the belief that the New Testament can only tangentially, as it were, give us access to Jesus himself. I see this as like the pseudo-problem of the hare and the tortoise, according to which the hare can never actually overtake the tortoise, since all it can do is continually halve the distance between itself and its slower neighbour. But, just as we all know that the hare does in fact overtake the tortoise, so we should recognize not only that the four canonical gospels were written in order to give the readers access to Jesus himself, not simply to the early Christian faith about him, but that they really do so in fact. The evidence, as I have argued at length elsewhere, is overwhelming. I do think that the sources tell us more than simply various things about the people that wrote them; they tell us about the things that were actually going on. It's not enough to say that 'Matthew tells us about Matthew's community and his theology, so we can't be sure [119] whether it tells us about Jesus'. No: remember the hare and the tortoise. This is an optical illusion. Of course writers tell you a lot about themselves, whatever they're talking about. You have to read them critically, but you have to be a realist as well. So: critical realism.

This, I suggest, is enormously important for the church's mission and apologetic. Remember the slogan of Melanchthon in the sixteenth century: it isn't enough to know that Jesus is a saviour; I must know that he is the saviour *for me*. I agree with Melanchthon, but I think we have to say it the other way round as well. We must today stress that it isn't enough to believe that Jesus is 'my saviour' or even 'my lord'; *you must know who Jesus himself was and is*. Without that, merely saying that I have Jesus 'within my heart' or that I 'have a sense that Jesus loves me' or whatever can easily turn into mere fantasy, wish-fulfilment. That has happened before, and it will happen again, unless it's earthed in actual historical reality. As a pastor, I am only too well aware of the problem of serious self-deception: more than one priest, defending indefensible actions, has said that he or she sensed the presence of Jesus, apparently endorsing their scandalous behaviour. It's not enough to say you feel something, even the presence of Jesus, very strongly. Lots of people feel all sorts of things very strongly. In order to know that you're not just making it up, not fooling yourself – and if you don't think that's a danger, your sceptical friends ought to tell you – you must be able to say that this Jesus, whom we know in prayer, this Jesus we meet when we are ministering to the poorest of the poor, this Jesus we recognize in the breaking of the bread, this Jesus is the same Jesus who lived and taught and loved and died and rose again in the first century. We must believe and confess that he did indeed inaugurate God's kingdom, die to bring it about and rise again to launch the consequent new creation. We must know who Jesus himself actually was and is. Generations of sceptics have swept Jesus aside in their efforts to prove that Christianity is a dangerous delusion. Richard Dawkins is only one of many examples. We have to be able to provide proper, well-grounded answers.

This is, if you like, the personal version of the larger point that Ernst Käsemann made in the 1950s: if we don't do historical-Jesus re-[120]-search, difficult though it may be, we are helpless against the ideology that manufactures a new Jesus to suit its own ends. When German scholarship wasn't doing historical-Jesus study in the 1920s and 1930s, Hitler's tame theologians were able to invent an Aryan Jesus, a non-Jewish Jesus, and nobody in Bultmann's tradition could stop them. It won't do to respond, as some have done, by saying, 'You ask me how I know who he is? He is who he is in the tradition of the church!' That is precisely the point that has been radically challenged over the last two hundred years, and to ignore that challenge, or wave it away as irrelevant, is to court disaster. You have to do the history, otherwise the church can be dangerously deceived. As John Calvin said, the human mind is a perpetual factory of idols. And one of those idols, those home-made gods, can be named 'Jesus' – not least by those who claim to be canonical or orthodox Christians. How are we going to prevent that happening?

This personal point came home for me when I found myself, as a young preacher thirty years ago, wrestling with texts in the quiet of my study and wondering what to say about them. I was faced with the constant problem that most of the commentaries I had been given to study, and many of the lecturers to whom I had listened, had made the rejection of this or that saying, this or that deed in the gospels, the touchstone of genuine, 'sophisticated' scholarship. You had to be able to say 'Jesus didn't really say this or that', or 'Of course Jesus never actually walked on water', or 'Jesus couldn't have thought of himself as divine because he was a first-century Jewish monotheist'; these were your passports to a world where you were taken seriously as a critical scholar. The result was that many of my contemporaries in seminary and elsewhere, training to be preachers, simply shut off their critical minds once they left college and went off to preach the old simple gospel they had learned long before. That, I guess, may be better than nothing when faced with questions to which one could not discover answers for oneself. But how much better it would have been, and is, to engage with the real questions and come through to real answers.

For myself, I found myself incapable of saying in the pulpit, 'As Jesus said, . . .' without asking myself the question, *But did he?* And I found [121] myself unwilling to say in that same pulpit, 'Some scholars say he said it; some say he didn't.' I know that some young clergy in the 1960s and 1970s were only too eager to share their professors' doubts with their congregations, but that seemed to me profoundly counter-intuitive. That isn't going to help most congregations most of the time. Should I then only preach from texts of whose historical value I had no doubt? Perhaps, but that could only ever be a stopgap. Nor was I prepared (despite what some of my own critics have said) to play the fundamentalist trump-card: 'The Bible says it.' I have always had a very high theology of the Bible, but I have always regarded that as setting the questions, not establishing the answers. (On this, see *Scripture and the Authority of God* [Wright 2011b].) The stronger your theology of scripture, I believe, the more the historical question ought to be pressed, precisely because Matthew, Mark, Luke and John do *not* appear to be saying 'Welcome to our non-historical storytelling world' but 'Here is a powerful lens through which to make sense of the events that actually happened in our midst'.

I did not know, in the late 1970s and early 1980s as I was wrestling with these questions, how strongly Ernst Käsemann (whose commentary on Romans I had devoured, though not I hope uncritically) had mounted a protest, thirty years earlier, against the non-historical readings of the previous German generation. Käsemann, to be sure, saw the difficulties of offering a properly historical account of Jesus himself, but as I said a moment ago he saw equally clearly the problems that had been caused by not making the effort. Käsemann was (from my point of view) fighting this battle with at least one hand tied behind his back, not only because of the legacy of earlier German *Wissenschaft* and the academic imperative to build on it, but also because he too was operating within a theological framework in which the first-century Jewish notion of God's kingdom was more or less out of reach. Instead, he and his contemporaries imagined Jesus to be talking about 'the near God' as opposed to a far-off deity, as though Jesus were trying to persuade his Jewish contemporaries not to be eighteenth-century deists. Käsemann's announcement of a programme thus far exceeded his ability to launch it successfully. But his programme remains important: without history there is no guarantee that the church will not reinvent yet more Jesus-figures, which turn [122] out to be projections or embodiments of this or that ideology.

That remains my main worry about the appeal to canon or tradition over against history. I believe in canon, and I believe in the holy spirit. But history has shown again and again that the church is well capable of misreading the canon, and that tradition can drift in many directions, some less than helpful, some decidedly destructive. To appeal to tradition and dogma as the framework for understanding Jesus is to say that not only the entire enterprise of biblical scholarship but also the entire protestant Reformation has been based on a mistake. Some may find it strange to hear me defending either of these (critical scholarship and the protestant Reformation!), but if the alternative is to say simply that tradition has got it mostly right I reply that the history of the church tells a very different story. It is that position, applied in moral and pastoral theology, that has landed the contemporary church (particularly, but not only, the Roman Catholic church) in some of its worst current dilemmas.

Käsemann's agenda was thus always going to be held back by his own academic and intellectual context. But help was at hand from a quarter to which, even after the war, he and his contemporaries had not expected to look: the freshly studied world of first-century Judaism. This, from one angle at least, is where I myself came in.

I had first felt a flutter of excitement in Jesus himself as a real, human figure of actual history when I heard the rock musical *Jesus Christ Superstar* in 1971. I still think it contains among the best lyrics Tim Rice ever wrote, and for that matter some of the least banal music Andrew Lloyd Webber ever penned, but that wasn't the reason for the fascination. For the first time I realized that it was possible to ask the question, 'What was Jesus actually thinking about?' I suppose that up till then I had taken it for granted that because he was the son of God he went through life unreflectively, going off to die for the sins of the world as a kind of supernatural robot. The thought that Jesus might have struggled with vocational questions – 'What am I supposed to be doing?' 'How ought I to address this next problem?' 'What is it going to be all about?' – these were fascinating possibilities. The musical evoked Jesus as a real person *who faced, and made, real and hard choices*. Some of [123] those, I believed, were misrepresented (the idea of Jesus, tired after a long day's healing, suddenly losing his temper and having to be soothed by Mary Magdalene – this belongs in a Dan Brown novel, not in history), but others seemed not to be. Tim Rice had caught the real dilemma of Gethsemane. He managed to express vividly, too, the clash between the disciples' expectations and Jesus' vision of God's kingdom, power and glory.

Haunted by all this, and by the fascinating questions it raised, I turned away into a decade of studying Paul, approaching questions of first-century Judaism through the lens of Romans 9—11 in particular. I recall a colleague in Merton College, Oxford, in the mid-1970s, asking me if there was a good recent book about Jesus in his historical context, and my having to confess that there didn't seem to be one. (Vermes's work seemed then, and seems to me still, best summed up in Henry Chadwick's verdict: 'A Rather Pale Galilean'.) But towards the end of that period, while completing my doctorate and teaching and pastoring in Cambridge, I read two books that rekindled my interest, one because it was massive and (mostly) wrong, the other because it was dense and (mostly) right. Schillebeeckx's *Jesus* projected a humanitarian Christology on to a fictive screen of source-criticism and 'discovered' the answer it started with. Ben Meyer's *The Aims of Jesus* possessed a philosophical sophistication and attention to first-century sources that was then without rival or peer, and has largely remained so. It was from Meyer that I learned critical realism, from Meyer too that I and many others learned that several Jesus-sayings that Bultmannian criticism had swept aside fitted like a key in a lock within the world of first-century Judaism. Once one had got over the obviously flawed 'criterion of dissimilarity', which by itself would have rendered a Jesus who was merely a freak, the exploration of the Jewish world, in a way that left Vermes more or less standing at the starting-gate, formed a rich context for exploring not so much 'whether Jesus could have said this or that' but the question, 'Supposing Jesus said this or that, what would that have meant at the time?' leading to the question, 'So what *did* Jesus mean at the time? What was he wanting to get across to his hearers? What was he trying to accomplish? What, in short, were his *aims*?' [124]

I think what was particularly liberating about this question was the recognition that Jesus was not simply telling people how to get to heaven. Most of Jesus' teaching, of course, doesn't look as though that's what he's saying, though his central slogan, 'God's kingdom', had for so long been understood in that way that it was almost impossible for Protestants, whether conservative evangelicals or radical Bultmannians, to hear anything else. I suspect, in fact, I was the more prepared to listen to Meyer because, in the mid-1970s, I had come to believe, as a matter of exegesis, that Paul had been saying far more than 'Here's how to go to heaven'. The so-called 'new perspective' was part of the same wave of studies as the Third Quest (which label, by the way, is justified particularly by Meyer's clear, detailed and sharp distinction between the post-Bultmannian New Quest and the kind of work he himself was doing, and which I picked up). Rather, I and others were becoming fascinated by the question, 'If Jesus wasn't simply saying, "Here's how to go to heaven when you die", what was he saying?' Why did some find his message utterly compelling, and why did others find it so dangerous and threatening that they determined to have him killed?

It was with those questions in mind that I arrived at McGill in the early 1980s and found myself, in late 1982, teaching an introductory course on the New Testament. I began, as you would expect with someone of my background (in classics and philosophy), with two streams of lectures, alternating between the ancient world of the Middle East from the Maccabees to John the Baptist and the modern world of critical scholarship from the mid-eighteenth century to the present. The two strands were designed to meet in the first chapters of the gospels, and when they did I found that I at least had become fascinated (I can't speak for the students) by the sweep and power and frustration of the Jewish story of the period and the way in which the different movements (scribes, Pharisees, Essenes and so on) appeared not nearly so much as 'religious' or 'philosophical' teachers but as people with an agenda, a programme about the national expectation and hope, a desire for God to act again and to do so decisively, a longing for a new Passover, a new exodus, a real 'return from exile' (though I didn't appreciate the [125] significance of that point until later). Whatever historical criticism might say about the gospels themselves, the story up to the mid-20s of the first century could be understood, from many sources and particularly of course Josephus, in a rich, multi-layered unity of history, hope, faith, worship, scriptural reflection, political intrigue, empire, revolution, taxes and crucifixions. Herod the Great fitted extremely well into this world; so did Hillel and Shammai, Samias and Pollio, Judas the Galilean, and the other figures about whom we know far, far less than Jesus of Nazareth but whose motives, beliefs, aims and objectives we can study – *not* as figures who live only in a story, whether that of Josephus or those of the later rabbis, but as persons within actual history. The hare easily and obviously overtakes the tortoise: the historian really does know about Herod himself, not simply about 'Josephus's narrative of Herod' or whatever. Nobody objects, when people write books about Hillel, that they are 'constructing a Hillel behind the text' and thus falsifying some cast-iron principle either of literary criticism or Jewish faith. To be sure, Josephus does construct a narrative of Herod and the rest, and the wise historian takes full account of what Josephus is trying to do. To be sure, there are many points in all such historical work where the same historian admits that the conclusions are only tentative. But that it is possible to write *about Hillel*, not just about other people's ideas of him, the historian has no doubt.

My course reached John the Baptist. Here too there was no problem. Indeed, once we'd understood the Herodian legacy on the one hand, the Roman objectives in the Middle East on the other, and the ordinary Jewish aspirations in the middle, John fitted into the context exactly. Indeed, he came up in three dimensions, not just as a 'voice in the wilderness', a disembodied prophetic word, but as a man with a mission and a hope. God was going to come and be king. Everything was going to be different. And by now we were treading on the sacred turf, not any longer of Josephus or the Scrolls or the rabbinic traditions, but of the gospels themselves. I remember thinking, when I got to that point in the lectures, *Is there any reason why we shouldn't go on doing the same kind of thing, in relation to Jesus and the gospels, that we have been doing with the Jewish sources?* The answer was clear: of course not. Jesus [126] was a figure within history, and the sense that he made he made within that history. He wasn't floating free somewhere in mid-air. He was precisely living in the middle of it all. The Word became *flesh*. A canonical Christian is presumably committed to that point. Were we about to be warned off by the anxious thought-police of the split-level world, insisting not only that one should not, today, allow one's faith to be sullied by history but also that the gospels weren't committing that crime either? Were we only to be allowed to speak of Matthew's (or the others') *narratives about* John the Baptist or Jesus, rather than John or Jesus themselves? I saw no reason to give such objections any space. If we could read the Jewish story from the Maccabees to the Baptist by using all the available historical sources (including coins, archaeology and so on, as well as literary remains), why shouldn't we go on doing so? Could we not at least make the thought-experiment of supposing that the story really *did* make historical sense – but not the historical sense of a Jesus telling people about a 'near God' as opposed to a distant one, or about 'how to go to heaven', but something that would be far more relevant and urgent to his Jewish contemporaries, something that actually enabled the parables and deeds of power to stand up straight at last, something that would be both compelling and crucifiable in that first-century world? That was the movement of my own thinking, out of which, over a decade later, there emerged *Jesus and the Victory of God*.

As I stepped out of the boat of safe, sanitized, 'critical' scholarship in answer to this strange summons, I had no sense at all of going 'behind the text' to a Jesus the texts had falsified or skewed. Rather, I had, and still have, the sense of discovering *the Jesus the gospels had been talking about all along* but whom the long tradition of western misreadings (catholic and protestant, conservative and radical) had failed or even refused to see. As a scientific historian using the hypothesis-and-verification method, I was keen to include the data within the big picture. Only in a determinedly anti-historical world could it be supposed that *leaving out lots of evidence* could be a virtue in a historian. Of course, the post-Bultmannian picture of the early church as the cheerful factory for 'fake' Jesus sayings has had a long run for its money, but the more we know about the early Christians the less, in fact, it appears that they made [127] up Jesus-sayings to suit their own new contexts. Nowhere in the gospels does Jesus address the key problems we know from Paul to have preoccupied the early church. The obvious example is circumcision.

Reflecting on this false either/or (Jesus 'within the gospels' versus Jesus 'behind the gospels') led me, and leads me still, to reflect that the real-history Jesus was a *public* figure making a *public* announcement. To be sure, as Ben Meyer had rightly pointed out, the Jesus of the gospels seems to have taught at two levels, speaking widely to the crowds and intimately to his close associates. But the content of his message was not private individual spirituality or salvation. It was about *what Israel's God was doing in history,* in real space, time and matter. I hadn't read much of Lesslie Newbigin at that point, but I think what I was stumbling on was the emphasis that we now associate especially with him: Christian faith is *public truth.* Christianity appeals to history; to history it must go. It is about creation. It isn't a form of Gnosticism, escaping this wicked world of history and earth. It is a form of creational theology in which history and earth, space, time and matter, are *redeemed.* The Word became flesh, not vice versa. Matthew, Mark, Luke and John themselves are convinced that God's kingdom was inaugurated not when they picked up pen and ink to write their gospels but when the living God took flesh and blood to inaugurate the kingdom, to live and die and rise again. In Matthew 28 the risen Jesus declares 'all authority in heaven and on earth' is given – not to the books Matthew and the others would write, but to Jesus himself. If there is such a thing as scriptural authority, that is a shorthand for God's authority, through Jesus, exercised and put into practice through scripture.

So I really do believe that the gospels give us access to what Jesus was thinking, to his worldview and his mindset, as well as to what he did. This is not a matter of trying to psychoanalyse him. We're trying to get at the things that Jesus chose to do and say. We can ask the same question about John the Baptist: why did he think it was a good idea to go down to the river and splash water over people? It wasn't an unreflective thing; it carried, and he must have intended it to carry, all kinds of symbolic resonances with the exodus and the entry into the [128] land, in other words with the events that constituted Israel as God's people and might now reconstitute Israel as such. So with Jesus. He didn't just wake up one morning and decide, on a whim, that he might as well go and talk about the kingdom of God and see what would happen. He wrestled with it. According to the gospels, he wrestled in prayer and fasting. We see in the gospels the things he did, but those pose the question, to any intelligent reader: what did he think he was about? What was he hoping to accomplish? What did he hope would happen next? Is there a credible first-century Jewish mindset within which such actions make sense? Unless we can answer that, teachers and preachers are going to be left saying to themselves, *Well, scripture says Jesus did this, or said that, but we can't be sure; there's a seed of doubt planted in my mind and my preaching will be affected by it.* And then what happens – which has happened for many generations now – is that the whole church shifts subtly, and decides that since we know 'Christ died for our sins' that's all we need to think about. All the specific incidents in the gospels can then just become little illustrations of this larger abstract theology. And with that not only is history lost but the kingdom of God, which is what the gospels are all about.

This affects both the content of Jesus' message and the way we access it through the study of the gospels themselves. Just as Jesus refused the protection of Peter and the others brandishing their futile swords in Gethsemane, so the gospels refuse to be placed within a cordon sanitaire whereby, as the private property of 'the church', they invite us into a world from which the muddled questions and muddy boots of the secular historian would be excluded. The gospels speak of the kingdom coming in and through Jesus' own work, and of misunderstanding, opposition, threats both human and satanic, political danger of several different kinds, and finally an unjust trial and a horrible death – at which point, the same gospels declare, Jesus is, however paradoxically, enthroned as 'King of the Jews'. The real falsification of the gospels – the real 'going behind the gospels to a different reality' – lies not in the attempt to understand, historically, the Jesus of whom they speak, but in the attempt to reconstruct the gospels as sacred story *and therefore not also profane story*. [129]

In particular, it seems to me radically counter-intuitive to suppose that the gospel-writers themselves would support the non-historical reading that is often still proposed. The gospels are not self-referential. They do not say, 'Come into our private world, and there you will find faith, hope and love.' To be sure, as good storytellers they do indeed create what can be called a fictive world (not that the events they are describing didn't happen, but that all selection and arrangement of events is a human creation, a 'fiction' in that sense), and they invite us to live in it. But they insist, on page after page, that this fictive world is one way of looking at *the real world of space, time and matter in which Jesus of Nazareth lived and died*. That, after all, is the point of Luke's careful placing of the story within the chronologies of world history and Jewish history. That, after all, is why Matthew's Jesus speaks of God's kingdom coming on earth as in heaven. It is, above all, what John meant when he spoke of the Word becoming flesh. The thought that they would be read as turning flesh back into word would have horrified the evangelists. They were Jews; creational monotheists; longing for Israel's God, the creator, to act *within* space, time and matter, not to create another world, a 'narrative world', within which certain things could be true in some Pickwickian sense whether they actually happened or not. To imagine that by invoking 'story' we are somehow escaping the public, historical world is to forget what sort of 'story' it is that the canonical evangelists (as opposed, say, to 'Thomas') think they are telling. Yes, it matters that we live within the story of Jesus as they have interpreted it. If the archaeologists came upon the court records of Pontius Pilate, that would of course be one of the most fascinating and important documents ever turned up by a spade. It would help us enormously in understanding what was going on. But we would not expect to construct our own worldview on the basis of the interpretation of the court proceedings that was offered by the official Roman stenographer. But recognizing that the canonical evangelists invite us to see the events through their eyes and with their interpretation doesn't mean they are not inviting us *to see the events*. For them, the most important thing is that these things – the inauguration of the kingdom, and Jesus' death and resurrection – actually happened. [130]

Within this, it made sense, and makes sense, as I said, to ask about the worldview and mindset of Jesus himself. Far too many Christians have been content to assume that because Jesus was and is the second person of the Trinity, he went about in a completely unreflective fashion, turning out those exquisite parables and engaging with people of all sorts in a richly human combination of severity and gentleness, of teasing and challenge, automatically and without thinking and praying through what the one he called 'Abba, Father' was summoning him to do. To say this is not to claim to know more than we should. It is to ask substantially the same question we might ask not only (as we saw) about John the Baptist, but also about figures such as Hillel or Herod: why did they do what they did? And it seems to me, despite what is sometimes said, that when it comes to Jesus the gospels themselves give us plenty of suggestions as to the answer: Jesus was 'deeply moved'; 'looking on him, he loved him'; 'he gazed round, grieved at their hardness of heart'. Creative fiction? I don't think so. This was Jesus as they had known him: a real human being, a historically available human being, not of course without mysterious depths (my closest and dearest friends, sharing my own culture and life, still remain mysterious), but knowable *by history as well as by faith*. That is what the gospels offer. And, to repeat, any attempt to speak about Jesus as though the resurrection, and the fact of Jesus' being alive today, would enable us to have a 'knowledge of him' that could enable us to bypass the knowledge which the gospels offer – that is the real 'going behind the gospels'.

The canon itself in fact supports, indeed urges, the kind of reading I have proposed. To appeal to the canon of scripture over against the historical study of Jesus seems to me a category mistake. Rather, the real divide comes, alas, between the canon on the one hand and certain aspects (by no means all) of later church-tradition on the other. I shall return to this point, but to make it briefly here: Matthew, Mark, Luke and John, all in their very different ways, insist that the full meaning of Jesus is to be found precisely as the climax of the canon, the point where the large and complex story of Adam and Abraham, of Moses, David and the prophets, all comes rushing together. It won't do to say, 'Oh, we can't go behind the text.' It isn't a matter of setting up a 'historical [131] Jesus' over against the 'canonical' one. It won't do to claim that historians like myself are opting for the former, as a construct of our own, over against the latter. The whole point is that the canonical Jesus *is* the historical Jesus, in the sense that Matthew, Mark, Luke and John all intend to refer to someone outside their own thought-world, the someone they knew as Jesus of Nazareth, and my judgment as a historian is that they are successful in that reference. The canonical story *is* the big story of scripture. In fact, if I am accused of having in my head a 'large narrative' that I then use as the template for interpreting the gospels, I plead guilty – and summon the four evangelists in my defence. This, demonstrably, is what they are urging us to do.

The real trouble is that for many centuries the church's tradition has refused to allow the four evangelists to say this to us, to allow the canon to be the canon. In fact, the church's perception of the canon has been very limited and distorted. This is the problem. The church has often colluded with shallow, one-dimensional readings of the canon and shallow, one-dimensional readings of who Jesus really was. For many traditional Christians it would be quite enough if Jesus of Nazareth had been born of a virgin and died on a cross (and perhaps risen again). But this leaves us with the baffling question: why then did he go about doing all those things in between? Why did the canonical evangelists take the trouble to collect and record them? Merely to provide the back story for the cross-based theology of salvation? Merely to show what the incarnate son of God looked like and got up to? Simply to demonstrate, by his powerful deeds, that he was the second person of the Trinity? Was he, at that point, simply a great ethical teacher (and if so, how does that relate to his saving death?)? Or was he living a sinless life in order that his sacrifice, when eventually offered, would be valid? All these have been proposed within 'the tradition' as ways of filling the blanks left by the great traditional omission of what the gospels are actually talking about, namely, the inauguration of God's kingdom. If you appeal to the canon, then let the canon correct the tradition, not the other way round.

Actually, there is in any case no such thing as a reading of the canon without reference to extra-canonical material. However much you may [132] say you're a canonical Christian, we all depend on non-canonical material, on extra-textual elements, even if it's simply the lexicon in which we look up the Greek words and find out what they meant at the time. Someone has constructed that lexicon from other non-canonical texts. Then there are archaeological finds, artefacts and so on, which help us understand how that world worked. You can't actually do a purely canonical reading. You can't actually do without history. Let us then embrace it and see where it takes us.

But I fear it is precisely the traditional church (I speak as a traditionalist!) that has invented another Jesus and superimposed that Jesus on the canon, greatly diminishing what the canon itself was actually trying to say. As a result, the church has again and again tried to fit its 'Jesus' into a different narrative, the story of how the second person of the Trinity revealed his divinity and saved people from their sins into a disembodied heaven. This, not surprisingly, has little continuity with the great canonical story into which the four evangelists hook their own work – not because Jesus is not indeed the second person of the Trinity, or because he did not indeed save people from sin, but because those theological shorthands are capable of being cashed out into many different narratives of which the genuinely canonical one is only one, and normally the ignored one. It is precisely the *canonical* Jesus who announces God's kingdom on earth as in heaven – something that 'tradition' managed to screen out from quite early on. It is precisely the *canonical* Jesus whose death was, in his own intention, intimately connected with his kingdom-agenda; again, one would not know that from later tradition. It is the western tradition, coming to a particular climax (but not the only one) in Bultmann and his predecessors (Kähler among them) and followers (the New Quest in particular), that has insisted on inventing a Jesus 'behind the gospels'. Sometimes this has been 'gentle Jesus meek and mild'; sometimes it has been the Preacher of the Word whose only real message is that he is indeed the Preacher of the Word, revealing simply that he is the revealer. Kähler's own famous protest about the danger of historians discovering a Jesus other than the one in scripture turns out to be sheer projection. The tradition – the traditional church! – which Kähler embodied at that point [133] did, and continues to do, exactly that. And the irony has been that the tradition has been so strong that nobody has even noticed. The gospels have remained at the centre of the church's life, but they have been muzzled and emasculated.

All of which leads us to the question, which looms up all the way from the mediaeval church onwards: what then are the gospels actually all about? I think that the western church has simply not really known what the gospels were there for. Here, at the heart of this paper, I have two main themes to explore. In both cases, rather than simply defending the project of the historical study of Jesus, I want to move to the attack, to expose and critique what seem to me demonstrable misreadings of the canonical gospels themselves.

Divinity and Humanity?

I begin with a point that may seem strange and even potentially heterodox, but which I believe is the high road to a genuine, canonical orthodoxy. The gospels are not primarily written to convince their readers that Jesus of Nazareth is the second person of the Trinity. They are not talking about that. Rather, they are written to convince their readers that he really was inaugurating the kingdom of God – the kingdom of *Israel's* God – on earth as in heaven. That is front and centre in the synoptic gospels, and not far behind in John (the rather few Johannine references to the kingdom (for example John 18.36) are none the less tell-tale). But it is almost entirely absent from 'the tradition' – as witness the entire line of thought from the great creeds and the Chalcedonian Definition through to much dogmatic theology in our own day. Jesus as kingdom-bringer has been screened out of the church's dogmatic proclamation. The church has managed to talk about Jesus while ignoring what the gospels say about him. That, indeed, is why there was a lacuna that liberation theology has tried to fill, sometimes with more success, sometimes with less. In fact, one might suggest sharply that it is the mainstream dogmatic tradition (arguing about the 'divinity and humanity' of Jesus) that has actually falsified the canon by screening out the gospel's central emphasis on the coming of the kingdom and by substituting for this the question of the divinity of Jesus, as [134] though the point of the gospels' high incarnational Christology were something other than the claim that *this is Israel's God in person coming to claim the sovereignty promised to the Messiah.* Psalm 2, front and centre in the baptism narratives, says it all; but it is folly to abstract 'You are my son' from the psalm, or the baptism story, as though this were a proof of Jesus' divinity, while ignoring the conclusion of the psalm that Israel's God is giving to this 'son' the nations of the earth as his possession. That, of course, is the context of the canonical account of Jesus' temptations: to gain the right end by the radically wrong means. And it is the full psalm, and the baptism story as resonating with the full psalm, that launches Jesus on a career – not of 'going about explaining that he was divine' but of going about explaining what it means that Israel's God is present and active, in and through him and his work, to claim his rightful sovereignty over the whole of creation.

Seen in this light the particularly eighteenth-century apologetic reading of the miracles is shown up as the shallow thing it is. Instead of the deep biblical (canonical!) resonances which indicate that this is indeed the new age for which Israel longed, the 'tradition' has read Jesus' mighty acts in terms of proofs of divinity. But this is an abstract divinity belonging more to the dry world of deism than to the rich world of Jewish faith and life. And, in any case, religious traditions, including the Jewish traditions, are full of strange stories about people doing surprising things, but, whether it's Elijah raising a child to life or Joshua making the sun stand still, nobody suggests that these things prove they are somehow divine. That is an eighteenth-century diminution of what the ancient stories were actually about. The so-called miracles do sometimes point to the strange secret of Jesus' ultimate identity. But they do so within their primary emphasis, which is on the arrival of God's saving sovereignty within the world.

By the same token, the early church's proper insistence that Jesus was also fully human always tended to screen out what the canonical gospels were saying, that the human Jesus was the Messiah of Israel, summing up Israel in himself and, with that, summing up the whole history of the human race. (Again, it is precisely the *canon* that would insist on this point, reading the gospels in the light of Israel's scriptures.) Seen [135] from this angle the Chalcedonian Definition looks suspiciously like an attempt to say the right thing but in two dimensions (divinity and humanity as reimagined within a partly de-Judaized world of thought) rather than in three dimensions. What the gospels offer is the personal story of Jesus himself, understood in terms of his simultaneously (1) embodying Israel's God, coming to rule the world as he had always promised, and (2) summing up Israel itself, as its Messiah, offering to Israel's God the obedience to which Israel's whole canonical tradition had pointed but which nobody, up to this point, had been able to provide. The flattening out of Christian debates about Jesus into the language of divinity and humanity represents, I believe, a serious de-Judaizing of the gospels, ignoring the fact that the gospels know nothing of divinity in the abstract and plenty about the God of Israel coming to establish his kingdom on earth as in heaven, that they know nothing of humanity in the abstract, but plenty about Israel as God's true people, and Jesus as summing that people up in himself. The Council of Chalcedon might be seen as the de-Israelitization of the canonical picture of YHWH and Israel into the abstract categories of 'divinity' and 'humanity'. I continue to affirm Chalcedon in the same way that I will agree that a sphere is also a circle or a cube also a square, while noting that this truth is not the whole truth. Here, perhaps ironically in view of our ongoing conversation, Richard Hays's forthcoming work on the use of scripture in the four gospels bids fair to point to the rich heritage which the gospels were evoking but which, I think, much of the tradition from the fourth century onwards has screened out. The gospels have a very high Christology; but this isn't about divinity in the abstract, but about *the God of Israel personally present and active*.

It is, in fact, the church's dogmatic tradition, through which the gospels have been forced to give answers to questions they were not addressing, or not addressing head-on, that has made the apologetic and historical tasks much harder. It is harder to retrieve the *canonical* Jesus (YHWH in person and Israel in person) because the whole church has taught itself to read the canon in ways that significantly diminish it, a problem that can only be remedied precisely by a fresh (however dangerous!) *historical* reading. But it is harder to retrieve a genuinely **[136]** *historical* reading – the historical reading to which the canonical evangelists were urging their readers, the history to which the canon gives access and was designed to give access – because of those same misunderstandings, which led people to say, with wondrous confidence, that the real Jesus 'could not have said or thought' this or that 'because he was a first-century Jew', while showing remarkably little knowledge of the rich world of actual Jewish discourse of his day. (The obvious example is monotheism: for generations, as I said before, it was a staple of historical criticism that no first-century Jew could think of incarnation, because they were all monotheists. Five minutes of serious study of Paul shows how mistaken this is.)

A further irony now emerges. It is precisely one of the founding principles of Protestantism that what Jesus did on the cross was unique, unrepeatable, *ephhapax*, one-off. 'He died for our sins once and for all', in a never-to-be-repeated sacrificial self-offering. But that principle, designed of course to ward off any supposed catholic suggestion that Jesus might be re-crucified in every mass, is itself the proper root of a genuinely historical reading. That is why historical criticism, for all its ambiguity over the last three centuries, is from one point of view a natural outgrowth of Protestantism, however much then the various strands of protestant tradition have introduced new quasi-catholic distortions; because, classically in Bultmann but in all kinds of other ways too, the whole critical enterprise that has sought to read the gospels as evidence not for Jesus but for 'early Christian faith' was designed to highlight the words and deeds of Jesus not as part of a one-off, unique and unrepeatable event, but to turn them precisely into a repeatable, timeless statement of 'the church's faith'. Bultmann, in other respects so ultra-protestant, was in this respect much closer to certain kinds of 'catholic' reading. But it matters that these things *happened*. Without that, one would turn this specific statement into a general truth about theology, spirituality or extra-historical salvation. That's not what the canonical writers were saying. They were saying that at one moment *in actual history* a great door swung open on its hinge, and the creator of the cosmos declared that the way was now open into his remade creation. He was making all things new. The story of Jesus is about the real world, the [137] actual space-time universe, not about the private spiritual experience of a specific group of people. The canonical story *is* the public story of the real Jesus and the real world, and to live within the gospel story – all that wonderful postliberal language about being the people of the story and so forth – is not to enter a private world, separated off from the rest of the space-time universe, but to enter the public world of space, time and matter, facing all its risks. To imagine that by entering the world of the gospels, or by saying the magic word *story*, we are immune from the risks of living in the public world is to fail to realize *what story it is that the canonical gospels are telling*. It is precisely the story of the *real world*, the world of space, time and matter, of actual events. My first real problem of not doing history properly is that we shrink the story of God and God's kingdom in Jesus, and the story of Jesus bringing Israel's story to its climax – which two stories are not two but one – to the thin, abstract categories of 'divinity' and 'humanity'. It is much safer, less risky, to do that; much more in line with 'the tradition'; but much less like the real gospels, or the real gospel.

This kind of reading could only be done, of course, once the unique event itself had become shrunk to one point: the crucifixion. This brings us to the second great point at which the entire western tradition has not known what the gospels are there for: the split, almost ubiquitous in tradition but never found in the canon, between Jesus' announcement of the kingdom and Jesus' pilgrimage to the cross.

Kingdom and Cross

The split between kingdom and cross is not simply a scholar's construct. Nor is it simply one element in the western tradition. It has radically shaped and coloured church life and thought in many traditions and at many levels. In my own ministry it is not too much to say that I have met this split again and again, and have had to deal with its effects in the life and work of the church. It is sometimes, actually, seen as a division between the gospels and Paul, with the gospels offering a kingdom-theology and Paul offering a *theologia crucis*. But actually it is better seen as a division within the gospel material itself. Schweitzer put it in terms of the stark question: did Jesus go to Jerusalem 'to work **[138]** or to die'? Does the central message of Christianity concern the kinds of things Jesus did, which other people must do as they follow him, or about his unique salvific death? If the former, why the cross? If the latter, why all the earlier material in the gospels?

This problem is easily seen acted out in church life. Some Christians, some congregations and some whole multi-congregational denominations have been grasped by the vision of Jesus announcing and inaugurating God's kingdom. Jesus went about doing good, healing people, feasting with sinners, bringing new life and hope in all directions. People today are still captivated by that Jesus, by that agenda. They sign on: *This*, they think, *is the man we want to follow!* And often they do wonderful things in his name. They really can, and sometimes do, make the world a better place. But then there comes a problem. How strange, how sad, that Jesus' public career was so brutally cut short! He was just getting going – he was on a roll! So much more needed to be done, so many more lepers to be healed, so many more people to catch his vision of a world set right. So what was the cross all about? And why do the evangelists seem to highlight it in the way they do? Some, indeed, have suggested that, for some of the evangelists at least (Luke comes to mind), the cross has no real interpretation, no atonement-theology attached to it: Jesus is simply putting into operation the agenda he announced at the start. Such a reading, of course, is bound to find Paul particularly opaque. It might be said that sometimes this has been convenient. 'Kingdom-churches', if we can call them that, have not always been happy with Paul's ethics. But actually the problem goes far deeper. Paul, obviously rooted in the death and resurrection of Jesus, and seldom mentioning the kingdom of God, has little appeal for those who glimpse Jesus at his kingdom-work and find themselves called to join in.

For other Christians, of course, the cross of Jesus is at the very centre of the faith. 'Christ died for our sins according to the scriptures'! Nor is this simply a protestant innovation. Mediaeval Catholicism produced a thousand pictures of the crucified saviour for every one image of Jesus healing, feasting or teaching. The gospels then appear – as some would-be critical scholarship has argued they should be read – as 'Pas-[139]-sion narratives with extended introduc-tions'. In Nick Perrin's phrase, the gospels simply supply the 'chips and dips', an optional hors d'oeuvre before we go on to the real main course, the real red meat, of Pauline theology. As we saw earlier, for many Christians it would have been quite sufficient if Jesus of Nazareth had been born of a virgin and died on a cross (and raised again afterwards). They have no real use for anything in between. So why did Matthew, Mark, Luke and John spend such a long time telling us about it all? Purely out of antiquarian interest? Certainly not. The four gospels are quite clear that the kingdom and the cross go together, but much of the later western church has found that conjunction very, very difficult, and has often played kingdom-theology off against cross-theology, because it's had one vision of reality about God making the world a better place and another vision of reality about God saving people from their sins, and never the twain shall meet. But both in canon and in real history they do meet. They belong together. For some, indeed, Jesus' death looks more and more strange: a bizarre event in itself, with no apparent connection to his kingdom-message (except insofar as the political power-brokers misunder-stood him). For Jesus in some sense to have *intended* his forthcoming death would make him, within our modern worldviews, simply 'weird' (as one writer actually said), as though the whole thing was a kind of strange assisted suicide with some peculiar theology stuck on top of it. And unless we are going to diminish everything into that fog of misunderstandings, we are bound to ask, as a matter of history: how, within a first-century Jewish mindset, might Jesus of Nazareth have thought about, conceived, imagined as a matter of vocation, a vision of the kingdom that would be accomplished through such an event – this vision of his own forthcoming death as the climax, the key moment, of his kingdom-programme?

This can be asked as a matter of historical investigation. Such historical work is not designed to replace the canon with a historian's reconstruction, but to offer a hypothesis to explain what the church has manifestly not explained or understood. What then is it that the evangelists are trying to tell us? They don't think there is a massive disjunction between kingdom and cross. How does it work for them? [140]

Before answering the question, let us look at the same puzzle from the opposite end. For some traditional Christians, Paul is everything (at least, a particular reading of Paul is everything), and the kingdom of God (on earth as in heaven!) is nothing, or next to nothing. The dangerous possibility that Jesus might want us to *do* things and thereby justify ourselves by our works has led generations of cross-centred Protestants to be very wary of the gospels with their detailed kingdom-agenda and kingdom-ethic. Think of the sheep and the goats in Matthew 25: is 'eternal life' and its horrid alternative really to be decided by what people *do*? Thus, in many churches the canonical gospels, or rather their dismembered fragments, are relentlessly translated into narratives that are 'really' about Jesus' salvific death. This of course is not a complete travesty, since the evangelists do indeed recount many of the incidents in Jesus' public career in such a way as to point forward to Calvary. But the strong tendency in this cross-centred reading of the gospels is to ignore, for instance, Jesus' bracing Jubilee agenda in Luke 4, or the striking commands about hospitality to strangers in Luke 14, or the cup of cold water in Matthew 10, or (again) the 'inasmuch' of the sheep and the goats in Matthew 25. At this point (ironically, considering the normal evangelical refusal of Bultmann and all his ways) the tradition that has focused on the cross to the exclusion of the kingdom adopts a more or less exactly Bultmannian hermeneutic: the stories about Jesus are really just reflections of different aspects of the cross-based kerygma – with the difference, of course, that whereas Bultmann thought they didn't actually happen, the evangelical tradition has insisted that they did. This, however, was not in order to explore their kingdom-meaning but in order to shore up an endangered belief in scriptural infallibility, which was in turn serving two quite different agendas (modern rationalist apologetic against modern rationalist scepticism, and protestant freedom over against the pope), neither of which were likely to send such readers back to the question of what Jesus might have thought he was doing when he announced that Israel's God was at last becoming king on earth as in heaven.

It is a question of history, as well as of canon, to ask how in fact, if at all, kingdom and cross belong together. History here (to repeat) is not **[141]** a way of going behind the canon or falsifying it, but of asking the question the canon itself raises but the church has been very bad at even noticing, let alone answering. This question, I suspect, has been marginalized in much western theology for a good deal longer than the five hundred years of Protestantism. The split has been instantiated in a variety of positions, both historical and theological. We might think, for instance, of the nineteenth-century picture of Jesus enjoying a successful 'Galilean springtime' as he goes about healing and teaching and winning approval – only then to discover that people start to fall away, at which point he moves to 'plan B', going to the cross to force God's hand. Worse, there have been plenty of portraits (popular and would-be scholarly) of Jesus the social activist, launching a protest movement to show people a different way to live and then accidentally falling foul of the authorities, or Jesus the fanatic, with a complex (supposedly biblical) atonement-theology in his head, going off to get himself crucified and somehow, inexplicably, healing and feasting and walking on water for a year or two before the moment came. These pictures have in their turn bred reactions in both directions, often picking up energy from the various social, cultural, ecclesiological and (not least) political contexts in which the story has been told, now this way, now that.

The second of those caricatures has been especially popular, all the way back to the great creeds. There, the virgin birth is followed directly by Jesus suffering under Pontius Pilate, and Jesus' endless kingdom is placed towards the end of the narrative, appearing to suggest that Jesus will only inaugurate this kingdom at the very end – which contradicts both the gospels and Paul. The creeds, of course, record the results of the church's major early contro-versies. It is a kind of washing list: this is the laundry that we needed to clean. But since the question of God's kingdom does not seem to have been among the problems to which an agreed solution seemed necessary, Jesus' kingdom-inauguration during the course of his public career, and through his death and resurrection, finds no mention in them. That is the problem about taking what is essentially a list of resolved disputes and then using it as the agreed syllabus for the church's teaching. But, to say it one more time, [142] there have been many Christians in the western world who, with the apparent encouragement of the creeds, would be quite satisfied if Jesus of Nazareth had been born of a virgin and died on a cross and done nothing very much at all in between. That, they would assume, would be what canonical or traditional Christianity was all about. But the canon itself suggests otherwise.

Some, of course, have filled in this blank theologically. Some have claimed that Jesus was teaching us how to go to heaven, which, as I've said, hardly fits with most of the gospel material. Some have suggested that he was leading a sinless life in order that his atoning sacrifice would be valid. This, though close to things that Paul and Hebrews both say, is not exactly highlighted in the gospels themselves. Some have gone further, suggesting that Jesus was fulfilling the Mosaic law in a life of 'active obedience', so that the right-eousness which would accrue to someone who fulfilled the law might then be imputed to all his people. There are verses in Matthew which can be read that way (Jesus' 'fulfilling all righteousness' in Matthew 3, and 'not coming to abolish but to fulfil the law' in Matthew 5). But the particular theological construct implicit in this third proposal is, again, not something one would discover on the surface of the text of any of the four canonical evangelists.

It looks very much as though all such proposals are ways of papering over the very large crack between the (abstract) doctrines of incarnation (Jesus' conception and birth) and atonement (the cross and its saving significance). Once again, perhaps it is these abstractions that are causing the problem. The technical terms *incarnation* and *atonement* are, I believe, true signposts. But what is the reality to which they are pointing?

As far as the canonical evangelists are concerned, *there is no split between kingdom and cross*. The long kingdom-narrative leads seamlessly up to the cross; the shadow of the cross falls on many kingdom-announcing incidents; when Jesus dies, his kingship is proclaimed, with heavy irony, by the *titulus* over his head: 'King of the Jews'! That, one might suggest, is actually a moment of real climax for the evangelists: having portrayed Jesus as Israel's Messiah all through the narrative, now at last this royal status is proclaimed to all – but only from the cross. This is hugely profound, and frequently ignored in the tradition. [143] For the evangelists, *the kingdom is the project that is sealed, accomplished, by the cross*, on the one hand, and *the cross is the victory through which the kingdom is established*, on the other. Neither can be reduced to terms of the other, either by reading 'kingdom' as the 'heaven' to which we go because Jesus died for our sins, or by reading the cross merely as 'the inevitable reaction of a wicked world and the "domination system" against people who try to live differently'. It is perfectly proper to ask the canonical evangelists how the kingdom and the cross might go together – how they went together in the evangelists' minds, as they clearly did, and how they went together in Jesus' intentionality, as the evangelists imply they did. This, again, in other words, is not to advance a project behind the backs of the canonical evangelists but rather to enquire whether their own vision of a single kingdom-and-cross reality corresponds to the aim and intention of Jesus himself. It is, in other words, to try to explain what the church for much of its life has manifestly not even begun to address, namely, what it is that the evangelists themselves are trying to tell us.

(We might note at this point, because it's out there in the media and popular culture, the massive and radical difference between the four canonical gospels and those other documents, like *Thomas*, which have from time to time attracted the title 'gospel'. These mostly gnostic or semi-gnostic texts have no interest in Jesus' death and resurrection, and for that reason alone have sometimes been hailed as more primitive or historical. But this is a complete misunderstanding. They offer a de-Judaized picture of a Jesus who was neither inaugurating the kingdom of Israel's God nor dying a meaningful – let alone salvific – death. They do not offer *news* about an *event* – something that has happened as a result of which the world is a different place – but *advice* about how to reorder one's private spirituality or to attain a disembodied salvation. Sadly, this is too close for comfort to some varieties of Protestantism and to some elements in post-Enlightenment culture. These two have sometimes made common cause and lurched towards the gnostic 'gospels' as if they, rather than the canonical ones, rendered the genuine historical Jesus. Such a move fits well in a culture that has become cynical about any kind of traditional Christian faith and regards it as [144] oppressive and self-serving, preferring instead some version of privatized self-help spirituality or soteriology. This is very like what happened in the middle of the second century, after the fall of the Bar-Kochba rebellion. But it is a matter of history, not canonical prejudice, to see this as an utterly false move. Christianity from the beginning, as we know in Paul, was a gospel movement about the events in which Israel's God had acted decisively in the Messiah, Jesus.)

The question to be asked, then, is this: what sort of a kingdom is it that needs the crucifixion of the kingdom-bringer for its completion? Or, conversely, what sort of meaning might one give to the cross – what sort of atonement-theology might we envisage – that effects the establishment of God's kingdom on earth as in heaven? The fact that this feels quite a strange question indicates worryingly that, as I have suggested several times, the entire western tradition appears not to have allowed the canonical gospels to make their full impact. Many kingdom-theologies seem to have no place for the cross, and many atonement-theologies, including 'sound' evangelical ones, have no place for God's kingdom on earth as in heaven. Something is badly wrong with this picture. It appears that our contemporary division between kingdom-work on the one hand and atonement on the other – which plays itself out in terms of the endless church debates between social ethics and saving souls – is radically misconceived. Our visions of social justice and of salvation have become cruelly detached from one another.

This is cognate with the problem I noted in *Evil and the Justice of God* [Wright 2006b], namely, that the philosophical problem of evil has been allowed to float free from the cross, while the cross, seen as atonement, has become quite detached from the massive and deeply troubling fact of evil, of all sorts, in the world. My working hypothesis is that the evangelists are reflecting a train of thought and prayer and vocation which was Jesus' own train of thought. Otherwise we'd have to suggest, once more, that Jesus was an unreflective sort of person who just went around doing odd things without really thinking them through or wondering where it would all lead, and that it was the evangelists who were the brilliant and innovative thinkers and theologians, the astonishingly versatile and innovative scripture-interpreters, who took these unre-[145]-flective actions and put them together into a fresh coherent whole. Such a proposal ought to be counter-intuitive, whether we approach the question from the tradition, the canon or from a warm but unthinking piety. That it is not counter-intuitive is thus a reflection, not just of critical scholarship, but of the context of western Christianity within which such scholarship could flourish.

In fact, the four canonical evangelists insist that it was Jesus himself who did and said what he did in such a way as to generate a web of meaning, leading on from Israel's scriptures, within which his kingdom-inauguration and his forthcoming death would be mutually interpretative. The evangelists intended to do what they in fact did, namely, to join up kingdom and cross and allow them to mean what they mean in reference to one another. They urge us not to enter into an ahistorical world of 'story' in which we might live without ever raising the question of Jesus' own intentionality and mindset, but to allow ourselves to be impacted by the one-off historical facts of a particular human being believing certain things about his own place in the divine plan and acting in accordance with those beliefs. More specifically, I think the evangelists are telling us on every page that Jesus of Nazareth believed that he was embodying Israel's God in launching his sovereign rule over Israel and the world, and that, as Messiah, he was embodying Israel's own destiny, and that this complex of beliefs would involve him (in fulfilment of ancient prophecy, psalm and story) in being himself apparently defeated at the hands of the pagans. The four canonical gospels thus offer, I believe, from their four different angles, a compelling hypothesis, not about the abstract narrative world they are constructing but about Jesus himself. When the earliest post-Easter tradition says, as it does, '[He] loved me and gave himself for me' (Galatians 2.20) or 'Having loved his own who were in the world, he loved them to the end' (John 13.1), it makes sense – specifically *Christian* sense, not just post-Enlightenment historiographical sense! – to ask: but was that true of Jesus himself prior to the cross? Did Jesus really live and think and feel like that? Was Jesus himself passionately and compassionately motivated by love? Or is that only true of the way believers now encounter and experience the risen Jesus? The evange-[146]-lists themselves portray a Jesus who really was that sort of person and had that sort of impact on people.

That reflection is not simply an interesting fact about the Jesus conveyed by the canonical gospels. It invites two further methodological elaborations. First, the Jesus of the canonical gospels is both sovereign and vulnerable. The fact that we believe him to be the second person of the Trinity must not for one moment raise him above the vulnerability of being mocked, spat on, beaten and killed – or the vulnerability of being open to sharp critical historical investigation. Yes, he acts as if he's in charge, and he explains his actions by saying that this is what it looks like when God's in charge. But at the same time there are plots and schemes against him, which reach their head in his arrest, trial, mocking, beating and crucifixion. This is the Jesus the canonical evangelists offer us, in line here with Paul who speaks of Jesus emptying himself and becoming obedient to the death of the cross. Later tradition (and some current proposals) appear to seek to protect Jesus from the historians' equivalent of the plots, trials, whips and nails, by removing him from the reach of those who ask the awkward did-it-really-happen historical questions, just as some of the gnostic writings have Jesus being snatched away just before things get nasty, so he doesn't have to suffer and die on the cross. But this, it seems to me, is the scholarly–theological equivalent of Peter's flawed attempt to protect Jesus in the garden. It misses the point. The point is that the kingdom is inaugurated precisely by the vulnerable, canonical, historical Jesus, because the kingdom must come on earth as in heaven. He became vulnerable to the world of his day; is there any reason why we in the church should now take it on ourselves to do what he forbade Peter and the others to do in the garden, that is, to defend him from attack and arrest? Is it not far more appropriate that we should respect him for who he is, rather than trying to make him into the sort of god with whom we would be able to live a lot more comfortably?

The second methodological elaboration highlights the meaning of love itself. Love does not sit still in safety and persuade the beloved to leap over a separating gap between them. Love goes to meet the beloved in the dangerous territory. Love is the highest mode of knowing, tran-[147]-scending the subject–object distinction that has formed the dilemma on which so much western thought has been impaled. The canonical gospels do not offer us a Jesus who can be grasped objectively, pinned to the page like a dead butterfly (to borrow Ben Meyer's graphic image from his discussion of D. F. Strauss).[1] Nor do they offer us a Jesus who is to be known only in the subjective appreciation and appropriation that arise when someone makes the narrative world of the gospels his or her own, without reference to events and persons in first-century Palestine. They invite us to a different kind of epistemology, one that corresponds to the driving motive of their central character.

---

1 Meyer 2002, 98f.

Kingdom and Resurrection

If it is problematic to put together the kingdom and the cross, there is also a problem about putting together kingdom and cross on the one hand with the resurrection on the other. There is much to say on this subject, but not here and not now. Of course I believe that the resurrection of Jesus is the vital moment in the story, the vital fact at the centre of all history, the vital element in the Christian worldview. Of course the gospel-writers themselves, and their first readers, were writing and reading the story of Jesus as the story of one who was alive, who was known in scripture and bread-breaking, in the *koinōnia* of the spirit and in the service of the poor. But the gospels never forget, what much protestant scholarship and popular thought, and much would-be orthodox or canonical Christianity, has conveniently forgotten, that the resurrection is precisely the resurrection of the kingdom-bringer, the crucified kingdom-bringer, and that these elements are not left behind in the resurrection but rather fulfilled. It is vital in the New Testament that the risen Jesus is known by the mark of the nails and the spear thrust in his side, and that the resurrection is not simply about his being alive again but about his *ascension*, his new status as the world's true lord – in other words, as the fulfilment of the kingdom-agenda he began in his public career. This contrasts sharply with the notion, which has been popular in many so-called liberal circles, that all that the early [148] church really meant by resurrection was that the spirit or influence of Jesus somehow lived on, as a spiritual presence, even though his body was mouldering in a tomb somewhere. The real objection to that is not simply, as conservative theology has responded, that this denies the great miracle, but rather that it makes no sense of the resurrection as the climax of Jesus' work of bringing God's kingdom on earth as in heaven. It deconstructs the narrative the evangelists are at great pains to tell. The four canonical evangelists see the resurrection and enthronement of Jesus as the conclusion of the story they had been telling all along. This, they are saying, is what it looks like when the agenda Jesus announced at the start is fulfilled.

Nor is the resurrection of Jesus seen by the evangelists as a straight-forward proof of Jesus' divinity in the sense people normally give that today. When Thomas makes his great confession, *kyrios mou kai theos mou*, the circle which is thereby closed with the Johannine prologue ('The Word became flesh . . . No-one has ever seen God, but the only-begotten God has revealed him', literally *exegeted* him) indicates that we are therefore to reread the whole gospel narrative as the story of God in human form, not simply to say, 'Well! So he was divine all that time', but rather, 'So that's what the incarnate God looks like; that's what he does; that's how he brings his kingdom and overthrows the ruler of the world.' Otherwise the 'proof of divinity' line leads only to a sigh of relief from the would-be 'orthodox' Christian: there we are, the box has been checked, we're all right. Instead, in the gospels the resurrection of Jesus leads to a quite different train of thought: Jesus really is God's Messiah (the verdicts of the courts have been reversed), and must have been Messiah all along; new creation has begun, and this must all along have been the point of God becoming king; all the forces of evil that stood in the way of God's rescue of creation and of Israel have been dealt with, and this must have been the meaning of the cross; Jesus is now to be enthroned as the world's true lord, having done what in scripture only Israel's God himself gets to do; and we, the witnesses of this event, are commissioned and equipped for the major task that lies ahead, establishing the fact of God's kingdom by the methods of God's kingdom. That is what the book of Acts is all about. [149] We must not short-circuit the Israel-dimension of the story the gospels are telling. We will falsify it, forcing it into a different mould of our own making, instead of opening up our worldview to the possibility that it might itself need remaking by God, precisely through the process of reading and living the canonical story.

It will not do, then, to hold up the resurrection as a way of avoiding, or sidelining, the ongoing historical task. The resurrection means what it means because it is the resurrection *of this Jesus*, not of someone else. The church will constantly be tempted to use the resurrection itself as a way of avoiding the challenge of being the kingdom-bearing people. Rather, the resurrection establishes Jesus' people as people of new creation in themselves but also, as the sign of this, people through whom new creation happens. And one of the tasks of that new creation is precisely telling and retelling the story of who Jesus always was. This is the ultimate answer to the line of thought that ran from Bultmann through Gerhard Ebeling to Hans Conzelmann and others: writing the gospels did not represent a failure of nerve on the part of the first or second generation of Christians. Rather, it represented a commitment to the new creation, to the kingdom of God on earth as in heaven, launched in the events to which the gospels give us genuine historical access and now let loose into the world through Easter and Ascension themselves and through the gift of the spirit to Jesus' followers. If Jesus was Messiah, and if his death was the kingdom-bringing event, then his resurrection means that new creation has begun. So often preachers at Easter say, 'Jesus is alive again; therefore he's in heaven; therefore we'll go to be with him one day.' That's not what the evangelists say. Rather, they say, 'Jesus is alive again; therefore new creation has begun; therefore we have a job to do.' And part of that job is precisely *to tell the story*, the story of Jesus as the climax of the story of Israel's God and the climax of the story of Israel, the means of the world's redemption.

Prospects

Where might all these reflections lead us? There are many tasks still remaining. Biblical scholarship in the western world has had a particular slant. It has not favoured big-picture thinking; it's been much easier, **[150]** for a long time, to earn a PhD in biblical studies if you are an ISTJ on the Myers-Briggs scale than if your first letters are ENF. This has to do, not least, with the left-hemisphere dominance of western culture, the propensity to privilege detail over insight, grasp over reach. (On this, see the remarkable work of Iain McGilchrist.)[2] But big-picture hypotheses are what we need just now. We need intuitive thinkers as well as details people. That, granted, is a problem when someone is doing a degree, for which accuracy in detail is an important requirement, but it's vital none the less. We need to look at the ways in which Jesus' kingdom-proclamation broke open the moulds of his day and perhaps of our day too. And there is plenty of room for this. The study of the gospels in the light of all we now know about first-century Judaism positively cries out for exploration of big, new subjects: Jesus and the Temple, Jesus and priesthood, Jesus and economics. There are literally thousands of exegetical and historical projects waiting to be undertaken from new angles of vision. I have no sense that my own previous work has solved all these problems. Think, as one example, of the meaning of the Last Supper: when Jesus wanted to give his followers the clue to the meaning of this forthcoming death, and how it related to the kingdom he'd been announcing and inaugurating, he didn't give them a theory; he gave them a meal, and a meal cannot remain an idea in your head. It feeds you; it strengthens and sustains you. You share it; you do it. It feeds you and other people too, and that is part of the meaning of the whole thing. We need to explore what all that might mean, in new ways. I hardly began to scratch the surface of all that in *Jesus and the Victory of God*, and it remains central and vital.

Work such as I am recommending, of course, is not exempt from the risk of being merely quirky. That's always the risk when you're reconceiving big ideas.

---

2   McGilchrist 2009.

But most of the supposedly leading gospel scholarship of the last century has itself been quirky in the extreme, proceeding (if I am even a quarter right) from wrong premises, addressing wrong questions and coming up with answers that did no justice either to Jesus or to the evangelists. We need, not least, a quite new form-[151]-criticism. It's a perfectly sensible question to ask why the traditions about Jesus got shaped the way they did. But Bultmann launched his form-criticism of the gospels on the basis of a hypothesis about early Christianity in which the earliest form of the faith was basically non-Jewish, so that reflection on Israel's scriptures must have come in at a second stage. The Jesus Seminar, including Dominic Crossan, followed Bultmann down this blind alley. We now know – or should know – that this was absurd. It is far more likely to be the other way round, with gospel traditions beginning with stories about Jesus that were initially told, by devout Jews with scripture in their heads and their hearts, in such a way as to echo that scripture, and developing into stories which, in a different context, were flattened down into something more like hellenistic *chreiai*. But that is only one example; there could be many more.

If there are new worlds of scholarship waiting to be opened up, what about fresh readings of the gospels in the service of the church? What is the 'so what'? This, I believe, is not basically about apologetics – the older I get, the more I become suspicious of that project in at least some of its forms – but about *mission*. Somehow, the whole complex of kingdom, cross and resurrection must play out into a full-orbed gospel-rooted mission which will be significantly unlike the 'social gospel' mission that forgot about the cross, or the 'Jesus died for you' mission that forgot about the kingdom. One of the great breakthrough moments for me when I was first struggling with historical-Jesus questions was John 20.21: '*As* the father has sent me, *so* I send you.' That derivative correspondence – the 'as' and the 'so', with Jesus' own mission the source and template for that of his followers, as they receive the spirit – suddenly opens up an entire hermeneutic world, demanding that the church again and again study the historical mission of Jesus not just to find out the back history of the crucified and risen one, but to realign itself with the shape and content of that mission in order to carry out its own. Jesus' own mission becomes the template and the energizing force for all that the church then has to do and be. We are to be for the world what Jesus was for Israel. You will only understand the mission of the church in the world if, instead of using the canon as a closed story, a [152] charmed circle in which it means what it means but which you can't break into or out of, you go back to Jesus himself, which is what the canon is pleading with you to do, so that you can then see who he was and is and then discern, in the power of his spirit, who we have to do and be. If you want to know what that looks like, read the book of Acts: a story of doing the kingdom, bearing the kingdom, suffering for the kingdom, and eventually announcing the kingdom under the nose of Caesar himself. That is what it looks like when the church goes out, with the breath of Jesus in our lungs, to tell the world that he is its rightful lord. Sometimes people get hurt; sometimes a thousand people get converted; sometimes all sorts of things in between take place; and somehow the gospel gets to Rome, to the centre of human power and authority, to announce there that Jesus is lord and God is king, openly and unhindered.

To do this, however, the church needs constantly to reconnect with the real Jesus, whom the canonical gospels give us but whom we have so badly misunderstood. The world will pull these things apart again, will lure us into the smaller worlds of *either* social work *or* saving souls for a disembodied eternity. Our various western worldviews will force on us political agendas that are culled from elsewhere, which we can feel good about because they don't have the cross attached to them. Gnosticism is so much *easier* than Christian mission: easier epistemologically, especially in today's western world, and easier socially and politically too. You don't have to worry about justice in the world if you take that route. Beware of atonement-theologies that deliver a type of evangelical preaching which is actually detached from what scripture actually says! (Two or three years ago a book was written that attempted to explain what the Bible says about the atonement. It had a lot of Old Testament, and a lot of Paul – but almost nothing about the gospels. A travesty. The gospels are not just the back story for Pauline theology.) And those who, in order to renounce Gnosticism, become glorified social workers will find all too easily that they are caught up in political agendas culled from elsewhere, which can be adopted with no need for the cross – the cross as the means of victory, the *only* means by which genuine kingdom-victories are won. For this we need the whole gospel story, [153] the whole story *as history*. History then; history now.

Once all that is in place, there is indeed an apologetic task. But this task is not (*pace* C. S. Lewis and others) to prove Jesus' divinity or anything like it, but to speak wisely and (historically) truthfully about Jesus and to show that the gospels – as they are, not as the tradition has shrunk them into being! – really do make sense. Historically speaking, the case still needs to be made in public that the overwhelmingly best explanation for the rise of early Christianity is that Jesus of Nazareth really was and really did and said what the canonical gospels say he was, did and said. It is no shame, in my view, to hear the questions of the sceptical historian and to answer them with all the first-century tools we can muster. It simply won't do to say, 'Never mind the history; feel the power of this story': every sensible sceptic knows how powerful stories are. As Dom Crossan once said in my hearing, Mark's gospel is a wonderful movie script, and because we all enjoyed the movie we all supposed it was true. Please note, I do not believe that historical research can compel faith. But, as I have said often enough in relation more specifically to the resurrection, genuine historical research is very good at cutting back the undergrowth behind which sceptical arguments have been hiding, and showing them up as worthless. This process, while not a full apologetic in the high modernist sense, can and should be a genuine *praeparatio evangelica*, clarifying and posing more sharply the ultimate challenge of the Christian message.

Otherwise – and this is my perceived problem with Karl Barth, or at least with those who have followed through some aspects of his thought – it really does appear to me that the gospel is presented as a closed, charmed circle, where we don't allow any natural theology, which protects itself against the ravages of negative historical scholarship at the massive cost of shutting itself off against any possibility of genuine enquiry from outside. There is no way out and no way in. It is all very well to say, 'Come inside this circle, and you'll see it all makes sense', but that is no real argument to someone who says, 'From outside I can see that you are living in your own deluded little world.' And that isn't simply a matter of apologetics; it applies to politics and similar spheres as well. What good is it if I say to the government, 'You ought [154] to remit Third World debt', or 'You ought to treat asylum seekers as vulnerable human beings, not as criminals', if they can retort, 'That's all very well from within your charmed faith-based circle, but we live in the real world and you have nothing to say to us'? No wonder Paul's speech on the Areopagus has had a bad press in neo-orthodox circles. Paul shouldn't have tried to build, they have said, on the signals of God in the Athenians' culture. Isn't it bound to end up in compromise? But the whole point of Israel's tradition – of Abraham's vocation! – was that Israel should be the people *through whom* God would go out and address the world, in order to rescue the world. When Jesus said, 'You are the light of the world', he expressly warned against putting a bucket over that light. He presupposes that the world can and will see the light when it's shining and will be attracted to it.

And it is precisely the canonical gospels that take us, not into a world simply suffused with the light of the resurrection, but into the pre-Easter world in which Jesus himself said such things. The fact that the gospels are written from the perspective of Easter both does and doesn't mean that they tell things in that light. Yes, they wouldn't have bothered to tell the stories if they hadn't believed that Jesus was risen. But they explicitly encourage us to see things through the lens of the disciples' pre-Easter understanding. The gospel-writers themselves stress that the disciples did not, at the time, understand; they want us, their readers, to get inside the minds not only of Jesus' first followers, struggling to work out what he was talking about, but also of Jesus himself at that same time, frustrated at their lack of comprehension. They want us to understand what it was like beforehand, even though from time to time (John 2.22; Mark 9.10) they show that they, the storytellers, can see the longer end in sight. It matters to them that we hold that perspective at one remove and grasp what it was like in the days before they had even understood that Jesus really did have to die, let alone that he would rise again. Of course, without the resurrection there is no gospel. But it won't do to say that all the gospels give us is the risen Jesus with some back-story material attached. That's just back to Bultmann. Of course *we* know Jesus *as* the risen one who is with us today. But we only know the resurrection, in a canonical–biblical fashion, if [155] we understand the resurrection precisely as the resurrection *of the crucified kingdom-bringer*. To understand the resurrection in any other way is to misunderstand it, to snatch it out of its canonical and biblical context and make it serve some other set of agendas.

Thus, even though they are telling the whole pre-Easter story because they believe that Jesus was raised from the dead and is therefore the Messiah, the evangelists are telling it in such a way as to insist that their readers need to know *what it was like then*, for the disciples and for Jesus himself. It is, after all, the pre-Easter Jesus who goes about doing and speaking the kingdom, and precisely if we say, with the letter to the Hebrews, that Jesus is the same yesterday, today and for ever, we cannot use that as an excuse for imagining a docetic Jesus as today's Jesus and then projecting that back on to the pre-Easter world, as so much would-be orthodoxy has done. No: we know him today, if we know him truly, as the kingdom-bringer, the crucified kingdom-bringer, the crucified and risen kingdom-bringer. We must continue to hold together what the gospels refuse to split apart. We only know the meaning of the resurrection, and hence of present Christian faith, in the light of the kingdom and the cross. Without that, the very word *resurrection* loses its meaning and becomes merely a cipher for 'the new spirituality'. The point about resurrection is that the risen Jesus, though now immortal and beyond the reach of suffering and death, *is nevertheless the same Jesus who went about announcing God's kingdom and dying to bring it about.*

For all this we need to be, as Paul puts it, 'transformed by the renewing of our minds'. It is history as well as faith that enables us to say 'He loved me and gave himself for me'. It will not do to shun history, to declare it off limits, just because there is such a thing as sceptical historiography – any more than we should shun the use of money because there is a god called Mammon, or make ourselves eunuchs because of the goddess Aphrodite. There is a proper history and an improper history, and though they may sometimes look alike they need to be distinguished, and the former not rejected because of the existence of the latter. There is a large task still waiting here, namely, the fresh articulation of a historical method that will not be dictated to from within the shrunken world of post-Enlightenment epistemology, but will, [156] rather, be open to genuine knowledge of the past and will not dismiss it on the spurious grounds that there is, after all, no real world outside the text. When faith says 'He loved me and gave himself for me', it can properly look to history to back it up. Otherwise we lay ourselves open once more to the obvious charge of fantasy – to which western Christianity, alas, has so often been prone.

Time would fail me to tell of the meetings with the risen Jesus in John 20—21, where these epistemological issues are played out in terms of wonderful human drama. Here is Mary, who recognizes the risen Jesus through her tears and at the sound of her name being called. Here is Thomas, who wants to touch and see and is invited to do so (rather than being told off for coming with the wrong epistemology). Here is Peter and the challenge 'Do you love me?', inviting Ludwig Wittgenstein's fascinating comment, 'It is *love* that believes the resurrection.' But here too are the encounters in the earlier parts of the gospels: with Peter in Luke 5, Mary of Bethany in Luke 10, Matthew in Matthew 9, and so on. Jesus meets the disciples where they are, as we see in the wonderful exchange between Jesus and Peter, where Jesus finally comes down to Peter's level: 'Simon, son of John, do you love me?', and then, when all Peter can say is 'Yes, lord, you know I'm your friend', phrasing his third question in Peter's terms: 'Simon, son of John, are you my friend?' We need these stories; we need this historical Jesus. If these are just fantasies, they are no good to us; because we need the real Jesus, with the dust of the Galilean streets on his feet, to meet us in our dusty worlds, with the dust of today's streets on our shoes and in our souls, with the worries and weight of the world on our shoulders, with fears and suspicions and prejudices and misunderstandings in our hearts and homes. It is the real Jesus, the historical Jesus, the Jesus of yesterday who anchors our hold on the Jesus of today and tomorrow, whom we know in the canonical gospels, through the proper historical research that discovers what those canonical gospels were really telling us rather than constructing a different Jesus behind or above them (as is done every time someone writes about Jesus without making front and centre the fact that he was the kingdom-bringer!) – it is this real Jesus who challenges the church, the scholar, the sceptic, the whole wide [157] world, with the cross and resurrection as the kingdom-establishing events. He presents himself afresh through the multi-dimensional historical work that opens up what the gospels were really trying to tell us, so that no-one will imagine for a moment (as he or she is bound to do when listening to the anti-historical post-Barthian construct) that this message is the preserve and prerogative of the church, which so many have rejected. He is, and remains, the Jesus who comes to seek and to save the lost; to rescue sinners, not the righteous. To all alike he gives the same command, the command that draws together kingdom, cross and resurrection: 'Follow me!'

If we are to obey that command, we need, not simply the knowledge of the post-Pentecost church that Jesus is alive and is with it in the present, but the knowledge the four canonical gospels give us of who Jesus was and what he did. He is the same yesterday, today and for ever; but we may be deceived, not least self-deceived, about who he is today, and only by regularly rerooting ourselves in the faithful stories of who he actually was can we be refreshed in faith and witness and enabled to avoid inventing an idol that, however much we call it 'Jesus', may be not quite the same person, and may serve our own ends. If the Messiah is not raised, said Paul, your faith is futile and you are still in your sins. And, we might add, if the Messiah who died is not the Jesus whose history we know through Matthew, Mark, Luke and John, our faith is groundless and we are still in our fantasies. We need the truly historical Jesus, not as a clever construct we can detect behind the canon or play off against it, but as the truly canonical and truly historical Jesus whom (thank God!) we can still detect behind the later traditions that have screened out what the canon itself was trying to say. Scripture is the witness to Jesus. Woe betide us if, for whatever reason, we turn this round and make Jesus merely the presupposition of something we then call scripture. You can always tell, because when Jesus takes a back seat things get out of balance: the kingdom out of balance with the cross, or the kingdom and the cross out of balance with the resurrection, or the kingdom, cross and resurrection out of balance with the life of the church. It is Jesus we follow, not (primarily!) Matthew, Mark, Luke or John. They are servants through whom we see Jesus, but Jesus is more [158] than the sum total of their sense perceptions or our perceptions of their sense perceptions. And it is Jesus himself who calls us to follow him, and calls us thereby into the wide-open world, the world where God remains sovereign and vulnerable, the world of historical reality, the world of tomorrow's challenges: God's world, the world over which Jesus is already lord and to which he will return to set all things right at last.

11

The Evangelists' Use of the Old Testament as an Implicit Overarching Narrative

Professor John Barton preceded me as a junior research fellow of Merton College, Oxford, in the mid-1970s. When I was ordained there in 1975 the then chaplain, the Revd Mark Everitt, was on sabbatical, and John was invited to return for six months as Acting Chaplain. Thus I, as 'Junior Chaplain', was, effectively, his curate – perhaps the only one he has ever had. We shared many moments of reflection on the daily and weekly scripture readings, and I quickly came to enjoy his many insights and his gentle, shrewd sense of humour. We were again colleagues in the Theology Faculty in Oxford in the late 1980s, and we kept in touch on and off thereafter, with John on one occasion preaching as my guest in Westminster Abbey. So when I was invited to contribute to his Festschrift I did so gladly, and it was natural to seek out a topic in which my main field, the New Testament, was organically linked to his, the Old.

Since this essay was published, Richard Hays's remarkable *Echoes of Scripture in the Gospels* has appeared (Waco, TX: Baylor University Press, 2016), and there are, predictably, many convergences between his larger argument and my smaller one. But I think the present piece still has its own distinctive contribution to make. On the question (central to this article) of the 'extended exile' in the second-Temple period, reference may now be made to chapter 2 of *Paul and the Faithfulness of God* (Wright 2013b), and to the many-sided discussions in J. M. Scott (ed.,), *Exile: A conversation with N. T. Wright* (Downers Grove, IL: InterVarsity Press, 2017).

[189] Early in 2011, the atheist philosopher A. C. Grayling published *The Good Book: A secular bible*.[1] It contains wise sayings and teachings from

---

1 Grayling 2011.

many cultures and centuries. It is cast into sections, beginning with 'Genesis' and including 'Lamentations', 'Acts' and 'Epistles'. It is divided into 'chapters' and 'verses'.

Writing in the *Times Literary Supplement* (*TLS*), David Martin pointed out that, despite the book's apparent echoing of biblical categories, it had no overall *story*.[2] The Bible, he said, provides 'a journey in mixed company from garden to city and from profound loss to grace and bounty'. In a subsequent letter, Gabriel Josipovici endorsed Martin's critique, but pointed out the difference between the narrative closure of the Christian canon and the open-endedness of the Jewish one.[3] 'It is fascinating', he writes, 'to see how a book can change in character when a new ending is tacked on, as happened with the Hebrew Bible and Christianity.'

Quite so. Clearly someone who reads the entire (Christian) Bible as a single narrative, however much of a break they may sense between Malachi and Matthew, will perceive closure in a way that someone who reads Israel's ancient scriptures will not. And that perceived closure will suggest all sorts of other interconnections. [190]

But to what extent were second-Temple Jews aware of their Bible as providing an overall narrative, albeit an unfinished one? And do the New Testament writers, and especially the four evangelists, show awareness of, so to speak, helping such a narrative to its appropriate destination? These questions are cognate with many that Professor John Barton has addressed, from various angles, throughout his career, and I am delighted to offer these reflections in gratitude for a long-standing friendship.

I An Overarching Jewish Story?

There are many kinds of story within the Bible, functioning in different ways both within their immediate contexts and within the canon (whether Jewish or Christian) as a whole. Small personal stories (sometimes, not always) nestle within larger narratives, and the larger narratives themselves are welded together canonically to form macro-stories. Thus the sense of completion at the end of Genesis-Exodus becomes the foundation for something greater

---

2   Martin 2011, 25.

3   Josipovici 2011. The same *TLS* carried (p. 28) a review of James Charlesworth's blockbuster, *The Good and Evil Serpent: How a universal symbol became Christianized* (Charlesworth 2010). Even if the review had been unsigned, we might have guessed that it was by John Barton, not only because of its shrewd summary and critique but because of the twinkle in the eye offered by the faint praise: 'As a rehabilitation of snakes, it could hardly be bettered.'

when the other three books of the Pentateuch are added. The addition of
Joshua to the Pentateuch then works backwards, as it were, to give a different
flavour again to the whole thing. If *that* was the 'ending', we read the earlier
parts differently. And so on.

But there are certain places in the ancient scriptures, and their deutero-
or extra-canonical successors, where we glimpse a larger narrative still that
points forward into the dark, expecting something decisive but not being
quite sure what or when. The classic exilic writings, notably Isaiah 40—66
and Ezekiel, promise a great restoration that nobody in the second-Temple
period thought had yet occurred. The key post-exilic prophets, especially
Zechariah and Malachi, strain forward towards some kind of an 'ending'
required by their own implicit narrative but not yet visible except to the
eye of faith and hope. Many post-canonical works pick up this sense of an
ending yet to come; many of them reflect the vision of four monsters in
Daniel 7, even though, as the angel helpfully explains to 'Ezra' in *4 Ezra* 12,
'it was not explained to him as I now explain to you or have explained it'.[4]
But it is Daniel that offers the most powerful and important 'unfinished
story', one that arguably shaped the understanding of a good many Jews
between the time of Herod the Great and the catastrophic outbreak of war
in AD 66.

In Daniel 9, the hero prays for the promised end of exile. Jeremiah had
said that Israel's time of desolation would last for seventy years; is that not
now over?[5] Back comes the answer (9.24): not seventy years, but seventy times
[191] seven. 'Seventy weeks', in fact.[6] This chronological prophecy fascinated
many people in the two centuries either side of Herod the Great. Various
movements calculated, and re-calculated, when the moment of redemption
would arrive.[7] This theme has, however, remained almost unnoticed in New
Testament scholarship, perhaps because the idea of a continuous history into
which Jesus and his first followers might fit has been almost entirely alien
to the post-Reformation western world. I have suggested elsewhere[8] that a
notoriously cryptic passage in Josephus, explaining why first-century Jews
were so eager for revolt, is best explained as a reference to Daniel – not only
to this passage in chapter 9, but to the book as a whole, and especially to the

---

4   *4 Ez.* 12.12.
5   Dan. 9.2; cf. Jer. 25.11–12; 29.10; 2 Chr. 36.21; Ez. 1.1; Zech. 1.12; 7.5.
6   This is further elaborated in 9.25–27. On all this see now Portier-Young 2011, 267–72.
7   See esp. Beckwith 1981 (= Beckwith 1996, ch. 8); and the discussion in Wright 1992a, 173, 197–8, 312–14.
8   Wright 1992a, 312–14.

predictions of chapters 2 and 7. I here summarize the argument, expanding one element that now seems to me more important than I had previously realized. What, more than all else, incited the Jews to revolt, says Josephus, 'was an ambiguous oracle . . . to the effect that at that time one from their country would become ruler of the world'.[9]

This oracle, Josephus goes on to explain, referred in fact to Vespasian, who was besieging Jerusalem at the time when he was proclaimed emperor.[10] This is of course itself ambiguous. Josephus was writing both for his Roman overlords, who might be glad for this unexpected 'ending' to a prophetic Jewish narrative, and for his Jewish kinsfolk, who might well scan his work for signs that, despite his outward pro-Flavian stance, he still cherished the more normal Jewish hope. There may well be something of both here. Certainly, there is good reason to suppose that the oracle in question was contained in the book of Daniel. No other candidate, in fact, fits the description, particularly the specific 'at that time', *kata ton kairon ekeinon*. No other biblical prophet (except for Jeremiah; but everyone knew his original seventy years were long gone) gives any kind of chronology for fulfilment; and the evidence of Daniel-based chronological speculation (from *Jubilees*, *1 Enoch*, the *Testaments*, Qumran and so on) fits well with the mood Josephus describes.

Nor should we suppose that he meant only Daniel 9 (chapter divisions are, of course, much later). There are signs that the book was being read as a whole – including the interesting phenomenon that when Josephus comes to summarize Daniel's prophecies in the *Antiquities* he draws a discreet veil over the crucial passages, the 'stone' of 2.44–45 and the whole of chapter 7, the former of which was certainly, and the latter arguably (on the basis at least [192] of *4 Ezra*), read as messianic prophecies in the first century.[11] And it is at the very moment when Josephus might have been expected to describe chapter 7 that he mentions once more the point about exact prophetic chronology. Indeed, Josephus stresses that Daniel stands out from other prophets in precisely this respect. Not only did he prophesy future things, as did the other prophets, but 'he also fixed the time (*kairon*) at which these would come to pass'.[12] This corresponds exactly to the passage in *War* 6, and to my mind clinches the case for the reference to Daniel.

---

9   *War* 6.312 (tr. Feldman in LCL).

10 Cf. *War* 3.399–408, where Josephus describes his own prophesying of this to Vespasian in person.

11 On the Stone, see *Ant.* 10.210, with Marcus's notes (in LCL) on 10.206, 209 and here. The omission of any account of Dan. 7 comes at 10.264–8.

12 *Ant.* 10.267 (tr. Marcus).

Did Josephus actually believe that the prophecies were fulfilled in Vespasian? Does he go suddenly quiet when expounding Daniel 2 because he really believes in a still-future Jewish victory, or is he simply trying to distract Roman attention from a blatantly nationalistic prophecy? It is hard to say.[13] We can be clear, however, that he provides strong evidence for a first-century reading of the history of Israel as a continuous, and as yet unfinished, narrative – a story that might conceivably be 'completed' in the most bizarre and paradoxical fashion by the exaltation to world sovereignty of the pagan monarch who was oppressing God's people, or might yet be 'completed' in the way *4 Ezra* still hoped, with the messianic lion defeating the pagan eagle. What he himself believed we cannot be sure. That many of his contemporaries continued to believe in the latter story there should be no doubt.

Of course, not all first-century Jews thought of themselves as living in an incomplete narrative of this sort. We might suppose that Josephus himself might have preferred the kind of apparently 'complete' narrative offered in Ben-Sirach 44—50, in which the long list of heroes reaches a magnificent climax in Simon son of Onias, the high priest in the generation before the Maccabaean crisis. Chapter 50, in fact, seems almost to be the equivalent, within the book, of Exodus 40 within the long story of Genesis and Exodus, or of the prophecy of Ezekiel 40—43 within that book. The second-Temple period, after all, lacks any suggestion that Israel's God had actually returned in person to dwell in the rebuilt shrine.[14] Malachi assures the bored priests that he will return, but that merely emphasizes the fact that he had not yet done so.[15] Perhaps Ben-Sirach was proposing the great liturgical scene in chapter 50 as a kind of equivalent. That on the one hand, and Josephus's prophecy about Vespasian on the other, are as near as we come to any sense of closure to the otherwise open-ended implicit narrative held by many second-Temple Jews. [193]

The other obvious source for an 'incomplete narrative' within second-Temple Judaism is Deuteronomy, whose closing chapters were taken by some in the second-Temple period as a prophetic scheme. God holds out the covenant to Israel: obedience will bring blessings, disobedience cursings (27—28). These warnings are reinforced in chapter 29, but it is assumed that Israel will in fact disobey and thus incur the curse, whose climax will be

---

13   On questions of this sort see esp. Barclay 2005.

14   Zech. 1.16 and 8.3 are sometimes interpreted as making a claim that such a return has already occurred, but in my judgment are better seen as promises for the future. That is certainly how the writer of 14.5 understands the matter.

15   Mal. 3.1–4.

exile (28.64–68; 29.20–28). Only then will the promise of Deuteronomy 30 come into play: restoration the other side of exile, a renewal in which God will circumcise the hearts of his people so that they will at last obey Torah from the heart (30.6–14). The whole scheme is then played out once more, poetically, in chapter 32.

There is widespread evidence that many Jews of the second-Temple period read these chapters in exactly this way, applying them to their own day on the assumption that the curses (particularly 'exile') had come on them and had not yet been properly removed or replaced by the great renewal. I have set out the evidence for this elsewhere, including a consideration of *4 Ezra, Jubilees,* the *Testament of Moses,* the *Psalms of Solomon* and of course Qumran.[16] There is, in addition, another tell-tale little passage in Josephus. Speaking of Moses writing Deuteronomy, he says that the final great poem contains 'a prediction of future events, in accordance with which all has come and is coming to pass'.[17] The last clause is telling: *kath hēn gegone ta panta kai ginetai.* As with his treatment of Daniel, Josephus is not going to tell his Roman audience too specifically what exactly Moses had been predicting. But he believes – or, at any rate, he reflects a current belief – that Deuteronomy 32 constituted a prophecy *that was coming to pass in his own time.*[18]

We have said enough to indicate that, though many Jews may well have been blissfully unaware of any such thing, many others believed themselves to be living in *a narrative in search of an ending,* specifically the great biblical narrative stretching back to the patriarchs and Moses, and behind them again to creation itself. This narrative had, for many, a specific shape: that of Deuteronomy's scheme of blessing–exile–restoration.[19] It had a specific schedule, that of Daniel's 'seventy weeks', variously calculated. And it had a specific goal: some kind of great reversal, involving some at least of the many elements of eschatology (including the eventual return of Israel's God) that swirled around, unsystematized, in the minds of scripture-reading second-Temple Jews. It was above all, however, a narrative in search of an ending.

All four gospels seem to me to be saying, in their different ways: 'This is the ending you were waiting for, even though it doesn't look like you thought it [194] would.' This is the claim that David Martin takes for granted and which Gabriel Josipovici, too, assumes is true of the Christian Bible, however

---

16 Wright 2006a; 2013b, ch. 2. This is not the place to address the objections that have sometimes been raised to this reading.

17 *Ant.* 4.303 (tr. Thackeray).

18 On Paul's use of Deuteronomy, see Hays 1989, 164.

19 This is visible especially clearly in 4QMMT section C.

challenging this may be for Jewish readers. It is, however, a claim that is remarkably silent in mainstream biblical scholarship itself.

2 The Gospels and the Jewish Story

There has, of course, been plenty of work on the use of Israel's scriptures in the gospels. The forms of quotation, the use of typology, the *pesher* method of exegesis, different apocalyptic and eschatological expectations – all this is familiar ground.[20] Excellent work has been done, in particular, on the way in which the exodus-narrative provides the evangelists with a powerful and almost omnipresent substructure.[21] What I miss, however, is the sense – which seems to me as clear in the gospels themselves as it does to a contemporary reader like Martin – of *bringing to its proper conclusion an already existing and presupposed narrative*. This is more than simply saying that Jesus fulfils promises that God made to Israel. That is of course regularly acknowledged as a theme in all four gospels, without any sense of a single continuous narrative. There is all the difference in the world between isolated themes, micro-narratives, with characters cropping up here and there, and a single unbroken story. *This* tennis set is not just another miscellaneous few games. It means what it means because of the four that have preceded it, leaving the match poised and awaiting a decisive climax.

Many other early Christian writings tell the story of Jesus precisely as the climax of the single continuous (if complex, dark and contested) narrative of Israel. Stephen's speech appears to do something like this, with the coming and death of Jesus as the strange fulfilment of a highly negative narrative.[22] Paul's speech in Pisidian Antioch strikes a more positive note, but still offers a long biblical narrative with Jesus as its climax.[23] Paul himself, in Romans, tells the story of Abraham, Isaac, Jacob, Moses and the exodus, the prophets and the 'remnant' – reaching its *telos* with the Messiah, through whom the promises of Deuteronomy 30 have at last come true, resulting in worldwide blessing.[24] The whole of the letter to the Hebrews makes the point that Israel's scriptures look beyond themselves to a further, more complete fulfilment, and chapter 11 offers a sustained narrative which reaches its climax with Jesus [195]

---

20 Classic studies include Lindars 1961; Longenecker 1975; Ellis 1991. The older work of Dodd 1965 [1952] remains important.
21 See particularly Swartley 1994. On the theme of 'new exodus' see esp. Watts 2000.
22 Ac. 7.2–53.
23 Ac. 13.16–39.
24 Rom. 9.6—10.21. See Wright 2002 ad loc.

himself.[25] Would it be so surprising if the gospels told the story of Jesus not only as a kind of detached fulfilment of various ancient prophecies, not only as the anti-type of various ancient 'types' (Moses, David, the Passover Lamb), not only as the decisive recapitulation of major ancient themes (especially the exodus), but as the point at which the single narrative in which all those were contained reached its dramatic destination?

'The time is fulfilled!' declares Mark's Jesus; 'God's kingdom is arriving!'[26] This declaration has proved controversial: has the kingdom already arrived, or is it about to do so? But that old puzzle often sidelined a key point. If (as many have thought) Mark is here echoing Daniel 7.22, then this indicates that for Mark at least the start of Jesus' public career was the moment when the great *narrative* of Daniel 7 (and, by implication, of Daniel 2 and 9 as well) was moving into its final phase. This was the moment when the 'fourth beast' was to be overthrown, and God's people vindicated. The *kairos* that arrived in Daniel 7 was the *kairos* that was 'fulfilled' in Mark 1.15.[27]

This is only, of course, the tip of the iceberg. The two quotations at the start of Mark – Malachi 3.1 and Isaiah 40.3 – are not isolated, detached prophecies floating in a non-historical vacuum, as tends to be implied when the gospels' scripture usage is discussed. Both of them refer to that moment in the implicit narrative at which, after the long wait, Israel's God would return to his people. They hook Mark's story in to the far longer, older story; Mark presents his Jesus-narrative as the proper, if shocking and unexpected, conclusion to the implicit story of God and Israel. For Mark, this is a *messianic* conclusion: Jesus is anointed as king in his baptism, confessed as Messiah by Peter at Caesarea Philippi, and 'enthroned' (that, for sure, is how Mark saw the crucifixion) with the words 'King of the Jews' over his head. The bridegroom has arrived at the wedding-party (2.19). The fresh seed is at last being sown, even if much appears to be going to waste (4.1–20). However paradoxical all this may be as a 'conclusion' to the glorious story of Israel – and it does seem almost as paradoxical as Josephus's idea that Israel's God had gone over to the Romans and was installing Vespasian as world ruler – there should be no doubt that this was how Mark intended his story to be heard.

---

25 Heb. 11.4—12.2.

26 Mk. 1.15.

27 This is so in both the LXX and Theodotion. The latter has *ho kairos ephthasen*, which Dodd argued was closely related to the underlying Aramaic of Dan. 7.22. Note also Mt. 12.28/Lk. 11.20, where *ephthasen* is found. See Dodd 1961, 36–7. Dodd's wider proposal about 'realized eschatology' has, I think, distracted attention from the question of how Mark saw Jesus fitting into the *narrative* of Daniel 7.

And if Mark, then rather obviously Matthew. Matthew's opening chapter makes it clear enough which way the wind is blowing. It is not enough to point out that the evangelists show Jesus giving 'a prominent place to the Old [196] Testament' in his teaching.[28] The genealogy tells the *continuous story*, with its only break being the question of how, if (as Matthew insists) Joseph is not Jesus' biological father, the family line from Abraham and David can be relevant. But Matthew's intention is clear. Jesus comes as the climax, after six sequences of seven generations: the seventh seven is now beginning. As in Daniel, so here (and in Matthew 18.22), the theme of Jubilee is not far away – the theme that, as we saw, was highlighted by some of the groups who were searching for the right interpretation of Daniel 9.[29]

The genealogy focuses on three 'moments' in Israel's long story: Abraham, David and the exile. It is not simply, as one might suppose at first glance, that the exile was a convenient marker, fourteen generations after David and fourteen before Jesus. Rather, Matthew shared the widespread first-century Jewish perception that 'exile' was a state of being, not merely of geography; that it had come about as a result of Israel's sin (see, again, Daniel 9); and that it had not yet been dealt with. The angel's announcement that Jesus 'will save his people from their sins' (1.21) is not referring to a timeless 'salvation'. Jesus will undo the condition of exile by dealing with its primary cause.[30] Jesus, for Matthew, does not simply recapitulate elements in the ancient scriptures, though of course he does that too. He brings that ancient story to its long-awaited goal.

Mark and Matthew between them highlight Daniel, especially, of course, the famous (even notorious) chapter 7. But this is not to be thought of as a detached 'messianic' interpretation of the 'one like a son of man'. Rather, as I and others have sought to show elsewhere, the point is again the overall narrative. The four-kingdom scheme of Daniel 2 and 7, coupled with the chronological pointer in chapter 9, provides a story-line in which Jesus can be portrayed as the one who is launching God's sovereign reign, on the one hand, and carrying the weight of the people's suffering at the hands of the 'beasts', on the other – all prior to his exaltation and enthronement. The story is not a separate narrative about Jesus almost randomly 'fulfilling' this or that

---

28 Ellis 1991, 77. Ellis does, however, point towards what seems to me the fuller and deeper truth when he says (p. 77) that 'the messianic hermeneutic continues, admittedly in a highly climactic manner, earlier prophetic interpretations of Israel's Scriptures in terms of the current acts of God within the nation'.

29 On the Jubilee theme in this connection see Portier-Young 2011, 270–2.

30 Among the many biblical passages that make this connection, see e.g. Lam. 4.22.

prophecy from some far-off seer. What we have in the gospels, rather, is the sense of a long journey reaching its destination – even though, on arrival, the travellers find the place not at all as they expected.

Luke stresses the note of fulfilment, with a divine necessity attached: this is how it 'must' be, whether for the twelve-year-old in the Temple or for the newly risen Jesus on the Emmaus Road. And at the heart of this theme we find the crucial claim: 'He began with Moses, and with all the prophets, and [197] explained to them the things about himself throughout the whole Bible.'[31] A later, atomistic exegesis has seen these passages in terms of a string of detached prophecies or proof-texts, such as Genesis 22 or Psalm 22, Isaiah 53 or (of course) Daniel 7. But such a list misses the point. The point is that what Jesus has been doing, the fate he has suffered, and now the resurrection itself, constitute the *completion of the story*. The sense they make is the sense of the ending to the much longer narrative that Jesus here invokes. This is what is meant, I take it, in the tradition repeated by Paul: the Messiah died for our sins, and was raised, *in accordance with the scriptures*.[32] This is where the narrative had been going all along. The great canticles, Mary's song and Zechariah's song, set carefully at the start of the story, explain it exactly. This is the fulfilment of what God promised Abraham long ago. Jesus says exactly the same in his quoting of Isaiah 61 in the 'Nazareth Manifesto'.[33]

John takes the whole thing right back to the beginning, with his obvious echoes of Genesis 1. But he, no less than the others, tells the story of Jesus as the long fulfilment of the story of Israel, with a special focus on the Temple. The people had been waiting for Israel's God to return, to pitch his tent in their midst and to reveal his glory. This, says John, is precisely what has happened in and through Jesus (1.14), even though it meant that when he 'came to what was his own . . . his own people did not accept him' (1.11). Central to John, as to almost every New Testament writer, is the clash between two conflicting visions of how the ancient scriptural story is to be told, and how, in particular, it is to reach its goal. Some ask, 'How can Jesus be the Messiah?' But others insist that he is (for example 7.31–52; 10.22–30). Jesus persists: when Moses wrote, he was writing about him; when Abraham believed God, he was looking forward to him.[34] The political implications emerge starkly in chapters 18 and 19 as Jesus confronts Pilate: this, for John, is the climax of the

---

31   Lk. 24.27; repeated in 24.44–45.
32   1 Cor. 15.3–4.
33   Lk. 4.18–19.
34   5.46; 8.30–59.

age-old scriptural stand-off between the kingdom of God and the kingdoms of the world. And Jesus' last word says it all: *tetelestai*. 'It is completed.' The story (of both creation and Israel) has reached its goal.[35]

There is much more, of course, that could and should be said about the way in which the four canonical gospels are written with the deliberate intent of telling the story of Jesus as the proper goal of the single narrative of Israel (and, in a measure, of creation). That, I have suggested, was a deeply Jewish thing to do, however unexpected and shocking to first-century Jews this 'ending' might have appeared. But I want to turn, in conclusion, to a striking parallel phenomenon that is not normally observed in this connection. There was, at the time, another great story being told with a striking new ending.

[198] 3 The Gospels in a World of Gospels

If we speak of 'other gospels' alongside the four canonical documents that normally bear that name, many might suppose we meant books like the so-called *Gospel of Thomas*. Indeed, one of the many differences between them and the canonical gospels is the absence of Israel's narrative, let alone any sense of its goal. But in the first century, before such things were thought of, there were indeed many 'gospels', many *euangelia*, namely, the repeated imperial announcements.[36] One of the gains of recent scholarship has been to relocate Jesus and his first followers in a world where the 'good news' of Augustus, then of his various successors, was well known, employing the usual imperial rhetoric: so-and-so has won a great victory, bringing peace, prosperity and justice to the world, so we will acclaim him as saviour and lord.[37]

What is not so widely noted is the way in which the four gospels, told as the climax of the much longer story of Israel, are thus engaged in an exercise strangely parallel to that undertaken, two generations before, by the writers of the Augustan court. Rome had a long, proud history of republicanism, with a deep inbuilt resistance to one-man rule. Yet Augustus's writers were able to put it about that in his reign the long traditions of Rome had been not subverted but rather fulfilled. Augustus had won great victories, and was therefore hailed as 'son of God'; he was technically that already, being the

---

35 19.30. Note the echo of Gen. 2.1–3.

36 There is now a huge literature on this topic. A good, suggestive introduction is that of Stanton 2004, ch. 2, with copious references.

37 Oakes 2000.

adopted son of the deified Julius, but had he not won at Actium the title would have been quietly forgotten. In similar fashion, the crucified Jesus was not the 'Messiah' anyone had imagined, but early confessions insisted that his resurrection proved him to be, indeed, 'son of God', the one through whom Israel's long story reached its goal.[38]

The first Roman writer to pull off this intellectual stunt, claiming that destroying the republic was really fulfilling it, was Livy. A lifelong friend of the princeps, he may have had private doubts about whether one-man rule was ultimately in Rome's best interests (rather like Josephus hailing Vespasian but still, perhaps, hoping for a more traditional fulfilment). But he told the story in such a way as to lead the eye up to Augustus, and was not above tweaking the older story to set up relevant political points.[39]

In the *Odes*, Horace offers a crescendo of support for Augustus. He prays that Caesar will be Zeus's vice-regent in his worldwide kingdom (1.12). **[199]** He celebrates his victory over Cleopatra (1.37), his various other military successes (2.9; 2.12) and his splendid return to Rome (3.14; cf. 4.2; 4.5; 4.15). All this could be seen as simple homage, without a previous narrative. But then he writes the *Carmen Saeculare*, a 'hymn to a new age', seeing Augustus as the long-awaited descendant of Venus and Anchises, locating him as the true heir to Rome's ancient traditions.[40] This offers a clear implicit narrative, which it was left to Rome's greatest poet to make more fully explicit.

The poet in question was of course Virgil. The famous Fourth Eclogue, describing the birth of the child who will see in the golden age, is probably not about Augustus. But the poet was personally close to the princeps while writing the *Aeneid*, and we are not surprised when, early on, Zeus prophesies that from the line of Aeneas will come 'a Trojan Caesar, who shall extend his empire to the ocean, his glory to the stars'.[41] Venus takes up the theme, prophesying to her son Aeneas the great coming triumphs of his mighty descendant.[42] But the classic passage is the 'prophecy' of Anchises himself, showing the young Aeneas the splendour of the future Age of Augustus.[43] Augustus, son of a god, 'will establish a golden age' and 'advance his empire . . . to a land which lies

---

38 Rom. 1.3–5 etc.

39 Cf. Livy 4.20, where Cornelius Cossus celebrates the *spolia opima*; it was important for Augustus that Cossus be seen not as a tribune, but as a consul, so as to deny such celebration to any potential rivals. Livy adjusts the record to suit imperial need.

40 The *Carmen Saeculare* is on pp. 262–7 of the LCL edn of Horace (tr. Rudd).

41 1.286–7 (tr. Fairclough, rev. Goold).

42 8.626–731, esp. at 678–81 and 714–23.

43 6.788–901.

beyond our stars'.[44] With the artistry of his grand narrative as well as in his poetic detail, Virgil thus creates a single story going back a millennium and reaching an otherwise unexpected (but now, we see, foretold) goal. His master is the one for whom, had it but known, Rome had been waiting all along.

So far as I know, this was as much of an innovation in the pagan world of late antiquity as the gospels were within the Jewish world. They stand in a strange parallel. Livy and Virgil were writing, of course, before the time of Jesus' public career; and no-one, I think, will suggest that the evangelists were trying to emulate the great Romans. Yet just as in Luke 2 we find Augustus lifting a finger in Rome and, with an enviable mastery of the law of unintended consequences, sending the pregnant Mary to Bethlehem, so in these two parallel narratives we have the kingdom of God and the kingdom of Caesar both claiming to tell the world that it has a rightful lord, who has at last brought peace and justice to birth. This, at the very least, offers some fresh angles of vision on both sets of writings, and on the ideologies they embody. Perhaps the contemporary interest in narrative (not least the sense of an ending) and the contemporary interest in counter-imperial readings of scripture are more closely intertwined than has commonly been supposed.

---

44 6.792, 795–6.

12

John, Jesus and 'The Ruler of This World': Demonic Politics in the Fourth Gospel?

Like many Pauline scholars, I have managed to write very little on the fourth gospel, apart from some (I hope) suggestive remarks in *The New Testament and the People of God* (Wright 1992a, 410–17) and the exploration of the resurrection in John in *The Resurrection of the Son of God* (Wright 2003, ch. 17). But when we scheduled an entire semester's worth of graduate seminars on the interface between the early Christians and the Roman empire, in the spring of 2014, including a memorable trip to the Augustus exhibition in the Capitoline Museum in Rome, it was clearly important that at some stage we should deal with John. There being no-one else willing to take on this challenge, I decided to investigate the matter myself. My then research assistant, Jamie Davies, provided copious assistance, and he co-authored the following article, which appeared under both our names in the Festschrift for Andrew Lincoln, whose scholarly company I have enjoyed over many years and whose contributions to the study of John's gospel remain something of a landmark.

[71] Introduction

One might think that of all the New Testament books the least likely to be caught up in debates about anti-imperial politics would be the gospel of John. The old nineteenth-century prejudices about John linger on. John is a 'spiritual' gospel, a 'theological' gospel, not like the rough-and-tumble synoptics, still less like that argumentative fellow Paul. John is about the incarnation of the Word, the love of God in sending the son, and the glory revealed on the cross. At the heart of John we find the 'farewell discourses', seen by many as the deepest and richest focus and source of Christian spirituality. What can all this have to do with the messy business of politics, still less the dangerous suggestion of a counter-imperial agenda?

And yet, before we even glance at contemporary scholarship, we should pause. John is a deeply *Jewish* book: the older prejudice which screened out John's [72] Jewishness in favour of non-Jewish hellenistic settings is just that, a prejudice. From the first two chapters we ought already to know that this author is soaked in Genesis and Exodus, in Isaiah and the Psalms, and not least in a Temple-theology from which both his Christology and his pneumatology gain their meanings. His closest cousins – different, but with family likenesses – are Ben-Sirach, the Wisdom of Solomon and indeed the Scrolls, rather than the Stoics or the Gnostics. The running battle in the fourth gospel between Jesus and the Judaeans (I call them that because 'the Jews' is obviously misleading, and it is not clear to me that John's *hoi Ioudaioi* always and only means 'the Jewish leaders') is a family squabble, and should not be seen as a non-Jewish gospel breaking free of Judaism altogether. And from all we know about first-century Judaism we have to say that the political agenda was never far from the surface. To put it no more strongly, if we are telling a story about a would-be Jewish leader, whose followers considered him to be Messiah, who clashed repeatedly with the Jewish authorities and was finally put to death by the Romans, then this story is a lot more 'political' than many older views would have allowed. And as for the farewell discourses – well, that is where Jesus warned his followers that the world would hate them, that they would be put out of the synagogues, and that (whatever this means) 'the ruler of this world', *ho archōn tou kosmou toutou*, was coming to get him, but that Jesus had conquered the world, *nenikēka ton kosmon* (15.18; 16.2; 14.30; 16.33). What does this mean, and how does it all fit together? Might there, after all, be some links, however submerged, to that other great Johannine book, the far more obviously political 'Revelation of St John the Divine'?

In offering this gift, in admiration, to a scholar whose company I have enjoyed in our shared pursuits over forty years or so, I should make it clear that I claim no long or deep acquaintance with contemporary Johannine scholarship. However, in some of my more popular speaking and writing I have frequently been drawn to the extraordinary scene in chapters 18 and 19 where Jesus and Pilate confront one another, representing the kingdom of God and the kingdom of Caesar, and I have ventured the suggestion that this is the heart of the New Testament's political theology.[1] So I want here to take a fresh look at that scene, drawing in some key strands from earlier in the gospel, and make some tentative suggestions. I am bracketing out any discussion of history, whether the actual events concerning Jesus or the putative situation

---

1   E.g. Wright 2012, esp. 144–7; 229–32.

of the Johannine community. I want to focus on the text and what seems to me its own inner dynamic, rhetoric and logic. [73]

Recent Study

Many recent studies of John have bypassed the theme of politics and empire altogether. Craig Keener's massive two-volume commentary says almost nothing on this subject. Richard Bauckham's collection of essays on John[2] does not address the subject, even in his quite substantial piece on Jewish messianism in the fourth gospel (ch. 10, pp. 207–38). The solid volume on *The Gospel of John and Christian Theology* that emerged from the St Andrews conference of 2003[3] seems to ignore the theme altogether, though there are some interesting related reflections in the essay by Sigve Tonstad (pp. 193–210). At the popular level, commentaries and introductions proceed as though there were nothing there to discuss, an example being the work of Andreas Koestenberger.[4]

Some of those who have written on empire in the New Testament have actually suggested that John's whole presentation is running in the other direction from the counter-imperial material that many discern elsewhere. The articles of Kvalbein and Hengel[5] are fairly adamant on the subject. A much more nuanced statement is found in Stephen Moore's book *Empire and Apocalypse*.[6] His chapter on John argues for two quite different strands. In one sense, he says, John is the most political of the gospels, recognizing the political dimensions and dangers inherent in Jesus' presence and mission. On another level, however, 'John is also the *least* political of the canonical gospels . . . because the same passion narrative seems to place Jesus' kingship front and centre only in order to depoliticize it'.[7] Moore at once applies a classic post-colonial hermeneutic of suspicion:

> If the Roman prefect's 'I find no crime in him' (18.38) is to be construed – approvingly and unequivocally – as meaning that the Jewish Messiah's brand of kingship is not, in the end, a threat to the Roman Emperor's brand, then pro-Roman apologetics would here seem to be extending themselves

---

2 Bauckham 2007.
3 Bauckham and Mosser 2008.
4 Koestenberger 1999.
5 Kvalbein 2003, 227f., following Hengel 1991, 51.
6 Moore 2006.
7 Moore 2006, 50f.

to the limit and paving the royal road to the fourth century and an unproblematic fusion of Christianity and Rome.[8] [74]

The irony then, says Moore, is that it is the chief priests who see Jesus as a political danger. However, though for Moore the fourth gospel thus appears to be the charter document of Constantinian Christianity – appearing to allow Rome the freedom to develop without the threat of imminent judgment that is found in the apocalyptic tradition in the synoptics and Revelation – it nevertheless contains embedded within it 'the most trenchant critique of Roman imperialism of any of the canonical gospels', partly through its inclusion of Rome within the 'world' that it denounces, partly through its structuring of the narrative of Jesus' trial and torture, and partly through 'the searing critique of the fundamental machinations of the *imperium Romanum*' within that same narrative structure.[9] As will become apparent, my conclusion about Moore is the same as Moore's about John: absolutely right in some ways, massively wrong in others.[10]

There has recently been a flurry of detailed 'John-and-empire' studies. There is a useful survey by Francis Moloney in the *Expository Times*,[11] pointing out some of the 'back-markers' in this discussion, and offering a brief and clear description of the three main recent works, those of Richey in 2007,[12] Carter in 2008[13] and Thatcher in 2009.[14] Warren Carter steps aside from the usual idea of positing a church–synagogue split behind the fourth gospel, and suggests that the anti-synagogue material is a 'hidden transcript' in which 'the Jews' are actually to be subsumed under the larger entity of Roman imperial power. Carter locates the whole drama in Ephesus, where the privileged Jewish elite have been over-accommodating to the empire, while John is urging Christ-believers to distance themselves from any such position. Moloney, summarizing Carter's position, says that, if Carter is right, 'everything written [about John] over the past 150 years will become marginal'.[15] I see this as itself a hidden transcript for Moloney's own view, which is that Carter has considerably overstated his case, not least where Carter suggests

---

8   Moore 2006, 52.
9   Moore 2006, 74.
10   Moore 2006, 74-5.
11   Moloney 2012, 424-6.
12   Richey 2007.
13   Carter 2008.
14   Thatcher 2008.
15   Moloney 2012, 424.

that we should read Johannine Christology in the light of Caligula's attempt in AD 40 to install in the Jerusalem Temple a statue of himself as Zeus. That is a cat-among-the-pigeons proposal which is so sharp and surprising that it deserves more study, certainly in the light [75] of the fourth gospel's Temple-focus. But at this point I am inclined to agree with Moloney that Carter has stretched the evidence further than it will go.

Lance Richey retains the usual view of a church–synagogue split, but he finds explicit anti-Roman polemic in several parts of the gospel. In particular, he offers a counter-imperial reading of the prologue that even I, straining my ears to catch such overtones, found hard to detect. He does, however, have an interesting discussion of the trial narrative, which as I have said I consider to be the heart of the matter.[16]

Tom Thatcher attempts to answer Stephen Moore. He, like Carter and Richey, focuses on Johannine Christology, arguing that 'imperial terms were foundational to John's Christology, and that his thinking about Christ was always informed by the premise that Jesus is greater than Caesar'.[17] Like Carter, he sees the Jewish authorities in John as a puppet aristocracy doing its best to maintain the status quo and thus effectively being a sub-branch of empire. This turns on its head a more usual reading of the gospel, in which the Jewish authorities are the real enemy throughout, with Pontius Pilate being wheeled on reluctantly at the end to do what the chief priests tell him. In particular, Thatcher goes against the grain in reading John 12.31, 'now this world's ruler is going to be thrown out',[18] as referring not to Satan but to Caesar.[19] That is important, and we must return to the point.

This is hardly a complete literature review on this topic.[20] But I hope it is sufficient to indicate that John belongs on the map of current studies of early Christianity and the Roman empire, and to form something of a platform for the close readings of the text to which I now turn.

---

16 Richey 2007, 153–84.

17 Thatcher 2008, 11.

18 For the English translations of scripture in this article, see the note in the preface to the present volume.

19 Thatcher 2008, 116–17.

20 In his work *Truth on Trial* (Lincoln 2000), Andrew Lincoln suggests that the 'ruler of the world' is Satan (106). But at several points in the book he firmly holds together the 'cosmic' nature of the 'trial' that is taking place with the 'political' dimension; though I think he is sometimes using the word 'cosmic' to indicate a universal, worldwide significance (as opposed to a merely local, Jewish one), e.g. 123–4; 256; 321 (the opposition is 'both supernatural and human', though the latter, the 'unbelieving world', is represented by 'the Jews'). At p. 258 Lincoln appears to distinguish between 'the ruler of this world' and the Jewish and Roman authorities. I hope in this tribute to bring some further clarity to these and related matters.

Before we move on, however, it is important to face one question in particular. Almost all commentators seem to take it for granted that the phrase *ho archōn tou kosmou* refers naturally and only to the devil or 'the [76] satan'.[21] But is this really the best way to take *archōn*? The entry in BDAG, when dealing with Luke and Paul, lists human officials, whether Jewish or pagan, as possible meanings; but when it comes to John, it classifies the word in reference to evil spirits, placing John 12.31, 14.30 and 16.11 alongside the *archōn tōn daimoniōn* of the synoptics (for example Matthew 12.24).[22] But this seems simply to beg the question. Walter Wink, in his quite thorough survey, points out that in the Septuagint the word always denotes human authorities, and that this holds true for Josephus and Philo as well, despite them having plenty to say about evil spirits.[23] The more we read John within an assumed broadly Jewish setting, the more the language of world rulership ought to remind us of the apocalyptic literature in which 'suprahuman' rulers are invoked in order to highlight the cosmological dimensions of earthly 'political' life, not to separate the one from the other. From this background, it would be natural to assume that a phrase like *ho archōn tou kosmou* in John could refer *both* to the devil/the satan *and* to the political regime of Caesar. John, like Daniel, would be seeking to reveal to his readers the 'spiritual' battles being fought behind the scenes of the 'political' empires of the world. That is, more or less, the case I now want to present.

John 12.20–36

As is well known, John's gospel divides into two distinct parts, breaking at the end of chapter 12. After the prologue, the first twelve chapters take Jesus to and fro between Galilee and Jerusalem. The narrative oscillates between the 'signs', starting with the wedding at Cana, and the 'discourses' that draw out

---

21 Though cf. Haenchen 1984, 98, who reads the phrase politically in 12.31, mentioning war, torture and the 'powers of state, business, and political parties, of the mass media'. Lindars 1972, 433, says that *ho archōn tou kosmou toutou* is 'obviously a reference to the Devil . . . though there is no precise parallel for it in Jewish literature'. Rensberger 1988, tellingly, has no listing in the index for Jn. 12.31, 14.30 or 16.11, despite the book being ostensibly about politics in the fourth gospel.

22 BDAG, 140.

23 See Wink 1984, 151–2. The exceptions are that Philo can use *archōn* for God himself; and that, in LXX Daniel, *archōn* is used for 'spiritual' authorities. In Daniel, of course, part of the point is that 'spiritual' realities are shown up as standing behind scenes of earthly political domination; see Portier-Young 2011. Wink reads the Johannine 'ruler of the world' as Satan (42 n. 9; 61), but links this with the Jewish authorities (9) and elsewhere says that the satan 'could scarcely avoid being identified as the special patron of Rome' (33–4).

their meaning. John's multiple themes are displayed from many angles: light, water, life and so on. The advance summary statement in the [77] prologue that 'he came to his own, and his own people did not receive him' is demonstrated in numerous confrontations, some very sharp, between Jesus and *hoi Ioudaioi*, 'the Judaeans', the inhabitants of Jerusalem and its immediate environs. Jesus is threatened with stoning for blasphemy, and his death is openly plotted, for nakedly political reasons, by Caiaphas and his colleagues at the end of chapter 11: 'If we let him go on like this, everyone is going to believe in him! Then the Romans will come and take away our holy place, and our nation!' (11.48). Caiaphas's answer is totally political and, for John, totally theological: 'This is what's best for you: let one man die for the people, rather than the whole nation being wiped out' (11.50). John comments that this was an unintended prophecy, since Jesus would die not only for the nation 'but to gather into one the scattered children of God' (11.52). That is the background to chapter 12, and in particular to 12.20–36.

In 12.20 'some Greeks' at the festival ask Philip if they can see Jesus. This has been prepared for by the continuing irony earlier in chapter 12, where Jesus rides into Jerusalem in fulfilment of the Zechariah prophecy, with the crowds all around him, and the Pharisees conclude that they can do nothing because 'the world has gone off after him' (12.19). The *kosmos* is of course another major Johannine theme, straddling the line (as all creational monotheism must do) between 'the world' as created by God, loved by him and to be redeemed, and 'the world' as the sphere of rebellion, corruption and death. Here the Pharisees mean it contemptuously. But, as with Caiaphas's prophecy, John believes that they have said more than they knew. Hence the arrival of the Greeks. 'The world' is the pagan world; who then is its present 'ruler'?

When Philip and Andrew tell Jesus about the Greeks' request, Jesus does not say, 'Very well; I will see them presently.' He appears to go off into quite a different subject: 'The time has come. This is the moment for the son of man to be glorified' (12.23). As often in John, however, within the apparent non sequitur we should discern a deeper theme. Jesus sees the arrival of the Greeks as the sign that the hour had come – 'the hour' which was 'not yet' from 2.4 up to this point. Does John intend his readers to understand that Jesus is invoking the scenario in Daniel 7, where 'one like a son of man' becomes lord and ruler of the whole world? As usual in John, we are not told. But clearly this glorification has to do with Jesus' death, with the grain of wheat that must fall into the earth and die in order to bear much fruit (12.24). Then comes the real 'response' to the Greeks. Jesus prays that the father would glorify his name, and the thunderous voice responds that this has been done and will be done. John's Jesus draws the conclusion, in other words, that *the arrival of the Greeks is the sign that he himself, through his death, is going to be the new ruler of the world, displacing the present one:* [78] 'Now comes the judgment of this world! Now this world's ruler is going to be thrown out! And when I've been lifted up from the earth, I will draw all people to myself' (12.31–32).

With this we are suddenly introduced to a new theme. The 'ruler of the world' has not been mentioned before in John. The parallels often adduced to this phrase are not exact. 2 Corinthians 4.4 speaks of 'the god of this *aiōn*', and Ephesians 2.2 of 'the ruler of the power of the air'; we might compare Ephesians 6.12, James 4.4, Luke 4.6; and, back in the Johannine literature, 1 John 4.4 and 5.19, the last of these speaking of the whole world lying *en tō ponērō*, in the power of the evil one. Taken together, even though none is exactly parallel, all these seem to indicate the conclusion that almost all commentators have reached: that 'the ruler of the world' here refers, unambiguously and only, to the satan, the devil. This then points on to some kind of *Christus Victor* reading of Jesus' death: the cross will be the means of the satan's overthrow.[24]

But ought we to accept this either/or so easily? Are we so sure that John, or any of the early Christians, would have pushed such a thick wedge between satanic power and political power? Granted the clearly political edge to the machinations of Caiaphas and his colleagues, and granted the clearly political hints earlier in the gospel – such as Jesus perceiving that the crowds want to come and make him king – I have my doubts. And these are confirmed when we look into both the farewell discourses and the trial narrative itself.

The Farewell Discourses

The farewell discourses (chapters 13 to 17) are so well known that we often fail to note their extraordinary rhetorical effect within the book as a whole. From the tense moments in chapters 7, 8 and 9, the narrative has been gathering pace. The 'good shepherd' discourse in chapter 10 is not, as it has been so often portrayed, a soft-focus pastoral scene. It is nakedly political: all who came before were thieves and brigands, *kleptai kai lēstai*, but the sheep did not listen to them. Jesus, however, will lay down his life for the sheep. We are not surprised when

---

24 See e.g. Barrett 1978 [1955], 426–7; Morris 1971, 597–8. An interesting exception is Temple 1945, 198–9, assuming without argument that the reference is to Caiaphas and Pilate.

things again turn ugly, and stoning is threatened. Jesus goes off to the Jordan, but then, despite the disciples' warnings, comes back to Judaea to raise Lazarus. The reader knows how this will end, and Caiaphas's prophecy confirms it. Then comes the triumphal [79] entry, and then the passage we have just seen: the grain of wheat falling into the earth, the world's ruler being thrown out and Jesus himself being lifted up to draw all people to himself.

By this time – this is my point about rhetorical effect – the reader is on tiptoe with excitement. Each time Jesus has been to Jerusalem, up to now in the narrative, there has been some kind of confrontation, usually in connection with one of the great festivals (Passover, Tabernacles, Hanukkah, now Passover again). Each time, we hear overtones from the prologue, where the Word became flesh and 'tabernacled' in our midst; from chapter 2 onwards we have been informed that Jesus himself is the new Temple, so that the long-awaited returning Shekinah is coming back to Zion at last. The prophecies, particularly of Isaiah, are now coming true. Now, therefore, the reader is agog: how is it going to play out? How will Jesus be 'lifted up'? What will happen in his final showdown with the authorities?

John surely knows what he is doing, but in narratival terms it feels very strange. Instead of taking us straight into the final flurry of activity, he leads us into the upper room, and holds us there for five chapters, nearly a fifth of the whole gospel. There is barely any activity, other than the initial footwashing, the departure of Judas, and the hint at the end of chapter 14 that the little party is leaving the upper room ('Get up. Let's be going', 14.31). The discourse is helped on its way by a few short questions, but these chapters consist almost entirely of teaching. What is John saying?

For a start, he is at last taking us, not into the present Temple in Jerusalem, but into what he has hinted all along is the true Temple. This is where heaven and earth meet, because this is where Jesus bares his heart and soul to his friends. Here he explains that through the spirit the Temple is now to be extended into all the world. This picks up the strange little passage in 7.38, where Jesus says that 'anyone who believes in me will have rivers of living water flowing out of their heart', in accordance with a scriptural prophecy that, though unnamed, must be Ezekiel 47.1–12, distantly echoing Genesis 2.10–14. All this reaches its peak in the so-called high-priestly prayer in chapter 17, where the long-promised revelation of the divine glory is to take place, not in the Jerusalem Temple, but in Jesus and his followers and in their common life.

One might say that all this was already 'political'. The Jerusalem Temple was after all the centre, not of a 'religion' in a modern sense, but of an embattled but proud community. It was the symbol of hope and, sometimes, of resistance. That was why Antiochus Epiphanes had paganized it two centuries earlier, and it was why Caligula wanted to do the same thing in the 40s. To say, as John's Jesus does, 'But *this* is the true Temple' is thus both to upstage the present Temple – and its hierarchy, of course – and to [80] reaffirm the central symbol of Jewish monotheism and culture against all pagan cult and culture, of which the most obvious new example was Rome. All this might be said, simply on the basis of a Temple-understanding of the farewell discourses.

But at key points in the discourses, not as their main theme, but as a persistent sub-plot, we hear a dark note that looks back to 12.31 and points forward to chapters 18 and 19. This is part of how the discourses work. Before we get to the trial and death of Jesus, John wants us to know what these events will actually mean. In the synoptics this is accomplished by (among other things) the Last Supper, through which Jesus says, in effect, 'This is how you are to understand what is about to happen.' John does something like this, only far more so: not only the footwashing, but the whole complex of the discourses, explains from one angle after another how the reader is to grasp, and then to live by, the meaning of Jesus' death and resurrection.

The dark note in question is the express mention of the satan. The dark powers feature less in John than in the synoptics. There has been one mention earlier, at the end of chapter 6: one of the twelve 'is a devil' (6.70); and in chapter 8 Jesus charges 'the Judaeans' that they are true children of 'their father the devil' (8.39–59). Now, in chapter 13, we are told in verse 2 that the devil (*ho diabolos*) had already put it into Judas's heart to betray Jesus; then, terrifyingly, at verse 27, Judas receives the bread from Jesus, and 'the satan entered into him', *ho satanas* rather than simply *ho diabolos*. This is the only explicit mention of 'the satan' in John, and it has its literal Hebrew force; it isn't just that Judas is demon-possessed, but rather that he becomes 'the accuser', setting the prosecution of Jesus in train. So he went out, says John; *ēn de nyx*, 'and it was night' (13.30).

I wonder whether we should hear a larger echo at this point. If in these chapters John is constituting Jesus and his followers as the true Temple, the place where God is dwelling with his people, then it is striking that in this company, as in the heavenly court in the Old Testament, we find a public prosecutor, namely, 'the satan'. But he, for his own reasons, leaves the company. Is there an echo of the satan being ejected from heaven, as in Revelation 12.8–9 and indeed Luke 10.18, both echoing Isaiah 14.12?

This is only a suggestion. But it might fit with other elements of the developing picture.

This scene, and the sense of excitement and joy that immediately follows Judas's departure, again indicates that, as with the arrival of the Greeks, John's Jesus is 'reading' these events as signals which show where the divine plan now stands. 'Now the son of man is glorified', he says, 'and God is glorified in him' (13.31) – an explicit glance back to 12.23. In its context, Jesus is recognizing that the battle with the dark enemy is coming to a head. But how will that happen? [81]

The end of chapter 14 provides at least part of the answer. 'The ruler of this world is coming (*erchetai*)', declares Jesus. 'He has nothing to do with me' – that's how I translate the somewhat compressed *en emoi ouch echei ouden* – 'but all this is happening so that the world may know that I love the father, and that I'm doing what the father has told me to do' (14.30–31). This passage, of course, likewise echoes 12.20–36. The theme introduced at that point is starting to expand and find its way into the interpretative grid through which John wants us to understand chapters 18 and 19.

In particular, it compels us to question whether 'the ruler of this world' in these passages can simply be 'the satan' or 'the devil'. What would it mean, in chapter 14, to speak of the satan as 'coming'? When we finally reach chapter 18, the one who 'comes' (*erchetai*) is Judas himself (18.3), with an entire cohort of Roman troops (a *speira*, under the authority of a *chiliarchos* (18.12), an officer above a centurion), as well as the police under the command of the chief priests and the Pharisees.[25] However we divide up this company, John seems to intend that we should see the arrest as fulfilling the prediction of 14.30; and, if that is so, we already find a further link with 12.20–36. 'The ruler of the world' may, in one sense, be the satan. But if we continue with that meaning we have to say that Judas, the one into whom the satan had entered (13.2, 27), was leading a Roman force, with Jewish assistance as well, that was doing the satan's work. As in chapter 12, the 'ruler' is the one who currently has charge of the gentile nations, and when the Greeks come to see Jesus, this is taken as a sign that Jesus, in being lifted up as the son of man, will cast out the world's ruler and draw all people to himself instead. I thus agree with, but go much further than, Craig Keener's suggestion that 'one might think of a coalescence of imperial and antichrist images'.[26] At this point I think we are looking at a

---

25 See Moore 2006, 53.

26 Keener 2003, 879–80, points out that in pagan literature phrases like 'ruler of the world' could be applied both to divinities and to the emperor.

phenomenon whose most obvious parallel would be in the book of Revelation, where the imperial power and the satanic force are somehow either combined or at least in close alliance, working hand in glove. One thinks of the dragon and the beast in Revelation 13.2.

This impression is strongly confirmed, for me at least, by the difficult passage in 16.8–11. The coming spirit, Jesus declares, will act not only as advocate on behalf of the disciples, but also, through them, as prosecuting counsel – against 'the world'. The spirit will 'prove the world to be in the wrong on three counts: sin, justice and judgment'. The tables will be turned. Instead of the world holding the church to account, through the spirit the [82] church is to hold the world to account. And 'the world' here cannot simply be the demonic power or powers that stand behind actual people and events. These are real humans, real human systems.

The critical charge, for our present purposes, is the third one. The first two matter as well, of course: the world is guilty of sin (of which disbelief in Jesus is the all-important symbol); the world is guilty in relation to justice (because God is vindicating Jesus, thereby proving that the world's judgment on him was wrong). But the third charge points to a further dimension: the world is guilty in relation to judgment itself, 'because the ruler of this world is judged'.

Once again, we have a clear echo of 12.31. Once again, therefore, we ask, who is 'the ruler of this world'? Is it enough to say that this is the satan, or more generally the diabolical force? I think not. When the satan is thrown out of heaven, the human powers that have attained their status through their Faustian pacts with the satan are overthrown as well. 'The ruler of this world' is coming to get Jesus: that is, Judas is coming with the Roman cohort, and with the Temple police to back them up. In the lurid imagery of Revelation 13, the beast from the sea is accompanied by the beast from the land. 'The world has gone after him', but now in a different sense (John 12.19).

But this is to be the moment, not of Jesus' defeat, but of his victory. The last word of teaching, before the prayer of chapter 17, is a shout of triumph: 'Cheer up! I have defeated the world! (*nenikēka ton kosmon*)' (16.33). This is again an unmistakeable *Christus Victor* statement, comparable to Colossians 2.14–15 and to the hint in 1 Corinthians 2.8, where 'the rulers of this world' put the lord of glory to death because they did not understand the 'hidden wisdom' of the gospel – a very Johannine passage. All this leads the eye up to the great scene with which John's gospel reaches its climax. John's readers are to leave the exalted world of the discourses, but they are to take with them, as they return to the messy and dangerous world of event, the rich and layered world of meaning that they have now been shown. The Word of chapters 13—17 becomes the Flesh of chapters 18 and 19.

John 18—19

There is a sense in which, for John, Gethsemane has already taken place in chapter 12, where Jesus' heart was troubled, wondering if he should pray for rescue but determining to pray for God to be glorified (12.27–28). We know, by now, that these events are to be the way in which God will be glorified: this is how Jesus will accomplish that goal, how he will conquer [83] and cast out the ruler of the world, and so draw all people to himself. The brief hearing before the high priest, interspersed with Peter's denial, leads the eye quickly to the main scene, which comprises 18.26—19.16. Here we find the three-cornered conversation between Pilate, Jesus and the chief priests, with 'the Judaeans' as the crowd in the background.

There are many points we could make here. Stephen Moore draws attention to the flogging and violent mocking coming in 19.1–3 – right in the middle of the 'trial'. This is how Roman justice works, and John may well be making that point. There are many levels of irony, particularly in what the chief priests say. There are many ways of reading Pilate's character and of suggesting the levels of motivation, manipulation and political machination that seem to be going on between him and the chief priests.[27]

But the themes that dominate this set piece are those of kingship, truth and power. This is where the kingdom of God finally confronts the kingdoms of the world; putting it like that will rightly reawaken echoes of Daniel, and once more of Revelation as well. This is a *political* scene that can only be understood through the lens of *apocalyptic* imagery. Just as, throughout his gospel, John has wanted his readers to think of the Logos whenever they look at Jesus, so, more subtly perhaps, he wants his readers now to think of 12.31, 14.30–31, 16.33, and perhaps especially 16.8–11, as they overhear the conversation between Jesus and Pilate. They are, in other words, to listen to Pilate and recognize the voice of 'the ruler of this world'. They are to listen to Jesus and realize that this is what it sounds like to convict the world of sin, of justice and of judgment. They are to watch the whole scene, ending with the

---

27 Moore 2006, 56–63.

crucifixion itself, and are to discern that this is what it looks like when the ruler of this world is defeated and cast out.

The main theme that arches across the whole discourse is kingship and kingdom. 'Are you the king of the Jews?' asks Pilate (18.33), who has obviously got this information from somewhere else because the chief priests, in this narrative, are remarkably reticent on the point. The theme returns again and again: Pilate uses the phrase 'king of the Jews' as a title when asking if he should release Jesus (18.39); the soldiers use it in mockery (19.3); Pilate, showing Jesus to the crowd, says 'Here is your king' (19.14), and then asks 'Do you want me to crucify your king?' (19.15). Then, of course, comes the greatest irony, when Pilate places the 'title' on the cross, 'Jesus of Nazareth, the King of the Jews' (19.19), deliberately offending the chief priests (19.21–22). Clearly, kingship – and the 'king of the Jews' motif in particular – is what John regards as the underlying theme of the entire scene. [84]

That goes part of the way to explaining the sudden introduction of the charge that Jesus made himself 'son of God' (19.7). This title is, of course, messianic, as in Psalm 2 and elsewhere.[28] Jesus' Messiahship, as well as his divine sonship, is as prominent a theme in John as in any part of the New Testament. But already by the time of Paul, and arguably for Jesus himself, the title had come to carry as well the idea of some kind of identity between Messiah and God himself.[29] That is part of the point of the prologue, as in its final flourish: the Word who became flesh and tabernacled in our midst is the only-begotten son of God who has uniquely made the father known (1.18). But to assume that the messianic (and hence political) meaning has thereby been relativized or abandoned is to capitulate once more to an older ideological disjunction which historical scholarship has been teaching us to overcome.

We should not, then, assume that with the charge that 'he made himself the son of God' in 19.7 the Jewish leaders have shifted to the 'spiritual' or 'theological' plane and hence away from the political one. Pilate's nervousness in 19.8 ('when Pilate heard that, he was all the more afraid') is often explained as the result of religious superstition, but I suspect that John intends something else. 'Son of God' or 'son of the deified' was of course a regular Caesar-title.[30] If Pilate were to release someone who had claimed that title, Caesar might have

---

28 Ps. 2.7; cf. 2 Sam. 7.12–14. See my discussion of 'son of God' as a messianic title in Wright 2013b, 690–701.

29 E.g. Rom. 1.3–4; 8.3–4, on which see again Wright 2013b, 692–700, 818–19.

30 See further Wright 2013b, 327–8.

something to say about it. This would fit exactly with the next move from the chief priests: 'If you let this fellow go, you are no friend of Caesar! Everyone who sets himself up as a king is speaking against Caesar!' (19.12). If we start our analysis with that verse and look back, we might well conclude that 'son of God' in verse 7 is at least as much about a challenge to Caesar as it is about Trinitarian Christology (and are we so sure that those two are on opposite sides of some great divide?). And the last line of the trialogue seems to confirm this. The chief priests come out with the crowning irony: 'We have no king except Caesar!' (19.15). They have turned the Jewish revolutionary slogan upside down: 'No king but God' has collapsed into total collusion with the imperial force. Ultimately, there are only two kingdoms, God's and Caesar's, and they have chosen the latter.

Already this suggests that, for John, Jesus' death is *in some sense or other* 'political'. That begs several questions, of course, but nobody with any knowledge of first-century Jewish messianism could miss the point. There [85] is no precedent for, as it were, a non-political 'king of the Jews'. If a 'king of the Jews' were to emerge, then, according to Psalms 2, 72 and 89, not to mention Isaiah 11, he would be king of the whole world. When the Romans led Simon bar-Giora at the back of Titus's triumphal procession and then had him killed, this was the ceremonial killing of 'the king of the Jews.'[31] We do not have an account of Bar-Kochba's last stand, but there is every reason to suppose that it would have had the same overtone.

But in what sense 'political'? And in what sense 'king'? Clearly John wants his readers to believe that, despite Pilate's cynicism, the title on the cross was true. But Jesus has already redefined what this 'kingdom' means in the much misunderstood verse 18.36. The Authorized (King James) Version, as is well known, has Jesus say 'My kingdom is not of this world'. Those words have been quoted times without number in support of a supposedly 'otherworldly', and hence non-political, kingdom. Faced with that regular misunderstanding I have translated that verse, 'My kingdom isn't the sort that grows in this world'. The Greek is *hē basileia hē emē ouk estin ek tou kosmou toutou*: my kingdom is not *from* this world. It does not take its origin from the present world – if it did, Jesus' followers would be fighting. His kingdom has a radically different character from that of Caesar. But the whole point of John's gospel, seeing Jesus and the spirit as the new Temple, is that Jesus' kingdom is *for* the world: for the world in the sense that the creator God is

---

31   On the death of Simon bar-Giora, see Jos. *War* 7.153–7; for his 'royal' aspirations, punished as such by the Romans, see Wright 1992a, 177–8.

decisively launching his project of new creation from within the heart of the old. There is therefore bound to be a clash: a clash of Pilate and Jesus, of Caesar's kingdom and God's, of the kingdom that comes from the world and the kingdom that comes from somewhere else. Jesus is the new king, over a new kind of community, a new *polis* that will challenge, defeat and displace all the other sorts.

There are two particular ways in which Jesus' kingdom is marked out. The first is striking: in Jesus' kingdom, his followers will not fight to defend him (18.36b). That shows how perilously close Peter came to ruining the whole project with his sword in the garden (18.10–11), but the point stands and is vital for the theology, not only of John, but of the New Testament as a whole. The victory that Jesus wins on the cross is, by definition, the victory of *love*. That is how the second half of the gospel begins: having always loved his own, Jesus loved them right through to the end (13.1) – which is John's introduction to the footwashing scene, a tableau that serves as both metaphor and metonymy for the themes of incarnation and crucifixion. The [86] note of love is often restated, as for instance in chapter 10, but it is far more often enacted, and never more so than in chapter 13.

The second qualification of Jesus' kingdom is found in another apparent non sequitur. Pilate pounces on Jesus' mention of a kingdom: 'So you *are* a king, are you?' (18.37). Jesus turns the question in an unexpected direction: 'You're the one who's calling me a king. I was born for this; I've come into the world for this: to give evidence about the truth. Everyone who belongs to the truth listens to my voice' (18.37). The most famous line here is of course Pilate's response: 'Truth! What's that?' (18.38), and many appropriate comments can be made about the way in which, in Caesar's kingdom, there is no such thing as truth – only power. But did Jesus just change the subject? What has 'truth' got to do with 'kingdom'?

This fits into another of John's major themes, not only 'truth' itself but, as in the title of Andrew Lincoln's book, 'truth on trial'.[32] The whole gospel is framed as a courtroom drama: indeed, if we are looking for 'forensic justification', John is a much richer place to start than Paul. And Jesus himself is, of course, the supreme witness to the truth. This goes to the heart, not only of John's soteriology, but of his cosmology, and that in turn provides the frame for the political point. Truth, for John, is neither simply 'the facts on the ground', nor simply 'the ideal' that one may infer behind them. John is neither an Aristotelian nor a Platonist. He believes that the world is God's world,

---

32 Cf. also the similarly titled work of Harvey 1976.

and that the world is being redeemed and remade in, through and around Jesus himself. Jesus himself *is* the truth, because he embodies God's new world; he is the new reality, the new creation. His death will be the means of breaking the grip of sin and death, the grip (in other words) of the satan on the old world; his resurrection will launch the new creation whose radical truth will reshape all other truth. Bearing witness to the truth means telling, and enacting, God's judgment on the untruth of the present world, and enabling the launch of the new one.

Caesar's empire, in the person of Pilate, can make neither head nor tail of all this. Nor can the priests and the crowd, who choose the truth of the old world when they choose Barabbas, the brigand. And that is where the flogging and the mocking begin: legalized violence is Pilate's real answer to Jesus' strange words about his kingdom. That, John is saying, is paradoxically the way in which Jesus reveals the truth. 'Look! Here's the man!' (19.5) answers directly to the *ho logos sarx egeneto* in the prologue: here is the Image of God, bruised and bleeding, in royal crown and robes. Here, on the sixth day of the week, is the son of man, now to be given glory and honour, [87] with all things in subjection under his feet, as he is lifted high on the cross, drawing all people to himself.

There are many points one could make here. Anyone with half an ear for irony would, by now, have seen that John is denouncing the empire of Caesar as a hollow sham. It doesn't care about truth; it doesn't know about justice; it has never heard of love. It is a kingdom 'from this world', full of the inevitable idolatry, self-aggrandizement and brutal dehumanization that goes with that. It is wrong about sin; it is wrong about justice; it is wrong about judgment. Anyone reading John's gospel would know that, if Jesus is indeed the truth, Caesar's world is based on a lie. Is that a 'political' statement? Of course it is.

And so to the final point, with even greater paradox. 'Don't you know', asks Pilate, 'that I have the authority to let you go, and the authority to crucify you?' (19.10). We might imagine that Jesus would say, 'Yes, but your authority comes from Caesar, who is a blaspheming tyrant!' Instead, Jesus says, astonishingly to our ears, 'You couldn't have any authority at all over me, unless it was given to you from above. That's why the person who handed me over to you is guilty of a greater sin' (19.11). Here is the balance that the early Christians seem to have kept and which subsequent generations have all too easily lost. Jewish-style creational monotheism insists that God wants his world to be run by obedient humans.[33] Even Caesar

---

33 Rom. 13.1–7; Col. 1.15–20; *Mt. Pol.* 10.2.

has his God-given place, like the Assyrian king in Isaiah or the Kittim in Habakkuk.[34] But he will be held accountable for how he exercises that role. So too will those who collude with him. 'The ruler of this world is judged.' And, as Jesus has thus convicted Pilate of sin, justice and judgment, the church – this is the point of 16.8–11 – must now look at this model and learn to do the same. 'As the father sent me,' says the risen Jesus, as he breathes the spirit on his disciples, 'so I send you' (20.21). That is why the farewell discourses are what they are.

These, I suggest, are the vital elements of a Johannine political theology. I think that, taken together, the passages at which we have glanced point strongly towards 'the ruler of this world' meaning *both* the satan *and* Caesar. Teasing out how that combination works has always been difficult, but I do not think we gain anything by screening out one of the two elements. This, I think, puts me within reach of writers like Thatcher, though without embracing his overall construction. It puts me in direct conflict with Hengel and Kvalbein and most commentators. It clarifies, I think, the combination of 'cosmic' and 'political' advocated here and there by **[88]** Andrew Lincoln. The danger here, as with Horsley and others in Pauline studies, is that one might fall into the trap of saying 'politics, therefore *not* theology': if any book is theological through and through, it is John.[35] That, indeed, is one reason why I think it is also political, because for John theology is about the God who loves the world, who judges the present ruler of the world, and who in Jesus the Messiah wins the victory over the world and launches his new world from within the old one. We cannot, as Stephen Moore would like to do, collapse a full-orbed political theology into a mere post-colonial critique, but nor can we allow the great Johannine themes of the Word becoming flesh, of his being lifted up to reveal the divine glory, of the love that sent the son into the world to save the world, and of the son's own love for his own, even to the uttermost, to float free of the world where real communities live under real empires and have to learn both how to navigate them wisely and how to hold them to account.

Conclusion

A test for any fresh reading of a book like John might include the question: how does this proposal contribute to a fuller or richer understanding of

---

34   Isa. 10.5–6; Hab. 1.5–6.
35   On the pitfalls of political readings of Paul see Wright 2013b, ch. 12.

the other great themes in this narrative? How does it contribute to incarnation, atonement, the new Temple, the new exodus, new creation itself? This would be a proper subject for a whole book, but let me say just two things in conclusion.

First, the large outer themes of John's gospel and indeed of the Bible – creation and new creation, and the role of humans within that – can never ignore their necessary political dimensions. Precisely because the one God wants his world to be wisely ruled by humans, and precisely because, in the truly human Word made Flesh, God was establishing, and now has established, his own rule of love and judgment in the heart of the world, all other human systems are called to account. Because they idolize themselves, they become blasphemous parodies of the truly human rule, and they use violence to sustain themselves in their power. In the second-Temple Jewish world, deeply informed by Daniel in particular, this bestial anti-empire was believed to have raised itself to its full height, at which point the one God was to take his judgment seat and vindicate 'one like a son of man'. Reference to Daniel is elusive in John, but this scenario illuminates the very passages we have been studying. John, I think, can be claimed as another example of a Daniel-based apocalyptic and therefore political message, in [89] which Rome becomes the fourth 'monster from the sea' who is judged as the son of man is vindicated. Jesus is now the true ruler of the world, and the church must figure out what that means in practice.

Second, by placing the *Christus Victor* motif at the heart of John's atonement-theology, defeating the powers at every level in order to provide the new exodus and thereby the new creation, we have not eliminated, but have rather properly contextualized, the many other strands of atonement-theology in the book. Indeed, John furnishes us with powerful reasons for thinking that atonement is not a theory but an acted narrative, a narrative that reached its climax on the cross, but that now continues in the form of a community.[36] The footwashing, itself a deeply subversive social action, was a pointer, not only to what Jesus was to do on the cross, but to what his followers were to do for one another. As many have discovered, communities that follow that model, whether literally or metaphorically, work quite differently from the ways in which empires normally work. And empires do not usually appreciate that.

John's gospel is notoriously open-ended. 'What is that to you?' asks Jesus to Peter. 'Follow me' (21.22). Yes, says John, ending with a comment that, though

---

36 For this theme see McKnight 2007.

typically cryptic, is nevertheless full of explosive political and theological charge: 'If all the other things which Jesus did were written down one by one, I don't think the world itself would be able to contain the books that would be written' (21.25).

13

Pictures, Stories and the Cross: Where Do the Echoes Lead?

The many friends and admirers of Richard Hays were delighted when at last he was able – in the teeth of a major illness – to complete his long-awaited book *Echoes of Scripture in the Gospels*, a natural follow-up to his ground-breaking *Echoes of Scripture in the Letters of Paul* (New Haven, CT: Yale University Press, 1989). We were even more delighted that, having seen off the challenge to his health against the normal odds, Richard was able to engage in the kind of ongoing debate that his book naturally demands. It was a special pleasure for me to contribute this essay, one more move in a discussion that has lasted over thirty years and shows no sign of abating, to an issue of the *Journal of Theological Interpretation* devoted entirely to his new work.

[49] The breathtaking new book with which Richard Hays has once more redirected a major field of research will be discussed for decades to come.[1] The story of its final production, done at speed and with help when the author was battling a life-threatening illness, adds an extra dramatic twist, but actually the thesis Hays argues, and the way in which he sets it out, was [50] already dramatic enough to keep scholars alert at their desks and awake at nights. The received wisdom used to be that John's gospel gives us the 'divine' Jesus while Matthew, Mark and Luke tell us the 'human' story (albeit with occasional overlaps in both directions). If Hays is even half right in his central argument, this well-worn theory cannot simply be lightly adjusted. It must be abandoned altogether. When we see the (very different) ways in which all four gospels use Israel's scriptures in retelling the story of Jesus, we are bound to recognize that all four see their central figure as the living embodiment of Israel's God. 'The low/high Christological categories collapse completely' (p. 280). If we listen

---

1 Hays 2016. References in this chapter are to this work unless otherwise indicated; italics within quotations indicate original emphasis unless otherwise noted.

hard, we may catch other echoes: of tearing paper as lecture-notes are ripped up, and of frantic typing as old textbooks are rewritten.

Not everyone will like it, of course.[2] Old habits die hard and there will undoubtedly be resistance. But the case is so strong, both subtle and supple, that going back to the old paths will carry with it a hint of wilful ignorance (if not actually of the more vivid metaphors offered by 2 Peter 2.22). If I were Hays, I would prepare to defend myself against two fairly obvious charges, which I mention here to clear the way for the different questions and proposals I shall then advance.

First, there is no attempt in this book to defend, or even to explain, the way 'echoes of scripture' are to be detected. Many critics of Hays's earlier 'echoes'[3] have raised good and serious questions at the level of method, and at some point it would be good to see Hays answering them. The discussions of method launched by that earlier book have been vigorous and wide-ranging, an example being the study of Ezekiel by my colleague Bill Tooman.[4] Hays's new book contributes to those discussions only obliquely, by the simple method of 'Watch and you'll see'. Hays works through many detailed examples in which scriptural echoes are not only detected but, individually and particularly cumulatively, point to a resounding and clear conclusion. Like some other kinds of revolution, this book doesn't wait for a negotiated settlement on points of principle, but simply creates new facts on the ground. Let methodological discussions follow fresh readings, for once, rather than precede them! Discussions of method can sometimes postpone, or even neutralize, actual exegesis; this way of proceeding has a bracing, refreshing quality. This is not so much a bomb on the theologians' [51] playground, then, but more of a sudden cold shower on the overheated heavy machinery of the exegetical industry.

A second problem is that Hays appears almost entirely to skip over the question of how other first-century writers were reading, and echoing, the same scriptural texts. Sirach receives somewhat more sustained treatment, but many other relevant texts such as the Scrolls, *4 Ezra* and the Wisdom of Solomon are noticed only in passing. Philo receives a brief mention (on the Logos) and a single footnote; Josephus, one footnote. In a sense, as with the comment above about method, this really does not matter. Hays's

2 I have not yet seen Daniel Kirk 2016, but by all accounts it offers a radical alternative to the views of Hurtado, Bauckham and Hays himself. A new wave of important debate appears to be gathering force.

3 Hays 1989.

4 Tooman 2011.

argument stands or falls on the sense his fresh readings make of the gospels as they stand. And, of course, to have attempted anything fuller by way of comparative study (on the model, say, of Francis Watson's remarkable *Paul and the Hermeneutics of Faith*[5]) would have doubled the size of the book. But at point after point his proposals cry out, it seems to me, for this kind of second-Temple grounding. When he says that early Christian reflection on Jesus was 'fundamentally conditioned by the biblical stories of God's dealings with the people Israel' (p. 5), many would want to stress 'as those stories were being retrieved by other Jews in the second-Temple period' – not, of course, to restrict interpretative possibilities to things the evangelists' contemporaries were already saying but to contextualize them. Hays writes of the assumed or ideal readers with their 'encyclopedia of reception' (for example pp. 195, 198, 229, offering thereby an implicit response to some of his methodological critics), but this could be considerably strengthened by demonstrating the ways in which that 'encyclopedia' was variously held by the evangelists' contemporaries.[6] It might also be strengthened by historical parallels to the combined idea of such an 'encyclopedia', on the one hand (that is, assuming that first-century readers already knew the texts to be echoed), with the proposal on the other hand that Luke at least, and to a considerable extent the others as well, were trying 'to encourage the formation of a certain kind of reading community' (p. 276; that is, assuming that readers might not yet know the texts but that his work would encourage them in that direction).[7] Thus, if there are parallel retrievals of crucial texts, it would be good to study them, not least to compare the potentially different treatments. If there are not (and if this seems not to be simply because of the accidents of preservation) then that, too, would be interesting, providing at least a sign that the scriptural echoes Hays is tracking were generated afresh as the first followers of Jesus, 'reading backwards' as in the title of [52] his short earlier treatment, discovered advance signs of the new thing they had witnessed. I suspect there would be plenty of both.[8]

These two comments relate to one of the rare moments when a debate with another scholar makes it into Hays's text rather than into the seventy and more pages of detailed, small-print footnotes. He quotes Udo Schnelle, among the best-known current German New Testament (NT) scholars, to the

---

5 Watson 2015 [2004].

6 Hays credits this idea of an 'encyclopedia of reception' to Eco 1979.

7 Hays speaks of the encyclopaedia 'that is presupposed both for the text's production and for its proper reception' (p. 289).

8 See Hays 2014.

effect that a 'biblical theology' is impossible for three reasons. First, the Old Testament (OT) does not mention Jesus Christ. Second, the resurrection of a crucified man 'cannot be integrated into any ancient system of meaning formation'. Third, although the OT may be the most important cultural and theological context for understanding the NT, it is by no means the only one.[9] I am not sure that Schnelle is in fact denying what Hays wants to affirm. By 'biblical theology' he seems to mean a single coherent historical account of the whole Bible through which one might read Israel's scriptures *in their own contexts* and see that they were 'teaching the same truths' as the early Christians. Because that kind of a project is still alive and well, the point seems to me still worth making. Hays's own proposal is precisely that the fresh readings of Israel's scriptures are generated by 'reading backwards' from the events concerning Jesus, rather than reading 'forwards' from the obvious original meaning of the scriptures. Hays naturally highlights Jesus' fresh interpretation of scripture on the Emmaus Road (Luke 24.13–35), but his treatment rightly emphasizes exactly Schnelle's point, that prior to this moment nobody, not even devout Jews, had any 'system of meaning formation' that could include a crucified and risen Messiah.[10] Hays is proposing a kind of *reborn* biblical theology; Schnelle is objecting to the 'once-born' kind. Hays cites Martin Luther as an exponent of 'figural exegesis', contrasting him with Schnelle, but I am not sure that Luther's 'figural' readings (such as Hays's opening example, in which Luther sees scripture as the manger in which the Christ-child lies) really advance his case. But more of that anon.

Like most of Hays's work, this book will be the foundation for many other subsequent projects. There are dozens, perhaps hundreds, of potential scriptural echoes in the gospels beyond those studied here; and there are several important gospel themes awaiting fresh study in terms of their biblical echoes. Hays has chosen to focus on the scriptural echoes that highlight the *identity* of Jesus in terms of Israel's God, and as I have stressed, this is both necessary, timely and revolutionary. But there is something strange [53] about this focus, excluding as it does certain other potential focal points. I have argued in various places that though the four gospels do undoubtedly understand Jesus in terms of the personal embodiment of Israel's God, this is the key in which the music is set rather than the tune that is being played. The music itself, played in this key, is the launching of God's kingdom on earth

---

9   Hays 3 (with 368 n. 6), quoting the German original of Schnelle 2009, 52.

10 Hays cites Williams 1998 [1979], 1, speaking of the 'experience of profound contradictoriness' at the heart of the apostolic faith; this, I think, is what Schnelle is meaning.

as in heaven, through the actions but particularly through the death of the one who was then raised from the dead. Christians in the modern west have grown used to the modernist critique that attacks the idea that Jesus might be 'God incarnate', and it is important to revisit our texts with this question. But when we do, we find the texts saying, in effect, 'Yes, yes, of course we believe that, *but look what happens as a result.*' Modernism has managed to keep off the agenda altogether the NT claim that with Jesus God's kingdom was launched on earth as in heaven. Often the churches have gone along for the ride.[11] Here, too, the evangelists echo scripture in a multiplicity of ways, and Hays's book ought to propel his readers forward to examine these echoes in their turn.

Pictures and Stories

As in Hays's earlier work, there are twin themes jostling together. It is not clear, or not to me, which one will receive the midwife's accolade of 'firstborn', or indeed whether the elder will end up serving the younger. Perhaps this is because the mother – the fertile mind of our author – seems to be in no Rebecca-like distress over these potentially antagonistic twins. In some of his earlier work, particularly *Echoes of Scripture in the Letters of Paul*, the picture seemed to be dominated by *figural* exegesis without obvious links to an overarching narrative (though narrative was always important in Hays's other work).[12] In some of his subsequent work, for instance the commentary on 1 Corinthians, he draws more on the implicit overall *narrative* of Israel's scriptures and the ways that narrative is retrieved by Paul.[13] In this work, we are introduced at once to 'figural' readings, as in the example from Luther cited above. There are many 'pictures' in the scriptures that, retrieved in the gospels, enable us to get a three-dimensional and theologically enriched sense of what the evangelists intend us to think. But as the book goes on, the sense of *a continuous narrative* becomes more and more important. I do not think this easily counts as 'figural', certainly not in the way many are using that term today to retrieve an explicitly non-historical [54] method of reading scripture.[14] What we are now dealing with is *historical continuity*, and it looks as though Hays intends the 'figural' readings to be understood *within that*

---

11 See Wright 2012.
12 As, obviously, in his dissertation, Hays 2002 [1983].
13 Hays 1989; 1997.
14 E.g. Radner 2016.

framework rather than as a separate method. The stories contextualize the pictures, or some of them at any rate. But these are quite different things, and those who have stressed the one have sometimes ignored the other, or even warned against it. Which twin is serving which?

This emerges in the treatment of Mark, where Hays traces the way in which Mark's Jesus, warning Jerusalem of its impending fate, is echoing the warnings of Jeremiah. 'As Judgment fell upon Israel in Jeremiah's time, so it looms once again over the Temple in the time of Jesus' (p. 29): the 'as' and the 'so' set the two in parallel. But Hays immediately continues by affirming 'the more fundamental promise of God's ultimate design to bring about Israel's deliverance and restoration' (p. 29). Mark 'has primed his readers to expect that his story will focus on the fulfilment of Isaiah's prophecy of a new exodus and the establishment of God's kingly rule in Jerusalem'. Mark's ideal reader, that is, 'any reader steeped in Isaiah's language', would get the point: Jesus is proclaiming 'the consummation of Isaiah's long-deferred hope' (p. 30), the hope 'that the moment of God's destined intervention is at last at hand' (p. 31). Thus, the coming of the kingdom 'is an apocalyptic event, fulfilling Isaiah's vision of a new exodus in which God will lead the people on a way through the desert to return in power to Zion' (p. 44). We might wish that the phrase 'apocalyptic event' could be wheeled off to a retirement home where it might eke out its days in penitence for past misdeeds, but leaving that to one side we find the question pressing: in what sense is this 'figural' exegesis; and, if it is not, does that matter?

When we turn to Matthew, similar questions arise. Hays's sensitive probing into the meanings of the opening genealogy highlights the narrative *continuity* 'between Israel's story and the story that Matthew is about to narrate' (p. 110). A single story-line runs through, all the way to Jesus, a story in which 1.17 (the mention of exile as the third marker, after Abraham and David) 'signals that the coming of Jesus portends the end of Israel's exile', so that 'the periodization of the genealogy outlines the *plot* of Israel's story' (p. 110). This in no way suggests that Matthew thinks of Israel's history as a progressive revelation, a smooth sequence leading up to the final revelation. On the contrary, the genealogy functions 'as a *Sündenspiegel*, a long and tortured narrative in which Israel sees its corporate sins reflected' (p. 111).[15] Matthew's Messiah, in other words, is 'the one [55] who saves his people from the consequences of their sins by closing the chapter of powerlessness and deprivation that began with "the deportation to Babylon"' (p. 111). This larger narratival

---

reading of the genealogy contextualizes, and refocuses, the figural meanings of characters within it. Tamar, Rahab, Ruth and Bathsheba are absolved from the normal imputations, exemplifying instead the inclusion of non-Jews within the family; blame is placed instead on David (and, by implication, Judah) (p. 112). These 'figural' readings work *within* the narrative, not independently from it, though when Matthew goes on to describe Jesus as Israel coming out of Egypt (2.13–15) this is, says Hays, a 'figural fulfillment' of the exodus-narrative (p. 113). Matthew is not merely 'looking for random Old Testament prooftexts that Jesus might somehow fulfill' but is rather 'thinking about the *specific shape* of Israel's story and linking Jesus's life with key passages that promise God's unbreakable redemptive love for his people' (p. 116). This too seems to be a figural reading (a specific shape 'back then' which is gloriously repeated 'now') set within a larger narrative continuity.

I do not think that Hays has ever made explicit the way in which these two very different hermeneutical moves relate to one another. The discipline of 'intertextuality' itself, to which Hays has made such a significant contribution and which, indeed, he has introduced into NT studies, may need to be sharpened. If Hays is right in his analysis of the underlying single narrative, the NT's use of the OT is not simply a special case of 'intertextuality' but a subtly different kind of thing altogether. If a later composer, writing a new symphony, 'echoes' themes from Schubert's 'Unfinished' symphony, that is one thing. If someone claims to be writing the missing final movement which will appropriately complete the earlier movements, that is something quite different.

That is the claim – that the events of Jesus' life, death and resurrection constitute the *narrative continuation and climax* of Israel's story – that Hays draws out particularly in discussing Luke. Luke, he says, is the most intentional and skilful of the evangelists in telling Jesus' story 'in a way that joins it seamlessly to Israel's story' (p. 191; also p. 277). Luke is constantly prompting his readers to consider how the events narrated are linked to earlier events, 'earlier chapters in the epic', so as to create 'a strong sense of historical continuity, an impression that Luke's story belongs integrally to an older series of stories that the reader is expected to recognize' (pp. 275–6). We might want to press the point, which Hays clearly affirms, that the 'series' is itself a single 'story', not simply a collection of smaller stories. At the same time ('pictures' within 'stories' once again) Luke's writing 'constantly folds OT patterns into its story', leaving us 'with a powerful but indistinct sense of analogy between God's saving acts for Israel in the past and the new liberating events coming to fulfillment in the story of Jesus' (p. 192). This seems to me exactly [56] right, but it raises the question, which Hays does not, as to how the continuous narrative and the figural echoes work together – especially, once again, granted that many who advocate 'figural' readings do so explicitly against any sense of actual historical continuity. Again for Hays, however, the stories seem to retain pride of place over the pictures: 'God's intent to reveal salvation to all flesh was part of Israel's plotted role from the beginning' (p. 199). Luke intends his readers to understand Jesus' story 'as the narrative continuation of Israel's story and as the liberating climax toward which that story had moved' (p. 200; so too, for example, p. 215).

The pictures, then, are largely held within the stories, or rather the single story of the divine purpose for Israel and also, so to speak, the divine purpose for God himself. Luke's Jesus is somehow to be identified both with Israel's God and with Israel/humanity (p. 245). Hays glimpses the huge problems that many will identify at this point, but apart from a few remarks he does not turn aside to ward off potential challenges. On the one hand, as we have seen with his reading of Matthew, he insists that the biblical presentation of the 'back story' of Israel is not a smooth Hegelian progress, such as has been imagined by the critics of 'salvation-historical' readings of the NT.[16] On the other hand, any claim that the events concerning Jesus were the unique fulfilment, the divinely intended climax, of the long story of Israel now routinely calls down on the interpreter's head the charge of being, in some sense or other, anti-Jewish. Hays appears at one point to be warding off this charge, but in fact simply repeats the point that many find objectionable. 'The theological effects of this hermeneutical program', he writes, 'are of wide-ranging significance', which is undoubtedly correct; but he continues:

> Rather than setting the church against Israel, Luke presents a continuous story of the one people of God. There has always been one elect Israel, and within that Israel, there have always been those who respond to God's redemptive action with faith, and others who turn away and are cut off. Luke sees this pattern continuing in his own time.
> (p. 277)

This again is undoubtedly correct, but it shows why many have insisted that such a reading, while admittedly not 'setting the church against [historic, biblical] Israel', does indeed set 'the church' over against those Jews of Luke's day who refused to believe the gospel, thus establishing a pattern of 'church

---

16 On this, see Wright 2015, Part II, esp. chs. 6, 7.

against [subsequent] Israel'. I have argued strongly elsewhere against this slur, not least on the grounds that the NT writers are not doing 'comparative religion' but rather *messianic eschatology*. If any second-Temple Jew claimed, as many did, that they knew who the Messiah was, this constituted a typically Jewish claim that *this*, rather than somewhere or somehow else, was how Israel's God was fulfilling his promises, and that the consequences of refusing to accept this claim [57] would be dire.[17] More needs to be done, I think, precisely if we are to hear and rightly interpret the echoes of scripture in the gospels, to think *historically* about the first-century situation and not to allow later polemics, of whatever sort, to cloud our vision.

There are surprises in store in Hays's treatment of John. John, he says, 'offers fewer signs of interest in narrative continuity than do the Synoptic Gospels' (p. 288, amplified variously thereafter). There are some senses in which this is true – no genealogies, for a start, and no explicit evocation of Malachi 3. However, the narrative of the returning divine 'glory', resonating with Exodus 40 and Ezekiel 43 and expressed specifically in Isaiah 40 and 52 in relation to the long-range promise of a rebuilt Temple, is central. Isaiah 40.3 appears on cue at 1.23, and Isaiah 53.1 and 6.10 are cited towards the climax of the twelve chapters of opening narrative (12.38, 40), with John's explicit comment that Isaiah said this 'because he saw his glory, and spoke about him' (12.41).[18] Hays's brief discussions of these passages (at, for instance, pp. 292–3) do not attempt to draw out this theme of the returning divine glory, which is all the more surprising in that Hays does see clearly that the gospels are picking up not only the unfinished narrative of Israel (when will the 'exile' be over?) but the unfinished narrative of God himself. Israel's God had promised to return to Zion, and the gospels pick this up and apply it to Jesus (for example pp. 252, 257).[19] But this obviously Temple-focused narrative fits far more closely with John's gospel as a whole, and with the scriptural echoes that indicate a great narrative, than Hays appears to allow. He offers a rich exploration of what is obviously a central Johannine theme, of Jesus as the new Temple. But this appears to remain, for him, at the 'figural' level rather than the narratival.

This seems to me a missed opportunity. The best-known scriptural echo in John, the opening words of the gospel, are of course an echo of Genesis 1.1,

---

17 See Wright 2013b, 806–10, and in the index under 'Supersessionism'.

18 For the English translations of scripture in this article, see the note in the preface to the present volume.

19 I have argued that Paul, too, exploits this theme, and that it is in fact at the heart of the earliest Christology: see Wright 2013b, ch. 9.

and, as Hays sees, a focusing of the creation story on Jesus as the one 'through whom' all things were made, resonating with later Jewish themes of 'word' and 'wisdom'. But Hays never explores the possibility that the line of thought from John 1.1 to John 1.14 (in which the Word 'tabernacles' in our midst so that 'we gazed upon his glory') is itself a narrative, and that at three levels at least.

First, it is the narrative of creation itself. The creation of human beings in the divine image (Genesis 1.26–28) completes the picture of the creation-as-Temple, which is the narrative of Genesis 1.1—2.3. Second, it is the narrative [58] of creation *and new creation*, involving the rescue, repair and renewal of the old; this points forward to Pilate's famous *ecce homo*, 'Here's the man', in 19.5, and then to the emphatic *tetelestai* of 19.30, which echoes the 'finished' in Genesis 2.1–2. This is not just a random echo out of historical sequence. John is inviting his readers to understand the events concerning Jesus, particularly his death, as the culmination of the vast story of creation and new creation; and, granted all the other things he is doing, this cannot be other than some kind of a *Heilsgeschichte*. That is why, after the 'rest' of the seventh day, John so strikingly opens his resurrection chapter with 'On the first day of the week' (20.1), rubbing in the point at 20.19. Jesus' resurrection is the launch of the long-awaited new creation, consequent on the victory over 'the ruler of this world' that was won on the cross, to which we shall return presently.

Third, and granted the all-pervasive Temple-theme in the fourth gospel, the line of thought from John 1.1 to 1.14 must be heard as a clear echo of the line of thought from the opening of Genesis to the end of the book of Exodus. The Pentateuch, as we just noted, begins with the creation of a 'Temple', the heaven-and-earth reality with the humans as the 'image'. After things go horribly wrong, the rescue operation, first of the human race (through Abraham and his family), and then of enslaved Israel (through Moses and Passover), leads to Exodus 40, where the Tabernacle is constructed, an explicit *microcosmos* or 'little world', with Aaron as the human figure in the middle of it. Genesis 1 and 2 are in principle recreated. The *skēnē* is constructed (Exodus 40.17–29), the cloud of the divine presence covers it (40.34a), and the tabernacle is filled with the glory of the Lord (*kai doxēs kyriou eplēsthē hē skēnē*). This is what John is echoing in 1.14 and, then, with multiple other echoes besides, in 1.15–18. And this makes sense of much of the rest of the book.

I was surprised, then, to find that Exodus 40 is not mentioned in Hays's book. But its absence makes it, perhaps, less surprising that Hays can suggest that there is no underlying eschatological narrative in John. When, however, we put the Isaiah references noted above within the triple implied narrative in the prologue, we are faced once more, as in the synoptics though by a very different route, with the story of exile and restoration, and in particular the story of the promised return of Israel's God to Zion, all reaching their shocking fulfilment in the events concerning Jesus. This means that in John, too, we would be right to see the manifold and multi-layered web of biblical allusion and echo as held within the large implicit narrative framework, in his case not only the story of Israel but the story of the whole creation. The pictures mean what they mean within the story. Here, not for the first time, one is struck by the theological similarity with Paul, despite the radically different mode of expression.

The implicit tension I observe between Hays's twin proposals, the 'figural' and 'narrative' readings of scripture, can be seen by reflecting for a [59] moment on what we might call the hermeneutical direction of travel. Here Hays's discussion has something in common with the proposals from the last twenty years concerning the 'apocalyptic Paul'.[20] His advocacy of 'reading backwards', as in his earlier and smaller book, sounds very like some of the would-be 'apocalyptic' proposals, and fits rather obviously within an overall Barthian reading strategy that refuses to make Jesus the result or product of anything else, including any story, and insists instead on starting with Jesus and working outwards from there. (This can be seen, for instance, in the various proposals regarding the 'plight' from which the gospel rescues people: was this problem well known, requiring the solution that was then provided, or did the first Christians reason backwards 'from solution to plight'?[21]) Hays's basic proposal sounds as though it is moving straight-forwardly down this line: first Jesus, then, in retrospect, various scriptural figures and themes spring to life. But in this book, as we have discerned, there is something else going on as well. When we 'read backwards' in this way *we discover a forward-moving story coming to meet us.*[22] Of course, when we 'read backwards' we see things in the story which had remained opaque, and would remain scandalous, to those without the same hermeneutical starting-point. But there were plenty of second-Temple Jews telling the story of Israel as the story of creator and cosmos, of the covenant God and the covenant people,

---

20 See again Wright 2015, Part II; and Goodrich, Blackwell and Mastin 2016.

21 As famously proposed by E. P. Sanders in Sanders 1977; discussed and nuanced in Wright 2013b, 747–71.

22 I owe this succinct way of putting it to a conversation with Dr J. Davies; see also Davies 2016.

as the story of an exiled people in need of restoration, of an enslaved people in need of a new exodus, of a leaderless people hoping for a Messiah. Hays fully recognizes this, though (again because of the scant attention given to second-Temple texts) he never really probes the ways these narratives worked at the time. Though he fully agrees with my own arguments about the 'end of exile', with 'exile' treated as a flexible metaphor for the long period of Israel's sorrow which began with Babylon, he never explores the way in which the all-important text, Daniel 9, was being read at the time. Even when discussing the scriptural echoes awoken in Matthew 18.21–22 when Jesus insists that forgiveness must happen 'seventy times seven', he goes quite naturally to Genesis 4.23–24 but not to Leviticus 25, and the Year of Jubilee, nor to Daniel 9.24–27 where the 'exile' is extended to 'seventy weeks of years'. Many things become even clearer when these are taken into account.[23] And the more we study the Jewish texts of the period, the more it becomes clear that the early Christians were by no means [60] the only people who were 'reading backwards'. That is what the Qumran pesherists were doing with texts like Habakkuk. That is what Daniel 9 does with Jeremiah; and it is what *4 Ezra* does with Daniel.

Anyway, the point is this. Reading backwards, we find forward-moving stories, indeed in many writings a single forward-moving story. However much the early Christians were compelled to tell that complex story quite differently, *that was that story they were retelling.* They did not say, 'Forget the old stories; we have a totally new narrative, for which the scriptures will provide us with non-historical figural illustrations.' They said – and Hays has launched a new way of demonstrating that they said – 'What has just happened in Jesus the Messiah is the true goal towards which those stories were aiming, even though we now see we had been telling them in a misleading fashion.' This is most obviously true in the Emmaus Road story in Luke 24, but the same point could be made all through. The problem with invoking 'figural exegesis' is sometimes that the narrative dimension is not only relativized but not wanted at all, lest its historical emphasis corrupt the supposedly pure truth. Hays's book raises these questions in a fresh way, and I think points to the right answer, but without this ever becoming explicit.

---

23 I was surprised at Hays's suggestion (p. 371 n. 2) that in my earlier work I might be understood to have advocated a literal interpretation of 'exile'. That, despite misrepresentations, has never been my view.

The Scriptures and the Cross

All this brings us to what, to my mind, is the strangest omission in this remarkable book. Hays has focused so centrally on the *identity* of Jesus, the theme which in classic theology used to be called his 'person', that he seems to me significantly to have downplayed his *achievement*, the theme that used to be called Jesus' 'work'. Here I can only begin to probe new possibilities, but it seems to me that, not least by following in the ways Hays himself has taught us, new lines of thought open up that somebody ought to pursue further.[24]

Many will be surprised that Hays is cautious about discerning echoes of Isaiah's 'suffering servant' in the famous Mark 10.45 (the son of man came 'to give his life as a ransom for many', pp. 86–7). Subsequent Christian readers, he says, will undoubtedly have heard such echoes, but Mark is pointing us rather to Exodus 24.8, to the suffering psalms, and to the 'apocalyptic visions' of Zechariah and Daniel. But without wishing to downplay the latter, it seems to me that a stronger case can be made for echoes of Isaiah at this point.[25] Hays questions whether the allusion can be sustained by the possible echo between 'a ransom for many' in Mark 10.45 and 'he bore the sin of many' in Isaiah 53.12. But things go deeper than **[61]** that. Isaiah's servant will make kings to shut their mouths (52.15), just as Mark's Jesus explains that present power-games of 'the kings of the earth' are confronted with a new sort of power (10.42). The Isaianic figure will, by his serving, justify many (53.11), and the whole context of a reversal of expectations, and of earthly power, focused on a redemptive death, fits extremely well with the whole sequence of thought in Mark 10.35–45. We might also cite Mark 14.24, where again, as with many commentators, a strong case can be made for seeing the blood 'poured out for many' as carrying Isaianic overtones.

However, this is a comparatively small exegetical detail. Mark clearly offers a scripturally rooted interpretation of Jesus' death. The only questions are which scriptures, and to what extent. More unexpected, precisely in terms of the echoes of scripture, is Hays's contention that Matthew 'has given surprisingly little attention to formulating a scriptural apologetic for the crucifixion of Jesus' (p. 159) and that Luke 'does not explain *why* the cross is part of God's plan' (p. 278). These sentences seem to me to beg for rebuttal. This cannot be done here at any length, but some starting-points may be noted.

---

24 Some of what follows is expounded further in Wright 2016a.

25 See e.g. Marcus 2004 [1992]; Watts 2000 [1997]. Elsewhere Hays follows Marcus and Watts fairly closely; it is not clear to me why he departs from them at this point.

I think that the key to it all, in all four gospels, is Jesus' announcement of God's kingdom. No surprises there – though the kingdom plays less of a central role in Hays's book than one might have supposed. What matters is *what the kingdom means* and *how it was to be accomplished*. On both counts, all four gospels offer scripturally rooted reflections that reach their climax (in the narrative of each book and in the larger implied narrative of God and Israel) with Jesus' crucifixion. And it is this theme, the kingdom achieved through the cross, that is the evangelists' explanation and interpretation of the cross, echoing scripture in both narrative and figure.

Take Matthew first. Hays rightly noted that the echoes of exodus in Matthew 2 were designed to portray Jesus as the new Israel. But there is more. Herod the Great plays the role of the wicked pharaoh, killing all the babies to try to stop the Israel-shaped divine plan going ahead. Acts 4 will quote Psalm 2 of a later Herod, coupling him with Pilate: the kings of the earth did their worst, and God's Messiah was exalted, winning the victory and claiming the whole world as his kingdom. I am inclined to think that Matthew is working with a similar theme. Jesus comes into the world with a price on his head, a price that will eventually be paid; but that ultimate price will result in the ultimate new exodus. And when Jesus goes into the desert, echoing the narrative of Israel's wilderness wanderings and quoting explicitly from Deuteronomy to ward off the equivalent of Israel's temptations, this is no detached figure, but part of the narrative of the obedient Jesus-as-Israel, whose obedience will be finally tested on the cross, where the same mocking voices assail him.[26] This and other points seem to provide [62] the basis for a far more thoroughgoing scripturally based interpretation of Jesus' death in Matthew than Hays allows, though of course part of the point is that the four gospels are not exactly expounding what the western church has meant by 'atonement' except insofar as that slippery category can be related to the notion which, as I have argued elsewhere, dominates the scene far more. The *victory* of Israel's God, through the public career and death of Israel's Messiah, is central, and not to be played off against other 'theories'. The creator has defeated all the dark powers that, Egypt-like, had enslaved Israel and the whole world. This seems to me a primary insight of earliest Christianity, reflected variously in the many traditions represented in the NT.

Similar things can and must be said about Luke. It has been just as fashionable to say that Luke has no 'atonement-theology' as it has been to say

---

26 Comparing Mt. 4.1–11 with 27.39–44; into which latter passage are also, of course, woven the echoes of Ps. 22 and, for good measure, Lam. 2.15, as well as the Wisdom of Solomon.

that he offers a human, rather than divine, Jesus. But just as Richard Hays has shown the latter proposal to be baseless, so I think we can show the former to be ill-conceived. Again, the scriptural clues are central.

The most obvious passage is the explicit quotation of Isaiah 53.12 in Luke 22.37: 'He was reckoned with the lawless'. This more than makes up for the fact that in Luke 22.23–27, in other respects similar to Mark 10.35–45, there is no equivalent of the 'punch-line' of 10.45, which, by its supposed allusions to Isaiah 53, has been regarded as the heart of Mark's theology of the cross. The clear echo of Isaiah 53 in 22.37 ought, one might suppose, to have been enough to start the ball rolling in what has been the unfashionable direction, particularly when it is linked to the strong sense, which Hays expounds so clearly, of Luke's narrative of Jesus seen as the climax of the story of God and Israel. In particular, we should not miss Luke 22.53: 'Your moment has come at last, and so has the power of darkness.' Luke understands the cross to be the point at which the dark powers of the world do their worst, in order then to be defeated.

Throughout Luke's Passion narrative, in addition, there are clear hints of what in shorthand we may call 'representative substitution'. Israel's Messiah dies innocently under the condemnation which Barabbas and the brigands had deserved; his innocence is confirmed by the centurion. Luke allows specific biblical echoes to ring out: as Jesus goes on his way he warns the crowds one last time of the coming Roman devastation.[27] The time is coming, he says, when people will start to say to the mountains, 'Fall on us!', and to the hills, 'Cover us!' This quotes directly from Hosea 10.8, linking the people's rejection of Jesus with ancient Israel's idolatry, the turning away from Israel's God. The point is focused sharply through 23.31, which may contain an allusion to Deuteronomy 29.19: if this is what they do to the green tree, what will happen to the dry one? This is a figure of speech, to be sure, [63] but a figure that means what it means within the narrative that is clearer in Luke, I think, than anywhere else, anchored ultimately not simply to the story of Israel but to the story of Adam himself (see the genealogy in Luke 3). Rome will be the agent of divine judgment on rebel Israel, but Jesus, the obedient servant, is dying that death in advance. He is the 'green' tree, much harder to cut or burn, but all around him are the dry sticks of young revolutionaries, eager for a fight with Rome that they cannot win. 'Not only in theological truth but in historic truth, the one bore the sins of the many': words of George Caird that I have quoted many times at this point in the argument. This is

---

27 See the earlier warnings in e.g. 13.1–9; 13.34–35; 19.42–44 – not to mention ch. 21 as a whole.

at the heart of Luke's theology of the cross, and it is both rooted in and expressed through his scripturally rooted narrative and its accompanying figural echoes.[28]

When it comes to the fourth gospel, nobody doubts that John provides a rich interpretation of Jesus' crucifixion. But there seems little agreement as to where the heart of that interpretation is to be located. The focus of the gospel, as we have seen, remains on the interplay between Jesus and the Temple. When Caiaphas warns his colleagues that it would be better for one person to die in the place of the nation, this is partly to ward off the danger the Pharisees have indicated, that the Romans will come and take away 'our place' – in other words, the Temple – as well as 'our nation' (John 11.48–50). John explains that Caiaphas has prophesied truly. Jesus will indeed die for the nation, 'and not only for the nation, but to gather into one the scattered children of God' (11.52).

This leads to one of John's most profound interpretations of the cross, which comes in the complex and (to our eyes) convoluted response to the request from 'some Greeks' that they might see Jesus (12.20–22). Hays briefly expounds the passage that follows, but to my mind he skips over the telling climax, focusing only on the 'grain of wheat [that] falls into the earth' (12.24) and the resultant 'bearing fruit', meaning that Jesus will draw all people to himself (12.32) – the ultimate answer for the Greeks. Granted that the passage is indeed dense and difficult, there is another theme that emerges if we follow the metaleptic link suggested by Jesus' quotation of Psalm 6.4–5 at 12.27: 'Now my heart is troubled . . . What am I going to say? "Father, save me from this moment"?' The psalm consists mostly of lament and prayer, but it doesn't stop there. The last three verses indicate how things will turn out:

Depart from me, all you workers of evil,
for YHWH has heard the sound of my weeping.
YHWH has heard my supplication;
YHWH accepts my prayer. [64]
All my enemies shall be ashamed and struck with terror;
they shall turn back, and in a moment be put to shame.
(Psalm 6.8–10)

This fits exactly, it seems to me, with the underlying message of this passage. The Greeks want to see Jesus, and Jesus interprets their request as an eschatological

---

28 See Caird 1965, 22; see Wright 1996b, 608.

sign. This is the moment when the son of man is to be glorified (12.23). That alone, with its obvious allusion to Daniel 7, ought to indicate where the passage is going. 'The Greeks' belong to the non-Jewish world that has been ruled over by the dark powers. The combination of Daniel 7 and Psalm 6 declares that these powers are to be defeated, not by Jesus escaping death but rather by him going through it, troubled soul and all. The result will be clear: 'Now comes the judgment of this world! Now this world's ruler is going to be thrown out! And when I've been lifted up from the earth, I will draw all people to myself' (12.31–32). Jesus, by his crucifixion – drawing here on the 'lifting up' motif that goes back to the figure of the serpent in 3.14–15 – will win the ultimate victory over the powers that have held the world captive. And that will be the moment when the pagan nations, set free from their ancient slavery, will come to worship Israel's God in and through Jesus. This takes place, after all, at Passover-time, the time for the ultimate pharaohs to be overthrown. I have argued elsewhere that this discourse has a political as well as a 'demonic' reference.[29] For our present purposes, we need only note that the metaleptic associations generated by Psalm 6 and Daniel 7 not only reinforce what the passage itself says but also point forward dramatically to Jesus' confrontation with Pilate in chapters 18 and 19, and thence to his shameful, but for John victorious, death.

Underneath all this there is another psalmic allusion that points in the same direction. This joins together Jesus' action in the Temple, which most now recognize (though Hays makes less of this than one might have thought) as crucial to the evangelists' understanding of Jesus' death, and his 'lifting up' both on the cross itself and then in resurrection and exaltation. This point, not recognized in any commentaries known to me, deserves much fuller study. I raise it here partly to celebrate the fact that once one starts enquiring after metaleptic resonances all sorts of texts emerge from the woodwork and ask to be taken into consideration.

In Matthew 21.15, we are suddenly introduced to 'children' who are shouting out 'Hosanna to David's son!' in the Temple. Some have linked these to the 'children' in Matthew 11.25, though there is no particular reason why the youngsters of that passage should suddenly reappear at this crucial point. However, Jesus' response to the chief priests and the scribes is to quote **[65]** from Psalm 8: 'You called forth praise to rise to you/From newborn babes and infants too!' Despite a widespread recognition that in the early church Psalm 8, linked with Psalm 110, formed one of the most important scriptural matrices for understanding the events concerning Jesus, nobody to my

---

29   See Wright and Davies 2015 (ch. 12 in the present volume).

knowledge has asked the Hays-type question of this passage: what is Psalm 8 doing here?[30]

As soon as we reflect on the wider themes of the psalm, a fascinating link appears. 'What are human beings', asks verse 4, 'that you are mindful of them, mortals that you care for them?' Literally, of course, this might be translated 'What is man ... or the son of man ... ?' And then the obvious point emerges, indicating that the evangelist was seeing the Temple-incident as already linked to the Danielic scene in which 'one like a son of man' is vindicated after a terrible ordeal:

You have made them a little lower than God,
and crowned them with glory and honour.
You have given them dominion over the works of your hands;
you have put all things under their feet,
all sheep and oxen,
and also the beasts of the field,
the birds of the air, and the fish of the sea,
whatever passes along the paths of the seas.
(Psalm 8.5–8)

The evangelist seems to be indicating that the Temple-incident is itself a vital part of a whole narrative in which 'the son of man' is to be exalted. As in Daniel with the 'beasts', and as in Psalm 110 with the 'enemies' who are to be placed under the feet of the coming king (Matthew 22.44), so in Psalm 8: the praise of the sovereign Lord that comes from babes and infants will 'silence the enemy and the avenger' (8.2). All this is framed by the introductory and concluding verses, which repeat: 'O YHWH, our Sovereign, how majestic is your name in all the earth!' In the Septuagint, this begins *kyrie ho kyrios hēmōn*, which provides an obvious link to the opening of Psalm 110 (LXX 109): *eipen ho kyrios tō kyriō mou* . . . leading to the promise that 'the Lord' will put 'all things under his feet', just as in Psalm 8 all creation is put under the feet of the human one(s). I think it is safe to say that there were multiple reasons for linking Psalm 8 with Daniel 7 on the one hand and with Psalm 110 on the other, and that together this combination formed a powerful unit, explaining not only that Israel's Messiah, the truly human being, would be vindicated

---

30 On the fusion of Pss. 8 and 110 and their importance in early Christian reflection, see e.g. Bauckham 2009, 21–3, 173. The obvious passages are 1 Cor. 15.20–28 and Heb. 1—2. For the present point see below, ch. 14 in the present volume.

after suffering but that in this whole narrative the 'enemies' – dark powers of whatever sort – would be conquered and subdued.

This, as I said, could be considerably explored and expanded. I suspect that there are more secrets there waiting to be uncovered. As that work proceeds, I would simply note a fascinating Johannine link at the same point. When John is describing Jesus' Temple-action in chapter 2, he says that Jesus drove out of the Temple not only the traders, as in the synoptics, but 'sheep, cows and all' as well (John 2.15). The Greek for the latter [66] phrase is *ta te probata kai tous boas*, which just happens to correspond to the LXX of Psalm 8.8, where the animals that are put in subjection under the feet of the human figure(s) are *probata kai boas pasas*, 'all sheep and oxen'. No commentator that I know even mentions this allusion, let alone discusses it. Without the Matthaean reference to Psalm 8 at a similar point in the equivalent narrative one might dismiss it as a trivial coincidence. But granted John's propensity not only for subtle allusion but also for drawing attention to the theme of the exaltation of the son of man, I think we should take it seriously. It begins to look as though, standing behind two very different gospel traditions, we are in touch with a very early interpretation of Jesus' Temple-action in which the whole story was seen as part of the messianic path (made a little lower than God, or the angels) to the messianic exaltation (crowned with glory and honour), resulting in victory over the dark enemies of God and his people and therefore the glad shout of universal praise (echoing the victory-song of Exodus 15) to God as creator and redeemer. From this point the exegete can glimpse, in the mind's eye, speculative history-of-tradition reconstructions stretching out in all directions. But the central feature is, I think, clear. Already by the time the gospels were being put together, Psalm 8 was so thoroughly soaked into the narrative of Jesus' journey to Jerusalem and his actions and fate when he arrived that it kept making its appearance, not only in Paul and Hebrews but in Matthew and John as well. All this, of course, reinforces my sense that Hays, by encouraging us to look for scriptural allusions and the metaleptic significance they may possess, has once again presented us with questions and challenges that will keep us busy for some time.

Conclusion

There are many ways in which one might draw together this brief discussion of one of the most important books on the gospels to be published in my lifetime. Rather than simply sum up, I would like to raise two questions that emerge obliquely but I think significantly.

First, it would be fascinating to explore the question Hays mentions when he says that the narrative typologies used by Matthew (and by implication the others as well) 'help to create the theological puzzles that Chalcedon and its successors sought to solve' (p. 189). I am inclined to think that this is the wrong way round. Why should it be thought that Matthew – and the other evangelists, and Paul, and Hebrews, and the author of Revelation – were creating a 'puzzle'? Were they 'puzzled' by it, or did it seem clear to them? Or was the puzzle something that emerged when, in subsequent generations, Christian readers were less in tune with the first-century Jewish world in which – despite the older prejudices! – this way of looking at things made the sense the early writers thought it made? Might it not be that some writers at least in subsequent centuries, forgetting the [67] Temple-theology at the heart of Jesus' understanding of himself and his vocation, turned the evangelists' rich web of metaleptic scriptural allusions into mere proof-texts on the one hand or allegories on the other? Might it not be the case that the church was moving, steadily though not smoothly, into an intellectual climate which was bound to distort the deep biblical truths the NT writers were expressing, and to regard as puzzling what the first Christians found rather obvious? Of course, once the questions had been formulated as 'puzzles' it was much better that they were given wise answers within the new contexts and idioms. But perhaps it would have been better still to regard the earliest Christian writings, not as fuzzy, half-formed statements of truths that would be clarified four centuries later, but as already crystal-clear statements, within their own scripture-soaked world, of a vision of God and Jesus that would only appear puzzling when that context was forgotten.

And what about history itself? On the penultimate page of the main text, Hays puts a whole paragraph in italics. This is the heart of it:

the God to whom the Gospels bear witness, the God incarnate in Jesus, is the same as the God of Abraham, Isaac, and Jacob. Either that is true, or it is not. If it is not, the Gospels are a delusional and pernicious distortion of Israel's story.

(p. 363)

A similar point emerges in an important footnote: 'Both the Old Testament type and the New Testament antitype stand together as concrete disclosures of God's activity in the world' (p. 433 n. 73). Both these clear statements point to a question which, though naturally and rightly bracketed out for the whole book, is bound to press back on the interpreter: did it really happen? Does it matter whether it did or not, and what sort of account ought we to give of that question and of the ways in which we might answer it? This is of course the question of history.

In one of the few places in the book where this question is noted, Hays falls back on a regular distinction. For the present project, he says, he is investigating the ways in which the gospel-writers employ biblical echo, not 'reconstructing the history *behind* the Gospels' (p. 389 n. 150). But, though this book clearly was not the place to address such matters, it seems to me that the better Hays has argued his case, the more pressing they become. There is today a new wave of writers – not NT scholars, admittedly, but often using the appearance of historical scholarship – arguing that Jesus of Nazareth never existed, or that, if he did, he did and said few if any of the things ascribed to him in the gospels. The 'Jesus Seminar' has come and gone. But many in our world, and in our churches, are still asking the same questions; and the more we recognize Matthew, Mark, Luke and John as highly skilled and sophisticated writers, the more we lay ourselves open to the challenge: 'So: what if it turned out that they made it all up, weaving delightful scriptural patterns but not actually reporting things that really happened?'

At this point, the propriety, indeed the urgent necessity, of 'going behind the text' emerges with full clarity. (This is where we return to the [68] point I made earlier, that though 'incarnation' is indeed the key in which the gospels' music is set, it is not the tune that is being played.) That phrase, 'behind the text', has carried in some quarters an implicit rebuke, made up I think partly of postmodern fears about extra-textual realities, partly of anxieties about leaving Christian faith apparently at the mercy of quirky individual reconstructions, and partly of an implicit appeal to 'the authority of scripture'. But, while fully granting that texts create their own worlds and invite readers to live within them, it is obvious that some texts at least intend to refer to extra-textual realities, and that if it can be shown that they are wrong then the 'world' they are creating might be exposed as a sham. When I read reports of a football match in two newspapers known to support the two different teams, I am invited by the one to enter a world of celebration, and by the other to share a world of disappointment. But I do not expect them to invent the score-line. Indeed, the celebration and the disappointment depend entirely on that extra-textual reality. Thus, though postmodernists may squeal and postliberals may sneer, all four gospels are claiming to tell us about the actual events that constituted the launching of God's kingdom 'on earth as in heaven'. That is the world to which the gospels intend to refer, the world that these texts help us grasp in its multi-dimensional glory. The gospels insist that it was those events that generated the new world of Christian discipleship that they are inviting us to enter, thus forbidding us to reduce that new world to an inner-textual construct or its correlate in personal or ecclesial belief and practice. Incarnation means incarnation. When it comes to the gospels, intertextu-ality pushes us inexorably towards extra-textuality. The scriptures were not creating a private world, let alone a Platonic world. Hays is right. The evange-lists, exploiting scripture's rich echoes, were indeed intending to speak of 'concrete disclosures of God's activity in the world'. And that means history. Once we recognize the four evangelists as first-century Jews soaked in Israel's scriptures and able to echo them with sophistication, subtlety and power, what is to stop us suggesting that similar things might be said, and perhaps should be said, of the one to whom all four ostensibly refer?

14

Son of Man – Lord of the Temple? Gospel Echoes of Psalm 8 and the Ongoing Christological Challenge

As I hinted in the previous essay in relation to Richard Hays's recent book, the echoes of Psalm 8 at a crucial point in the gospel narratives of Matthew, and arguably John as well, seem to indicate not only that the psalm was seen by the evangelists as loadbearing for their understanding of Jesus, but also that it formed part of the very early reflection of Jesus' first followers. The present paper probes into the relevant texts with this in mind. I am particularly grateful to Dr Max Botner, the research assistant with whom I originally brainstormed this possibility. I am also indebted to Professors John Barclay and Francis Watson who hosted an earlier presentation of the paper at Durham University, and to Professor Walter Moberly for his shrewd and helpful comments on that occasion.

[77] Introduction

Richard Hays's recent book, *Echoes of Scripture in the Gospels*, has already been hailed as a masterpiece which, like several of Hays's books, has opened up new vistas of exegetical and theological possibility.[1] I have elsewhere discussed some of the questions it raises, and in the present paper I want to develop one point I mentioned there in passing.[2] Hays concentrates on the ways in which the biblical allusions and echoes in all four gospels indicate that all of them, not only John as has so often been said, understand the Jesus they portray as the living embodiment [78] of Israel's God. I will suggest that we

---

1 Hays 2016; see also Hays 2002 [1983]; 1989; 2005. I offer these reflections with great respect to John Nolland, and with gratitude and admiration for his sterling contributions to New Testament scholarship. I am grateful to Dr Max Botner for his help in preparing this paper, and to Dr Michael Bird and Dr Crispin Fletcher-Louis for their comments on an earlier draft (though I have by no means always taken their advice, and they are not responsible for what follows).

2 Wright 2017 (ch. 13 in the present volume).

can go further with this than Hays does, but that in order to do so we need to bring into play the question of Jesus and the Temple.

As I proceed towards my opening exegetical observations, I note that these involve an initial acceptance of Hays's now well-known view of metalepsis: that a single line quoted from a biblical passage may constitute an invitation to the reader to supply at least some of the larger context, and that when this is done surprising and stimulating results often arise.[3] A measure of scepticism about all this has been common in some circles, but I shall put that to one side for the moment.[4] Like Hays in his recent book, I will allow the data, and the sense which a metaleptic reading might offer, to reflect back on method, rather than vice versa. I want to draw attention to two potential metaleptic echoes from Psalm 8. The use of this psalm in Paul and Hebrews is well known; one might also discuss Acts 7.56 and 1 Peter 3.22.[5] As others have shown, Psalm 8 was of considerable significance in Jewish thought both before and after the New Testament.[6] But for this study, I concentrate on Matthew and John.

Matthew 21

I begin with Matthew 21.16. Matthew, unique here among the synoptists, adds to the story of Jesus entering Jerusalem, and driving out the traders from the Temple, a note about children singing 'Hosanna to the Son of David!' (21.15). The chief priests and scribes, who have been watching the remarkable things Jesus has been doing, object to this, and Jesus replies [79] with a reference to Psalm 8.2: 'Out of the mouth of babes and sucklings you have brought praise'.[7] No further comment is made. Jesus leaves the city and, as usual, goes out to Bethany.

The quote is clear, but Matthew's alert reader may already have spotted an echo of an earlier verse from the psalm.[8] Matthew, again without parallel,

---

3   See Hays 1989, 20; 2016, 11–12.

4   See e.g. Paul Foster's contention that Hays's approach lacks the necessary criteria for weeding out spurious intertextual proposals (Foster 2015). See too R. W. Moberly's article in the *Journal of Theological Interpretation* 11(1) (Moberly 2017): Moberly is not sceptical about metalepsis in general, but warns against its over-use.

5   For Paul, see 1 Cor. 15.27; Eph. 1.22; Phil. 3.21; less obviously but still I think importantly, Rom. 8.18–30 (a point I owe to Dr Haley Goranson). On the logic of Ps. 8 in Heb. 2 see Moffitt 2011, 120–9. On 1 Pet. 3.22 see e.g. Elliott 2000, 687.

6   See, for a start, Moloney 1981.

7   As John Nolland points out (Nolland 2005, 848), Jesus' question, 'Have you never read . . .?' is echoed at 21.42 where Jesus quotes from Ps. 118.22, with the use of *thaumastē* there echoing *thaumasia* here (and see nn. 8 and 11 below).

8   So already Davies and Allison 1997, 142. Davies and Allison note the wider christological use of this

speaks of people witnessing the remarkable deeds of Jesus, which he calls *thaumasia* (a New Testament *hapax legomenon*). This echoes the opening and closing of Psalm 8: 'O Lord our Lord, how remarkable (*thaumaston*) is your name in all the earth' (8.1, 9). Mention of that repeated line at once reminds a hearer of the more familiar psalm echo, that of Psalm 110.1, where YHWH says to 'my lord', 'Sit at my right hand until I make your enemies your footstool.'[9] Interestingly, when Matthew and Mark quote Psalm 110 they implicitly link it with Psalm 8. Both psalms speak of people being placed underfoot, Psalm 8 referring to 'all things' and Psalm 110 to 'enemies'. The LXX for the phrase in Psalm 8 is *hypokatō tōn podōn autou* whereas in Psalm 110 it is *hypopodion tōn podōn sou*, but Matthew and Mark, quoting Psalm 110, use the wording of Psalm 8 (while Luke reverts to *hypopodion* as in the LXX).[10] A further link between the two psalms is provided by the mention in both of [80] 'enemies'. In Psalm 110.1–2, explained further in verses 5–7, these appear to be foreign armies; in Psalm 8, unspecified 'enemies' who will be 'silenced' because of the 'bulwark' founded by what the 'babes and infants' will say. Already, therefore, a case can be made for seeing the quotation of Psalm 8.2 in Matthew 21 not simply as an explanation for the children's excited acclamation but, in company with Psalm 110, as a hint of a coming major theme, including part at least of the explanation for Jesus' action in the Temple.

It is worth noting at this point a widespread Jewish tradition that linked Psalm 8, not least the mention of children singing God's praise, to the exodus, and particularly to the Song of Moses and Miriam in Exodus 15.1–21. This is reflected in many sources, an obvious one being Wisdom 10.21, where after the exodus 'Wisdom opened the mouths of those who were mute, and made the tongues of infants (*glōssas nēpiōn*) speak clearly'. This tradition was developed in rabbinic and other writings from at least the second century onwards.[11] Granted that Matthew, describing an incident at Passover-time, has put into

---

psalm in the NT but not the specific point to be made below. France 2007, 790, notes that *thaumasia* is unique in the NT but not its link with Ps. 8.

9 Quoted in Mt. 22.44 and par., alluded to in 26.64 at the climax of the hearing before Caiaphas. MT Ps. 8.2, 10 reads *yhwh adonēnu*; Ps. 110.1 reads *n'um yhwh laadonai*; LXX 8.2 is *kyrios ho kyrios hēmōn*, while 109.1 reads *eipen ho kyrios tō kyriō hēmōn*.

10 Mt. 22.24 following Mk. 12.36; Lk. 20.42. On the linking of Pss. 8 and 110 in early Christian texts, see Hays 1989 [1973], 35–7; Bauckham 2008, 173, 176. Bauckham points out that 'it is *in conjunction with Psalm 110:1* that these other texts [Dan. 7 and Ps. 8] play their principal roles in the New Testament' (173, his emphasis).

11 See e.g. Davies and Allison 1997, 142, with copious references; also Luz 2005, 13, and e.g. Horbury 2003, 261, citing *Mekhilta*, Shirata 1, on Ex. 15.1; Nolland, 2005, 38, 848, pointing out that 'the relevant part of Ex. 15:2 is identical to Ps. 118:14, the psalm to which the children's acclamation relates, which was used in Mt. 21:9 and will be used again in v. 41 [*sic*: 42?] and 23:38 [*sic*: 39?]'.

the mouth of Jesus a line from the psalm which points across to this theme, it seems quite possible that he, too, understands Psalm 8 as (among other things) a celebration of the exodus. And, granted the main setting of Matthew 21 (Jesus' Temple-action and its various explanations), we notice that Exodus 15 celebrates not only the rescue from Egypt but also the prospect of building the sanctuary in Zion (15.17) – a text linked at Qumran to the eschatological Temple and the coming Davidic king.[12] It is also important to note that here Jesus uses a psalm which speaks of praise offered to Israel's God to justify praise offered to himself.[13] **[81]**

The possibility that Matthew has the whole psalm in mind, not just the third verse, is further strengthened by exploring another echo, which takes us to the heart of my proposal. The psalm goes on to raise the question: when I look at your heavens, the work of your fingers, the moon and the stars that you have established, *what are human beings that you are mindful of them, the son of man that you care for him*?[14] It goes on:

> Yet you have made them a little lower than God/the gods
> [or: angels, as LXX; Hebrew *Elohim*][15]
> and crowned them with glory and honour.
> You have given them dominion over the works of your hands;
> you have put all things under their feet . . .
> (Psalm 8.5–6)

A moment's reflection on Matthew, never mind any other early Christian writers, will remind us that he does indeed exploit the idea of a 'son of man', first humiliated and then set in authority over all things. Matthew has already emphasized this in chapter 9. In 9.6, paralleled in Mark and Luke, Matthew's Jesus heals the paralysed man 'to let you know that the son of man has authority on earth to forgive sins'. Matthew then adds, in verse 8, that the crowds were frightened 'and praised God for giving authority like this to humans'. This is a clear thematic allusion to Psalm 8, though not a verbal one; Matthew's *exousia*

---

12 4Q174, linking Ex. 15 to 2 Sam. 7 and Ps. 2: Vermes 1997, 493–4. The Hebrew of Ps. 8.3 says that God has brought 'strength', *'oz*, from the children, echoing Ex. 15.2; but the word was frequently understood to mean, in some sense, 'praise': see the note in France 1971, 251–2.

13 So France 2007, 789, and France 1971, 152: 'Unless he is here setting himself in the place of Yahweh, the argument is a *non sequitur*.'

14 Translating the last phrase literally. NRSV has 'mortals that you care for them' with a marginal note about the Hebrew original.

15 On the (relatively unimportant) distinction here between God and angels see Middleton 2005, 58–60.

is not used in the psalm, but the question of the *exousia* claimed implicitly by Jesus in his Temple-action is raised in Matthew 21.23, shortly after the quote from Psalm 8.[16] Then, to look at the most obvious passage, Matthew frames chapter 26 with just this theme. Unlike Mark or Luke, who cut straight into the plot against Jesus' life, Matthew gives Jesus an opening sentence: 'In two days' time, as you know, it'll be Passover! That's when the son of man will be handed over to be crucified' (26.2). Then, as the fast-paced scene reaches its climax, Jesus answers Caiaphas's (presumably scornful) question by declaring that 'from now on you will see "the son of man sitting at the right hand of the Power, and coming on the clouds of heaven"' (26.64). Matthew is presenting to his [82] readers a 'son of man' who is betrayed and will be crucified, but who will then be vindicated, exalted, so that, as in 28.18, matching 9.6, he is given 'all authority in heaven and on earth'. This narrative has exactly the same trajectory as the small story of 'the son of man' in Psalm 8 and indeed Daniel 7. I suggest that the metaleptic echo in chapter 21 is already pointing in this direction.

The context of these passages offers a further echo and thereby a further interpretative clue. In chapter 21, the reference to Psalm 8 is part of Jesus' explanation of his violent action in the Temple, or at least an oblique scriptural vindication of the acclamation he is receiving because of it.[17] In Matthew 24.2, Jesus declares that the Temple will be destroyed (*katalythēnai*). In chapter 26, his statement to Caiaphas (26.64) is part of his answer to the earlier charge (26.61; repeated at 27.40, again with a sneer, by the mockers at the cross), that Jesus had been threatening to destroy (*katalysai*) the Temple and build it again in three days. Confrontation with the authorities, focused on suspicions about Jesus and the Temple, provides a further resonance with Psalm 8 at the point mentioned a moment ago. In Psalm 8, the 'babes and sucklings' give perfect praise, 'because of your enemies' – which in Matthew's context would obviously be the Temple and the chief priests – and the object of this is 'to silence the enemy and the avenger' (Psalm 8.2). 'Silence' translates the Hebrew *lĕhašbît*, which the LXX renders as *katalysai*, 'destroy', the same verb that is used in Matthew in relation to the Temple's imminent destruction. It looks as though language and themes from the psalm have been woven

---

16 The word *exousia* occurs four times in Mt. 21.23–27, looking ahead to 28.18. The other obvious echo is Dan. 7.14, where (LXX, not Theodotion) the 'one like a son of man' receives *exousia*. The trouble with invoking Dan. 7 is that it can then drown out other echoes.

17 Some (e.g. Luz 2005, 13; earlier, e.g. Lindars 1961, 166) have seen the unexpected 'children' in Mt. 21.16 as a reference back to the *nēpioi* to whom divine revelation is given in Mt. 11.25. That seems quite a stretch, though it is possible that Mt. 11.25, too, is a distant echo of Ps. 8.

surreptitiously into Matthew's account of Jesus' Temple-action. Matthew's Jesus is indeed warning of the Temple's downfall, and connecting that with his own vindication.

How might we explain this? And what contribution, however small, might the echo of Psalm 8 make towards such an explanation? There are three inter-locking answers, and we must look briefly at each of them. Some see these as mutually exclusive alternatives; I think they are complementary.

The obvious answer from Matthew's gospel as a whole, and particularly chapters 21 and 22, is that Jesus is presented as the royal, Davidic Messiah; that this is reflected in the echo of Psalm 8; and that this [83] sets Jesus in an adversarial relation with the Temple and its hierarchy, expressed in dramatic symbol in his Temple-action. The Davidic theme is clear all through. Matthew quotes the royal prophecy from Zechariah;[18] the procession with palm branches recalls the incipiently royal entry-processions of the Maccabees;[19] the crowds, and then the children, are shouting out 'Hosanna to David's son!';[20] the presence of the blind and the lame in the Temple seems a deliberate and healing echo of David's decree in 2 Samuel 5.8;[21] Jesus' answer to the question about authority evokes the baptism of John, normally seen as a royal event;[22] the parable of the wicked tenants focuses on the owner's son, normally taken as messianic;[23] and the final dialogue in the sequence focuses on Psalm 110.1, an explicit evocation (not a denial, as is sometimes thought) of David and his son.[24] To this immediate context we can add the question of Caiaphas, whether Jesus is 'the Messiah, God's son'; the charge before Pilate; the 'royal' overtones in the mocking; and the 'title' on the cross.[25] We need only add the worldwide authority claimed by the risen Jesus in Matthew 28, echoing the royal promises in the Psalms, Isaiah and (arguably) Daniel, and the picture is complete.[26] Matthew is not subtle. He sees Jesus as the Davidic Messiah. If we detect an allusion in his use of Psalm 8 to the humiliation and exaltation of 'the son of man', the

---

18 Zech. 9.9, cited in Mt. 21.5.

19 Both of Judas Maccabaeus (2 Macc. 10.7) and later of Simon Maccabaeus (1 Macc. 13.51).

20 21.9, 15.

21 21.14; this interpretation (as e.g. Harrington 1991, 295) is mentioned as an option by Davies and Allison 1997, 140; but see the cautionary note in Luz 2005, 13. France 2007, 788, points out the implied contrast between Jesus and David.

22 21.23–27; cf. 3.17 (with 16.16).

23 21.33–46.

24 22.41–46; see Davies and Allison 1997, 254: 'neither the title nor its content is rejected or denigrated'.

25 26.63; 27.11; 27.28–29, 42–43 ('he's the King of Israel'); 27.37.

26 Mt. 28.18; cf. e.g. Ps. 2.7–11; Isa. 11.1–10; Dan. 7.13–14.

most natural assumption is that Matthew is seeing that as a coded messianic reference.[27] [84]

This is supported by the well-known Jewish interpretation of Psalm 8 in which, through its obvious echoes of Genesis 1.26–28, it is seen as a statement of kingly authority. This is simply assumed by many scholars.[28] Evidence sometimes cited includes *4 Ezra* 6.53 ('over all these you placed Adam, as ruler over all the works that you had made'); *2 Enoch* 30.12 ('I assigned him to be a king, to reign [over] the earth, [and] to have my wisdom'); and Philo *Opif. Mun.* 136–50, especially 148:

Quite excellently does Moses ascribe the bestowal of names also to the first man: for this is the business of wisdom and royalty (*sophias gar kai basileias to ergon*), and the first man was wise with a wisdom learned from and taught by Wisdom's own lips, for he was made by divine hands; he was, moreover, a king (*kai proseti basileus*), and it befits a ruler to bestow titles on his several subordinates.

We may also recall Wisdom 10.2, where God gives Adam strength to rule all things (*kratēsai pantōn*); Sirach 49.16, where Adam is 'above every other created being', higher even than Shem and Seth who are 'glorified' (*edoxasthēsan*); *Jubilees* 2.14, which more or less repeats Genesis 1.28; and the *Apocalypse of Moses* 24.4, which speaks to Adam, after the fall, of the animals over which he had ruled. This catena is not massive, but it covers quite a spectrum of Jewish writings, and reveals a basic assumption that the first man is some kind of a king; or, to put it the other way round, that the true king will be in some sense the true Adam. This is strongly supported by the wider evidence from the Near Eastern world, and from hellenistic philosophy.[29] [85]

---

27 This is taken for granted by e.g. Moloney 1981, 658: '[the children] have properly understood the messianic role of Jesus'. Moloney's article, though dated in some respects, is still important, not least for his Targumic explorations.

28 E.g. Fishbane 1975, 20 n. 34; Collins and Collins 2008, 110; Middleton 2014, 141; Jipp 2015, 104–6, citing copious primary and secondary sources. For rabbinic links between Ps. 8 and Gen. 2.19–20 see Anderson 1997, 96.

29 For details see e.g. Marcus 2003, e.g. 59 n. 82, with copious references; Fishbane 2014, 402, citing the *Enuma Elish* and the Akinu festival; see too the Egyptian evidence in G. H. R. Horsley et al., eds *New Documents* 9.15. From the hellenistic world see e.g. Plut. *Princ. Iner.* 780e5–f2. Once we add in wider biblical themes the royal and/or priestly echoes of Dan. 7 come naturally to mind. Among older literature see e.g. May 1962, esp. 170f., citing Bentzen, Mowinckel and Ringgren, saying that 'the royal terminology is evident and a kingly First Man at least implicit', referring to the king putting all his enemies under his feet in 2 Sam. 22.39 and 1 Kgs. 5.3, and suggesting that Ps. 8 'may reflect an earlier form of the creation story than that now found in Gen 1'; Brueggemann 1972, esp. 12 (though focusing on Gen. 2, not on Gen. 1 and its echo in Ps. 8).

How justified are we then in taking Psalm 8 as a whole, metaleptically referred to in Matthew 21, as a reference to Jesus as the true king, the Davidic Messiah? The link in thought might work like this:

1 Matthew 21 as a whole is about the kingship of Jesus, displayed in his dramatic action which claims authority over the Temple and portends its doom;
2 when challenged, Jesus quotes Psalm 8;
3 Psalm 8 offers a poetic restatement of the human vocation to sovereignty as in Genesis 1 and 2 (especially 1);
4 that original human vocation was seen by some Jewish writers as explicitly 'royal';
5 elsewhere in Matthew 21 and 22 Jesus explains his Temple-action in cryptic but converging language about his messianic vocation;
6 Matthew's denouement in chapters 26 to 28 concerns the 'son of man' who is humiliated and killed but then exalted to a position of cosmic authority;
7 meanwhile the Temple and its authorities are warned of imminent judgment.

It looks as though Matthew at least is trying to say, through this veiled but powerful echo, that in Jesus' Temple-action we are to see the outworking of his vocation as Davidic Messiah, pointing forward both to his own humiliating death and to his vindication over his 'enemies', in this case the present Temple (which will be 'destroyed') and its ruling authorities.

For some, the phrase 'son of man' would by itself be enough to sustain the weight of this argument, particularly because of Daniel 7. There, too, a strong case can be made for saying that in the first century at least the 'one like a son of man' in Daniel 7.13 was seen by some as a royal Messiah. That, at any rate, is the interpretation given by *4 Ezra* 11—12, explicitly [86] described as a fresh interpretation of Daniel (12.11–12) and focused on the 'lion' who is the coming Davidic Messiah (12.32). It is usual here as well to point out that Josephus's silence in interpreting Daniel 7, corresponding to his sudden coyness over the end of the vision of the statue in Daniel 2, indicates well enough that he sees both passages as indicating a coming Messiah.[30] When we then add Daniel 7 to the picture already built up, and see it quoted, along with Psalm 110,

---

30 See the discussions in Wright 1992a, 312–17; and Wright 2013b, 116f., 130f., 293. Josephus's exposition of Dan. 2 is at *Ant.* 10.206–9; the telling omission of what might have been an exposition of Dan. 7 is after 10.263.

in Jesus' answer to Caiaphas in Matthew 26.64 – as part of the answer to a charge about conspiring against the Temple! – the circle appears complete. Psalm 8 speaks of God overthrowing his 'enemies', and of the exaltation of 'the son of man'; Jesus, faced with the challenge of the chief priests and scribes in Matthew 21 and of Caiaphas in Matthew 26, quotes Psalm 8 to the first and Psalm 110 and Daniel 7 – both closely linked with Psalm 8 – to the second. Matthew's Jesus claims to be the Davidic Messiah who, as heir to David and Solomon, has authority over the Temple. He will be exalted, while, according to 24.2, the Temple will be overthrown.[31]

The circle appears complete; but perhaps appearances deceive. An alternative account of 'son of man' in Daniel, and by implication in Psalm 8, would shift the emphasis from a Davidic Messiah to a coming high priest. Assuming that the phrase 'son of man' in the second-Temple world would carry at least a reference back to Adam, we note that there are certain texts in which Adam is seen not, or not only, as a king, but as a priest. It has frequently been pointed out that this emerges from, for instance, *Jubilees* 3.26–27 (Adam offering sweet-smelling sacrifices), the *LAE* [=*Apocalypse of Moses*] 29.3–6 (Adam taking spices from Eden with him at the expulsion so he can thereafter offer them to God) and several rabbinic sources.[32] The first-century *Liber Antiquitatum Biblicarum*, conscious of Adam's failure and the disasters that followed, holds back from making him a priest, but in doing so bears witness to a strong tradition which pointed in that direction.[33] In recent years the prime mover in [87] advocating a 'priestly' interpretation of Adam, and of 'the son of man', is Crispin Fletcher-Louis, whose case includes particularly a reading of the Hebrew version of Sirach 49.16 and a combined reading of the Day of Atonement liturgy of Leviticus 16 and the exaltation of 'one like a son of man' in Daniel 7. The 'son of man' is therefore the true Aaronic priest.[34] The jury is still out on this; but I find the most convincing argument in this direction to be the narrative arc from Genesis 1 to Exodus 40: if the tabernacle is the *microcosmos*, the small new working-model of creation, against the day when Israel's God will complete the project and flood the whole world with his glory (Numbers 14.21), then Aaron takes the place within this little world

---

31 The interpretation of Mt. 24, especially vv. 29–35, is beyond the scope of this paper. See Wright 1996b, ch. 8.

32 See the important article of Hayward 1992, here at 7.

33 Hayward 1992, 19: *LAB* attacks the tradition, but thereby bears witness to its wide dissemination.

34 See, as the most recent example of this thesis (but not yet the end of the story), Fletcher-Louis 2015, with full bibliography of earlier studies. Fletcher-Louis's detailed arguments demand far more engagement than is possible here; as will become apparent, I believe his emphasis can and should be contained within a larger picture.

that was occupied by Adam and Eve in the garden.[35] This then, for me, makes sense of the possible link of Adam and the high priest in Sirach, rather than the other way round.

I do notice, however, that the key texts which stress Adam's role as priest come from periods either when there was no reigning king in Judaea or (since we cannot be sure of dates) only one that the writers might well disapprove of, such as a Hasmonean or Herodian. At such a time, and also because the writers might have been priests themselves, there may have been pressure to emphasize potential 'priestly' meanings of key texts and to downplay 'royal' ones. It is, of course, hard to say; and in many ways it does not matter so much for the interpretation of the New Testament, since the most important text for early Christology, Psalm 110, draws together priesthood and kingship. It is, of course, a subversive priesthood, 'after the order of Melchizedek': an originally Jerusalem-based priesthood, still powerfully evoked both in Genesis and in the Psalter.[36] It was a priesthood to which even Abraham owed allegiance, as the letter to the Hebrews insists.[37]

The first option, then, is that Matthew is giving 'son of man' a royal connotation; the second, that he is understanding a priestly one. I do not regard these as mutually exclusive; and the use of Psalm 110 in the passage that concludes the sequence offers a way of combining them. [88] But there is a third possibility for interpreting this incident and perhaps the phrase 'son of man'. If Matthew's Jesus is the 'Emmanuel',[38] he is already in person the one who *embodies* the reality to which the Temple had all along pointed. That is why Jesus performs an acted symbol of the destruction of the Temple: not (as has been suggested by many, Jews as well as Christians) because the Temple and its cult were primitive, representing an earlier stage of a putative religious evolution, but because the reality has appeared, and the signpost is no longer necessary. The sense this makes is not one of comparative styles of religion, but of a *narrative* in which the divine purposes for creation's rescue and restoration, focused on a new Passover and new exodus, were drawn together in the story of the archetypal human being who, it turned out, was also 'God with us'. This seems to me profoundly Matthaean, though obviously not unique to him.

From this quick survey of quotations, allusions and echoes of Psalm 8, in particular relation to Matthew 21, we might take a leaf out of Matthew 9 and

---

35   See e.g. Morales 2015, 39.

36   Gen. 14.17–20; Ps. 110.4.

37   Heb. 7.4–10.

38   1.23; cf. 'I am with you' at 28.20.

apply it to the matter now in hand. In Matthew 9, Jesus, as son of man, is lord of the sabbath. Here in Matthew 21, I suggest, the echoes awoken by Psalm 8 indicate that he is also lord of the Temple. It is a commonplace of Jewish studies that the sabbath is to time what the Temple is to space. Jesus appears to be claiming authority over both, to be *embodying* both. He is bringing the long-awaited new day, the inauguration of God's reign. He, the Emmanuel, is now the place where heaven and earth come together at last.

Before asking where all this might lead us in terms of Christology and related issues, I turn to my second main text.

John 2

As is well known, the story of Jesus' Temple-action, though found in the synoptics at the close of his public career, is in John set very near the start, in chapter 2.13–22. So far as I can discover, no commentator has noticed that here, too, there appears to be an echo of Psalm 8, albeit a more distant one. Jesus finds in the Temple people selling oxen and sheep (*boas kai probata*), and also doves, and also the money-changers at their tables. Making a whip of cords, he drives them all (*pantas*) out of the Temple, *ta te probata kai tous boas*, 'both the sheep and the oxen'. He overturns the tables and pours out the coins, and tells the dove-sellers to stop making 'my father's house' a market-place. [89]

The first fascinating thing here is that John, unlike the synoptists, spells out twice which animals it is that Jesus is driving out, switching the order of the reference in the previous verse so that it corresponds exactly to Psalm 8, *ta te probata kai tous boas*. Continuing the previous quotation from the psalm:

> You have put all things under their feet,
> all sheep and oxen (*probata kai boas pasas*),
> and also the beasts of the field,
> the birds of the air . . .
> (Psalm 8.6–8)

I would not wish to overplay this hand by suggesting that John has these psalmic birds in mind with his line about the dove-sellers, though with John it's hard to set limits. But I do think that the sheep and oxen, and the switching of the order to echo the psalm, and the fact that this echo of Psalm 8 is placed, like that in Matthew, in relation to Jesus' action in the Temple, ought to be taken into account in understanding John 2 and the Temple-Christology to which it points. This might explain the surprising reference to oxen.[39] It would render unnecessary the various forced allegorical interpretations of the sheep and oxen that have been offered from time to time.[40] It would also help to explain the odd construction with 'all' (*pantas*): this echoes the repeated root in Psalm 8 (v. 7: you put all things (*panta*) under his feet; v. 8: all sheep and oxen (*probata kai boas pasas*)).[41] In other words, I suggest that some of the puzzles that have **[90]** been observed in this text are best explained by detecting here another echo, albeit a fainter one, of Psalm 8 and of the 'son of man' in particular. And this gives added force to the proposal that I see emerging out of Matthew: that Jesus' claim to fulfil the son-of-man prophecies of Psalm 8 (linked with Psalm 110) and Daniel 7 lies behind his Temple-action, seen as a coded prophetic warning of imminent destruction, and also points to the underlying explanation, in this case that Jesus himself is the true Temple towards which the present Jerusalem Temple is simply an advance signpost.

The larger context all points in this direction. John's Temple-Christology is evident from the prologue itself, with Jesus as the true *skēnē* where the divine glory is at last revealed. He is, in other words, the equivalent of the tabernacle at the end of Exodus, so that John 1.1–18 gives the christological version of the narrative arc from Genesis 1 to Exodus 40. This finds dramatic expression at the end of chapter 1, where Nathanael is assured that he will 'see heaven opened, and God's angels going up and down upon the son of man' (1.51). Like Jacob's Ladder in Genesis 28.10–22, obviously echoed here, this is a Temple-image, with heaven and earth coming together 'upon the son of man'. As in 1.14, the human one is not simply the image at the heart of the new Temple; he *is* the new Temple in person, the place where and the means by which heaven and earth are now joined together.[42] This point is then glimpsed from another angle in the wedding at Cana (2.1–11), symbolizing the marriage of heaven and earth and the transformation of the Jewish cult (v. 6). And it

---

39 Klawans 2006, 224, suggests that the idea of oxen being sold in the Temple is 'rather unlikely', citing Safrai 1985, 147; see too Sanders 1992, 87–8. Sanders's arguments are important, though perhaps magnified by his polemic at this point against J. Jeremias. Lindars 1972, 138, cites Epstein 1964, as arguing that the inclusion of oxen was an innovation by Caiaphas.

40 E.g. that Jesus was leading out his sheep (cf. 10.1); these and others noted by Keener 2003, 521 n. 268.

41 See e.g. the debate noted in Chilton 1991, at 331–3. J. B. Lightfoot, in the recently discovered commentary, suggests that *pantas* refers to all the sellers, with *ta te probate* indicating '*and* the sheep . . .' (Lightfoot 2015, 122); so too Barrett 1978 [1955], 197–8, pointing out that many have seen the extra phrase *ta te probate kai tous boas* as an editorial addition.

42 Hays 2016, 312–13, makes this clear, but without reference to Ps. 8.

then emerges in startling fashion as Jesus explains his Temple-action: 'Destroy (*lysąte*) this Temple, and I'll raise it up in three days' (2.19); here Jesus says explicitly what he is accused of saying in Matthew and Mark. John explains: 'he was speaking about the "Temple" of his body' (2.21). All these hints go together: Jesus, the Word made flesh, is the true tabernacle or Temple, the one through whom heaven and earth are joined at last. And this will be put into decisive operation through his death and resurrection, the humiliation and exaltation of the 'son of man' spoken of in Psalm 8. **[91]**

For John, as for Matthew, this is seen as the vocation of the royal Messiah. Jesus is hailed by John the Baptist as 'God's lamb' (1.29, 36); but the word that then goes around between Andrew and Simon, and between Philip and Nathanael, is that Jesus is Israel's Messiah, Israel's king, as foretold in scripture (1.41, 45, 49). This opens a sequence of Johannine claims that Jesus is Israel's Messiah, claims which culminate in the sharp debate with Pilate and the 'title' on the cross.[43] There are of course many more obvious scriptural echoes in the Temple-scene, not least Psalm 69.9 in 2.17. This is certainly one of the passages to which John refers when he says that after Jesus' resurrection 'they believed the scripture' and the word that he had spoken. But John, like Matthew, seems to want us to have Psalm 8 in the mix as well, providing the implicit narrative of the humiliation and exaltation of the son of man and, with that, the further echo of Genesis 1 to go with the prologue.

The implications of all this are clear enough in John. Jesus is himself the ultimate reality; the Jerusalem Temple is indeed 'my father's house' but he is the father's son. Thus John is not, to use Klawans's term, 'antiTemple'; nor does he have an anti-cultic 'attitude'.[44] He sees the Temple as the God-given forward pointer to the new (but always intended) reality now unveiled in the Messiah.[45] As Christopher Rowland takes up the story from the end of John 1:

The manifestation of divine glory exemplified by the sign at Cana in Galilee means that the locus of that divine glory is now focused pre-eminently, and perhaps exclusively, in the Word become flesh and in the demonstration of glory in the lifting up of Jesus on the cross (Jn 3.14; 12.32–33). As Jesus tells the Samaritan woman, Gerizim and Zion have had their day. True worship

---

43   Jn. 18.33–37 on Jesus' kingship; 19.3, 12, 14, 15, 19, 21–22. I regard the discussion about Jesus' Davidic ancestry in Jn. 7.40–44 as Johannine irony, assuming his readers know the synoptic traditions of Jesus' birth at Bethlehem (so e.g. Barrett 1978 [1955], 330).

44   Klawans 2006, 241–3.

45   On all this, see esp. Beale 2004.

is worship in spirit and in truth (Jn 4.20–24). The Temple has to take second place to this definitive manifestation of divine glory.[46] **[92]**

And for John at least the all-important connection seems to be the affirmation that Jesus is thus in some sense challenging or upstaging the Temple precisely in his identity as 'son of man', the Messiah who perfectly expresses the human vocation as in Genesis 1 or Psalm 8. Caiaphas, saying more than he knew in John 11.48, warned that if Jesus went on doing what he was doing it might mean the end of both Temple and nation, and that Jesus must therefore die instead of the nation (11.50) – which John (11.51–52) interprets as a true prophecy. But this is not a new point. John's whole gospel is as much about Temple as about people, claiming Jesus as the true 'tabernacle', the place where the divine glory has at last come to dwell in fulfilment of scriptural promises. And this extraordinary and far-reaching claim – a claim all but ignored in most New Testament theological writing over the last two hundred years, a point to which I shall return – is to be made good through a *narrative*, a real-life story. The narrative in question is the *sequential story* in which the truly 'human one', the 'man' and 'son of man' of Psalm 8, is first humiliated and then exalted. The 'human one' of Psalm 8 obviously corresponds to the image-bearing human of Genesis 1, again strongly echoed in the Johannine prologue. John is saying, among many other things but centrally among those other things, that the God of Israel is now made known, in the eschatological climax to which both Temple and scripture had pointed all along, in and as this God-bearing, God-imaging human called Jesus of Nazareth, Israel's Messiah, and that this makes the sense it makes not statically, as though in a tableau, but through the story of his humiliation and exaltation. John 2, in other words, is reinforcing what the end of John 1 had proposed in striking symbolic terms: we are to hear the story of the truly human one and to see it, exactly in line with the prologue, as the story of the true, or ultimate, Temple. The Johannine son of man, having claimed authority over the sabbath, is lord also of the Temple.[47]

Here, then, are my two pieces of evidence: echoes of Psalm 8 in Matthew 21 and John 2, and both in connection with Jesus' messianic authority and his encoded warning against the Temple. I am not of course suggesting that the reference I detect in both passages to Psalm 8 as concerning the humiliation and exaltation of the son of man in relation to the Temple becomes

---

46 Rowland 2007, 472.

47 On Jesus and the sabbath in John see e.g. 5.1–18, 27; 9.1–17.

the key to unlock all exegetical doors. But I think what we have seen raises questions that are worth following up. Along with the more obvious passages like Psalms 110 and 118, and Daniel 7, all of which have obvious links with Psalm 8, Psalm 8 itself should be given greater weight than usual as forming part of the very early christological [93] reflection – so early that though it has left echoes it seems to have taken a step back and been squeezed out of more regular arguments. If I am right in detecting these echoes, it might appear that Psalm 8 was part of the very early Christian reflection on the meaning of Jesus' Temple-action; and, since that action was seen by all the evangelists as decisive for understanding what Jesus was all about, the psalm must be considered central to early Christology. One could suggest, of course, that Matthew and John have introduced it into a tradition where it was previously unknown. But the cryptic nature of the echo in both cases (along with the use of the psalm in the rest of the New Testament) suggests rather that it was there earlier on and, being taken for granted, lost emphasis in the retelling. I am not much enamoured of hypothetical tradition-history, but there may be questions there still worth exploring. It may well be that others, contemplating the same evidence, will come up with different proposals to explain why this quiet but persistent hint should have appeared in the first place and why, having appeared, it should have stayed shyly in the background.

Concluding Reflections

All this raises wider issues, similar to those now evident in a range of writing which is rolling back an older tide and insisting that a Christology of 'divine identity' (as Richard Bauckham calls it)[48] is to be found not only in John and Hebrews but in the synoptics as well. The combination of Jesus' Temple-action and the explanatory use of Psalm 8 has something to add here, reinforcing the conclusions of Hays and others but offering a different dimension. Hays makes little of the Temple, except when discussing John. Bauckham and Hurtado do not include it, or not in the way I think we should. But Mark opens his gospel with two biblical quotations (Malachi and Isaiah) which speak explicitly, in their contexts, of the return of YHWH to Zion (Malachi 3.1; Isaiah 40.3).[49] These are not what we think of as *messianic* predictions; they are about Israel's God coming back to the Temple in power and visible glory. Mark, like John, is inviting us to see these predictions fulfilled in Jesus. But the second-Temple

---

48 Bauckham 2008, 18–59.
49 See Marcus 1992, 12–47; Watts 2000, 53–90. For Hays's own discussion see Hays 2016, 20–4.

[94] question, faced with these prophecies, was: what will it look like when he does that? Will it be cloud and fire, a throne-chariot with whirling wheels, or what? The four gospels answer: the revelation of the divine glory has been given, in and as *a human being*, the ultimate human of Genesis 1 and Psalm 8, Israel's representative, the Messiah. And this glory is revealed not in a static vision but in a *story*: the story of the humiliation and exaltation of the son of man and the overthrow and replacement of the Temple. The son of man is lord also of the Temple.

John is the most explicit about how and why this makes sense, with his reprise of Genesis 1 and with Jesus as simultaneously the image-bearer (John 1.14 corresponds, within the prologue, to verses 26–28 within Genesis 1) and the ultimate tabernacle. Paul and the others add their own material. But Matthew and John, linking Psalm 8 with Jesus' challenge to the Jerusalem Temple, seem to be saying that the humiliation and exaltation of the 'son of man' – his joining earth and heaven, perhaps – is the way to understand how it is that the God of Israel is appearing in paradoxical power and glory to accomplish the promised redemption. Jesus as Temple; Jesus as Adam; the story of Adam as a descent followed by exaltation: I do not think that anyone prior to Jesus of Nazareth had put these elements of biblical narrative together in this fashion. But when Jesus' first followers, 'reading backwards', followed the biblical hints Jesus himself had given in deed and word, these great eschatological themes were ready to hand.

Jewish writers from early days to the present have seen the later christological formulae as unJewish, and they have a point. Some Christian theologians have seemed quite happy about this. But this does not mean that the earliest ways of speaking of Jesus, combining the narratives of Temple and Adam, were unJewish. Far from it. Arguably, trying to do Christology without reference to those underlying narratives was bound to give hostages to fortune. Perhaps the exegete has, despite the common prejudice, something new to say to the systematic theologian.

Look at it like this. According to the received critical orthodoxy since at least Harnack – in fact, going back a long way behind him, but he was responsible for summing it up so clearly and launching it on the twentieth century – the New Testament was innocent of Trinitarian theology, and it was only when the early church forgot its original simplicity and went in for complex Greek philosophy that such ideas started to emerge, thereby falsifying an original faith which would have been shocked by such a distortion, or at least dilution, of basic monotheism.[50] [95]

---

50 von Harnack 1984–1989, 1:43–50.

At a superficial level Harnack was obviously right. Technical terms like 'substance', 'nature' and 'person' are not found in the first Christian century, or not (at least) in their later sense. But Harnack's view has bred a reaction in our own day, namely, that the fourth and fifth centuries did indeed develop the Trinitarian dogmas as we know them, *and that this was a right and proper development* to which the first Christians pointed forward, if at all, in a semi-coherent, arm-waving fashion, seeing through a glass darkly and creating 'puzzles' for those who came after.[51] The New Testament, on this view, gave advance signposts towards later orthodoxy, but it is to the Fathers that we should look to see, in effect, what the early Christians had struggled to express with primitive and inadequate equipment. This view has picked up steam, I think, from the frustration of some systematicians with those exegetes who appear, from the theologians' point of view, stuck in a kind of reductionist historicism.[52]

A healthy corrective to all this can be found in a fresh christological focus on Jesus' Temple-actions and Temple-sayings, *combined with his Adam-actions and -sayings*; exactly the focus, in other words, of Matthew 21 and John 2. Jesus receives messianic acclamation and interprets it in terms of the mighty acts of Israel's God expressed through the humiliation and exaltation of the son of man. He embodies the divine Word and reveals the long-awaited divine glory precisely through his human descent and his elevation to world sovereignty. As I said a moment ago, the untapped source of New Testament Christology is the expectation of YHWH returning to the Temple.[53] The scriptural narratives of Genesis, Exodus, the Psalms and Isaiah – to look no further – provide a more than adequate account of how a second-Temple Jew might hold a framework of thought within which it might make sense to see the returning divine glory in and as a human being, specifically the Messiah or the high priest. [96] I am not saying that any pre-Christian Jews really did think like this; merely that we have here a framework, quite different from later patristic frameworks, within which the early Christians were able to explore their central beliefs. The rich, contoured and layered categories of earliest Christology were later flattened out

---

51 This is how, for instance, I read Hill 2015; and see even Hays 2016, 78, 189, speaking of 'puzzles' left – or even created! – by the New Testament writers which the later Fathers had to 'solve'.

52 I detect this reaction in the early pages of Radner 2016. Part of the problem there is methodological: exegetes are trained at least by implication to think that the only proper way to argue is by induction, while systematicians are trained to work by deduction. Each shakes its head sorrowfully at the other, neither realizing that *abduction* is different from both of those, and is in fact the best way to go – in fact, is always what really happens! – in both exegesis and systematics. But I think it goes a lot deeper as well.

53 See e.g. Wright 1996b, 612–53; 2013b, 644–56.

into the notions of 'divinity' and 'humanity'. Those bare and static categories always were, arguably, attempts to put the wind of biblical narrative into the bottle of philosophically driven abstractions.

It is true (in other words) that the later technical language is missing from the New Testament. But this is not because the early Christians did not believe, in their own terms, pretty much what the later theologians worked their way round to saying. They did believe it – and they expressed it in concepts which, so far as I can see, were much less likely to result in giving hostages to fortune, much less likely to make the whole thing look like a confidence trick, much less in danger of being accused of trying to have one's theological cake and eat it. Harnack was right to say that the technical language was a later development, but wrong to suppose that the reality to which that later language intended to refer was absent from early Christian reflection. The newer orthodoxy is right to affirm the positive relation between earliest Christian belief and Chalcedonian Christology, but wrong to suppose that the former consisted of fuzzy, ill-formed original expressions and the latter of clear, untroubled truth. The difficulty is, I think, that from the fourth century onwards the Fathers, like many New Testament scholars until recently, seem to have ignored the tabernacle and the Temple, on the one hand, and, on the other, the resources like Psalm 8 which offered the story of Adam as the vital interpretative grid. The words 'divinity' and 'humanity' are, at best, one-dimensional signposts pointing back to that three-dimensional reality. The early Fathers were trying to reconstruct in their own terms something the early Christians had done, far more easily and with far less ambiguity, in *their* own terms.

It is as though people of a generation a thousand years from now were to discover a box of piano music but, because of the spoiling of the planet, were unable to build pianos any more. They might succeed in making, out of the wrong materials, instruments that would produce a recognizable version of the music, though without the intended subtlety and resonance. The New Testament scholar, paying historical attention to the rich and dense biblical and Jewish context and especially to the Temple on the one hand and the image-bearing human vocation on the other, may in fact still have a piano or two in a storeroom, and we might just be able to get them in tune once more. And when we do that I suspect that Psalm 8 will provide part of the resonance which the later instruments have never been quite able to match.

15

Son of God and Christian Origins

One of the joys of academic life at St Andrews is the succession of international conferences that assemble scholars from many backgrounds to discuss key topics. In the 2016 conference it fell to me to sum up the proceedings and to explore one of the most central questions concerning Christian origins: how did the phrase 'son of God', with its various meanings in the Jewish and non-Jewish worlds, come to carry so much significance for the followers of Jesus? The debate continues.

[118] The conference papers from June 2016 that now make up this volume [see Allen et al. 2019] cover a wide range of topics, and it would be inappropriate to try to sum them up. The contributors brought to the table a wide range of methods, starting-points and personalities. Many scholars are attracted to biblical and related studies because they like the microscopic analysis of complex fragments; that is indeed vital, but some of us prefer to locate such work within its larger context, and it is that larger context that I want to address here. As we remind ourselves of the need to see the texts we study in their larger setting, it is also important to see our own studies within the larger world of biblical and theological scholarship that has brought the relevant disciplines to the complex places they find themselves today. So the first third of my paper will attempt this kind of retrospective scene-setting. The second segment will then highlight and discuss what seems to me an intriguing and puzzling phenomenon at the heart of it all. In the third segment, I will offer some suggestions for ways forward.

'Son of God' within the Study of Christian Origins

First, then, the notion of divine sonship within the study of Christian origins. Why has this topic mattered to scholars, and how have the changing answers to this question affected the way we have seen things? Discussions of the phrase 'son of God' as they occur in fragmentary texts from Qumran and elsewhere gain their significance not simply from the desire to interpret this or that scrap of text but from the implication that these texts might have within an assumed larger world of discourse.[1] Particularly for those coming relatively new to this topic, it's **[119]** important to be aware of the back story. A pastoral analogy suggests itself: when a young couple fall in love and head off into the sunset, they may imagine that they come to the relationship totally fresh. But as any counsellor will tell you, they are carrying, whether or not they know it, all kinds of baggage from the past few generations. So it is in scholarship. When we are deep in relishing the latest debate about one line of an Aramaic papyrus, exciting as it is, we ought not to ignore the package of scholarly genes that have brought us to this point.

To begin with, there is the larger agenda of the classic Enlightenment scholarship from Hermann Samuel Reimarus (1694–1768) onwards. Reimarus assumed, and tried to argue, that Jesus was a Jewish revolutionary and that what we know as Christianity, including the ascription to him of divine honours, was invented by the early church after his failure.[2] Reimarus saw the phrase 'son of God' as an honorific phrase for humans, particularly kings, specially beloved by God.[3] William Wrede (1859–1906), at the other end of Albert Schweitzer's famous survey, developed the theory that Mark had invented the notion of a messianic secret to cover up the fact that Jesus had not been thought of as Messiah during his lifetime.[4] Wrede did not, I think, distinguish the notion of a *messianic* 'son of God' from the notion of a *divine* 'son of God'.[5] He assumed that these were much the same, an assumption shared in popular and scholarly circles until comparatively recently. Even Schweitzer, paying far more attention to the Jewish context, ended up with Jesus as a different kind of Jewish failure.[6] The various responses of the 1920s and 1930s to these (as they were perceived) threatening accounts of Christian

---

1 One of the particular focuses of our symposium was the 'Son of God Text', 4Q246. This fragmentary text has sparked a tremendous amount of debate about the figure designated 'son of God' and 'son of the Most High'. See e.g. Fitzmyer 1997 [1979], 102–7; Martinez 1992, 162–79; Steudel 1996; Collins 2010, 171–88; Ferda 2014; Segal 2014. See also George Brooke and Reinhard Kratz's contributions in the original volume. I think it is safe to say that the ambiguous nature of the text ensures that debate concerning the identity of this 'son of God' figure will continue well into the future. I am grateful to Max Botner for his help and advice with preparing this paper for publication.

2 Reimarus 1970 [1778].

3 Reimarus 1970 [1778], 74–90.

4 Wrede 1901.

5 Wrede remarked, 'Die immer wiederkehrenden Versuche, ihm [i.e. to Mark] eine Unterscheidung der Begriffe Messias und Gottesohn beizulegen, ich meine, eine *Wert*unterscheidung, müssen prinzipiell als falsch erkannt werden' (Wrede 1901, 76–7).

6 Schweitzer 1901; 1906.

origins [120] produced proposals such as Bultmann's demythologized existentialism and Jeremias's warm-hearted pietism. Jeremias knew more of the Jewish world than Bultmann. But both still assumed that the phrase 'son of God' carried some kind of 'divine' meaning far above any specific Jewish-messianic context, which for them as for many would have been an earthly irrelevance beside Jesus' supposedly spiritual kingdom.[7]

This assumption, indeed, has continued to pervade popular discussions. If a journalist asks me, as happens from time to time, whether I think that Jesus was 'the son of God', neither the journalist nor any ordinary church members overhearing the conversation will have in mind 3 *Enoch*, Apocryphon of Daniel (4Q246) or even Psalm 2. Asking whether Jesus was 'the son of God' will be heard simply as a way of saying, 'Was Jesus "divine" or wasn't he?' In the same way, the word 'Christ' itself, in popular discourse to the present time and in academic theological discourse at least until recently, has had the same confusing connotation. When Eduard Schillebeeckx produced his massive two volumes, the first called *Jesus* and the second called *Christ*, the first was about the human Jesus – the Jesus of history, if you like – and the second was about the early church's belief in Jesus' divinity.[8] Books used to appear with monotonous regularity under titles like *Jesus Who Became Christ*, with the word 'Christ' meaning not 'Israel's Messiah', but 'the divine one, the second person of the Trinity', and so on. And the question has then been heard, and answered, within a frame of reference very different from the one that is assumed by scholars discussing texts from the second-Temple period. On the one hand, more conservative Christians will say that Jesus did claim to be 'the Christ', so that 'the claims of Jesus' or even 'the claims of Christ' is a popular topic among certain kinds of apologetics. On the other hand, some variant of the Reimarus–Wrede–Bultmann position is widely held: Jesus didn't think this kind of thing, perhaps even Jesus *couldn't have thought* this kind of thing, but the church made it up and read it back. And so on. Thus, until quite recently and still in many circles, someone reading John 20.30–31 ('These things are written so that you may believe that Jesus is the *Christos*, the son of God') would simply assume that the fourth gospel was written to convince people that Jesus was divine. Any potential 'messianic' meaning – however we factor that in to such a passage – would be ignored, despite its

---

7 Jeremias 1966, 15–67. Rudolf Bultmann accounts for divine sonship primarily in terms of the *theios anēr* and gnostic motifs (Bultmann 1953, 120–32). Jeremias does, however, recognize that some of the earliest divine sonship language has 'Jewish', and thus 'messianic', roots (Jeremias 1966).
8 Schillebeeckx 1979; 1980.

being highlighted explicitly in John 1.45–49, 4.45 and 11.27. This meaning of *Christos* persists in liturgical use as well. **[121]**

This gives us the context within which the protests of the 1970s came as a shock. When Geza Vermes published *Jesus the Jew* in 1973, it wasn't just the title that people felt as a slap in the face.[9] Vermes, picking up where Reimarus and others left off, pointed out that the phrase 'son of God' could be used in the first century to mean many things other than 'the second person of the Trinity'.[10] He suggested that Jesus was basically a Galilean holy man and wonder-worker, of which there were others, but whose later followers, particularly Paul, radically changed his Jewish existentialist message into a hellenistic cult. This wasn't new, of course, as we shall see in a moment. But when Bousset and others had said similar things about the transition from a Jewish Jesus to a hellenistic cult of Christ as lord, they were trying to present a modified version of Christianity for a modern, post-Kantian world. When Vermes said it, his aim was to undermine Christian faith altogether.

Not long after Vermes, there came that extraordinary volume *The Myth of God Incarnate*.[11] This book made a big splash at least in the UK, written as it was not by a Jewish critic but by theologians and clergy mostly within the church. There, too, we were forcibly told that 'Messiah' and 'son of God' were human titles, not divine ones; that no good Jew, and indeed no sane human being, could think that he or she was God incarnate; and that, granted the way the modern world now thought, it was impossible to see the traditional doctrine as anything other than a myth.[12] It had been, perhaps, a helpful myth for its time. But it now needed radical re-expression.

I touch on all this because it still forms the backdrop of current discussions. The explosion of research into second-Temple Jewish texts has, in a measure, been a filling out of these questions and also an attempt to respond to them. It was in the 1970s that C. F. D. Moule produced his *The Origin of Christology* and Martin Hengel his smaller but powerful *The Son of God*.[13] They were seen by many as a scholarly response, albeit obliquely, to the challenges that had been offered. But to understand the impact of these, we need a further word about contextualization.

---

9   Vermes 1981.

10 Vermes 1981, 192–222.

11 Hick 1977.

12 This move was, in fact, simply a return to the dogma of so much early life-of-Jesus research. Note e.g. H. J. Holtzmann's declaration: 'Kein namhafter protestantischer Theologe vertritt heute noch die Zweinaturenlehre der Symbole' (Holtzmann 1907, 100).

13 Moule 1977; Hengel 1977.

Discussions of 'son of God' were not simply set within the polarized positions of Reimarus or his opponents. They were set within the so-called history-of-religion debates. As I have argued in the first chapter of *Paul and His Recent Interpreters*, this was already a decision for a particular slice of history.[14] Two assumptions [122] were being made. First, it was assumed that early Christianity was an example of something called 'religion' – with 'religion' here defined within the Enlightenment's new paradigms rather than those of the first century, thus excluding supposedly non-religious elements of both history and language. I shall return to that presently. The second assumption, easy to make after a century of German liberal Protestantism, was that Judaism was the wrong sort of religion, so that the quest was launched to discover the supposed roots of early Christianity, and particularly of ideas like divine sonship, within the *non*-Jewish world of the time. Hence theories about the mystery-religions, about a hypothetical early Gnosticism, about a *theios anēr* myth, and so on: anything rather than a Jewish context, which might give to Christianity the undesirable Jewish flavour of a nationalistic or military religion (though the imperial cult might have pointed in that direction) or even that ultimate protestant bugbear, 'works-righteousness'. An early Christian use of 'son of God' must therefore be essentially non-Jewish.

This widely prevalent would-be Christian assumption was all the easier to make since it had pervaded a great deal of systematic theology from some of the Fathers onwards. Jewish frameworks of thought were either forgotten or ignored and were replaced with forms of Platonism or pagan religion. And this, of course, left the door wide open to Jewish critics, of whom Vermes was only one more, pointing out that, as Jews had always supposed, Christianity was a corruption of the pure early Jewish teaching of Jesus himself. This, in turn, then joined up, from a different angle, with the normal Enlightenment critique, from Reimarus onwards.

All this changed after the Second World War, both for obvious historical and political reasons and for other less obvious ones, such as the discovery of the Dead Sea Scrolls. Suddenly, Jewish ideas were 'good' and pagan ideas were 'bad'. W. D. Davies led the way in the English-speaking world, and in the 1970s Martin Hengel performed the same service in Germany. I recall a seminar one year at Studiorum Novi Testamenti Societas where I was cautiously trying out some ideas about the parallels (now widely recognized) between imperial cultic language and the poem in Philippians 2 when the late

---

14   Wright 2015, 8–25.

lamented Earle Ellis rounded angrily on me and told me not to reintroduce all that wretched *religionsgeschichtliche* stuff we had just got rid of with such a sigh of relief. But if Jewish ideas were suddenly 'good', then did this mean that the earliest Christology was after all Jewish and therefore 'low'? That is what was then argued by James Dunn and others, though since the studies of Hurtado and Bauckham, not to mention my own work, rather few have followed him.[15] There has been in the last generation a groundswell of [123] support for an 'Early High Christology Club', in which divine sonship is to be seen not as a pagan import but as meaning what it means within a Jewish context. There is as yet no agreement on exactly how such a belief emerged, but the movement has already reached the point where something of a backlash is becoming evident.

But what Jewish context are we talking about? Here, at last, is the impetus for some of our present research. Is there, in fact, any solid evidence for a pre-Christian Jewish use of the idea of divine sonship that might serve as an explanatory matrix for what we find in John, Paul and Hebrews – and perhaps even in the thought and teaching of Jesus himself?

While we ponder that, we should note that the wind has suddenly swung round, and at least one gust is blowing from the opposite direction. Daniel Boyarin, in his book *The Jewish Gospels*, reverses the old Jewish line of thought.[16] Instead of saying that the idea of a divine redeemer-figure is an obvious pagan corruption, he says, more or less, that all the key ideas in early Christianity were already there in the Jewish world. The jury is still out on that book, though my own sense is that Boyarin has considerably overplayed his hand. And the fact that the same rather small base of evidence can be appealed to in so many different directions ought to give us pause before we say that the mystery has been solved.

Indeed, it would be surprising if that were so. While all this supposed history of religion has been going on, the much wider, and probably more interesting and fruitful, study of actual multi-dimensional history has been making a come-back. The history-of-religion paradigm has done its work mostly within a philosophically idealist world, cut off from the rough-and-tumble of real life. As Michael Peppard's work reminds us, the world of the first Christians was full of coins and processions, of temples and sacrifices,

---

15 Dunn 1980. Contra Dunn: Hurtado 1988; 2003; Bauckham 2008. For my part, see Wright 1991, 56–135; 1996b, 615–53; 2013b, 619–709.
16 Boyarin 2012.

of sex and shopping, of slavery and subsistence farming.[17] Setting our question within that much larger world – all of which, of course, was shot through with religion in the first century in a way that the Enlightenment did its best to hush up – might produce some very different results. Ed Sanders not long ago wrote an interesting article bemoaning the fact that Barth and Bultmann put a stop to real historical research on the key questions in the first half of the twentieth century.[18] Neither ever visited the holy land. Neither attempted to follow up Deissmann. [124]

At this point, other contemporary issues come into play. I presume that Martin Hengel's firm refusal of imperial allusions in *The Son of God* had something to do not just with his preference for Jewish sources over pagan ones but also with his preference for a Lutheran two-kingdoms theology over a Calvinist, or even a catholic – or even, dare I say, a Jewish – vision of all of life coming under divine rule and/or the rule of the Messiah. Yet that is the point that several psalms make quite explicitly, and that is reinforced by the risen Jesus in the strikingly Trinitarian passage at the end of Matthew. Saying this ought to alert us to the prospect that the question of divine sonship is far more complex than we have supposed and that it will include, at least in principle, all those imperial references.

This is where I have myself regularly made the distinction between derivation and confrontation.[19] The history-of-religions movement was itself part of a Hegelian attempt at genealogy, tracing the immanent development of ideas as a form of explanation. This project is even more fraught with danger than its equivalent in etymology, where we have all learned that you can't tell where a word is going to by discovering where it's come from. And what we find in the New Testament, unquestionably, are ideas and phrases, not least 'son of God' itself, going to places for which any possible prehistory would struggle to provide an explanation. Thus, as I have argued in relation to some other ideas and phrases as well, one possible working hypothesis is that, in earliest Christianity, we are looking at Jewish roots and pagan targets – a hypothesis all the more likely in that many second-Temple Jewish texts have those same pagan targets in mind. In addition, I do not doubt that there was a spectrum of viewpoints in the early church on the question of gospel and empire: a range of viewpoints with collusion at one end and confrontation at the other. But having thus sketched some of the necessary background to our discussion, it is time to

---

17   See Michael Peppard's contribution in the original volume and his monograph (Peppard 2011).
18   Sanders 2008, 32.
19   Wright 2013b, 1271–319.

move to the second part of my paper and examine the puzzling phenomenon at the heart of our subject.

Awkward Conjunction or Effortless Confluence?

One of the great dangers of our shared disciplines is related to one of our greatest strengths. We are brilliant at analysing the orthography, grammar, syntax and setting of tiny fragments, but it's easy to be so absorbed in that necessary and fruitful work that we forget to stand back and look around at the larger picture. As we have discussed 'son of God' texts, we have taken care to stick closely to the script, to the phrase or at least something like it. But I sense that there are various things missing. We have noted that Israel in Egypt is called God's son, but we have not begun to think about how that language of sonship functions within [125] the complex but vital narrative of the exodus as a whole and how it relates to the other elements within the same story – slavery, Passover, the role of Moses, Sinai and Torah, wilderness wandering, the promise of inheritance, and not least the setting up of the tabernacle. Israel's divine sonship means what it means within this narrative, which was frequently retrieved in our period, especially by Jesus himself and his first followers.[20] In the same way, scholars often glance at Paul's usage of 'son of God' but do not always comment on the way in which most of his ascriptions of that phrase to Jesus are closely related to statements about Jesus' death and its saving effects.

We have looked with interest at 2 Samuel 7 but have not commented, I think, on the fact that the whole passage is about the building of the Temple, about the royal and divine son as the Temple-builder and perhaps, at least with hindsight, as the human Temple in himself. (God's reply to David was, after all, that he was going to build him a house. Again, with hindsight, it looks as though part of the prophetic answer was that, though God might take up residence in a house of stone and timber, God's real project would be to dwell among his people as a human being.) In the same way, at least some of the early Christian language about divine sonship is closely allied with strong echoes of the wisdom tradition. We may adduce Colossians 1.13–14, leading in to the great poem of 1.15–20; or indeed the Johannine prologue with its spectacular conclusion; or, of course, the language of the 'sending' of the son

---

20   Wright 1992a, 215–338; 2013b, 108–39.

in Romans 8.3 or Galatians 4.4. Just as lexicographers try to track not only the etymological roots of a word but its behaviour within different clusters of meaning, so we should do the same with 'son of God'. This would inevitably mean complexifying our search. But it should also mean a greater chance of coherent, if many-sided, analysis.

What happens when we even begin to do any of this? We find, I suggest, something so striking and fascinating that it is easy to ignore it. We find something for which neither western theology as a whole nor projects like the ill-fated *Religionsgeschichtliche Schule* had prepared us. We find that the early Christians seem to have held together various things that have seemed for a long time in western culture, not least in western Christian culture, so radically unalike that we have assumed that those early Christians must have meant either one thing or the other but not both.

The early Christians said three things about divine sonship. If we have a problem holding them together, I think Paul and John at least would tell us it was our problem, not theirs. We feel this as an awkward conjunction; for them, it appeared an effortless convergence. That is the surprising thing. [126]

The first point is that the New Testament clearly uses the language of divine sonship to insist that Jesus was and is Israel's Messiah. It is now widely recognized that there was no single, uniform messianic expectation.[21] But if we step away from idealist constructions and embrace realism for a moment, there were things that most people knew that a Messiah, should a candidate be proposed, might be expected to do; or, to put it another way, even those Jews who were not particularly interested in the possibility of a Messiah would be able to understand what was being claimed by those hailing this or that figure as the long-expected king. Such a figure was supposed to rescue Israel, to defeat the pagans, to rebuild or cleanse the Temple, to establish a worldwide rule of justice and peace.[22] The fact that Jesus hadn't done any of those things meant that the disciples on the Emmaus Road said '*We had hoped* that he was the one to redeem Israel' (Luke 24.21); in other words, his crucifixion had put paid to any putative messianic identity. But Luke, in company with all the other early Christian writers, insists that he *was* the one to redeem Israel and that, in his death and resurrection and the spirit-driven mission of the church, this messianic agenda, this son-of-God task, was indeed being fulfilled. The way the early Christians drew on messianic psalms (whether or

---

21   Novenson 2012.

22   This is, of course, a truncation of a much longer discussion. See e.g. Wright 1992a, 307–20; 1996b, 481–9.

not all or even most Jews of the time would have seen them as such is not the point) tells its own story. 1 Corinthians 15.20–28 is a case in point: for Paul, Jesus has fulfilled, and is fulfilling, the messianic hope of Israel. One can imagine, in the first two years of Bar-Kochba's brief reign, some enthusiastic supporters saying similar things about him: 'He must reign until he has put all things under his feet.' Granted, Paul's language about Jesus goes further. Jesus has defeated, and will defeat, even death itself. Jesus, then, is seen as the messianic son of God. But none of this implies in and of itself that Jesus was seen as a divine being.

Second, the New Testament obviously uses the language of divine sonship for Jesus' followers. This is already clear in the widespread use of *adelphoi* for people who are not blood-relatives. They are siblings because they all have God for their father and Jesus for their older brother, as Paul says explicitly in Romans 8.29. And in Galatians 4 this sense is directly linked to Jesus' own 'sonship': God sends the son to redeem the slaves and make them sons as well and heirs to boot (this is exodus language, of course, though remarkably enough some commentators ignore this fact). We have seen that both in Israel's scriptures and in later Jewish literature this combination (a single 'son of God' and a corporate 'son of God') is rare if not absent; we do not find 'the messianic son' and 'Israel as son' side by side, let alone joined in a logical sequence.[23] Certainly, too, such a link would make no [127] sense within the Roman imperial 'son of god' language. But there it is in the New Testament, taken for granted, not argued for, just assumed.

In the same way, third, the New Testament writers also use the language of divine sonship to refer to Jesus as the living human embodiment of Israel's God. Obvious passages such as John 1.1–18 – where the unambiguously divine Logos (cf. John 1.1–3) is now to be known as the 'only-begotten God [or son] who is in the father's bosom' – come to mind.[24] We might also instance passages such as Romans 5 and 8, where the giving of the son to death is the supreme expression of the father's love, which only makes sense if there is a strong identity between them. The context of these two and others like

---

23 The closest we come to this, it seems, is 4Q174, wherein the community awaiting God's son, the 'branch of David' (I, 10–14), is described as 'his messiah' in Ps. 2.2 (I, 19). While it is possible that the interpreter has 'democratized' Ps. 2.2 *tout court*, his discussions of the coming descendant of David may suggest a more fluid interpretation of the psalm, one in which 'his messiah' may have both communal and individual referents (cf. Ac. 4.25–31; Rev. 2.26–28). See also *T. Jud.* 24, though here there is a strong possibility that the author/redactor is working with Christian material.

24 It remains disputed whether one should read *monogenēs theos* or *monogenēs hyios* in Jn. 1.18. For a brief discussion, see Metzger 1994, 169–70. I have followed NA (28) and UBS (5), reading *monogenēs theos*.

them leave no option, I think, for an explanation in terms of derivation from imperial language. John 1.14, the climax of the paragraph that holds together the Logos at the start and the *monogenēs theos* or *hyios* at the end, refers strikingly and unambiguously to the long-awaited return to the Temple of the divine glory: the Word became flesh, *kai eskēnōsen en hēmin*, and we gazed upon his glory, glory as of the father's only son. Here we find, all in a rush, the new Genesis of John 1.1 completed by the new Exodus, the construction of a human tabernacle in which the divine glory comes at last to dwell. One might almost think John had been reading 2 Samuel 7, not just verse 14 but the whole wider context. But this is to run ahead of myself.

The main point I want to make, at the heart of this paper, is that the early Christians seem to have used the language of divine sonship in all these three senses, that they did so with these senses in close proximity to one another, and that they give every appearance of supposing that these three senses fit together easily and naturally. The point is that *they take all this for granted.* They do not argue for it; there is no controversy about it. Paul never writes, 'How can some of you say that Jesus isn't the son of God?' We have evidence of all kinds of controversies and puzzles in the early church, but not on this topic. The heretics in 1 John doubt Jesus' full humanity, not his divine identity. In particular, there is no evidence that the early Christian worship of Jesus, within a strongly reaffirmed Jewish monotheism, was the occasion of persecution; this is regularly assumed, but I see no evidence for it. Rather, it seems to me that the problem the early Christians faced was not what was being said about this man, but that what was being said was being said about *this* man in particular. The problem came in ascribing this 'son of God' language to the crucified Jesus of Nazareth, the unlikeliest son of God one could imagine. [128]

We should also note, in line with Richard Hays's detailed arguments in his recent book *Echoes of Scripture in the Gospels* (sketched in his previous shorter treatment, *Reading Backwards*), that the synoptic gospels, no less than John, offer us a Jesus who is somehow to be identified with the God of Israel arriving in person.[25] In terms of the history of modern scholarship, this is one of the most revolutionary proposals ever; we may dream of the day, though sadly I doubt it will be soon, when nobody any longer supposes that the synoptics give us the 'human' Jesus and John the 'divine' Jesus.[26] In fact, we may look forward to the day when these questions are no longer discussed in terms of the abstract 'humanity' and 'divinity' and are instead

---

25   Hays 2016; 2014.
26   Daniel Kirk 2016.

posed in terms of the God of Israel and the people of Israel and/or its anointed representative. None of the first Christians was thinking in abstractions like 'humanity' and 'divinity', and to translate the specific things they say into such generalized terms is anachronistic. I regard this as one of the major points in today's discussions where historical exegesis has serious questions to pose to systematic theology – though, granted the way in which those disciplines have run on separate tracks for many years, I am not holding my breath as I wait for a reply.[27]

All this opens up the possibility not that pre-Christian Jews expected a divine Messiah but that there were categories of thought within the second-Temple world within which – to put it cautiously – it might not be a category mistake to suppose that Israel's God might reveal himself, might return to his people, in and as a human being. This is, of course, a vast and difficult question, but I think there are at least some ways of approaching it that are less inadequate than some others. The most obvious way in must be via the early Christian rereading of scripture. That brings me to the third and final section of this essay.

'We Had Hoped': The Backward Look at the Forward Story

I cited Richard Hays's book *Reading Backwards* just now, and that must be where we start. When we see how the early Christians re-used Israel's scriptures, we are struck again and again by fresh exegetical proposals that appear to have been generated by the early Christian belief that the crucified and risen Jesus was indeed Israel's Messiah and had indeed launched the long-awaited kingdom of God. Since (despite Boyarin) there is no clear evidence that Jews of the period were expecting [129] a crucified and risen Messiah such as we find in the gospels, let alone one who had embodied Israel's God, it was inevitable that Jesus' followers would search the scriptures for clues to a new way of telling the story. And they found them. Such proposals went on being controversial, of course, through to Justin's *Dialogue with Trypho* and beyond. But their claim was that these made sense of the scriptural narrative in a way nothing else had done or could do.

But if they were reading backwards, starting with Jesus and looking back from there, what they were looking at was a story that had already been

---

27   I have argued at length in Wright 2013b that Paul saw Jesus both as the personal embodiment of Israel's God (ch. 9) and as the anointed representative of Israel (ch. 10).

unfolding for quite some time. 'Beginning with Moses and all the prophets, he interpreted to them in all the scriptures the things concerning himself' (Luke 24.27). I do not think that Luke, or for that matter Paul in quoting the early formula about the Messiah's death and resurrection 'in accordance with the scriptures' (1 Corinthians 15.3–4), were simply imagining a number of isolated or atomized proof-texts. They were insisting on a fresh, backwards-discovered reading of the forward-moving story from Abraham, David and the exile to their own day (Matthew); from Isaiah's prophecy of the new exodus and Malachi's of the Coming One (Mark); from the books of Samuel (Luke); and, above all, from Genesis and Exodus (John). The attempt to discover a non-narrative early Christianity was always a foolish, perhaps even a Marcionite, quest, and ought now to be abandoned. Pointing out that the early Christians read their scriptures backwards doesn't mean that those scriptures were not themselves telling a story that was moving forwards.

The story in question was the long story of Israel and, behind that again, the story of all creation. The story was focused, as Israel's scriptures show again and again, on the sense of exile: exile from the garden, exile from the land, exile that ends in Babylon literally and metaphorically, exile that constitutes slavery. And slaves, particularly slaves who are in some battered sense 'God's son', need a new exodus. That is promised in many scriptural texts, not least texts retrieved afresh in the early church. And, above all, Jesus himself chose Passover as the moment to do what he had to do. He wove Passover into a new shape so that it wasn't just about release from slavery but was also, as required by the extended exile, forgiveness of sins. All of this demands much fuller exposition for which there is no space here.[28]

But when we look at some of the texts that the early Christians used, we see parts of the exodus pattern repeated. The exodus itself was about the slaves who were also God's son, about their rescue, their wandering, their Torah, their promised inheritance, and above all their tabernacle, where their God came to dwell with them and lead them home. When we look at Psalm 2, arguably just as central in early Christianity as the exodus story itself, it has a similar shape. The pagan nations rage and threaten, but Israel's God acts in power, exalting his 'son' and [130] promising him an inheritance – this time, the entire world. When we look at 2 Samuel 7, we see David wanting to build a house for Israel's God and God declaring that he would build David a house – in the sense of the son who would be born, who would be God's own son, and who would build the house for God's name. No slavery, no rescue,

---

28   For my most recent treatment of these themes, see Wright 2016a.

but two exodus elements none the less: God's son, who will construct the replacement for the wilderness tabernacle. And with 2 Samuel 7, there is one of the most radical exegetical innovations of all. There is no evidence (as far as I am aware) that pre-Christian Jews read *wehaqimothi eth zar'a* in terms of the *resurrection* of David's 'seed'. The Septuagint reads *kai anastēsō to sperma sou*, but since nobody at the time thought David's ultimate seed would die, nobody read that literally. But the early Christians, reading backwards, found this text springing into new life, as we see for instance in Romans 1.3–4.[29] That new life provided a Temple-shaped Christology in which the risen Messiah would constitute in himself the place and the means of the returning divine glory. Back to John 1.14 – and also to many other texts, the Pauline ones that I discuss in chapter 9 of *Paul and the Faithfulness of God*.[30]

All this is rooted in the promise of divine return. It remains my contention, from which I am not distracted by the objections of some, that the second-Temple Jewish question of divine presence remains foundational for New Testament Christology. The great promise of Isaiah 40 and 52 was that Israel's God would return one day in visible glory, with mountains being flattened and valleys filled in to make a way for him. The watchmen would shout for joy as in plain sight they witnessed the divine return. The later rabbis, gloomily cataloguing ways in which the second Temple was inferior to the first one, included the Shekinah as among the items missing, almost as though it were just another piece of furniture (cf. bYom. 21b).[31] This is borne out by Ezekiel's promise of divine return (cf. Ezekiel 43.1–9; 48.35), and echoed in both Zechariah and Malachi, writing at a time when the second Temple was up and running but where something was still perceived to be lacking. It is not part of my case that all Jews of the period thought like this or that there was no continuing sense of divine presence. The Western Wall in Jerusalem to this day still has that sense, but nobody would claim that Israel's God has returned to it in glory and power. It is central to my case that several different early Christian texts employ, when speaking about Jesus, scriptural texts which promise this glorious return (see below).

The heart of my constructive proposal, then, is this: we have been looking in the wrong place in searching for pre-Christian texts about a divine Messiah. [131] We should have been looking at the texts, there in plain sight, that speak of the divine return. And we should have noticed that, among them, there are

---

29 Duling 1973, esp. 72–3; Whitsett 2000.
30 Wright 2013b.
31 See my discussion in Wright 2013b.

texts that speak – mysteriously to be sure (how could it not be so?) – both of the fulfilment of Davidic promises (of a coming individual son of God) and of new-exodus promises (of a people who would be the corporate divine son).[32] The promise of divine return is translated into the affirmation of Jesus as the divine son and of Jesus' followers as the new-exodus people.

This could generate a whole other essay or even monograph, but let me focus at once on the obvious passage – obvious both in itself and in the fact that so many early Christian texts refer to it. Isaiah 40—55 is all about the new exodus: the real return from exile, the forgiveness of sins, the defeat of the pagan powers, the renewal of all creation. The energy that drives this poem is the promise that Israel's God will return in person and in power, revealing his glory and unveiling his *tsedaqah*. And just as Genesis 1 places the responsibility for the carrying forward of the creator's purposes in the hands of his image-bearing human creatures, so the vision of new creation in Isaiah 40—55 is placed in the hands of the servant of the Lord. As is well known, the portrait of the servant in Isaiah 42 owes much to the royal pictures in Isaiah 9 and 11.[33] The strangely royal servant is Israel, yet stands over against Israel, doing for God's people (and the world) what they cannot do for themselves. And the 'servant of YHWH', the *'ebed adonai*, is not translated by the Septuagint as the *doulos kyriou*, but as the *pais*, the child.

This has caused some puzzlement, but it is actually an important clue. There is good evidence, in passages where we have the same trains of thought and that resonate in the same parts of the New Testament, that the messianic son of God and/or the corporate Israelite son of God could be spoken of in this way, not to avoid *hyios* for whatever reason but precisely to join together, as *pais* can though *hyios* cannot, the two ideas of servant and son – the two ideas that, we note, are fused together in the heavenly voice at Jesus' baptism (cf. Mark 1.11).

There is, on the one hand, Wisdom 2 and 5, which I take to be part of a single narrative about the suffering and vindication of the righteous. The righteous person has claimed to be God's *pais* (2.13) and says God is his father (2.16), but in 2.18, he is God's 'son', *hyios*, and in 5.5 the vindicated martyrs,

---

32 This point is drawn out in Scott 1992, though I suspect that Scott presses the issue too far in his reading of non-Pauline texts.

33 The mysterious identity of the servant-figure in Isaiah 42 did not stop later Jewish and Christian interpreters from concluding that this was the same figure as the one depicted in Isaiah 11 (e.g. *1 En.* 37—71, *Tg. Neb.* Isaiah, Matthew). This connection was facilitated, first, by the link between the designation 'my servant' and a scriptural strand of royal ideology (e.g. Pss. 89.4; 39—40; 51—52) and, second, by the observation that the servant's vocation is roughly the same as that of the 'shoot of the stump of Jesse'.

now plural, have been shown to be 'among God's sons', *en hyiois theou*. This is regularly taken to mean joining the assembly of angels, but granted the emphasis in chapter 2 and the **[132]** retelling of exodus later in the book, it is at least arguable that it refers to the vindicated people of God.[34] Thus, in the large-scale retelling of the exodus-narrative, the Egyptians eventually acknowledge Israel to be God's son, *hyios* (18.13). Wisdom, as well as providing a large-scale exegesis of Psalm 2 itself, seems also to be echoing the theme of the suffering and then vindicated servant in Isaiah.[35]

There is, on the other hand, the use of Psalm 2 in Acts 4. In what I take to be a bit of primitive atonement-theology, the threatened group of disciples prays Psalm 2: the nations, in the persons of Herod and Pilate, had gathered together to wage war against God and his anointed and are overthrown. The church is invoking the whole psalm, which climaxes in the exaltation of the Messiah with the Davidic claim, *hyios mou ei sou*. It is introduced with a reference to David as God's *pais* (4.25a), and the church then prays that God will look on their threats ('He who dwells in heaven will laugh them to scorn') and grant to his servants (*dos tois doulois*) to speak his word with all boldness, while God stretches out his hand to heal, and signs and wonders are performed in the name of his holy child Jesus (*tou hagiou paidos sou Iēsou*; 4.29–30). In both cases *pais* might be thought to stand for the *hyios* of the psalm. And if we ask why not *hyios*, one answer might be that, in the light of an early Isaianic interpretation of Jesus' death, Psalm 2 was already being fused together with the servant songs (as also by implication in the heavenly voice at the baptism), so that the enthronement in the psalm was seen in inextricable mutual relation with the suffering of the servant. David was already being seen as God's 'servant child', and the fusion of roles, familiar from Mark 1, was obviously applied to Jesus.

There is then one emerging possibility in Isaiah 53 itself that ties together the strands of what I have been saying. Throughout Isaiah 40—55, one of the great images for the coming of Israel's God in rescuing power is the 'arm' of the Lord. His arm rules for him (40.10); the prophet summons the 'arm' to 'awake' (51.9), since it was this power that effected the first exodus (Exodus 15.16; Deuteronomy 4.35; 5.15; echoed in Psalm 77.15 and elsewhere).

---

34 For an angelic interpretation of the 'sons of God' in Wis. 5.5, see Nickelsburg 2006.

35 Wisdom echoes the language of the psalmist's refrain addressed to 'the kings and the rulers of the earth' (cf. Ps. 2.10) at the open and close of the first major section of the book (Wis. 1.1; 6.1, 21). The writer also avers that the Lord 'will laugh' at those who have dishonoured his righteous one (Wis. 4.8), just as he laughed at those who rose up against his anointed king (Ps. 2.4). For a discussion of the final servant-poem in Wisdom, see Nickelsburg 2006, 83–8. See also Hengel 1996, esp. 81–2.

The divine 'arm' will now be against the Chaldeans (48.14). Then, in the climactic kingdom-passage in 52.7–12, the watchmen see in plain sight the return of the divine glory to Zion, because 'YHWH has bared his holy arm before the eyes of all the nations; and all the ends of the [133] earth shall see the salvation of our God'. This will mean that many nations will be startled at his appearing, and kings will shut their mouths because of him.[36] A fresh revelation, previously unimagined and indeed unthinkable, will dawn on them: 'Who has believed what we have heard? And to whom has the arm of YHWH been revealed?' Nobody, looking at this *pais*, this *'ebed*, this child, this servant, would have imagined for a moment that this would be what the powerful arm of the Lord would look like when finally revealed in rescuing action. But that is what the prophet seems to be saying.

The rest is well known. But it seems to me that when the New Testament writers, looking backwards, retrieve this forward narrative of new exodus, of the long-awaited divine return, they are making exactly this creative fusion of themes, of the messianic servant-task with the promise of the divine return. This would explain why, for them, what seemed from at least the third century to be a strange theological conundrum or even a confidence trick was nothing of the sort but something that, though it could not have been foreseen, makes dramatic retrospective sense. After all, if the creator made humans in his own image, to serve him by ruling his world, what more natural than that he should himself come as a human being? And if Israel's God called Israel to be his servant people for the sake of the world, as in Isaiah 49 and elsewhere, what more natural than that he would come himself in the person of Israel's representative? If we postulated something like this, would it not make sense of the otherwise puzzling evidence?

This leads us, of course, into many labyrinthine theological as well as exegetical pathways. But I submit that we have here at least one plausible account of a way to understand how the first Christians came so soon, so unambiguously, and (for them) so uncontroversially, to speak of Jesus of Nazareth both as the messianic divine son and as the unique son who embodied the very divine presence – and to speak of his people as themselves the promised seed, the 'sons' plural. From that starting-point it would be easy to show (since both Psalm 2 and Isaiah 40—55 are cheerfully fierce polemics against the pagan hordes) that this early high Christology was used to saying that Jesus was lord and that Caesar wasn't, so that among the early formulations we find

---

36 The writer of the Parables of Enoch picks up Isa. 52.13—53.12 as well (cf. *1 En.* 62—63), albeit in quite a different direction from that of the vindication of the crucified Messiah.

parodies of imperial narrative such as Philippians 2. And for Paul to start a letter to Rome by declaring that the royal Jesus has been powerfully declared as 'Son of God in Power', ruling the world and demanding allegiance because in him the divine justice is revealed, we might reflect that this was extremely unwise, not to say stupid – *unless* he had wanted to imply from the start that the real son of God is Jesus, not Caesar. But I think this is confrontation, not derivation. [134]

There are so many other ramifications of all this that the world itself might not contain them. But these things are written so that we may contemplate the possibility that the messianic 'son of God' texts come into new coherence when read backwards from the crucified and risen Jesus and that, contemplating this, we may have historical and exegetical fruitfulness in his name.

16

History, Eschatology, and New Creation in the Fourth Gospel: Early Christian Perspectives on God's Action in Jesus, with Special Reference to the Prologue of John[1]

One of the exciting innovations at St Andrews in recent years has been the Logos Institute for Analytic and Exegetical Theology, led by Professor Alan Torrance. As well as devising new graduate-level courses designed to draw together disciplines that normally ignore one another, this institute has laid on conferences; and I was honoured to be asked to give the opening lecture at the first one. As I explain at the start, I had already decided to focus on the prologue to John's gospel – as being a place where exegesis and theology are almost bound to converge – before I realized that of course the Johannine focus on the Logos, the Word of God, was in any case the obvious place for the Institute to begin, both for the conference and for any serious mutual engagement thereafter.

The challenge of historical exegesis of scripture remains – whether acknowledged or not! – at the heart of all Christian theology. Sadly, many theologians, having seen the ways in which exegetes have said they were doing 'history' while in fact smuggling in some of the negative presuppositions of the Enlightenment, have reacted by proposing uses of scripture that bypass historical meaning. As a case in point, the prologue to John's gospel has often been read in a 'theological' way which ignores the rather obvious inner-biblical context. But, when read in that context (of the Old Testament and second-Temple Judaism), the prologue strongly implies that with Jesus the creator God has accomplished the 'new Genesis', with Jesus as the 'image'.

---

1   Lecture for the inaugural Logos Conference, June 2017, given at the Logos Institute for Exegetical and Analytical Theology, St Mary's College, University of St Andrews, UK.

With that, it offers the story of Jesus as a 'new Exodus', with Jesus as the divine glory dwelling among humans, unveiling the creator's covenant love. This 'tabernacle' or 'Temple' theme, which extends throughout the fourth gospel, urgently needs to be reintegrated into systematic and analytic theology, from which it has all too often been absent. This applies particularly, and with great potential, to categories such as 'humanity' and 'divinity', or 'natural' and 'supernatural'.

This lecture looks forward in several interlocking ways to the Gifford Lectures which I then delivered in Aberdeen in the spring of 2018, and which are now published as *History and Eschatology: Jesus and the promise of natural theology* (2019).

[1] *En archē ēn ho logos.* John's opening line must be one of the most famous initial sentences in all literature, ranking with Virgil's *Arma virumque cano* or Shakespeare's 'If music be the food of love, play on'; or even Melville's dark and haunting 'Call me Ishmael.' And it is obvious even at first glance why John's simple opening is so profound: it echoes the first line of Genesis, *běrēšît bārā' 'ělohîm 'ēt hašāmayim w'ēt hā'āreṣ; en archē epoiēsen ho theos ton ouranon kai tēn gēn.* Curiously, I decided to begin with John 1.1 before I even reflected on how appropriate it is as a starting-point for this, our first Logos conference! So be it. [2]

Different Ways of Construing History, Eschatology and Theology

John's opening move is, of course, bold. It borders (one might think) on blasphemy: are you really sitting down to write a new Genesis? Yes, replies John; because that is the truth to which I am bearing witness. I am telling a story about something that has happened in which heaven and earth have come together in a whole new way, about the long and dark fulfilment of the creator's purposes for his creation. And, John might continue, since I am writing in the tradition of the Hebrew Bible, it won't surprise you that I am telling this story of creation and new creation in terms of the fulfilment of the divine purpose in, for and through Israel.

Thus, if we were to bring our categories of 'history' and 'eschatology', let alone 'theology' itself, to John, I think this is how he would anchor and expound them: that by 'history' he might mean the course of events in the creator's world, and by 'eschatology' he might mean the ultimate purposes of the creator for his world, to be accomplished through his purposes for Israel.

And in both cases, again obviously, these purposes are laid bare, for John and for the other early Christians, in the events concerning Jesus of Nazareth.

I want to begin with John, not least the prologue, rather than with an exposition of these larger abstractions, for programmatic reasons. I have long had the sense that theology, not least philosophical theology, and perhaps even analytic theology, has tended to start with its own abstract concepts and, in expounding and adjusting them, has drawn in bits and pieces of scripture on the way. That, I suppose, is better than nothing; but it can provide the illusion of engagement with the text rather than allowing the text to lead the way.

Of course, a suggestion like that will today meet the slings and arrows of outraged postmodernism: what is this 'text', and how can it possibly 'lead the way'? But part of my proposal is precisely that a *historically responsible* reading of the early Christian writings, allowing them to be themselves in their actual historical setting, will lead to an *eschatologically attuned* reading both in terms of the text's apparent intention and in terms of its reappropriation by later generations, including our own; and that this eschatologically attuned reading must be understood in terms of the new creation, which, in John's book, was launched in Jesus and continues to make its way in the life-giving power of the spirit.

Only when we have begun to glimpse this can we then make our way to a historically grounded critique of the hermeneutical traditions that have pulled and tugged at both exegesis and theology over the last two hundred years. Obviously there will only be time for a brief sketch of all that, but I hope at least to open up some issues and to do so, as I say, on exegetical grounds.

Exegesis is a branch of history, and we have suffered from a misperception about historical exegesis. People sometimes talk of the 'historical-critical method', as though there were one and only one thing that might be so called. [3] Karl Barth, famously, asked Ernst Käsemann the meaning of the two words, and particularly the meaning of the hyphen between them; I do not know what Käsemann replied, though that itself might be significant. The phrase has, however, been used as a slogan for a kind of negative criticism, following through an eighteenth-century desire to do something called 'history', but which in fact was running a philosophical a priori through the material, with Hume in the background and with the Epicureanism of the Enlightenment supplying the framework.

And sometimes the phrase has then acquired the apparent high moral ground of a supposed relentless intellectual honesty: we today cannot believe this or that because we live in the modern world. The response to this has been varied, with some capitulating and producing a reductionist account of Jesus and the first Christians, some doing their best to shore up the historical foundations, and some escaping into a second-order world where the truth of the gospel is not dependent on whether this or that actually happened.

These debates about Jesus and his first followers, and the theological and hermeneutical questions that are raised, go closely together with the larger questions of theology proper (if there is such a thing?): what can and must we say about God, about God's world and God's relation to that world, and how do we say it?

The large question of so-called 'natural theology', in particular, and whether any such thing is desirable let alone possible, turns out to be another way of addressing the same question as the question of God's action in Jesus. In other words, the question as to whether we can start with the study of this small bit of history and work up to truth-statements about God turns out to be a specific case of the question as to whether we can start with observations of the natural world and work up to God from there.

And hovering over both those projects, and their apparent intertwining, is the question as to whether that was the right question to ask in the first place. Those are among the larger issues that I will now leave in the background as we dive in and look at what John seems to be doing in his prologue and in the gospel as a whole.

It would be possible to run this thought-experiment with Paul, or indeed, especially following Richard Hays's remarkable recent book, *Echoes of Scripture in the Gospels*, with the three synoptic gospels, or indeed with Hebrews or Revelation; but in the light of time constraints I will stick with John.[2]

John: New Creation, New Temple

Let me then follow through on the basic insight that John thinks he is writing a [4] new Genesis. This offers a framework for the gospel, since chapter 20, the Easter account, seems to me to match the prologue quite closely, with the early morning, the darkness preceding the light, and Mary's appropriately mistaking Jesus for the gardener. This is common knowledge but the corollary is not always observed: that for John, as for Paul and the others, new creation means new *creation*, the *renewal* of the present world rather than its

---

2 Hays 2016.

abandonment and replacement by some other kind of world altogether. The resurrection is the reaffirmation of the goodness of creation following decisive divine judgment on the dark forces that have corrupted the present world; or, to put it the other way, when John depicts the arrival of the kingdom of God on earth as in heaven it is, truly, *on earth* as well as in heaven, with the risen and spirit-giving Jesus forging the ultimate link between the two.

But there is more to seeing John as a new Genesis than just this. Five things, closely related, stand out, each of which I regard as vital for understanding how the early Christians spoke of God's action in Jesus, each of which I think ought to form part of the framework for a fresh and creative collaboration between exegesis and theology in tomorrow's confused world.

I The Temple – Link between Heaven and Earth

The first is that John sees creation and new creation, and Jesus in the middle of them, in terms of the Temple. Jewish and Hebrew Bible scholars have been writing about ancient Temple-theology for quite some time, but it's only recently that New Testament scholars have picked up on it, not always (in my view) very helpfully; and my impression is that this has had little if any impact on systematic or analytic theology.[3]

It is now common coin among Genesis scholars that the ancient world would see Genesis 1 in terms of the creation of a temple, a heaven-and-earth reality in which the two spheres or realms are held together and seen as compatible, if dangerously so. The seven stages of creation are the stages of building this heaven-and-earth palace for God and humans to live in, and the 'rest' on the seventh day is not simply God taking a day off but rather God entering into his new home to enjoy possession of it as Lord. That's the language used later on for the Jerusalem Temple: Zion is God's resting-place, the house where he comes to take his ease among his people, through whom he rules creation.

Did John then think, in writing a new Genesis, that he was writing a new Temple-theology? The question answers itself: of course he did. The Temple is one of the major themes throughout the book, with Jesus himself as the focal point; hence, in the prologue itself, the decisive verse 14, where 'the Word became flesh, and lived among us'; the Greek is *kai eskēnōsen en hemin*, which literally means that the Word 'tabernacled', pitched his tent, in our midst. [5]

---

3 For what follows see now my Gifford Lectures, Wright 2019, ch. 5.

This theme grows and swells, through the reference to Jacob's Ladder at the end of chapter 1 (with heaven opened and angels ascending and descending, 1.51), into the wedding at Cana in chapter 2 (the wedding symbolizing the coming together of heaven and earth), followed at once by the Temple-scene where Jesus is 'speaking about the "temple" of his body' (2.21); and so on.[4]

As with several of John's themes, not least the Word itself, these are stated emphatically at the start in order that the reader may then hold them in mind while, so to speak, watching the action unfold: this, we are to understand, is what is really going on.

When, on Easter morning, Mary sees the two angels in the tomb, they are sitting one at the head and the other at the feet of the slab where Jesus' body had lain – a reflection, as some have pointed out, of the mercy-seat at the heart of the sanctuary. This is where the living God meets with his people. In particular, all this has to do with that overarching Johannine theme, the revelation of the divine glory. As we shall see, the ancient Jewish hope for the divine glory was for a renewed Temple, as in Ezekiel, to which the glorious presence would return at last.

But that is to anticipate the third of my four points.

2 Humanity as Image of God

The second point, closely allied to the themes of new creation and new Temple, is the role of humans in God's image. The climax of Genesis 1 comes at verses 26–28. If Genesis 1 is the great cosmic Temple, then humans are the divine image placed within that Temple. This rules out at a stroke centuries of puzzle as to what aspect of humanity might be supposed to be the divine 'image'; that isn't the point. The picture is *vocational* (and indeed to see it like that sets in quite a new context all the great questions of sin and salvation, as I have argued elsewhere).[5]

The 'image' in a temple is there for a purpose, indeed for a double purpose: so that the worshippers may bring their worship to the image and thus to the god who is imaged, and so that the power and protection and stewardship of the god may flow out through the image to the world around. This would be true of any pagan shrine and image, and it is what Genesis is saying about the vocation of human beings within the heaven-and-earth Temple we call the cosmos. In both paganism and the Bible, the deity is *present in and as* the

---

4 For the English translations of scripture in this article, see the note in the preface to the present volume.

5 See Wright 2016a.

image. Psalm 8 picks up this theme and, in later usage, applies it not least to Israel's king, and perhaps also to the high priest.

When we read John 1 in this light we see that at more or less the same point in the story where Genesis has the creation of humans in God's image (at the climax [6] of the narrative), John has the Word becoming flesh. And the close thematic parallels to this passage in Colossians 1 and Hebrews 1 ought to leave us in no doubt that John wants us to make exactly that connection. Jesus is the true human, the ultimate image-bearer, the one *in* and *as* whom the creator is now present in, with and for his creation.

John emphasizes this most strongly when Jesus stands before Pilate on the Friday, the sixth day of the week, and Pilate declares *ecce homo*, 'Here's the man!' (19.5). John's narrative is nearly complete at that point. Still, if we follow through the themes of creation and new creation, we see that Jesus goes to his death with the word *tetelestai* ('It's all done'), echoing Genesis 2.1–2. The six-day work is finished; and on the seventh day God rests, this time in the darkness of the tomb, before the new creation, which, as John emphasizes, happens 'on the first day of the week' (20.1).

But if John is writing a new Genesis, then verse 14 is also an indication that he is including a new Exodus at the same time.

3 The Exodus–Tabernacle Complex – God Coming to Dwell with His People

This brings me to the third point. One of the themes to emerge from recent work on ancient biblical Temple-theology is the reading of Genesis and Exodus as a single narrative arc. (When I originally wrote that sentence I mistyped 'arc' as 'ark', which was also appropriate, but from another angle.) From early days, and particularly in the second-Temple writings, the wilderness tabernacle and then the Jerusalem Temple were seen as small working-models of the whole creation. They were not 'religious' buildings seen as an escape from the rest of the world, signalling access to a remote divine sphere; they were advance signposts, eschatological pointers, indicating (like Noah's ark itself) that, despite the vocational failure of the image-bearers, the waters of chaos would not overcome the world.

The calling of Abraham in Genesis 12 – with Abraham seen very much as the new Adam – points ahead to the whole exodus-narrative with its climax in the tabernacle, into which the divine glory comes to dwell (Exodus 40.34–35). This, it seems, is the purpose of Israel, Abraham's family: to be the guardians of the tabernacle, the carriers of the promise that there would be new heavens and new earth.

The slavery in Egypt, and then the exodus, speak volumes about how the people of Israel, themselves part of the Adam-problem, can fulfil this vocation. The giving of Torah seems, in this light, to be the preparation for the coming of the tabernacle and particularly of the divine glory that will dwell in it.

All this is vital for John as he unfolds this major theme: that when the Word becomes flesh and 'tabernacles' in our midst, *we gazed upon his glory, glory like that of the father's only son, full of grace and truth*. There are multiple echoes here of the exodus story in which God reveals to Moses that he is full of ḥesed [7] and 'ĕmet (Exodus 34.6–7). Even the Johannine theme of Jesus as the Passover Lamb is, I think, subordinate to this point. In Exodus the new working-model of creation has its own divine image within it in the person of the high priest, Aaron himself.

Then, in the second-Temple period, we find the theme that I have come in recent years to regard as the major clue to all the early Christian accounts of God's action in Jesus. Ezekiel 10 tells of the divine glory, riding on the throne-chariot, abandoning the Temple to its fate because of the persistent idolatry of people and priests alike. But in the final dream-like sequence of the book, the Temple is rebuilt; and in Ezekiel 43 the divine glory returns at last.

This is the point, as well, of the whole poem of Isaiah 40—55: the watchmen will see the divine glory returning to Zion – though when they look closely what they will see is the figure of the 'servant'. And the point is this: in two of the major so-called post-exilic books, Zechariah and Malachi, the Temple has been rebuilt, but the promise of YHWH's glorious return remains unfulfilled. Both of these prophets insist that it will be fulfilled, that YHWH will indeed return, but that very insistence is powerful evidence that he hasn't done so yet.

Of course, the people are offering sacrifices, and praying, in the newly restored Temple, because that's how sacred space works. It is the same with the Western Wall in Jerusalem to this day, where devout Jews and even visiting presidents go to pray, even though no Jew supposes that Israel's God is really in full and glorious residence on the old Temple Mount. But when the later rabbis make a list of things that Solomon's Temple had, which the second Temple didn't have, they include the Shekinah, the glorious divine presence.[6]

And the whole New Testament, Mark as well as John, Luke and Paul alike, insist that this is how we are to see Jesus: as the living embodiment

---

6   bYom. 21b; see also jTa'an. 2.1 (65a) and parallels.

of the returning God of Israel. The place to start if we are to understand New Testament Christology, I suggest, is with the second-Temple narratives in which Israel's God had made promises about the new Temple (which, from what I said before, is obviously the sign and means of new creation). But we also need to reckon with the way the logic of that Temple-discourse works in terms of the simultaneity of the returning divine glory and the appearing of the true divine image. The coming of God and the appearance of the truly human one seem to be literally made for each other.

These are the themes that harmonize in the music that is the food of love. Those whose ears can only hear one note at a time will find it strange to be told that all these notes – Temple, image, divine glory, high priest, Messiah – can somehow come together. John's exposition of divine love will be our fifth point, which we shall reach in a moment. [8]

In John we should not be surprised that, even though this Temple-theme has not usually been explored, people have nevertheless seen chapter 17, one of the climactic moments of the whole narrative, as a 'high-priestly' prayer. And just as other themes are fused together, like the varied rainbow colours brought back into the pure white light from which they came, so Jesus turns out to be *both* the true Temple *and* the true Image within that Temple, *and also* the high priest . . . *and*, of course, the victorious Messiah.

4 The Victory of God's Kingdom

But the fourth point is where we switch from Shakespeare to Virgil. 'Arms and the man I sing'; that is the classic Roman ideology, the song of a nation whose vocation was war.

Throughout John's gospel, but reaching a peak in chapter 12 and then again in 16 and the dialogue with Pilate in John 18 and 19, John presents Jesus as the one who, like David confronting Goliath, is going out to do battle with 'this world's ruler' (12.31). Most have taken this as a reference simply to the unseen forces, the dark satanic power that must be dethroned. That is certainly part of it, but I think that John, like other writers of the time, doesn't make so clear a separation between what we call 'spiritual' and what we call 'political' powers. When Jesus says that 'the ruler of the world is coming' (14.30) he seems to mean troops, not demons, though it is the satan entering into Judas that will 'accuse' him, will hand him over (13.2, 27; 18.3).

The theme is stated most clearly in 12.31–32. Some Greeks at the feast have asked to see Jesus, and Jesus appears to regard this as a sign that the last battle is near: if his message is to bear fruit in the wider world, the grain of wheat must fall into the earth and die: the dying fall, perhaps, of the music of love.

What is required for the whole world to be able to receive, and respond in faith to, the news of God's kingdom is for the dark power that has kept the whole world in captivity to be overthrown.

This is new-exodus language: Pharaoh must be defeated for the slaves to be freed. And this will happen through Jesus' death: 'Now comes the judgment of this world! Now this world's ruler is going to be thrown out! And when I've been lifted up from the earth, I will draw all people to myself' (12.31–32).

As with other preliminary statements, John wants his readers to hold this image of the victorious battle in mind throughout what follows, particularly when Jesus confronts Pilate – arguing about kingdom, truth and power – and then going to his death as Rome does what it does best, only to discover that it has been lured into a trap, leading to the moment when God does what God does best, namely creation and new creation. [9]

This is the heart of the New Testament's theology of atonement, the heart of what the early Christians believed about God's action in Jesus.

We see it – to look outside John for just a moment – in the fourth chapter of Acts, where the disciples, having been threatened by the authorities, pray a prayer based closely on Psalm 2, celebrating the fact that the nations did their worst and that, when their power was exhausted by their rage against the Messiah, God exalted and enthroned the Messiah and served notice on the powers of the world that their time was up and that they had better come into line. Thus the song of Virgil is overcome by the song of Moses and Miriam, the victory song of the exodus-people – which in Exodus 15 ends, of course, with the establishment of the Temple itself (Exodus 15.17). The dark waters of chaos are overcome with the creation of the heaven-and-earth reality of the original cosmos. The dark waters of the flood are overcome with the ark, itself symbolizing a new Temple. The overcoming of the Red Sea leads to the construction of the tabernacle. In Daniel 7 the monsters come up out of the sea, the same terrifying symbolism that Melville exploited in *Moby Dick*, and God vindicates the true human, not now an Ishmael but 'one like a son of man', giving him authority over the monsters and through him establishing his kingdom on earth as in heaven (Daniel 7.13–14).

John has built all of this and more into his account of God's action in Jesus. Jesus as Israel's Messiah wins the victory, the lion of Judah over the eagle of Rome, the God-reflecting human against the monsters, the 'son of man' as himself the ladder between earth and heaven (1.51). His body, the ultimate 'Temple', will be destroyed and rebuilt in three days (2.19–22); here, too, we are to hold this picture in our minds as we read the story of the crucifixion and resurrection in chapters 19 and 20, so that, for instance, the breathing of Jesus' spirit on the disciples in 20.19–24 is itself an important Temple-moment, with the disciples thereby constituted as the new-Temple people for the world.

The tabernacle and Solomon's Temple were always designed as small working-models of the intended new creation. Now, with the preparation of the farewell discourses behind them, the disciples are to be the living and active Temple in which the spirit dwells – the new reality corresponding to the promise of Ezekiel 43 – with the living water flowing from this Temple, as from the garden of Eden, to refresh and irrigate the whole world.

The Johannine theme of divine victory, like the equivalent moments in Hebrews 2 or Colossians 2, not to mention the synoptic gospels and Revelation, is bound up with the theme of the Temple, which is itself a central way, perhaps *the* central way, in which the early Christians thought and spoke of God's action in Jesus and what it meant. [10]

5 And the Greatest of These Is Love

There remains one theme, vast and all-embracing. John's music is indeed the food of love, and by *agapē* he means the covenant love of God for his people and, through his people, for the world. 'He had always loved his own people in the world; now he loved them right through to the end (*eis telos*)' (13.1). This is yet another heading that functions as a lens through which we are to see the events of arrest, trial, crucifixion and resurrection. It looks back to the famous 'This is how much God loved the world' in 3.16 and on to the challenge to Peter ('Simon, son of John, do you love me?') in 21.13–17.

Here, as with Paul, I think we often fail to draw out the fact that this is *covenantal* language, whose natural home is in Exodus and Deuteronomy, in the Psalms and in Isaiah, particularly in the promises of restoration after the exile. That is, for John, the ultimate meaning of incarnation and cross: the word *agapē* does not feature in the prologue, just as the word *logos* is conspicuously absent in the rest of the gospel. But the reality is everywhere, with creation itself as the act of overflowing divine love and the covenant with Israel the agonizing subsequent phase of that same love, all held together in the love of father and son for one another, which is the deepest secret of both the prologue and of the gospel as a whole.

And this is the final prayer of Jesus as the high priest at the end of chapter 17: 'so that the love with which you loved me may be in them, and I in them.' This language of divine indwelling is Temple-language. It is thus the language of creation and new creation, of Jesus as the image, and the disciples, receiving the spirit, as themselves the new-image-bearing new Temple; it is the language of the new world that will emerge once the final battle with the dark powers has been fought and won. All these themes converge, with much more for which there has been no time here.

We could have told a very similar story from Paul, from the synoptics, from Hebrews, from 1 Peter or from Revelation. Here, I think, we are near the heart of what the first Christians thought and wished to say about God's action in Jesus.

Johannine and Systematic Reflections on History, Eschatology and New Creation

Most of us exegetes, faced with this rich multi-layered food of love, will find so much to satisfy us that we wonder why we should be troubled with theological or philosophical schemes from which much of the above has been carefully screened out. This is the problem at the heart of the Logos project, the dream of bringing together 'analytic' and 'exegetical' theology.

All that I have said so far is a matter of *historical exegesis*. I have come as a first-century historian, paying particular attention to the echoes and resonances [11] that the author of the fourth gospel has allowed us to hear within the echo-chamber, the cultural encyclopaedia, of his day, and particularly of his Jewish world.

I haven't had time to go into the partial parallels in the Wisdom of Solomon or indeed Ben-Sirach, or the fascinating ways in which the biblical wisdom-traditions, particularly Proverbs 8, have contributed.[7]

But my point is that from this essentially historical project – from the exploration, as much as we can determine, of what a particular text meant in the first century – we have an extraordinarily powerful, whole and integrated theological picture, which, like all the best theological pictures, is open-ended in that it positively summons its readers to live within its world: these things are written that you may believe.

And it leads me to be suspicious of any approach to Christian understanding that would sit light to this rich tradition, which would simply use it as a back-marker while exploring other ways of talking about God and Jesus. If systematic or analytic theology has no room for these themes of Temple and image, of Israel as the Temple-guardians and Jesus as the

---

7 Nor have I addressed the motif of God's action through the *word*, found not only in the Hebrew Bible (where God creates by *dābār*) and in the Targums (where both creation and redemption come through the *memra* of YHWH).

Temple in person, of the Paschal victory through which the new Temple is to be established – *not just as decoration around the edge of something else, but as central loadbearing themes* – then such theology has a hollowness at its heart.

In particular, I think the Temple-theme is of enormous help when we address the issues of history and eschatology as they have emerged in recent centuries. It is not difficult to see why the Temple has been sidelined. In New Testament studies in particular, dominated for the last two centuries by German Protestants wrestling with the world bequeathed to them by Kant and Hegel, the Temple seemed, on the one hand, so Jewish, and it was taken for granted that Judaism was the wrong sort of religion. And it seemed, on the other hand, so catholic, with a similar comment. So it was reduced to the status of metaphor – which is why, incidentally, that tradition could never understand Mark 13 and parallels, since the fall of the Temple in AD 70 was not, for people who thought like that, an event of any great theological significance; and that points to another important story to which I shall return presently.

In particular, the Temple-theology of John and the others is the larger and more appropriately multiplex world of which the later patristic categories of 'divinity' and 'humanity' are less nuanced imitations; as though one were to try to play Tallis's forty-part motet with a string quartet. But the food of love cannot be so easily reduced to the fast-food outlets.

When we talk of 'divinity' and 'humanity', John would understand what was [12] being said, but he would insist that from the start God's world was made as a Temple, a single bifocal reality, and that humans were made from the start to stand at the threshold of heaven and earth, the royal priesthood reflecting God to the world and the world back to God. Temple-theology does effortlessly – and the early Christians all knew it did effortlessly – what later formulations struggled to do, often with a sense of *credo quia impossibile*. And, in particular, Temple-theology insists that if earth and heaven are made for one another, then earth matters, and continues to matter. Saying this does not detract from, but rather enhances, all that one might want to say about heaven.

The heart of it all is, of course, that for John and Paul, for Matthew, Mark, Luke and the rest, incarnation is not only *not* a category mistake; *it is the very fulfilment, the eschatological unveiling, of the divine purpose from the beginning.*

Eschatology must not be allowed to play a supposedly 'vertical' role over against history's 'horizontal' role. The very notion of eschatology itself emerges from within the Jewish world. Ancient paganism supplies very little to match, apart from the political eschatology of Augustus's court poets, which forms a fascinating parallel, not least because the narrative of Rome's rise to imperial glory was obviously not copied from Israel's stories, nor they from it.[8] To understand Jewish eschatology aright we must understand the second-Temple world and the way in which the early Christians rethought that world around Jesus and the spirit.

In particular, the Temple-theology I have briefly sketched stands firmly over against some of the main currents of thought in the eighteenth-century world, which still exercises a powerful magnetic pull today. Despite the critiques of postmodernity, despite the many attempts, at the time and subsequently, to put imagination back alongside reason, the modernist split world has remained the assumed presupposition.

I do not think this split world is well described in the words 'naturalism' and 'supernaturalism'. Those terms themselves all too easily play into an assumed deist order, in which the naturalist assumes an absent and non-interventionist god and the supernaturalist assumes the same deist divinity, but supposes that this divinity sometimes reaches into the world from the outside, as it were, does things and then goes away again. This of course – heaven help us! – is how many Christians today think about the entire drama of incarnation and then ascension.

The real problem is not 'naturalism' but Epicureanism, which was already well in place a century before Charles Darwin ever boarded ship to look at finches [13] and turtles. The rediscovery of Lucretius in 1417 enabled subsequent generations to formulate philosophical schemes in opposition to the vast mediaeval synthesis, and by the eighteenth century this produced, within a few years, Edward Gibbon's *Decline and Fall of the Roman Empire* (history in a godless world), Adam Smith's *The Wealth of Nations* (economics in a godless world), the French Revolution (politics in a godless world), Erasmus Darwin's theories (science in a godless world) and, not least, Reimarus's attempt to write about Jesus *etsi Deus non daretur* ('as if God does not exist').[9]

These belong together and create a climate in which it is almost impossible to understand Temple-theology, since this theology is grounded in a

---

8   See Wright 2013a, 189–200.

9   Although this maxim first appears in fourteenth-century scholastic theology (as a thought-experiment in the debate about objectivist and voluntarist ethics), its modern use is usually traced to Hugo Grotius's 1625 treatise on the legal status of war, *De iure belli ac pacis*. On the signs of Epicureanism within the eighteenth-century 'Enlightenment', see Wright 2019, ch. 1.

worldview in which heaven and earth are made for one another, with humans as the fragile and vulnerable midpoint.

It is, however, from within the world bequeathed to us by the eighteenth century that the word 'history' has often been used to indicate, in true Epicurean style, a random process of cause and effect. And the word 'eschatology' then came to be seen in terms of an essentially 'other' god bringing this whole process to a shuddering halt and establishing something totally different instead.

That is why, towards the end of the nineteenth century, Weiss and Schweitzer were able to write about the early Christian hope of the coming of the kingdom in terms of 'the end of the world'. They could only reach this conclusion by screening out the natural environment of the Jewish apocalyptic texts to which they were referring. That natural environment was (what we would call) socio-political: not about 'the end of the world', but about the end of the present *world order*.

This is the great irony of Schweitzer's claim that Jesus passes by our century and returns to his own. It was precisely in Schweitzer's time that some radicals in both France and Germany, anxious about the arrogance of a Hegelian 'progress', were talking openly about 'the end of the world'. Had they begun with the Temple-theology within which the heaven-and-earth visions of the apocalyptists actually belong, they might have realized that such writers, poised between the promises of Isaiah and Ezekiel and the ongoing realities of second-Temple life, were looking not for the abolition of the space-time world, but for the proper integration of heaven and earth, of which the Temple was the ultimate symbol, with victory over the pagans and the healing of earth's injustices as part of the package. Of course, the texts in question are not monochrome. There are passages, for instance in *1 Enoch* 42, which seem to indicate that things on earth are so bad that nothing can now be done for it. But these are, I think, the exception. [14]

In particular, what Weiss and Schweitzer, and their greatest successor Rudolf Bultmann, never seem even to have imagined is that the heaven-and-earth language of the apocalyptists had a strongly *political* reference. The Lutheran 'two kingdoms' theology, in an unholy alliance with neo-Kantianism, kept this at bay in German New Testament scholarship for much of the nineteenth and twentieth centuries, but the cat is now well and truly out of the bag.

As Hebrew Bible scholars know, when the prophet speaks of the sun and moon being darkened and the stars falling from heaven, this is not a cosmic weather forecast. It is an attempt to draw out the full significance of the coming overthrow of Babylon, the city that had seemed to hold the world together.[10] This is where, again, the Temple-theology comes into its own, with the biblical theme of Temple and victory, which we briefly noted in John (and could also have noted in Acts, Paul or Revelation).

All this remains invisible to the Epicurean eye. And the neo-Kantian eye, seeing that something important is going on there none the less, can only translate it into the Platonic vision of an ideal world which sits at an oblique angle to the present world, rather than, as in a biblical vision, transforming the present world by winning the victory over the powers and so launching new creation itself. (I often have to remind students that, if we go to the first century looking for someone who believes that we humans are exiles from our true home in heaven and that we are looking forward to our souls going back there one day, the person we're after is Plutarch. That is Middle Platonism, not Christianity.)

What we have seen in much modern theology, including – alas – biblical exegesis, is a de-Judaized, dehistoricized version of the New Testament, which, hardly surprisingly, cuts little ice in terms of either genuine human transformation or genuine Christian political witness.

In particular, the combination of Epicureanism and neo-Kantianism, which has dominated at least my field, has made it almost impossible to speak biblically about the resurrection. Indeed, the whole Enlightenment project has squeezed it out: if world history reached its climax, and humans came of age, in western Europe in the eighteenth century, then this cannot have happened in Palestine in AD 30. There cannot be two climaxes of history.

But, as has often been shown, the implicit eschatology of the Enlightenment ('now that we live in the modern world' and all that) is, in fact, a parody of Jewish and Christian eschatology, producing in turn its own version of *inaugurated* [15] eschatology, where the great revolution has happened but is also still to happen – the source of much tension in Europe and America right now.

That is another story. But my point is that the underlying philosophies have made it almost impossible to believe in the resurrection, and hence even to glimpse that in the Bible, and especially the gospels and Acts, Paul and Revelation, resurrection is all about the new creation, which is both the fulfilment of the purpose of Genesis, the real hope of Israel, the unveiling of genuine humanness, the victory over the power of death itself and hence over

---

10 See e.g. Isa. 13.6–10. For a study of the this-worldly references of apocalyptic texts, see Middleton 2014, ch. 6: 'The coming of God in judgment and salvation' and ch. 9: 'Cosmic destruction at Christ's return?'

all tyranny for whom death is the final weapon, and above all the powerful revelation of love. The sea-monsters have been defeated; Roman arms can do nothing before the rich multi-part biblical music, which is both the revelation of love and the food of love. It is all summed up in John's opening paragraph: 'In the beginning was the Logos'; and 'the Logos became flesh and lived [tabernacled] in our midst', enabling us to gaze 'upon his glory, glory like that of the father's only son, full of grace and truth'.

One might wish at this point to say a word about the reframing of a natural theology within this Johannine Temple-theology; but I will let John say it for me: 'Nobody has ever seen God. The only-begotten God, who is intimately close to the father – he has brought him to light.' Literally, 'he has *exegeted* him' (1.18).

Yes, we need all the analytic tools available for our tasks. The very words 'history' and 'eschatology' themselves are blunt instruments, and we need to sharpen them up. The word 'Logos' itself contains so many layers of meaning that the world itself might not contain the books that would analyse them. But we must make a start. And how better for the Logos project to begin than by allowing the biblical categories themselves, for a change, to set the agenda. *En archē ēn ho logos . . . kai ho logos sarx egeneto, kai eskēnōsen en hēmin.* Let's start there.

17

Son of Man and New Creation: The Biblical Roots of Trinitarian Theology

I was delighted to be invited – as the only biblical specialist – to speak at the Pusey House Conference on the Son of Man. I am particularly grateful to the principal of Pusey House, the Revd Dr George Westhaver, for the invitation and his generous welcome. Most of my meta-reflections on the conference, and my role within it, are in the paper itself.

Introduction

The conference on Christology that Pusey House hosted in July 2018 was remarkable for many reasons, but for me as a biblical specialist it stood out because I was the only professional exegete within a glittering array of historical and systematic theologians. I speculated at the time whether I might turn out to be the exegetical fly in the theological ointment, or perhaps the biblical Daniel in the theologians' den. Daniel, indeed, was obviously relevant, since the phrase 'son of man' in the conference title is inevitably linked to the vision in Daniel chapter 7. But my lonely position invited two preliminary reflections before we turned to the text.

Exegesis and theology have been going their separate ways. They no longer share a common table; they hardly even recognize one another in the street. The systematician might comment that exegesis has dug itself into a series of smaller and messier holes from which no clear meaning ever emerges; and that, since Athanasius, Aquinas and the rest all read their Bibles and prayed for the spirit's guidance, we should assume they knew what they were talking about and take it from there. Scholarly oral tradition recalls that Paul Tillich once remarked to C. H. Dodd that the systematician can't be expected to sit there waiting for some useful nugget of exegesis to come down the hall from the biblical specialists. One might wait a long time. The exegete will respond that systematic and historical theology appear to be playing an in-house game in which the large concepts invented by later generations are endlessly rearranged with scant reference to the first-century historical reality to which they ostensibly refer. Anyway (both sides will comment) there's no time to say more, because academics these days need to get on with the next project in the field, and don't usually have time, or get any extra praise, for speculative cross-disciplinary interaction.

The phrase 'son of man', at the heart of the conference, is a case in point, and leads to my second introductory remark. Generations used to be taught – perhaps still are – that 'son of God' and 'son of man' indicated Jesus' 'divinity' and 'humanity' respectively. This has worked its way into popular discourse. When journalists ask a bishop if Jesus really was 'the son of God', they want the prelate either to affirm or deny an almost docetic belief in Jesus' 'divinity'. When a Christmas carol speaks of Jesus as the one who loves to be known as 'the son of man', it means, uncomplicatedly, that Jesus is 'one of us', a human among humans. But this was not what those phrases meant in the Jewish world of Jesus' day – a world increasingly opaque once apocalyptic messianism had been abandoned following the failure of the Bar-Kochba revolt, and a world still more opaque, for quite different reasons, in the increasingly Epicurean cosmology of the Enlightenment and the movements of critical thought within it.[1]

It was within the latter framework that Adolf Harnack famously sketched an early Christianity in which the simple timeless gospel of Jesus was muddled up by hellenistic philosophy, which invented strange things like the Trinity, unknown in the early period. The fact that Harnack was wrong in most respects makes it harder to argue the point which still needs to be made, to which this paper will contribute: that there was indeed a turn from the first-century Jewish context to the world of the third and subsequent centuries, but that the classic doctrines of the high patristic period, particularly Trinity and Christology, were clearly expressed by the earliest Jesus-followers, albeit in an idiom, and within a conceptual framework, which was all but ignored once its original Jewish context had disappeared in the disasters of 70 and 135. The question would then be: do the subsequent retrievals of the doctrines, within the very different idioms and conceptual worlds of the fourth and fifth centuries, successfully display all that the early texts were saying? Or are

---

1   On the radical change in the second-Temple worldview following the Bar-Kochba revolt, see Wright 1992a, 161–6, 199f. On the resurgence of Epicureanism in the modern period see my Gifford Lectures, Wright 2019.

we forced to concede, like Henry Chadwick in his article on Chalcedon, that, though we affirm Chalcedon itself, something of what the New Testament was saying seems to have slipped through its fingers?[2]

I assume that even non-exegetes will know the remarkable turn of the tide in the last generation towards an 'early high Christology'. The old picture of an early 'human Jesus' who gradually 'became' more 'divine' as the church moved away from its roots in Jewish monotheism is still popular, not least among those for whom Geza Vermes had said what they wanted to hear so that they didn't bother to read anything else.[3] But the work of Larry Hurtado and Richard Bauckham, and most recently of Richard Hays on the four gospels, has shown this up as a historically unwarranted fiction, happily embraced, though for quite different reasons, by many liberal Protestants and many Jewish scholars.[4] In fact – and this will be the heart of my own proposal in this paper – the more we understand the first-century Jewish world, particularly its key narratives and symbols, the more we see how the early high Christology of Paul and all four gospels, not to mention Hebrews and Revelation, belongs within that world – as an explosive new reality, to be sure, but a reality which makes the sense it makes precisely within that world.

The narrative world of the first-century Jews is on display in the various retrievals of the obvious text, Daniel 7, to which I now turn.

Daniel 7 and the First-Century Jewish Hope

Daniel 7 poses several historical puzzles, but some of them are irrelevant for the first century. We do not need to know the prehistory, angelic or otherwise, of the phrase 'one like a son of man'.[5] What matters is how the text was read in the first century. Here we have five converging pieces of evidence.

The first is the text of Daniel itself, as a whole.[6] The book is clearly about the creator God vindicating his suffering righteous people. The stories of Daniel and his friends in chapters 1, 3 and 6 and of divine judgment on arrogant pagans in chapters 4 and 5 give grounding to the visions of chapters 2 and 7. These then set the tone for the further visions of chapters 8 and 10, the prayer

---

2 Chadwick 2017.
3 E.g. Vermes 1973 and many subsequent works.
4 See e.g. Hurtado 2003 and several other works; Bauckham 2009 and other works; Hays 2016.
5 On which, see the full treatment by Collins 1993, ad loc.
6 See Wright 1992a, 291–7; 1996b, 513–19.

of chapter 9 and the promise of final deliverance in chapter 12. The different genres contribute to the common theme: the one God will establish his reign over the wicked nations, and the faithful, vindicated after suffering, will share this divine rule. That is how first-century readers would understand chapter 7: when violent pagan arrogance reaches its height, God will rescue his people and exalt them to share his newly inaugurated worldwide regime:

> The kingship and dominion and the greatness of the kingdoms under the whole heaven shall be given to the people of the holy ones of the Most High; their kingdom shall be an everlasting kingdom, and all dominions shall serve and obey them.
> (Daniel 7.27)

That is what the text itself insists is meant by 'one like a son of man' 'coming on the clouds' to the Ancient of Days. It means both vindication and installation into a position of authority. It resonates, in fact, with the way in which Daniel is regularly promoted to positions of high authority in Babylon.[7]

Two notes about this reading of Daniel itself. The symbolism of the four monsters coming up out of the sea, and the exaltation of 'one like a son of man', would be obvious to first-century Jews. The narrative is familiar from Psalm 2, with the warring nations confronted by God's exaltation of the king; or, indeed, from the book of Exodus (with Pharaoh's troops overthrown in the sea, and Israel rescued) or the Wisdom of Solomon chapters 1 to 5. Daniel 2 presents substantially the same scenario: the multi-metalled idolatrous statue is demolished by the stone. Psalm 46 repeats the point: the nations are in uproar, the kingdoms totter; but God utters his voice and the earth melts; the Lord of hosts is with us, the God of Jacob is our refuge. In a sense, this is Israel's only story, the theme that generated many variations, finding expression in symbol, liturgy and political action.

The second note follows from this: what to the modern world has appeared as 'apocalyptic', a strange dark world of dualistic fantasy distinct from older prophecy, was nothing of the sort.[8] Expressing the horrible this-worldly realities of brutal empires through the well-known metaphor of the beasts from the sea was a way of aligning political realities with the ancient cosmology reflected in Genesis 1 – the waters of chaos overcome

---

7 See Dan. 2.48; 5.29; 6.28.

8 On the much-misunderstood term 'apocalyptic' see particularly my Wright 2015, Part II; and Wright 2019, ch. 4.

by the good creation – and the parallel soteriology of Exodus, both evoking earlier ancient Near Eastern mythology. Daniel 7 was a way of saying that the vicious imperial rule of the post-Babylonian empires was the accumulated violence of the chaos to which the creator's answer would be a great act of new creation. Genesis 1 and 2 would be recapitulated at last, with the human one sovereign over the monsters. The vision of 'one like a son of man' means what it means, in the first century, within this well-known and widely shared narrative.

So far, the reading of 'one like a son of man' in Daniel 7 could be simply incorporative: Israel, the righteous sufferers, will be vindicated like the humans over the animals. The other four points, though, indicate from different angles that many Jews in the period were reading it in terms of the coming king, the Messiah. There was no single, unified 'messianic expectation' at the time.[9] Many Jews hoped for a coming king, drawing variously on scriptural prophecies, but their visions didn't always agree, and many were unsure or sceptical. Nevertheless, Daniel's 'one like a son of man' was certainly interpreted by some as Israel's representative, the coming Messiah.

The second of the converging pieces of evidence is found in the second 'Similitude' of Enoch (1 Enoch 45—57). This is still controversial, not least because of textual and dating difficulties. These are irrelevant for our purposes. What matters is that the author is clearly reading Daniel 7 messianically.

Much more important, third, is the vision of the eagle and the lion in 4 Ezra chapters 11 and 12. The eagle is transparently Rome; the lion, equally obviously, is Judah's Messiah. The interpreting angel explains that 'the eagle that you saw coming up from the sea is the fourth kingdom that appeared in the vision to your brother Daniel. But it was not explained to him as I now explain to you' (12.11–12). The Messiah will judge the wicked nations but have mercy on the remnant of God's people (12.31–34). This vision, dateable to the generation after AD 70, shows both that Daniel 7 was being read as exemplifying the narrative I sketched a moment ago (the sovereign God overcoming wicked chaos and giving authority to a human being) and that it was focused on a coming Messiah.

Fourth, the most important evidence is that of Josephus. What most of all drove his contemporaries to revolt in AD 66, he says in the Jewish War, was an oracle in their scriptures which prophesied that at that time a world ruler

---

9 See Novenson 2012.

would arise from their country.[10] Josephus doesn't give the reference. But when he discusses Daniel in the *Jewish Antiquities* (10.267) it becomes clear. In the *War* passage, he reinterprets the oracle: it was, he says, a prophecy about Vespasian, who went from besieging Jerusalem to be emperor in Rome. Josephus was of course living on an imperial pension at the time. For the same reason, he radically tones down his interpretation of Daniel. When expounding chapter 2, he skips over the obviously messianic 'stone'; and then, after a detailed description of chapters 3 to 6, he jumps over the crucial chapter 7 altogether and goes straight on to 8. He knows only too well what chapter 7 was about. He then insists, however, that Daniel is unique among the prophets, in that he not only prophesied what would happen but also put a specific time on it. This can only be a reference to Daniel 9, where the time of 'exile', when Israel was ruled by the pagans, would last not for seventy years, as in Jeremiah, but 'seventy weeks of years', in other words, 490 years, a sabbatical of sabbaticals. We know that many Jews in the first century were indeed calculating that 490 years, mostly arriving some time in what we call the first century AD.[11] Josephus thus, despite his cautious approach, bears witness to a first-century reading of the book in terms of a prophecy about a coming worldwide ruler arising from Judaea 'at that time'. The 'one like a son of man' would be brought to sit alongside the 'ancient of days', and the dark, chaotic power of pagan empire would be condemned at last.

This reading is confirmed, fifth and finally, by the controversy at the Bar-Kochba revolt in 132. Rabbi Akiba, supporting Bar-Kochba, used Daniel 7, which speaks of 'thrones' being placed in heaven before the 'one like a son of man' arrives there: 'One for the Ancient of Days', he explains, and 'one for David'.[12] This confirms three points. First, Daniel 7 was still being read messianically. Second, the apocalyptic genre was understood to refer to political or revolutionary events, investing them with theological significance. Third, here at least Daniel is presumed to teach that the coming Messiah, a successful revolutionary leader, will *share the very throne of Israel's God* – a point deemed blasphemous by some of Akiba's contemporaries, perhaps not least because it sounded suspiciously like some of the things the Jesus-followers had been saying.

---

10 Jos. *War* 6.312–15. See the discussions in Wright 1992a, 312–14; and in Wright 2013b, 117, 130, 142, 293, 1065.

11 See the texts cited and discussed in Wright 1992a, as above.

12 On all this see the now classic study of Segal 1977.

All this, I suggest, gives us a sense of the exegetical, theological and political possibilities inherent in a reference to the 'one like a son of man' in Daniel 7. The idea of this figure being 'human' in the sense of being 'one of us' is irrelevant. That isn't the question on the table. First-century Jews had rather few books, but the main ones they had – Torah, Prophets and Writings – were extremely well known, studied, prayed and sung. The echoes awoken by Daniel 7, as a whole and in its parts, would resonate with the large narratives of both creation and exodus. The one God wins the victory over the waters of chaos, and over the political monsters that gain their power from that dark force.

But in scripture the story doesn't stop there. In Exodus 15, in Psalm 2, and not least in Isaiah 52, this goes with the launching of God's kingdom, the establishment of the Temple, and particularly the personal and visible return of Israel's God to that restored Temple. This complex of vast interlocking themes, I have argued elsewhere, was not only well understood but also, in various forms, taken for granted as part of the overall biblically resourced hope: not that humans in general, or Israel in particular, would be rescued from this present world to live somewhere else, but that Israel's God would finally come to dwell amid his people and, through that indwelling, would rescue and transform the whole creation, suffusing it with his glorious presence.[13]

All the lines converge at this point. Central to the royal vocation, from the Psalms and Isaiah to Qumran, the *Psalms of Solomon* and beyond, is the task of defeating the enemy, building or cleansing the Temple, and so preparing the way for the return of the glorious divine presence.[14] Equally central is the task of doing justice and mercy, especially on behalf of the poor, the widow and the orphan, so that, as in Psalm 72, the glorious divine presence may fill the whole earth. The two go together. Imagery from the creation story (chaos waters overcome by God's creation, and the human authority within it) is applied to what we call political realities; equally, the order and structure of the tabernacle and Temple is seen to reflect, and to reflect on, creation itself, and thereby to point ahead to creation's ultimate renewal and filling with divine presence. Tabernacle and Temple were seen – at least by the editors of the Pentateuch – as small working-models of the whole creation, signs of the ultimate divine intention. Architecture and decoration alike spoke of the larger cosmos; the high priest, going into the shrine once a year, stood in for Adam in the original garden-Temple. The Temple was thus an

---

13   See Wright 2019, ch. 5.

14   On the 'royal' vocation see e.g. Wright 1996b, 481–6; 2013b, 817–25.

eschatological symbol, a forward-looking signpost for what the creator God intended to do for the whole creation. Israel's vocation was to be the guardian, not simply of a building, but of the promise signified by that building: that there would be a new creation, a time when heaven and earth would come together at last so that the earth would be filled with the knowledge and/or the glory of God as the waters cover the sea. This glorious divine return, as I have argued elsewhere, is the hidden clue to early Christology and pneumatology.

All this forms the implicit echo-chamber within which an allusion to Daniel 7, and to the 'one like a son of man', would make sense in the first century. But there is one further element before we move to the synoptic tradition. This is the sabbath. As Jewish scholars have long pointed out, the sabbath was to time what the Temple was to space. If the Temple was where heaven and earth overlapped, pointing forward to the day when they would be joined together for ever, the sabbath was the regular day when the 'age to come' appeared in the midst of the present age. Thus in Jesus' Jewish world there were twin symbolic themes, taken for granted then but largely opaque to modern scholarship: the Temple, signifying the joining of heaven and earth; the sabbath, signifying the advance appearing of the age to come.

All this thrives in the first-century Jewish worldview. It lives in symbol and story, and is easily retrieved when facing challenge or innovation. And that's what happens when the synoptic Jesus speaks of the 'son of man'.

'Son of Man' in the Synoptic Gospels

Three introductory remarks. First, Geza Vermes was correct to point out that the phrase 'son of man' could simply mean 'someone like me', an oblique self-reference.[15] But Vermes was reacting against an older assumption that 'son of man' meant 'Messiah' in an unnuanced sense of 'a divine redeemer figure', so he screened out Daniel 7, just as he screened out the significance of Jesus' action in the Temple. Once scholarship had moved on with Ben Meyer and Ed Sanders, making Jesus' Temple-action and associated sayings central rather than marginal to the tradition, it became natural, and far more credible historically, to situate Jesus within the more complex and multi-layered first-century world.[16] Vermes's Jesus was basically a Jewish version of Bultmann's dehistoricized existentialist sage.

---

15   See the refs. in Wright 1996b, 517.
16   See Meyer 1979; Sanders 1985.

Second, many scholars have assumed that the three categories of 'son of man' sayings – authority, suffering and future 'coming' – are incompatible, so that Jesus couldn't have said them all.[17] Debate has then been derailed by the stand-off between 'conservative' scholars, deeming the sayings all genuine for the sake of their inerrant Bible, and 'liberal' scholars, wanting many of them to be inauthentic for the sake of their errant one. Both 'conservatives' and 'liberals', though, read the 'coming on the clouds' sayings as referring to the second coming, the latter insisting that it didn't happen and the former that it still would. But when we bear in mind the larger Jewish contexts of meaning – in a way quite foreign to those earlier debates – then everything looks different.

In particular (my third introductory remark on 'son of man' in the synoptic gospels), the context of Daniel 7, and its retrieval by *4 Ezra* and the loud silence of Josephus on the subject, indicates that the 'coming' of the son of man is not his *second coming* but rather his *vindication and exaltation*. In Daniel 7 the 'one like a son of man' comes on the clouds to be presented to the Ancient of Days, there to receive kingly authority. The movement is upward, not downward. Nor must we imagine this 'coming' in terms of a literalistic three-decker universe. Three-decker language was serving the Jewish vision, common in other cultures as well, that the domains of gods and humans might overlap, the focal point of overlap being of course a temple; a temple with an image.

This is certainly how the 'coming of the son of man' was taken among Jesus' first followers. In 1 Corinthians 15, claiming to build on very early common tradition, Paul pulls together Psalms 2, 8 and 110, weaving in echoes of Daniel 7, to say that Israel's Messiah *is already reigning*. He has already inaugurated the age to come, and is now working to bring all things into subjection.[18] Paul doesn't use the phrase 'son of man', but the whole chapter is framed within explicit exegesis of Genesis 1—3, Adam and the Messiah, with Psalm 8 vital to its climax.

A further word about this now-and-not-yet inaugurated eschatology. Some have recently suggested that this is a modern way of getting off the hook of an apparently unfulfilled promise.[19] The world didn't end, and nobody came to earth riding on a cloud. This is simply unhistorical. When Simeon ben-Kosiba

---

17 See the discussion in Wright 1996b, 510–19; and, for a thorough survey, Hurtado 2012.

18 For this point and what follows, see Wright 2018a; and the further discussion in Wright 2019, chs. 2, 4.

19 See e.g. Congdon 2015, 10f.

was hailed as Messiah in 132, that *inaugurated* a three-year rule over a small independent kingdom. The coins say Year One, restarting the calendar like the French Revolutionaries. The kingdom had begun. But that was only the start. They still had to defeat Rome and rebuild the Temple. The age to come was *anticipated*, as with the sabbath itself. That's how kingdom-claims worked in the Jewish world of the time.

So when Jesus responds to Caiaphas's question about Messiahship, he is not saying that the high priest will see him, Jesus, or anyone else, flying downwards on a cloud. That would both literalize the apocalyptic metaphor and reverse the direction of travel. He is asserting, rather, that Caiaphas *will see Jesus vindicated* through events which will carry the message that he really was the Messiah, that he really did have authority over the Temple, and that he was indeed replacing the Temple as the place where, and the means by which, heaven and earth were coming together. Matthew and Luke, perhaps clarifying Mark, insist that Jesus is talking about a more or less immediate vindication. 'From now on', *ap'arti* in Matthew (26.64) and *apo tou nyn* in Luke (22.69), the son of man will fulfil both Psalm 110 and Daniel 7: seated at the right hand of Power, coming on the clouds of heaven. Psalm 110, perhaps the most frequently alluded-to biblical text in the New Testament, carries here the extra meaning that Jesus is claiming a priestly status which, as the letter to the Hebrews would later draw out, was effortlessly superior to the Levitical or indeed Aaronic line. No wonder Caiaphas shouted 'Blasphemy'.

Matthew insists on this again later. The risen Jesus claims, in Matthew 28.18, that 'all authority in heaven and on earth has been given to me' – another clear echo of Daniel 7. This global rule had been offered him by the dark enemy in chapter 4, in return for a switch of allegiance.[20] Now it is granted by the one God instead, as the result of Jesus' obedient suffering. This sovereignty is the foundation, here as in Paul, for the mission of the church. The enslaving enemy has been defeated, and the true king enthroned. The church's mission is not to offer people a new religious experience, or to invite them to escape earth and attain heaven instead. It is rather about enlisting people in the present time for the work of the kingdom, against the still-future day when heaven and earth will be one. That future day is of course reaffirmed in the tradition, but not, in my judgment, either in the saying to Caiaphas or in the similar saying in Mark 13 and parallels. There, the emphasis falls on the vindication of the son of man in the coming events of resurrection, ascension and the fall of Jerusalem, the city and the Temple that had refused

---

20   Mt. 4.9; more clearly in Lk. 4.6.

the gospel way of peace. Rather, the future 'coming' or 'return' of Jesus will be to complete the work 'on earth as in heaven', to effect the cosmic transformation promised in Romans 8, and the equivalent personal transformation promised in Philippians 3.[21] All this would take us into many fascinating areas for which there is no space here.

We can now fill in the picture with the other 'son of man' gospel sayings. Once we read the 'coming' sayings seen in terms of 'vindication', it is relatively easy to see both the 'authority' and the 'suffering' sayings within the same implicit narrative. Jesus claims authority to forgive sins as part of his kingdom-inaugurating public career.[22] This is the Jubilee, the seventy-weeks moment, when 'the time is fulfilled' so that 'the kingdom is at hand': the real return from exile, which is itself the forgiveness of Israel's sins, is taking place, *and Israel's God is now returning in person to judge and save.*

How does this work out? Not straightforwardly in our terms. Christology has often been short-circuited in the modern period, with even the word *Christos* being treated as a 'divine' title, and once more with conservatives insisting that this divine meaning was present to Jesus and liberals insisting that it wasn't and couldn't have been. This merely throws dust in the eyes.

What matters, once again, is the narrative, and the symbols that encode it. When we go back to Daniel 7, the 'one like a son of man' is clearly interpreted as 'the people of the saints of the most high'. When this is reapplied in the first century by *4 Ezra* and Josephus (and probably earlier in the Similitudes) the corporate figure has become an individual. Here are the roots of Paul's incorporative messianic theology: *the Messiah represents Israel within the divine purposes.* The authority that in Daniel 7 is vested in the saints is now vested in Jesus, because God has done for him, in raising him from the dead, what in Israel's traditions was to happen to all the righteous at the end of time. Jesus' resurrection is the key to inaugurated eschatology, as indeed to more or less everything else.

The 'authority' sayings are associated in particular with the sabbath.[23] Here is a classic interpretative riddle. Generations were taught that Jesus broke the sabbath because it was a piece of restrictive Jewish legalism while he believed in freedom; in grace, not law. That is an irrelevant anachronism. Jesus acted as he did on the sabbath, and justified his actions in that way, because *the time was fulfilled*; the seventy weeks of years were up; the kingdom was breaking

---

21 On both of which see Wright 2007.
22 E.g. Mk. 2.10. For the 'suffering' sayings see e.g. Mk. 10.45.
23 E.g. Mk. 2.28.

in then and there. The sabbaths had been forward-looking signposts to the coming age, when heaven and earth would be joined as always intended. They were now upstaged.[24] You don't put up a sign saying 'This way to Oxford' in the High Street. And if the son of man has authority over the sabbath, he also claims authority over the Temple. Both Matthew and John, describing Jesus' dramatic Temple-action, echo Psalm 8. Matthew has Jesus quoting, 'Out of the mouths of babes and sucklings you have drawn perfect praise'; John, echoing the authority of the son of man in the psalm, has Jesus casting out *ta probata kai tas boas* (the sheep and the oxen). It looks as though, in very early tradition, Jesus' Temple-action was associated with his status as the implicitly royal 'son of man' of Psalm 8. This picks up the older idea that the 'image' in Genesis 1 was itself a royal motif, now democratized to include all humans, but still available for specifically royal use.[25]

For Jesus thus to claim authority over both Temple and sabbath was to say, in symbol as well as word, that the new day was dawning towards which both symbols had been pointing. Forward-looking symbols become redundant when the reality arrives. 'Something greater than the Temple is here' (Matthew 12.6); and the humans for whom the sabbath was made can now enjoy the reality of which it spoke. Jesus, in fact, went about redefining 'kingdom of God' itself, around what he was doing and saying. *This is what it looks like*, he was saying, *when God becomes king as promised!* And central to that redefinition was suffering. Jesus took the theme of suffering – of exile, of martyrdom, of the persecution of the prophets – and, in making it his own, redefined it. No longer would it simply be the dark pathway *through which* the righteous would walk to attain the new day. Now, the suffering would be *the means by which* the eventual redemption would be won. This is where, of course, Jesus invoked Isaiah.

As with 'the son of man' itself, the 'suffering servant' has been off limits to many scholars. This was partly in reaction to the over-concentration on the passage by one strand of exegesis, and by the limiting of that exegesis to a particular theory of atonement. But when we step back from those older discussions, the conclusion is clear. In the 2018 St Andrews conference on the atonement in Jewish and early Christian thought, it was remarkable how often Isaiah 53 turned up as the key allusion in Jewish texts of the second-Temple period, irrespective of Christian interpretation. Different groups, of course,

---

24   See Wright 2011b, ch. 9; 2019, ch. 5.
25   See Wright 2018c (ch. 14 in the present volume).

read that chapter differently.[26] Some, like 2 Maccabees, took it as a prophecy about the redemptive quality of the martyrs' deaths – but not as in any sense messianic. Some, as with the later Isaiah Targum, saw it as a messianic prophecy, but turned the 'suffering' references the other way round so that they became, as in Psalm 110, the suffering the Messiah would inflict on God's enemies. It looks as though Jesus himself made the creative exegetical and vocational move to hold these together, so that the Messiah himself would become the ultimate redemptive martyr; and to hold together with that, too, the entire narrative of the 'one like a son of man', so that Isaiah 40—55 as a whole, and the book of Daniel as a whole, would come true together in the same way. Isaiah spoke of the personal return of Israel's God to Zion, with the 'servant'-poems woven into the larger pattern to reveal the means by which this redemptive return would be accomplished. 'Who would have believed', asks the prophet at the start of chapter 53, 'that he was the Arm of the Lord?' The servant embodies the promised divine return. The result, in chapter 54, is covenant renewal. This leads, in chapter 55, to the renewal of creation itself. Several psalms make the same point..

This is picked up in the opening of Mark's gospel. The two biblical passages with which he begins, Malachi 3 and Isaiah 40, are not about an Elijah-figure preparing the way for Israel's Messiah; they are about preparing the way for Israel's God.[27] Mark 1 is full of allusions to both creation and exodus: Jesus comes out of the water, with the spirit like a dove descending on him, and the voice proclaims his identity and vocation in terms of Psalm 2 and Isaiah 42. After his sojourn in the wilderness, he announces that the time is fulfilled and God's kingdom is at hand.

Mark's redefinition of what it will look like when God comes back emerges from Jesus' own redefinition of the kingdom. It will involve healing and celebration; it will involve victory, not over Rome, but over the dark power that has lent its weight to Rome and also, tragically, to Israel's misguided leaders and revolutionaries. It will involve the destruction of the present Temple and the establishment of something else that will do the job towards which the Temple had been pointing. It will involve the arrival of the age to come in such a way that the sabbath will no longer be needed as a forward signpost. All this and more Jesus declares in hints and riddles, with the parables teasing people towards a larger and shockingly redrawn picture of how the scriptures were to be fulfilled.

---

26 See the discussion of different interpretations of Isa. 53 in Wright 1996b, 588–91.
27 Mk. 1.2–3, quoting Mal. 3.1; Isa. 40.3.

At its heart is the redrawn vision of power itself. What will it look like, Jesus is asking, when God becomes king? James and John assume it will be a normal kingdom, with men to the monarch's right and left to enforce his decrees.[28] No, says Jesus, that's how the rulers of the world do it, but we're going to do it the other way. Someone who wants to be great must be your servant; anyone who wants to be first must be slave of all, *because* the son of man didn't come to be served but to serve, and to give his life, a ransom for many. That last line has been wrenched out of context to serve abstract theories of atonement, but part of the point is that to begin with the cross was at the heart of the redefinition of power, because the cross was the ultimate means through which God's kingdom would be established. All the evangelists insist on this point, with Jesus crucified as 'King of the Jews'. Later theology has found it hard to hold together kingdom and cross. The two have drifted apart in exegesis, in theology and in church agendas. But for the gospels there is no split, just as Isaiah 53 and Daniel 7 are fused together, as they cry out to be, into a single kingdom-bringing narrative, the story of the personal return and redemptive accomplishment of Israel's God.

The three strands of synoptic 'son of man' sayings – authority, suffering, vindication – likewise fit together into a fresh but perfectly recognizable construal of the many-stranded first-century Jewish narrative. Jesus really did believe that the events he was precipitating would be the point around which world history, cosmic history, would turn. He did not of course believe in the coming literal 'end of the world'. That is nineteenth-century German mythology projected back, with breathtaking anachronism, on to the first century.[29] He was a Jew, living from within the scriptures in which the creator God had promised to dwell on the earth. He was heir to the promises which spoke darkly about how that would be accomplished despite the failure and exile of the promise-bearing people. Paul understood this already, but it's clear he didn't invent it. The four gospels reflect all this in their different ways. But they, too, go on to make new points from it. They are not inventing it from scratch. Once we do our best to locate our reflection on Jesus and early Christianity within the larger first-century Jewish symbolic, narratival and conceptual world, all sorts of fresh options open up: new highways in the desert . . .

---

28   Mk. 10.35–45.
29   See Wright 2018a; 2019, chs. 2, 4.

From Exegesis to Theology

The options open up for theology as well as exegesis. By starting with 'son of man' in Daniel and the gospels, we have reached a vantage point for some wider reflections. Perhaps the most important is that, in some readings of Daniel 7 in the period, the 'one like a son of man' is *both* the literary figure who stands in for 'Israel as a whole' *and* the messianic embodiment of that Israel-shaped vocation – *and* the one who then shares the very throne of the one God himself. How all this can be held together we see in passages like John 1 or Colossians 1, which invoke Genesis 1 so as to let the Messiah appear as the true Image, the ultimate human being, while being also the one 'through whom all things were made'. It looks as though the first Jesus-followers, trying to understand just who it was they had known as friend and master, reached for the text that spoke of humans being made to reflect the stewarding power of the creator into his world and the worship of the world back to the creator. The Image stands at the heart of the ultimate Temple, which is creation itself. And, as in other passages like Hebrews 1, 1 Corinthians 8 and Philippians 2, the human who is now exalted is identified with the one who all along was equal with the creator. *The phrase 'son of man' does not of itself indicate Jesus' divine identity, but the narrative that it evokes generates the world in which that makes sense.*

The earlier critical assumption, then, was wrong. Many of us were told as students that the idea of incarnation itself was a category mistake. The first followers of Jesus begged to differ, not because they were primitive while we were modern, but because they were Jewish while we were late-flowering Epicureans for whom any commerce between heaven and earth would be off limits. Instead, John 1, Colossians 1, Philippians 2 and other passages are saying that Genesis 1, with humans called to be image-bearers, is itself, like Temple and sabbath, a forward-looking signpost: God made humans in his own image, to reflect his personal presence into the world, so that in due time he might himself become human in order to embody his own intention. That long-range plan was not thwarted by the vocational failure of the humans. Rather, it called forth a fresh dimension of the same generous love through which creation came to be in the first place. God called Abraham and his family to be the means of redeeming the world, so that in due time he might himself become the world's redeemer by embodying in himself the dark vocation of Israel, a vocation initially enacted in the slavery and redemption of Egypt and exodus and reaching its climax in cross and resurrection. These purposes were then expressed in the symbols of Temple and sabbath, with the image-bearing humans always central, and the royal and priestly vocations occupying a kind of liminal space, poised between the purposes of heaven and the paradoxes of earth. The New Testament then represents the astonished celebration and exploration of exactly this, with Jesus as himself the royal priest who simultaneously embodies *both* Israel's returning God *and* Israel's own act of utter self-offering worship, and reveals that those two vocations are not two but one. He is the Image of the invisible God; no-one has seen God, but the only-begotten God has unveiled him, explained him, made him known. I have long been of the opinion that, if Christology would begin here, many other questions would appear in a fresh light.

Where then does the spirit come into the picture? The authority that Jesus claims as 'son of man' in the gospels is exercised in the power of the spirit which anointed him at his baptism, and this provides one clue. The purpose of it all, of the whole biblical narrative, is not to save humans away from the world but for the living God to flood all creation with his presence, effecting the new creation spoken of in Isaiah and the Psalms. Jesus' healings are then to be seen, as he pointed out to John the Baptist, in terms of the new-creation prophecies of Isaiah 35. The healing, world-renewing spirit is then the one through whom the creator God will in the end be 'all in all' (1 Corinthians 15.28), not in a kind of eschatological pantheism but in a fusion of heaven and earth. Each will be truly itself while being perfectly united with the other, an image for which, as in John 2 or Ephesians 5, marriage is both metaphor and metonymy. In one passage after another – and not in writing only, since Paul at least saw the practical work of the church in these terms – the spirit is at work in the present to fill Jesus' followers with new and transforming life as itself a sign and anticipation of what is intended for the entire cosmos at the end. The present equipping of the church with the spirit's varied gifts in Ephesians 4 is to the end of the eventual 'filling of all things' that results from the Messiah's exaltation and enthronement. It is, in other words, the outworking of the Daniel 7 moment, the time when the risen Jesus fulfilled Psalm 110 and obtained executive authority over the whole world.

Of course, that executive authority, like Jesus' authority in his public career, was always to be fulfilled by the same kind of power, the new power of suffering and healing love. That is why the Sermon on the Mount is what it is. The regular objection, that things still don't look as though Jesus is in charge, is the equivalent of the objections people raised to Jesus himself when they asked for signs. Jesus gave them the sign of Jonah, launching the new creation in his own risen body, not only thereby possessing authority to renew the creation but embodying and modelling that new creation in himself. This is where the vindication of the son of man joins up with the larger prophetic narrative: Daniel 7, pointing back to Genesis 1 and 2, points on to the rescue and renewal of creation itself.

The spirit that is thereby let loose – since Jesus has overcome in his death the dark powers that had held the world captive – is spoken of by Paul, within twenty-five years of Jesus' death and resurrection, in terms reminiscent of the pillar of cloud and fire that accompanied the Israelites in the wilderness. For Paul to refer to the personal presence of the divine glory as the appropriate image for the indwelling spirit was to state as high a pneumatology as you could have, though it took the Fathers centuries to catch up. In Galatians, which I take to be the very first New Testament writing, Paul declares that after their former idolatry the converts had 'come to know God, or rather to be known by God'.[30] And the God he is referring to in the previous verses is the God of redemption, the God of the exodus, the God who sent the son and the God who sent the spirit of the son.[31] There is the choice, starkly presented in (I think) the late 40s AD. You either have this threefold God or you have paganism.

And that is why, though I love the church's great traditions and revere its great teachers, I cannot escape the sense that the Jewish roots of Christology and Trinitarian theology, long pruned to below ground level by the sceptical agendas which have called themselves 'historical criticism', are actually full of sap, ready to sprout, blossom and flower once more. By all means let us translate them into new idioms, as the spirit leads us, to address new contexts. But let us be sure that it is these that we are translating. Even if we were to take the phrase 'son of man' in its misleading popular sense, this much ought to be clear: we are followers of the first-century Jew called Jesus, and we need to think into his world. This means taking the risk of history, if we are to understand him in his own terms and those of his first followers. But if we then take the phrase 'son of man' seriously in that first-century context, as I have sketched in this paper, then we are invoking the larger narratives of Daniel 7, and of Genesis, Exodus and the Psalms which that passage itself invokes, as well as the symbols of Temple and sabbath which form the symbolic matrix for first-century interpretation. And, once we are there, we will find striking possibilities both for systematic theology, not least Trinity and Christology, and also for the practical mission of the church. Perhaps those vocations are part of what is really involved in 'knowing and loving the son of man'.

---

30 Gal. 4.9.
31 Gal. 4.4–7; more fully in Rom. 8.18–30.

Bibliography

Alkier, S. 2005. 'From text to intertext: intertextuality as a paradigm for reading Matthew.' *HTS Teologiese Studies* 61:1–18.

Allen, G. V., et al. 2019. *Son of God: Divine sonship in Jewish and Christian antiquity*. University Park, PA: Eisenbrauns.

Anderson, G. A. 1997. 'The exaltation of Adam and the fall of Satan.' Pages 83–110 in *Literature on Adam and Eve: Collected essays*, ed. G. Anderson, M. Stone and J. Tromp. Leiden: Brill.

Bailey, K. E. 1983. *Poet and Peasant / Through Peasant Eyes*. Grand Rapids, MI: Eerdmans.

——. 1991. 'Informal controlled oral tradition and the synoptic gospels.' *Asia Journal of Theology* 5:34–54.

Bammel, E. 1984. 'The revolution theory from Reimarus to Brandon.' Pages 11–68 in *Jesus and the Politics of His Day*, ed. E. Bammel and C. F. D. Moule. Cambridge: Cambridge University Press.

Bammel, E., and C. F. D. Moule, eds 1984. *Jesus and the Politics of His Day*. Cambridge: Cambridge University Press.

Barbour, R. S. 1993. *The Kingdom of God and Human Society: Essays by members of the Scripture, Theology and Society Group*. Edinburgh: T&T Clark.

Barclay, J. M. G. 2005. 'The empire writes back: Josephan rhetoric in Flavian Rome.' Pages 315–32 in *Flavius Josephus and Flavian Rome*, ed. J. C. Edmondson, S. Mason and J. B. Rives. Oxford: Oxford University Press.

Barr, J. 1961. *Semantics of Biblical Language*. London: Oxford University Press.

Barrett, C. K. 1978 [1955]. *The Gospel According to St John: An introduction with commentary and notes on the Greek text*. 2nd edn. London: SPCK.

Barth, K. 1933. *The Epistle to the Romans*, tr. E. K. Hoskyns. London: Oxford University Press.

Bauckham, R. 1981. 'The worship of Jesus in apocalyptic Christianity.' *New Testament Studies* 27:322–41.

——. 2007. *The Testimony of the Beloved Disciple: Narrative, history, and theology in the gospel of John*. Grand Rapids, MI: Baker Academic.

———. 2008. *Jesus and the God of Israel: God crucified and other studies on the New Testament's Christology of divine identity.* Grand Rapids, MI: Eerdmans.

———. 2009. *Jesus and the God of Israel.* Grand Rapids, MI: Eerdmans.

Bauckham, R., and C. Mosser, eds 2008. *The Gospel of John and Christian Theology.* Grand Rapids, MI: Eerdmans.

Bauer, W., F. A. Arndt and F. W. Gingrich, eds 2000. *A Greek-English Lexicon of the New Testament and Other Early Christian Literature.* 3rd edn. [BDAG] Chicago, IL: University of Chicago Press.

Beale, G. K. 2004. *The Temple and the Church's Mission.* Downers Grove, IL: InterVarsity Press.

Beasley-Murray, G. 1986. *Jesus and the Kingdom of God.* Grand Rapids, MI: Eerdmans.

Beckwith, R. T. 1981. 'Daniel 9 and the date of Messiah's coming in Essene, hellenistic, Pharisaic, Zealot and early Christian computation.' *Revue de Qumran* 40:521–42.

———. 1996. *Calendar and Chronology, Jewish and Christian: Biblical, intertestamental and patristic studies.* Leiden: Brill.

Bockmuehl, M. J. 1994. *This Jesus: Martyr, lord, Messiah.* Edinburgh: T&T Clark.

Borg, M. J. 1984. *Conflict, Holiness and Politics in the Teachings of Jesus.* SBEC 5. New York, NY: Edwin Mellen Press.

———. 1987a. *Jesus: A new vision.* San Francisco, CA: Harper & Row.

———. 1987b. 'An orthodoxy reconsidered: the "end-of-the-world Jesus".' Pages 207–17 in *The Glory of Christ in the New Testament: Studies in Christology in memory of George Bradford Caird*, ed. L. D. Hurst and N. T. Wright. Oxford: Clarendon.

———. 1994a. *Jesus in Contemporary Scholarship.* Valley Forge, PA: Trinity Press International.

———. 1994b. *Meeting Jesus Again for the First Time: The historical Jesus and the heart of contemporary faith.* San Francisco, CA: HarperSanFrancisco.

Boucher, M. 1977. *The Mysterious Parable: A literary study.* CBQMS 6. Washington, DC: Catholic Bible Association.

Bowker, J. W. 1973a. *Jesus and the Pharisees.* Cambridge: Cambridge University Press.

———. 1973b. *The Sense of God.* Oxford: Clarendon.

———. 1978. *The Religious Imagination and the Sense of God.* Oxford: Clarendon.

Boyarin, D. 2012. *The Jewish Gospels: The story of the Jewish Christ.* New York, NY: New Press.

Brandon, S. G. F. 1967. *Jesus and the Zealots: A study of the political factor in primitive Christianity*. Manchester: Manchester University Press.

Brueggemann, W. 1972. 'From dust to kingship.' *Zeitschrift für die altestamentliche Wissenschaft* 84:1–18.

Bultmann, R. 1934. *Jesus and the Word*, tr. L. P. Smith and E. H. Lantero. New York, NY: Charles Scribner's Sons.

———. 1953. *Theologie des Neuen Testaments*. Tübingen: Mohr Siebeck.

Burkitt, F. C. 1954 [1910]. Preface to A. Schweitzer, *The Quest of the Historical Jesus: A critical study of its progress from Reimarus to Wrede*. 3rd edn., tr. W. Montgomery. London: A&C Black.

Caird, G. B. 1965. *Jesus and the Jewish Nation*. London: Athlone.

———. 1976. 'Eschatology and politics: some misconceptions.' Pages 72–86 in *Biblical Studies: Essays in honour of William Barclay*, ed. J. R. McKay and J. F. Miller. London: Collins.

———. 1980. *The Language and Imagery of the Bible*. London: Duckworth.

———. 1982. 'Jesus and Israel: the starting point for New Testament Christology.' Pages 58–68 in *Christological Perspectives*, ed. R. Berkey and S. Edwards. New York, NY: Pilgrim.

———. 1983. 'The one and the many in Mark and John.' Pages 39–54 in *Studies of the Church in History: Essays honoring Robert S. Paul on his sixty-fifth birthday*, ed. H. Davies. Allison Park, PA: Pickwick.

Carter, W. 2008. *John and Empire: Initial explorations*. New York, NY: T&T Clark.

Catchpole, D. R. 1993. *The Quest for Q*. Edinburgh: T&T Clark.

Chadwick, H. 2017. 'The Chalcedonian Definition.' Pages 101–14 in *Selected Writings*, ed. W. G. Rusch. Grand Rapids, MI: Eerdmans.

Charlesworth, J. H. 1988. *Jesus within Judaism*. ABRL. New York, NY: Doubleday.

———. 2010. *The Good and Evil Serpent: How a universal symbol became Christianized*. New Haven, CT: Yale University Press.

Chilton, B. D., ed. 1984. *The Kingdom of God in the Teaching of Jesus*. IRT 5. London: SPCK; Philadelphia, PA: Fortress.

———. 1987. *God in Strength: Jesus' announcement of the kingdom*. SNTU 1. Freistadt: Plöchl 1979. Repr., BibSem 8. Sheffield: JSOT Press.

———. 1991. '[ὡς] φραγέλλιον ἐκ σχοινίων (John 2:15).' Pages 330–44 in *Templum Amicitiae: Essays on the second Temple presented to Ernst Bammel*, ed. W. Horbury. Sheffield: JSOT Press.

———. 1992. *The Temple of Jesus: His sacrificial program within a cultural history of sacrifice*. University Park, PA: Pennsylvania State University Press.

Chilton, B. D., and C. A. Evans. 1997. *Jesus in Context: Temple, purity, and restoration*. AGJU 39. Leiden: Brill.

Collins, A. Y., and J. J. Collins. 2008. *King and Messiah as Son of God: Divine, human and angelic messianic figures in biblical and related literature*. Grand Rapids, MI: Eerdmans.

Collins, J. J. 1993. *Daniel*. Hermeneia. Minneapolis, MN: Fortress.

——. 2010. *The Scepter and the Star: Messianism in light of the Dead Sea Scrolls*. 2nd edn. Grand Rapids, MI: Eerdmans.

Congdon, D. W. 2015. *Rudolf Bultmann: A companion to his theology*. Eugene, OR: Cascade.

Crossan, J. Dominic. 1988. *The Cross that Spoke: The origins of the Passion narrative*. San Francisco, CA: HarperSanFrancisco.

——. 1991. *The Historical Jesus: The life of a Mediterranean Jewish peasant*. Edinburgh: T&T Clark; San Francisco, CA: HarperSanFrancisco.

——. 1995. *Who Killed Jesus? Exposing the roots of anti-semitism in the gospel story of the death of Jesus*. San Francisco, CA: HarperSanFrancisco.

——. 1998. *The Birth of Christianity*. San Francisco, CA: HarperSanFrancisco.

Cupitt, D. 1979. *The Debate about Christ*. London: SCM Press.

Daniel Kirk, J. R. 2016. *A Man Attested by God: The human Jesus of the synoptic gospels*. Grand Rapids, MI: Eerdmans.

Davies, J. 2016. *Paul among the Apocalypses*. London: Bloomsbury.

Davies, W. D. 1948. *Paul and Rabbinic Judaism*. London: SPCK.

——. 1964. *The Setting of the Sermon on the Mount*. Cambridge: Cambridge University Press.

——. 1980. *Paul and Rabbinic Judaism*. 4th edn. Philadelphia, PA: Fortress.

Davies, W. D., and D. C. Allison. 1988. *A Critical and Exegetical Commentary on the Gospel According to Saint Matthew*. Vol. 1. ICC. Edinburgh: T&T Clark.

——. 1997. *A Critical and Exegetical Commentary on the Gospel According to Saint Matthew*. Vol. 3. ICC. Edinburgh: T&T Clark.

Dodd, C. H. 1961. *The Parables of the Kingdom*. London: Fontana.

——. 1965 [1952]. *According to the Scriptures: The sub-structure of New Testament theology*. London: Fontana.

——. 1971. *The Founder of Christianity*. London: Collins.

Downing, F. G. 1988. *Christ and the Cynics: Jesus and other radical preachers in first-century tradition*. JSOT Manuals 4. Sheffield: Sheffield Academic Press.

——. 1992. *Cynics and Christian Origins*. Edinburgh: T&T Clark.

Drury, J. 1985. *The Parables in the Gospels: History and allegory*. London: SPCK.

Du Maurier, D. 1966. *What I Believe*, ed. G. Unwin. London: George Allen & Unwin.

Duling, D. 1973. 'The promises to David and their entrance into Christianity: nailing down a likely hypothesis.' *New Testament Studies* 20:55–77.

Dunn, J. D. G. 1980. *Christology in the Making*. London: SCM Press.

Eco, U. 1979. *A Theory of Semiotics*. Bloomington, IN: Indiana University Press.

Edwards, R. A. 1971. *The Sign of Jonah in the Theology of the Evangelists and Q*. London: SCM Press.

Elliott, J. H. 2000. *1 Peter: A new translation with introduction and commentary*. New Haven, CT: Yale University Press.

Ellis, E. E. 1991. *The Old Testament in Early Christianity: Canon and interpretation in the light of modern research*. Tübingen: Mohr Siebeck; US edn.: Grand Rapids, MI: Baker, 1992.

Epstein, I. 1959. *Judaism*. Harmondsworth: Penguin.

Epstein, V. 1964. 'The historicity of the gospel account of the cleansing of the Temple.' *Zeitschrift für die neutestamentliche Wissenschaft* 55:42–58.

Evans, C. A. 1995. *Jesus and His Contemporaries: Comparative studies*. AGJU 25. Leiden: Brill.

———. 1999. 'Authenticating the words of Jesus.' Pages 3–14 in *Authenticating the Words of Jesus*, ed. B. D. Chilton and C. A. Evans. NTTS 28/1. Leiden: Brill.

Farmer, W. R. 1956. *Maccabees, Zealots, and Josephus: An inquiry into Jewish nationalism in the greco-roman period*. New York, NY: Columbia University Press.

———. 1964. *The Synoptic Problem: A critical analysis*. London: Macmillan.

Ferda, T. 2014. 'Naming the Messiah: a contribution to the 4Q246 "son of God" debate.' *Dead Sea Discoveries* 21:150–75.

Fishbane, M. A. 1975. 'The sacred center: the symbolic structure of the Bible.' Pages 6–27 in *Texts and Responses: Studies presented to Nahum N. Glatzer on the occasion of his seventieth birthday by his students*, ed. M. A. Fishbane and P. R. Flohr. Leiden: Brill.

———. 2014. 'The sacred center: the symbolic structure of the Bible.' Pages 389–408 in *Cult and Cosmos: Tilting toward a Temple-centered theology*. Leuven: Peeters.

Fitzmyer, J. A. 1985. *The Gospel According to Luke X—XXIV*. AB 28a. New York, NY: Doubleday.

———. 1997 [1979]. *The Semitic Background of the New Testament. Vol. 2: A Wandering Aramean: Collected Aramaic essays*. Grand Rapids, MI: Eerdmans.

Fletcher-Louis, C. 2015. *Jesus Monotheism*. Eugene, OR: Cascade.

Flew, R. N. 1938. *Jesus and His Church*. London: Epworth.

Foster, P. 2015. 'Echoes without resonance: critiquing certain aspects of recent scholarly trends in the study of the Jewish scriptures in the New Testament.' *Journal for the Study of the New Testament* 38:96–11.

France, R. T. 1971. *Jesus and the Old Testament*. London: Tyndale.

——. 1982. 'The worship of Jesus: a neglected factor in christological debate.' Pages 17–36 in *Christ the Lord: Studies in Christology presented to Donald Guthrie*, ed. H. H. Rowdon. Leicester: IVP.

——. 2007. *The Gospel of Matthew*. NICNT. Grand Rapids, MI: Eerdmans.

Freyne, S. 1988. *Galilee, Jesus and the Gospels: Literary approaches and historical investigations*. Philadelphia, PA: Fortress.

Funk, R. W. 1973. *A Greek Grammar of the New Testament and Other Early Christian Literature*. 5th edn. Chicago, IL: University of Chicago Press.

——. 1996. *Honest to Jesus: Jesus for a new millennium*. San Francisco, CA: HarperSanFrancisco.

Funk, R. W., and R. W. Hoover, eds. 1993. *The Five Gospels: The search for the authentic words of Jesus*. New York, NY: Macmillan.

Funk, R. W., B. B. Scott and J. R. Butts, eds. 1988. *The Parables of Jesus: Red letter edition. A report of the Jesus Seminar*. Sonoma, CA: Polebridge.

Goodrich, J. K., B. Blackwell and J. Mastin, eds 2016. *Paul and the Apocalyptic Imagination*. Minneapolis, MN: Fortress.

Goppelt, L. 1981. *Theology of the New Testament. Vol. 1: The Ministry of Jesus in Its Theological Significance*, tr. J. Alsup. Grand Rapids, MI: Eerdmans.

Goulder, M. D. 1989. *Luke: A new paradigm*. Sheffield: Sheffield Academic Press.

Grayling, A. C. 2011. *The Good Book: A secular bible*. London: Bloomsbury.

Haenchen, E. 1984. *John: A commentary on the gospel of John. Chapters 7–21*. Minneapolis, MN: Fortress.

Harrington, D. J. 1991. *The Gospel of Matthew*. Collegeville, MN: Liturgical Press.

Harvey, A. E. 1976. *Jesus on Trial: A study in the fourth gospel*. London: SPCK.

——. 1982. *Jesus and the Constraints of History: The Bampton Lectures, 1980*. London: Duckworth.

——. 1987. 'Christ as agent.' Pages 239–50 in *The Glory of Christ in the New Testament: Studies in Christology in memory of George Bradford Caird*, ed. L. D. Hurst and N. T. Wright. Oxford: Clarendon.

Hay, D. 1989 [1973]. *Glory at the Right Hand: Psalm 110 in early Christianity*. Atlanta, GA: SBL.

Hays, R. B. 1989. *Echoes of Scripture in the Letters of Paul*. London: Bloomsbury.

———. 1997. *First Corinthians*. Louisville, KY: John Knox.

———. 2002 [1983]. *The Faith of Jesus Christ: An investigation of the narrative substructure of Galatians 3:1—4:11*. 2nd edn. Grand Rapids, MI: Eerdmans.

———. 2005. *The Conversion of the Imagination: Paul as interpreter of Israel's scriptures*. Grand Rapids, MI: Eerdmans.

———. 2014. *Reading Backwards: Figural Christology and the fourfold gospel witness*. Waco, TX: Baylor University Press.

———. 2016. *Echoes of Scripture in the Gospels*. Waco, TX: Baylor University Press.

Hayward, C. T. R. 1992. 'The figure of Adam in Pseudo-Philo's Biblical Antiquities.' *Journal for the Study of Judaism* 23:1–20.

Hengel, M. 1971 [1970]. *Was Jesus a Revolutionist?*, tr. W. Klassen. Biblical Series 28. Philadelphia, PA: Fortress.

———. 1973 [1971]. *Victory over Violence: Jesus and the revolutionists*. Philadelphia, PA: Fortress.

———. 1974. *Judaism and Hellenism: Studies in their encounter in Palestine during the early hellenistic period*, tr. J. Bowden. 2 vols. London: SCM.

———. 1977. *Der Sohn Gottes: Die Entstehung der Christologie und die jüdisch-hellenistische Religionsgeschichte*. 2nd edn. Tübingen: Mohr Siebeck.

———. 1981a. *The Atonement: The origins of the doctrine in the New Testament*, tr. J. Bowden. London: SCM Press.

———. 1981b. *The Charismatic Leader and His Followers*, tr. J. C. G. Greig. Edinburgh: T&T Clark.

———. 1991. 'Reich Christi, Reich Gottes und Weltreich im Johannesevangelium.' Pages 163–84 in *Königsherrschaft Gottes und himmlischer Kult in Judentum, Urchristentum und in der hellenistischen Welt*, ed. M. Hengel and A. M. Schwemer. Tübingen: Mohr Siebeck.

———. 1996. 'Zur Wirkungsgeschichte von Jes 53 in vorchristlicher Zeit.' Pages 49–91 in *Der leidende Gottesknecht: Jesaja 53 und seine Wirkungsgeschichte*, ed. B. Janowski and P. Stuhlmacher. FAT 14. Tübingen: Mohr Siebeck.

Hick, J., ed. 1977. *The Myth of God Incarnate*. London: SCM Press.

Hill, W. 2015. *Paul and the Trinity: Persons, relations, and the Pauline letters*. Grand Rapids, MI: Eerdmans.

Holtzmann, H. J. 1907. *Das Messianische Bewusstsein Jesu: Ein Beitrag zur Leben-Jesu-Forschung*. Tübingen: Mohr Siebeck.

Hooker, M. D. 1972. 'On using the wrong tool.' *Theology* 75:570–81.

———. 1975. 'In his own image?' Pages 28–44 in *What about the New Testament? Essays in honour of Christopher Evans*, ed. M. D. Hooker and C. Hickling. London: SCM Press.

Bibliography

Hoover, R. W. 1971. 'The *harpagmos* enigma: a philological solution.' *Harvard Theological Review* 64:95–119.

Horbury, W. 2003. *Messianism among Jews and Christians: Twelve biblical and historical studies.* London: T&T Clark.

Horsley, G. H. R. et al., eds. 1981–. *New Documents Illustrating Early Christianity.* North Ryde, NSW: The Ancient History Documentary Research Centre, Macquarie University.

Horsley, R. A. 1987. *Jesus and the Spiral of Violence: Popular Jewish resistance in Roman Palestine.* San Francisco, CA: Harper & Row.

Hurtado, L. 1988. *One God, One Lord: Early Christian devotion and ancient Jewish monotheism.* London: SCM Press.

——. 2003. *Lord Jesus Christ: Devotion to Jesus in earliest Christianity.* Grand Rapids, MI: Eerdmans.

——. 2012. *Who Is This Son of Man? The latest scholarship on a puzzling expression of the historical Jesus.* London: T&T Clark.

Jeremias, J. 1966. *Abba: Studien zur neutestamentlichen Theologie und Zeitgeschichte.* Göttingen: Vandenhoeck & Ruprecht.

Jipp, J. W. 2015. *Christ Is King: Paul's royal ideology.* Minneapolis, MN: Fortress.

Johnson, L. T. 1994. Review of N. T. Wright, *The New Testament and the People of God. Journal of Biblical Literature* 113:536–8.

——. 1995. *The Real Jesus.* San Francisco, CA: HarperSanFrancisco.

——. 1999. *Living Jesus: Learning the heart of the gospel.* San Francisco, CA: HarperSanFrancisco.

Josipovici, G. 2011. 'The Good Book.' Review of A. C. Grayling, *The Good Book: A secular bible. Times Literary Supplement* 10 June: 6.

Käsemann, E. 1964. 'The problem of the historical Jesus.' Pages 15–47 in *Essays on New Testament Themes*, tr. W. J. Montague. London: SCM Press.

Keener, C. 2003. *The Gospel of John: A commentary.* Peabody, MA: Hendrickson.

Klawans, J. 2006. *Purity, Sacrifice, and the Temple: Symbolism and supersessionism in the study of ancient Judaism.* Oxford: Oxford University Press.

Kloppenborg, J. S. 1987. *The Formation of Q: Trajectories in ancient wisdom collections.* Philadelphia, PA: Fortress.

——. 1990. '"Easter faith" and the sayings gospel Q.' *Semeia* 49:71–100.

Koch, K. 1972 [1970]. *The Rediscovery of Apocalyptic: A polemical work on a neglected area of biblical studies and its damaging effects on theology and philosophy*, tr. M. Kohl. SBT 2.22. London: SCM Press.

Koestenberger, A. I. 1999. *Encountering John: The gospel in historical, literary, and theological perspective.* Grand Rapids, MI: Baker.

Koester, H. 1990. *Ancient Christian Gospels: Their history and development.* London: Trinity Press International.

Kvalbein, H. 2003. 'The kingdom of God and the kingship of Christ in the fourth gospel.' Pages 215–32 in *Neotestamentica et Philonica: Studies in honor of Peder Borge*, ed. D. E. Aune, T. Seland and J. H. Ulrichsen. Leiden: Brill.

Ladd, G. E. 1966. *Jesus and the Kingdom: The eschatology of biblical realism.* London: SPCK.

Lightfoot, J. B. 2015. *The Gospel of St John: A newly discovered commentary*, ed. B. Witherington and T. D. Still. Downers Grove, IL: InterVarsity Press.

Lincoln, A. T. 2000. *Truth on Trial: The lawsuit motif in the fourth gospel.* Peabody, MA: Hendrickson.

Lindars, B. 1961. *New Testament Apologetic: The doctrinal significance of the Old Testament quotations.* London: SCM Press.

———. 1972. *The Gospel of John.* London: Oliphants.

Lohfink, G. 1984. *Jesus and Community.* Philadelphia, PA: Fortress; New York, NY: Paulist Press.

Longenecker, R. N. 1975. *Biblical Exegesis in the Apostolic Period.* Grand Rapids, MI: Eerdmans.

Luz, U. 2005. *Matthew 21—28.* Hermeneia. Minneapolis, MN: Fortress.

Mack, B. L. 1987. 'The kingdom sayings in Mark.' *Forum* 3(1):3–47.

———. 1988. *A Myth of Innocence: Mark and Christian origins.* Philadelphia, PA: Fortress.

———. 1992. 'Q and the gospel of Mark: revising Christian origins.' *Semeia* 55:15–39.

———. 1993. *The Lost Gospel: The book of Q and Christian origins.* San Francisco, CA: HarperCollins; Shaftesbury: Element.

Maier, G. 1977. *The End of the Historical-Critical Method*, tr. E. W. Leveranz and R. F. Norden. St Louis, MO: Concordia.

Manson, T. W. 1931. *The Teaching of Jesus.* Cambridge: Cambridge University Press.

Marcus, J. 1992. *The Way of the Lord: Christological exegesis of the Old Testament in the gospel of Mark.* Louisville, KY: Westminster John Knox.

———. 2003. 'Son of man as son of Adam.' *Revue Biblique* 110:38–61, 370–86.

———. 2004 [1992]. *The Way of the Lord: Christological exegesis of the Old Testament in the gospel of Mark.* 2nd edn. Edinburgh: T&T Clark.

Martin, D. 2011. 'Heapeth Up Riches.' Review of A. C. Grayling, *The Good Book: A secular bible. Times Literary Supplement* 3 June: 25–6.

Martinez, F. G. 1992. *Qumran and Apocalyptic: Studies on the Aramaic texts from Qumran.* STDJ 9. Leiden: Brill.

Martinez, F. G., and E. J. C. Tigchelaar, eds. 1998. *The Dead Sea Scrolls Study Edition*. Leiden: Brill.

May, H. G. 1962. 'The king in the garden of Eden: a study of Ezekiel 28:12–19.' Pages 166–76 in *Israel's Prophetic Heritage*, ed. B. W. Anderson and W. Harrelson. London: SCM Press.

McEvenue, E., and B. F. Meyer, eds. 1991. *Lonergan's Hermeneutics: Its development and application*. Washington, DC: Catholic University of America Press.

McGilchrist, I. 2009. *The Master and His Emissary*. New Haven, CT: Yale University Press.

McKnight, S. 2007. *A Community Called Atonement*. Nashville, TN: Abingdon.

McNicol, A. J. et al., eds. 1996. *Beyond the Impasse: Luke's use of Matthew*. Valley Forge, PA: Trinity Press International.

Meadors, E. P. 1995. *Jesus the Messianic Herald of Salvation*. WUNT 2.72. Tübingen: Mohr Siebeck.

Meier, J. P. 1991. *A Marginal Jew: Rethinking the historical Jesus. Vol. 1: The Roots of the Problem and the Person*. ABRL 3. New York, NY: Doubleday.

——. 1994. *A Marginal Jew: Rethinking the historical Jesus. Vol. 2: Mentor, Message, and Miracles*. ABRL 9. New York, NY: Doubleday.

Metzger, B. M. 1994. *A Textual Commentary on the Greek New Testament*. 2nd edn. Stuttgart: Deutsche Bibelgesellschaft.

Meyer, B. F. 1979. *The Aims of Jesus*. London: SCM Press.

——. 1989. *Critical Realism and the New Testament*. Allison Park, PA: Pickwick.

——. 1991. 'A caricature of Joachim Jeremias and his work.' *Journal of Biblical Literature* 110:451–62.

——. 1992a. *Christus Faber: The master-builder and the house of God*. PTMS 29. Allison Park, PA: Pickwick.

——. 1992b. 'Jesus Christ.' *ABD* 3:773–96.

——. 1994. *Reality and Illusion in New Testament Scholarship: A primer in critical realist hermeneutics*. Collegeville, MN: Liturgical Press.

——. 2002. *The Aims of Jesus: With a new introduction by N. T. Wright*. London: SCM Press. Repr., San Jose, CA: Pickwick.

Middleton, J. R. 2005. *The Liberating Image: The imago dei in Genesis 1*. Grand Rapids, MI: Brazos.

——. 2014. *A New Heaven and a New Earth: Reclaiming biblical eschatology*. Grand Rapids, MI: Baker Academic.

Miller, R. J. 1992. *The Complete Gospels: Annotated Scholars Version*. Sonoma, CA: Polebridge.

Moberly, R. W. L. 2017. 'Scriptural echoes and gospel interpretation: some questions.' *Journal of Theological Interpretation* 11(1):5–20.

Moffitt, D. M. 2011. *Atonement and the Logic of Resurrection in the Epistle to the Hebrews*. Leiden: Brill.

Moloney, F. J. 1981. 'The re-interpretation of Psalm VIII and the son of man debate.' *New Testament Studies* 27:656–71.

———. 2012. 'Recent Johannine studies. Part Two: Monographs.' *Expository Times* 123(9):417–28.

Moore, S. 2006. *Empire and Apocalypse: Postcolonialism and the New Testament*. Sheffield: Phoenix.

Morales, L. M. 2015. *Who Shall Ascend the Mountain of the Lord? A biblical theology of the book of Leviticus*. Downers Grove, IL: InterVarsity Press.

Morgan, R. 1987. 'The historical Jesus and the theology of the New Testament.' Pages 187–206 in *The Glory of Christ in the New Testament: Studies in Christology in memory of George Bradford Caird*, ed. L. D. Hurst and N. T. Wright. Oxford: Clarendon.

Morris, L. 1971. *The Gospel According to John: The English text with introduction, exposition and notes*. Grand Rapids, MI: Eerdmans.

Moule, C. F. D. 1967. *The Phenomenon of the New Testament*. London: SCM Press.

———. 1977. *The Origins of Christology*. Cambridge: Cambridge University Press.

Neill, S. C. 1964. *The Interpretation of the New Testament 1861–1961*. London: Oxford University Press.

Nickelsburg, G. W. E. 2006. *Resurrection, Immortality, and Eternal Life in Intertestamental Judaism and Early Christianity*. Expanded edn HTS 56. Cambridge, MA: Harvard University Press.

Nolland, J. 2005. *The Gospel of Matthew: A commentary on the Greek text*. NIGTC. Grand Rapids, MI: Eerdmans.

Novenson, M. 2012. *Christ among the Messiahs: Christ language in Paul and Messiah language in ancient Judaism*. Oxford: Oxford University Press.

Oakes, P. 2000. *Philippians: From people to letter*. Cambridge: Cambridge University Press.

Patterson, S. J. 1993. *The Gospel of Thomas and Jesus*. Sonoma, CA: Polebridge.

Peppard, M. 2011. *The Son of God in the Roman World: Divine sonship in its social and political context*. Oxford: Oxford University Press.

Perrin, N. 1970. *What Is Redaction Criticism?* Philadelphia, PA: Fortress.

Perrin, N., and D. C. Duling. 1982. *The New Testament: An introduction*. 2nd edn. New York, NY: Harcourt Brace Jovanovich.

Petersen, N. R. 1978. *Literary Criticism for New Testament Critics*. Philadelphia, PA: Fortress.

Portier-Young, A. E. 2011. *Apocalypse against Empire: Theologies of resistance in early Judaism*. Grand Rapids, MI: Eerdmans.

Potok, C. 1974. *My Name Is Asher Lev*. Harmondsworth: Penguin.

Radner, E. 2016. *Time and the Word: Figural reading of the Christian scriptures*. Grand Rapids, MI: Eerdmans.

Reimarus, H. S. 1970 [1778]. *Fragments*, ed. C. H. Talbert, tr. R. S. Fraser. Philadelphia, PA: Fortress.

Rensberger, D. 1988. *Johannine Faith and Liberating Community*. Philadelphia, PA: Westminster.

Riches, J. K. 1980. *Jesus and the Transformation of Judaism*. London: Darton, Longman & Todd.

Richey, L. B. 2007. *Roman Imperial Ideology and the Gospel of John*. CBQMS 43. Washington, DC: Catholic Biblical Association of America.

Roberts, J. M. 1992. *The History of the World*. 2nd edn. Oxford: Helicon.

Robinson, J. M. 1959. *A New Quest of the Historical Jesus*. London: SCM Press.

Rowland, C. C. 2007. 'The Temple in the New Testament.' Pages 469–83 in *Temple and Worship in Biblical Israel*, ed. J. Day. London: T&T Clark.

Ruether, R. R. 1974. *Faith and Fratricide: The theological roots of anti-semitism*. New York, NY: Seabury.

Runnals, D. R. 1983. 'The king as temple builder: a messianic typology.' Pages 15–37 in *Spirit within Structure: Essays in honor of George Johnston on the occasion of his seventieth birthday*, ed. E. J. Furcha. Allison Park, PA: Pickwick.

Safrai, S. 1985. *Pilgrimage at the Time of the Second Temple*. Jerusalem: Akademon.

Sanders, E. P. 1977. *Paul and Palestinian Judaism: A comparison of patterns of religion*. Philadelphia, PA: Fortress; London: SCM Press.

——. 1985. *Jesus and Judaism*. Philadelphia, PA: Fortress; London: SCM Press.

——. 1991. 'Defending the indefensible.' *Journal of Biblical Literature* 110: 463–77.

——. 1992. *Judaism: Practice and belief, 63 BCE – 66 CE*. London: SCM Press; Philadelphia, PA: Trinity Press International.

——. 1993. *The Historical Figure of Jesus*. London: Penguin.

——. 2008. 'Comparing Judaism and Christianity: an academic autobiography.' Pages 11–41 in *Redefining First-century Jewish and Christian Identities:*

Essays in honor of E. P. Sanders, ed. F. E. Udoh et al. South Bend, IN: University of Notre Dame Press.

Sanders, E. P., and M. Davies. 1989. *Studying the Synoptic Gospels.* London: SCM Press; Philadelphia, PA: Trinity Press International.

Schillebeeckx, E. 1979. *Jesus: An experiment in Christology,* tr. H. Hoskins. London: Collins.

———. 1980. *Christ: The experience of Jesus as lord.* London: Collins.

Schnelle, U. 2009. *Theology of the New Testament.* Grand Rapids, MI: Baker Academic.

Schoeps, H. J. 1959. *Paul: The theology of the apostle in light of Jewish religious history,* tr. H. Knight. London: Lutterworth.

Schulz, S. 1972. *Q: Die Spruchquelle der Evangelisten.* Zürich: Theologischer Verlag.

Schweitzer, A. 1901. *Das Messianitäts- und Leidensgeheimnis: Eine Skizze des Lebens Jesu.* Tübingen: Mohr Siebeck.

———. 1906. *Von Reimarus zu Wrede: Eine Geschichte der Leben-Jesu-Forschung.* Tübingen: Mohr Siebeck.

———. 1925. *The Mystery of the Kingdom of God,* tr. W. Lowrie. London: A&C Black.

———. 1954. *The Quest of the Historical Jesus,* tr. W. Montgomery. 3rd edn. London: A&C Black.

Scott, J. M. 1992. *Adoption as Sons of God: An exegetical investigation into the background of ΥΙΟΘΕΣΙΑ in the Pauline corpus.* WUNT 2.48. Tübingen: Mohr Siebeck.

———, ed. 2017. *Exile: A conversation with N. T. Wright.* Downers Grove, IL: InterVarsity Press.

Segal, A. 1977. *Two Powers in Heaven: Early rabbinic reports about Christianity and Gnosticism.* Leiden: Brill.

Segal, M. 2014. 'Who is the "son of God" in 4Q246? An overlooked example of biblical interpretation.' *Dead Sea Discoveries* 21:289–312.

Smith, M. 1977. 'Palestinian Judaism in the first century.' Pages 183–97 in *Essays in Greco-Roman and Related Talmudic Literature,* ed. H. Fischel. New York, NY: Ktav.

Stanton, G. N. 1974. *Jesus of Nazareth in New Testament Preaching.* Cambridge: Cambridge University Press.

———. 2004. *Jesus and Gospel.* Cambridge: Cambridge University Press.

Steudel, A. 1996. 'The eternal reign of the people of God: collective expectations in Qumran texts (4Q264 and 1QM).' *Revue de Qumran* 17:507–25.

Swartley, W. M. 1994. *Israel's Scripture Traditions and the Synoptic Gospel: Story shaping story.* Peabody, MA: Hendrickson.

Temple, W. 1945. *Readings in St. John's Gospel (First and Second Series)*. London: Macmillan.

Thatcher, T. 2008. *Greater Than Caesar: Christology and empire in the fourth gospel*. Minneapolis, MN: Fortress.

Theissen, G. 1986. *Der Schatten des Galiläers: Historische Jesusforschung in erzählender Form*. Munich: Kaiser.

Thiselton, A. C. 2000. *The First Epistle to the Corinthians: A commentary on the Greek text*. NIGTC. Grand Rapids, MI: Eerdmans.

Tooman, W. 2011. *Gog of Magog: Reuse of scripture and compositional technique in Ezekiel 38–39*. Tübingen: Mohr Siebeck.

Tuckett, C. M. 1986. *Nag Hammadi and the Gospel Tradition: Synoptic tradition in the Nag Hammadi library*. SNTW. Edinburgh: T&T Clark.

——. 1988. 'Thomas and the synoptics.' *Novum Testamentum* 30:132–57.

——. 1996. *Q and the History of Early Christianity*. Edinburgh: T&T Clark.

Vaage, L. 1994. *Galilean Upstarts: Jesus' first followers according to Q*. Valley Forge, PA: Trinity Press International.

Valantasis, R. 1997. *The Gospel of Thomas*. London: Routledge.

Vermes, G. 1973. *Jesus the Jew: A historian's reading of the gospels*. London: Collins.

——. 1981. *Jesus the Jew: A historian's reading of the gospels*. 2nd edn. Philadelphia, PA: Fortress.

——. 1983. *Jesus and the World of Judaism*. London: SCM Press.

——. 1993. *The Religion of Jesus the Jew*. London: SCM Press; Minneapolis, MN: Fortress.

——. 1997. *The Complete Dead Sea Scrolls in English*. London: Allen Lane.

von Harnack, A. 1984-1989. *History of Dogma*, tr. Neil Buchanan. 7 vols. London: Williams & Norgate.

Wansbrough, H. 1991. *Jesus and the Oral Gospel Tradition*. JSNTSup 64. Sheffield: JSOT Press.

Watson, F. B. 1985. 'Why was Jesus crucified?' *Theology* 88:105–112.

——. 2015 [2004]. *Paul and the Hermeneutics of Faith*. 2nd edn. Grand Rapids, MI: Eerdmans.

Watts, R. E. 2000 [1997]. *Isaiah's New Exodus in Mark*. Rev. edn. Grand Rapids, MI: Baker.

Wedderburn, A. J. M. 1999. *Beyond Resurrection*. London: SCM Press.

Whitsett, C. 2000. 'Son of God, seed of David: Paul's messianic exegesis in Romans 2:3–4.' *Journal of Biblical Literature* 119:61–81.

Williams, R. 1998 [1979]. *The Wound of Knowledge*. Eugene, OR: Wipf & Stock.

Wink, W. 1984. *Naming the Powers: The language of power in the New Testament.* Philadelphia, PA: Fortress.

Witherington, B. 1990. *The Christology of Jesus.* Minneapolis, MN: Fortress.

——. 1994. *Jesus the Sage: The pilgrimage of wisdom.* Minneapolis, MN: Fortress.

——. 1995. *The Jesus Quest: The third search for the Jew of Nazareth.* Downers Grove, IL: InterVarsity Press.

Wrede, W. 1901. *Das Messiasgeheimnis in den Evangelien: Zugleich ein Beitrag zum Verständnis des Markusevangeliums.* Göttingen: Vandenhoeck & Ruprecht.

Wright, N. T. 1980. 'The Messiah and the people of God: a study in Pauline theology with particular reference to the argument of the epistle to the Romans.' DPhil diss., Oxford University.

——. 1982. 'Towards a third "Quest"?: Jesus then and now.' *ARC* 10(1):20–7.

——. 1985. 'Jesus, Israel and the cross.' Pages 75–95 in *SBL Seminar Papers 1985,* ed. K. H. Richards. Atlanta, GA: Scholars Press.

——. 1991. *The Climax of the Covenant: Christ and the law in Pauline theology.* Edinburgh: T&T Clark; Minneapolis, MN: Fortress.

——. 1992a. *The New Testament and the People of God.* COQG 1. London: SPCK; Minneapolis, MN: Fortress.

——. 1992b. 'Quest for the historical Jesus.' *ABD* 3:796–802.

——. 1994. 'Gospel and theology in Galatians.' Pages 222–39 in *Gospel in Paul: Studies on Corinthians, Galatians and Romans for Richard N. Longenecker,* ed. L. A. Jervis and P. Richardson. JSNTSup 108. Sheffield: Sheffield Academic Press.

——. 1996a. 'Jesus.' Pages 43–58 in *Early Christian Thought in Its Jewish Context: Festschrift in honour of Morna Hooker's sixty-fifth birthday,* ed. J. Barclay and J. Sweet. Cambridge: Cambridge University Press.

——. 1996b. *Jesus and the Victory of God.* COQG 2. London: SPCK; Minneapolis, MN: Fortress.

——. 2000. 'A new birth? An article review of John Dominic Crossan's *The Birth of Christianity: Discovering what happened in the years immediately after the execution of Jesus.' Scottish Journal of Theology* 53(1):72–91.

——. 2002. 'Romans.' Pages 393–770 in *The New Interpreter's Bible,* vol. 10, ed. L. E. Keck et al. Nashville, TN: Abingdon.

——. 2003. *The Resurrection of the Son of God.* COQG 3. London: SPCK; Minneapolis, MN: Fortress.

——. 2006a. '4QMMT and Paul: justification, "works," and eschatology.' Pages 104–32 in *History and Exegesis: New Testament essays in honor of Dr. E.*

Bibliography

Earle Ellis on his eightieth birthday, ed. S.-W. Son. New York, NY: T&T Clark.

——. 2006b. *Evil and the Justice of God*. London: SPCK.

——. 2007. *Surprised by Hope*. London: SPCK; San Francisco, CA: HarperOne.

——. 2011a. *The New Testament for Everyone* (US edn., *The Kingdom New Testament*). London: SPCK; San Francisco, CA: HarperOne.

——. 2011b. *Scripture and the Authority of God*. 2nd edn. San Francisco, CA: HarperOne (UK edn., London: SPCK, 2013).

——. 2012. *How God Became King*. London: SPCK; Minneapolis, MN: Fortress; San Francisco, CA: HarperOne.

——. 2013a. 'The evangelists' use of the Old Testament as an implicit overarching narrative.' Pages 189–200 in *Biblical Interpretation and Method: Studies in honour of John Barton*, ed. K. J. Dell and P. M. Joyce. Oxford: Oxford University Press.

——. 2013b. *Paul and the Faithfulness of God*. COQG 4. London: SPCK; Minneapolis, MN: Fortress Press.

——. 2015. *Paul and His Recent Interpreters*. London: SPCK; Minneapolis, MN: Fortress.

——. 2016a. *The Day the Revolution Began: Reconsidering the meaning of Jesus' crucifixion*. San Francisco, CA: HarperOne; London: SPCK.

——. 2016b. *God in Public: How the Bible speaks truth to power today*. London: SPCK.

——. 2017. 'Pictures, stories and the cross: where do the echoes lead?' *Journal of Theological Interpretation* 11(1):49–68.

——. 2018a. 'Hope deferred? Against the dogma of delay.' *Early Christianity* 9(1):37–82.

——. 2018b. *Paul: A biography*. London: SPCK.

——. 2018c. 'Son of man – lord of the Temple? Gospel echoes of Psalm 8 and the ongoing christological debate.' Pages 77–96 in *The Earliest Perceptions of Jesus in Context: Essays in honour of John Nolland on his seventieth birthday*, ed. A. W. White, D. Wenham and C. A. Evans. London: Bloomsbury.

——. 2019. *History and Eschatology: Jesus and the promise of natural theology*. London: SPCK; Waco, TX: Baylor University Press.

Wright, N. T., and M. Borg. 1999. *The Meaning of Jesus: Two visions*. London: SPCK; San Francisco, CA: HarperOne.

Wright, N. T., and J. P. Davies. 2015. 'John, Jesus, and "the ruler of this world": demonic politics in the fourth gospel?' Pages 71–89 in *Conception, Reception, and the Spirit: Essays in honor of Andrew T. Lincoln*, ed. J. G. McConville and L. K. Pietersen. Eugene, OR: Wipf & Stock.

Acknowledgments

The author and publisher are grateful for permission to reproduce the following material listed below in this volume.

Chapter 1: 'Towards a Third "Quest"? Jesus Then and Now.' Reprinted with permission from *ARC* (journal of the Faculty of Religious Studies at McGill University, Montreal) vol. 10, 1982, pp. 20–7.

Chapter 2: 'Jesus, Israel and the Cross.' Reprinted, with permission, from *SBL 1985 Seminar Papers*, ed. K. H. Richards. Chico, California: Scholars Press, 75–95.

Chapter 3: '"Constraints" and the Jesus of History.' Reprinted from *Scottish Journal of Theology* 39.2, 1986, pp. 189–210.

Chapter 4: 'Taking the Text with Her Pleasure: A Post-Post-Modernist Response to J. Dominic Crossan, *The Historical Jesus: The Life of a Mediterranean Jewish Peasant* (T&T Clark, HarperSanFrancisco, 1991) (With apologies to A. A. Milne, St Paul and James Joyce).' Reprinted with permission from *Theology* 96, 1993, 303–10.

Chapter 5: 'Jesus', in *Early Christian Thought in Its Jewish Context*, ed. John Barclay & John Sweet. Cambridge: Cambridge University Press, 1996, 43–58.

Chapter 6: 'Five Gospels but No Gospel: Jesus and the Seminar.' Reprinted with permission from *Authenticating the Activities of Jesus*, ed. Bruce Chilton and Craig A. Evans. Leiden: Brill, 1999, 83–120. Slightly revised from earlier publication in W. R. Farmer (ed.), *Crises in Christology: Essays in Quest of Resolution*. Dove Booksellers, Livonia, MI, 1995, 115–157.

Chapter 7: 'Resurrection in Q?' Reprinted with permission from *Christology, Controversy and Community: New Testament Essays in Honour of David R. Catchpole*, ed. D. G. Horrell and C. M. Tuckett. Leiden: Brill, 2000, 85–97.

Chapter 8: 'Introduction to the Second Edition of B. F. Meyer, *The Aims of Jesus*.' Princeton Theological Monograph Series no. 48. San Jose, CA: Pickwick, 2002, 9a–9l: reprinted by permission.

Chapter 9: 'Kingdom Come: The Public Meaning of the Gospels.' Reprinted by permission from *The Christian Century*, June 17 2008, 29–34, an edited version of a lecture originally given at the Annual Meeting of the Society of Biblical Literature in November 2007.

Chapter 10: 'Whence and Whither Historical Jesus Studies in the Life of the Church?' Reprinted with permission from *Jesus, Paul and the People of God: A Theological Dialogue with N. T. Wright*, ed. Nicholas Perrin and Richard B. Hays. Downers Grove, Ill.: IVP Academic, 2011, pp. 115–58.

Chapter 11: 'The Evangelists' Use of the Old Testament as an Implicit Overarching Narrative.' Reprinted with permission from *Biblical Interpretation and Method: Studies in Honour of John Barton*, ed. K. J. Dell and P. M. Joyce (Oxford: Oxford University Press, 2013), pp. 189–200.

Chapter 12: 'John, Jesus and "The Ruler of This World": Demonic Politics in the Fourth Gospel?' Reprinted with permission from *Conception, Reception and the Spirit: Essays in Honor of Andrew T. Lincoln*, ed. J. G. McConville and L. K. Pietersen (Eugene, OR: Wipf and Stock, 2015), pp. 71–89.

Chapter 13: 'Pictures, Stories and the Cross: Where Do the Echoes Lead?' Reprinted with permission from *Journal of Theological Interpretation* 11.1, 2017, pp. 49–68.

Chapter 14: 'Son of Man – Lord of the Temple? Gospel Echoes of Psalm 8 and the Ongoing Christological Challenge.' Reprinted with permission from *The Earliest Perceptions of Jesus in Context: Essays in Honour of John Nolland on His 70th Birthday*, ed. A. W. White, D. Wenham and C. A. Evans, ch. 5. London: Bloomsbury/T&T Clark, 2019, pp. 77–96.

Chapter 15: 'Son of God and Christian Origins.' Reprinted with permission from *Son of God: Divine Sonship in Jewish and Christian Antiquity*, ed. G. V. Allen, K. Akagi, P. Sloan and M. Nevader. University Park, PA: Eisenbrauns, 2019, pp. 118–34.

Chapter 16: 'History, Eschatology, and New Creation in the Fourth Gospel: Early Christian Perspectives on God's Action in Jesus, with Special Reference to the Prologue of John.' Reproduced with permission from the *Canadian-American Theological Review* 8.1, 2019, pp. 1–15.

Chapter 17: 'Son of Man and New Creation: The Biblical Roots of Trinitarian Theology.' To be published in *Christ Unabridged: Knowing and Loving the Son of Man* (Papers from the Pusey House Conference, July 2018) (London: SCM Press, 2020). Used with permission.

Index of Ancient Sources

Index of Ancient Sources

Index of Modern Authors

The New Testament in Its World

An Introduction to the History, Literature, and Theology of the First Christians

N. T. Wright and Michael F. Bird

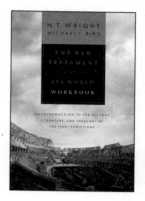

The New Testament in Its World is your passageway from the twenty-first century to the era of Jesus and the first Christians. In short, it brings together decades of ground-breaking research, writing, and teaching into one volume that will open your eyes to the larger world of the New Testament. It presents the New Testament books as historical, literary, and social phenomena located in the world of Second Temple Judaism, amidst Greco-Roman politics and culture, and within early Christianity. Book, workbook, and video/audio resources are available.

Available in stores and online!